FRANZ LISZT

FRANZ LISZT

The Man and the Musician

RONALD TAYLOR

GRAFTON BOOKS

A Division of the Collins Publishing Group

LONDON GLASGOW
TORONTO SYDNEY AUCKLAND

Grafton Books
A Division of the Collins Publishing Group
8 Grafton Street, London W1X 3LA

Published by Grafton Books 1986

British Library Cataloguing in Publication Data
Taylor, Ronald, 1924–
Franz Liszt: the man and the musician.
1. Liszt, Franz   2. Composers—Hungary
—Biography
I. Title
780'.92'4   ML410.L7

ISBN 0-246-12116-5

Typeset by Columns of Reading
Printed in Great Britain by
Mackays of Chatham Limited

To the memory of my parents

Contents

List of Illustrations

Preface   xi

1   'Le petit Litz'   1

2   The Galley Slave of Love   21

3   Conqueror of Europe   64

4   The Prince and Princess of the Altenburg   100

5   'Mephistopheles in the Guise of an Abbé'   167

6   'My Three-pronged Life'   192

7   The Weariness of the Nomad   228

Postscript   258

Bibliography   265

General Index   275

Index of Liszt's Musical Works
Referred to in the Text   283

List of Illustrations

Anna Liszt, pastel by L. Demarey, 1832 – Richard-Wagner-Museum, Eisenach

Adam Liszt, gouache by an unknown artist – Franz Liszt Conservatoire, Budapest

Liszt's birthplace, painting by an unknown artist – Liszthaus, Weimar

Liszt at fourteen, lithograph by Charles Motte *ca.* 1825 – Liszthaus, Weimar

Liszt in Rome, 1839, sketch by Ingres – Richard-Wagner-Gedenkstätte, Bayreuth

Countess Marie d'Agoult, portrait by Henri Lehmann, 1839 – Richard-Wagner-Gedenkstätte, Bayreuth

Liszt's children, portrait by Amélie de Lacépède, 1843

Liszt at the piano, painting by Josef Danhauser 1840 – from a collotype plate in the Goethe-Nationalmuseum, Weimar (original in West Berlin, Staatliches Institut für Musikforschung)

Recital by Liszt in Berlin, caricature by Adolf Brennglas (i.e. Adolf Glassbrenner), 1842 – Märkisches Museum, Berlin

Weimar *ca.* 1810, etching by G.M. Kraus – Schlossmuseum, Weimar

Villa Altenburg, watercolour by Carl Hoffmann, 1859 – from a photograph by Louis Held, Weimar (original painting lost) – Goethe-Nationalmuseum, Weimar

Princess Carolyne von Sayn-Wittgenstein, lithograph by C. Fischer, *ca.* 1844 – Liszthaus, Weimar

Franz Liszt, portrait by G.P.A. Healy, 1868 – Newbery Library, Chicago

Buda and Pest, 1854, lithograph by F. Sandmann – Budapest National Museum

Liszt in Wahnfried, engraving after G. Papperitz – Richard-Wagner-Gedenkstätte, Bayreuth

Liszt in 1883, photograph by Nadar – Mansell Collection

Liszt's Bechstein grand piano – Liszthaus, Weimar

Manuscript of Liszt's Hungarian Rhapsody No 4 – Goethe- und Schiller-Archiv, Weimar

Letter from Liszt to Lina Schmalhausen – Goethe- und Schiller-Archiv, Weimar

Liszt's funeral procession – Richard-Wagner-Gedenkstätte, Bayreuth

Preface

In June 1878 a Great Universal Exhibition, a display of ostentation already familiar from London and New York earlier in the century, was held in Paris. Dignitaries and household names flocked to France from all over the world. But there was one man above all whom everyone clamoured to see and speak to – 'the most famous personality in the whole of Europe', the critic Eduard Hanslick called him. 'Everybody knew, at least from pictures, the gaunt figure in his Abbé's soutane and broad-brimmed hat, with his sharp features and his Jove-like head set around with its snow-white mane.' The Jove-like figure was Franz Liszt.

Among poets, artists, musicians whose personal histories and reputations have reached beyond the immediate public for their art – figures like Villon, Byron, Van Gogh, Wagner, Oscar Wilde, men whose names are heavy with associations and images – Liszt has long had his own particular place. The child prodigy, the society beau, the peerless virtuoso, the indefatigable Don Juan, the cassocked abbé of the Roman Catholic Church – all these Liszts are set hard in the general imagination, whatever may, or may not, be known about symphonic poems, Hungarian rhapsodies, transcendental studies and the other original creatures of his mind. The crises that befell a Schubert or a Mendelssohn, the events that stirred a Chopin or a Brahms, do not force themselves upon the attention of those not concerned with the internal minutiae of these composers' biographies or with the specific relationship between their lives and their art. Liszt, on the other hand, often with the unpremeditation of the innocent but always with the sense that it could not be otherwise, thrusts himself into our consciousness with each move he makes, as though fate is determined that we shall not escape an awareness of his every step. Somebody once divided the world into quiet people and loud people. Liszt, like his son-in-law Richard Wagner, could be deafening.

But there is a great deal in his life to tell, a great deal to enjoy and to ponder. Of the generation of Chopin, of Schumann, of Mendelssohn, of Wagner, of Verdi, Liszt has his special place in the context of nineteenth-century Romantic art, and through the circumstances of his birth, as through the contingencies of his career, he embodies a cosmopolitanism under which many of the tendencies and values of European Romanticism can be subsumed. The once fashionable jargon-word 'seminal' is played out. But there remains in the phenomenon Liszt a core of meaning vitally relevant to the central issues of nineteenth-century Romanticism, both in music and in the other arts, and this hundredth year since his death offers an appropriate moment to restate these issues and feel our way into the mind of this larger-than-life character who spent much of his life in their exploration.

Biographical material on such a figure lies thick on the ground. Few whose paths crossed his at one moment or another denied themselves the pleasure of recording for posterity their reminiscences of what he said and did. Still more have left their accounts of what others told them he said and did. According to Charles Suttoni's admirably thorough researches ('Franz Liszt's Published Correspondence: An Annotated Bibliography', *Fontes Artis Musicae* 26, 1979), some 6,000 of Liszt's letters have been published in 300 different books and articles since the first collection edited by La Mara (Marie Lipsius) between 1893 and 1905, and the existence of thousands more is known, to say nothing of the unpublished thousands written to and about him by correspondents all over the world. On the one hand there is thus a substantial body of personal evidence at the biographer's disposal, on the other the awareness of a great deal of material still to be brought into the argument.

Similarly with Liszt's music. The only extensive edition, the Carl-Alexander-Ausgabe in thirty-three volumes (1901–36), no doubt provides most people with most of what they need but also sadly ignores a large number of significant works. Busoni described the difficulties facing the editor of a would-be complete edition as fourfold: 1) the absence of opus numbers for the known works; 2) the extraordinary number of different publishers involved, some reissuing pieces already published by others; 3) the existence of various versions of one and the same work, sometimes even of the same piece under different names; 4) the disappearance from the market of each older edition the moment a new edition appeared. Whether the *New Liszt Edition* (1970–) will redeem these deficiencies remains to be seen. It has in any case been emerging so sluggishly, slim volume by slim volume, that many scholars will already be across the great divide by the time the complete musical truth has been told.

'Do not confuse yourself with too many details,' said Liszt to Lina Ramann, his first thorough biographer, adding, with a jesting sense of what the future held in store, 'the story of my life is far more a matter of invention than of documentation.' I have tried to keep his injunction before my eyes, lest at the end the reader fails to see the trees for the wood. But even more anxiously have I sought to avoid falling prey to Liszt's other roguish insinuation. For he has been the predictable victim of more invented biographies – or of assemblages of wilfully manipulated evidence, which is not very different – than the subject of honestly documented ones. It is a life that lays more temptations in the biographer's path than most, temptations to tint and to embroider, to refashion and even to fabricate. Like any other historian of events I have a view of my subject, a set of beliefs and conclusions which has enabled me to bring some order to the scattered chronicles that claim attention. But wherever possible I have worked outwards from these sources, and I hope that at the end the result – craving the master's forgiveness – has been more a matter of documentation than of invention.

In the forefront of my narrative stands Franz Liszt the man in all his chameleonic colours: the lover, the father, the pianist, the gypsy, the composer, the teacher, the abbé. I have tried to present a portrait of his personality, both in its own right – what it was like to be Franz Liszt, so to speak – and through its impact on his environment, tracing the serpentines of consonance and discord, of adulation and scorn, of emotional agitation and spiritual serenity across the restless surface of his life. It is a life of extraordinary paradoxes and fascinations – but then, he was a paradoxical and extraordinarily fascinating man, and it would be as fruitless to try and resolve the paradoxes as it is misplaced to set about dissembling the fascinations.

From this confusion of opposites descends the bewildering contradiction of verdicts on the man and his music. By the one standard the smirking indulgence of a life of Bohemian hedonism and frivolity, by the other the shocked disapproval of a shameless moral laxity and irresponsibility; on one side the claim to a striking originality of artistic conception and an exuberance of musical expression, on the other the sneering rejection of a self-indulgent superficiality and a tasteless flamboyance. Few composers, both during his lifetime and since, have provoked such a polarization of opinion. Anton Rubinstein, pianist and composer, to Liszt the greatest keyboard virtuoso of the century, spoke for many: 'Liszt was perpetually posing – in his Church music before God, in his orchestral works before the public, in his song transcriptions before the composer, in his Hungarian Rhapsodies before the gypsies.' But so did Ravel: 'An entire century will be able to live on Liszt's music.' And Busoni: 'In the last analysis we are all descended from Liszt, and we owe to him whatever inferior things we have been able to achieve.' All are right, according to their lights, and Liszt in his fullness can be grasped only as an agglomerate of characteristics whose apparent irreconcilability, like that of the German and Hungarian cultural traditions which he inherited and inhabited, must be accepted, not resented, still less resisted.

The nature of the aim I have tried to follow in this book has meant that Liszt's compositions are brought into the discussion primarily as creative expressions of his intellectual and spiritual energy, not as a body of music for analysis in its own technical terms. When the focus of attention has moved from his physical and psychological life to his creative aspirations and achievements, significant works representative of these moments have naturally taken their place in the centre of the stage. But although I hope I have done some kind of spiritual justice to these works, and have tried to provide coherent contexts for others, to examine thematic relationships, analyse issues of form, illustrate matters of keyboard and orchestral technique and the like have lain outside my brief. By the same token the Bibliography centres on personal and circumstantial issues and makes no attempt to identify other than the most general and accessible works on Liszt's music.

For the purpose of my narrative I have called to as full a degree as possible on contemporary documentary sources, whether the utterances of Liszt himself or the testimony of those who were eye-witnesses to the one or other sequence of events in which he was involved. Quite a number of these sources, especially those held in the Goethe-und-Schiller-Archiv in Weimar, still seem to be almost unknown – or if not unknown, at least almost unused. I have spent many intriguing hours in the impressive Archive building across the road from Liszt's Villa Altenburg, rummaging through Liszt's manuscript jottings and other contemporary material, and although much more still awaits the scholar's attention, I believe that I have incorporated some revealing information which has not hitherto been brought into the picture.

One can never be *for* Bach, *for* Beethoven, *for* Mozart, *for*

Chopin – because one can never be against them. But many choose to declare themselves as being anti-Liszt, as others – or are they largely the same? – profess themselves anti-Wagner. Maybe it has something to do with their extreme tone of voice, or an extrovert, sometimes importunate manner that can cause embarrassment, especially when accompanied by lapses of taste. One can indeed, if one feels so inclined, make out a prosecutor's case against Liszt – which tacitly concedes that there is a substantial issue at stake and that the 'defendant' has a stature which requires him to be treated with appropriate seriousness and respect.

But I am not here to play the role of defending counsel, still less to hand down judgement from the bench. Rather I have been concerned to relate what I have found, to describe the pattern of physical and psychological events, be they logical or contradictory, ordered or confused, exhilarating or banal, that constitute the life of Franz Liszt the man and Franz Liszt the musician. If a modicum of the biographical and musical excitement of that life communicates itself to my readers, I shall be well content.

It is my pleasure to thank the staff of the various libraries and archives whose resources I have used, in particular the colleagues of the Goethe-und-Schiller-Archiv of the Nationale Forschungs- und Gedenkstätten der klassischen deutschen Literatur in Weimar. The typing of my manuscript was shared by Mrs Pat Samuels and Mrs Rita Goldman, to whom I express my sincere thanks, while to my wife Brigitte, who spent many hours with me sifting through archive material, and who also prepared the index, I owe a special debt of gratitude. Finally a warm thank you to Janet Law for her keen scrutiny of my manuscript, to my young friend David Harman for helping me with the proofs and to Richard Johnson of Grafton Books for seeing the book on its way to publication.

ONE

'Le Petit Litz'

On the wall of a farmhouse in the Austrian village of Raiding, nestling between rolling pastures and vineyards on the eastern fringe of the Burgenland, two plaques are to be seen. One, erected in 1881 in the presence of the man it commemorates, reads: *'Itt született Liszt Ferencz 1811 Oktober 22-én. Hódolata jeléül a Soproni iroldalmi és müvészeti kör'* (Here was born Franz Liszt on 22 October 1811. As a token of homage. The Sopron Association for Literature and Art). The other, which also bears a portrait relief, carries the inscription: *'Hier wurde Franz Liszt 22 Oktober 1811 geboren. Diese Gedenktafel weiht dem deutschen Meister das deutsche Volk'* (Franz Liszt was born here on 22 October 1811. This memorial plaque is dedicated to the German Master by the German people).

In one sense these rival claims need merely provoke an indulgent smile and recall the unproductive squabblings over whether Handel should be claimed for England, or Chopin for France – although, to be sure, where an artist freely chooses to live and work does indeed symbolize the values to which he attaches the greatest value at that moment, becoming the public to whom he makes his overtures and the immediate community that he serves. But the issues may lie deeper than this. There arises the question of roots – personal, social and spiritual. What blood flows through his veins? To what traditions, national, intellectual, aesthetic, does he feel he belongs – or do we claim he belongs? The answer may lie on the surface and the question barely arise. Beethoven and Wagner are as vitally and unmistakably lodged in nineteenth-century German Romanticism as is Michelangelo in the Italian Renaissance or Shakespeare in Elizabethan England. Dostoevsky is as Russian as Debussy is French. But Liszt?

At the time of his birth, and throughout his lifetime, his native village bore the German name Raiding, and Liszt always called it such (the Hungarian name is Doborján). But the administrative

1

county of Sopron (the German Oedenburg) in which it stood, some fifty miles south-east of Vienna, had a predominantly Magyar population. This was Esterházy country and had been in the hands of that powerful dynasty since the sixteenth century. Like all the magnate families, the Esterházys had become loyal supporters of the ruling house of Habsburg and moved ever closer to Vienna in social and cultural affairs, yet although they never entirely lost their national spirit, the classes below them, right down to the peasants, preserved a proud and often defiant sense of Hungarian identity far stronger than that of their semi-Germanized lords and masters.

So in whatever other cultures he came to move during the course of his life, and although his nomadic cosmopolitanism symbolized his inability to commit himself to one country alone, Liszt was born Hungarian, and constantly reasserted his pride in the fact. Yet he never learned the language. There were family, social and cultural reasons for this, but he never concealed his regret, almost shame, that it should be so, and anxiously begged his compatriots time and again to believe that it in no way diminished his patriotism.

The record of his baptism on 23 October 1811, the day after his birth, is in the register of the Catholic village church, together with the names of his parents, godparents and the officiating priest, who, as the final column shows, also shared responsibility for the neighbouring village of Lók:

23.	Franciscus L.	List Adamus ovium Rationista Principis Ester-hazy et Lager Maria Anna	Reiding	Patrini: Zambothy Franciscus et Szalay Julianna	Mersits Georgius Capellanus Lookiensis

That the family name is here written in the German form 'List' gives no ground for postulating, as some biographers have, that the family was of German origin and adopted the Hungarian form 'Liszt' because 'List' in Hungarian would have been pronounced 'Lisht'. The orthography of personal and place names can be fickle – witness also the 'ei' for 'ai' in Raiding – and matters little, especially in an area where two languages exist side by side. If 'Liszt' is the original Hungarian form, 'List' would be merely the German phonetic equivalent. Georg Adam, Franz's grandfather,

2

sometimes signed his name 'List', sometimes 'Liszt'. Many years later Franz wrote to his uncle Eduard: 'In Hungarian our name means "flour". Let us see to it – you and your children – that we supply high-quality wheaten flour.'

This uncle Eduard always maintained that according to 'family tradition' the Liszts were descended from a noble line of Hungarian Catholics. Yet at least as far back as Franz's great-grandfather they can be traced as German peasants and craftsmen in the Esterházy territories, so that the 'wheaten flour' seems to have come – and why not? – from a hybrid strain. Adam's language was German; a register of Esterházy employees records that he also had 'some Hungarian and Latin'.

Adam Liszt was thirty-five when his only child was born. Like his father, he was a steward on the estates of Prince Nicholas Joseph Esterházy, and to his no great pleasure had been transferred to the remoteness of Raiding from the Prince's palace at Eisenstadt the previous year. He had attended a *Gymnasium* (grammar school) in Pressburg (now Bratislava in Czechoslovakia) and at nineteen had become a Franciscan novice but left the order two years later 'because of his fickle and wayward temperament' (*inconstantis et variabilis ingenii*), as the record none too gently put it. It is a scrap of knowledge not without its place in the chequered career of his son, the future Abbé Liszt.

In Raiding, as Franz's baptismal entry states, Adam Liszt was business manager in charge of the Prince's huge flock of sheep – there were over 4,000 of them, Franz later remembered being told – and here, soon after his arrival, he married the twenty-two-year-old Maria Anna Lager, whose father had kept a draper's store in the Lower Austrian town of Krems, on the Danube. The ninth of eleven children, Anna had a hard life behind her. She was only seven at the death of her father in 1796; her mother died a year later, and after the residual family capital had been spent, Anna had to leave home and work as a chambermaid in Vienna. How she found her way to Raiding, we do not know, but a match with the gifted Adam Liszt, well-established employee of the Esterházys, gave her life a new purpose and offered her a security she had not known before. She was a buxom, homely, efficient woman who bequeathed to her only son a fundamentally excellent health for which he frequently thanked her. 'That's what I call a sound and healthy woman!' exclaimed the admiring Wagner to Liszt after meeting her in Paris in 1849. And, different as their appearance, their nature and their temperament were – 'the contrast between them is so marked', wrote an observer twenty

3

years later, 'one could believe that he was not her son at all but that she had stolen him' – he was always generous towards her and solicitous of her well-being. In the will he made in 1860, six years before she died, he again made sure that the world knew how much he owed to her:

> With reverence and tender affection I express my gratitude to my mother for the goodness and love that she invariably bore me. As a boy I was called a good son, but little of the credit for this belonged to me. How, indeed, could I have been other than a good son to so self-sacrificing a mother?

Adam Liszt's own special contribution to his son's development lay in a quite different realm. His father, Georg Adam, who had sired twenty-six children by three wives in the course of his eighty-nine robust years, was a farm manager on the Esterházy estates at Eisenstadt and used his position to secure his son's engagement in the Prince's employ. Inheriting certain musical gifts, and by dint of a great deal of private reading, Adam Liszt educated himself above his station and was already in his youth a versatile and talented musician, to the extent, his son later recorded, 'of taking his place among the cellos at court concerts'. In this capacity he frequently played under Haydn, who had been appointed to the Esterházy court in 1761 and remained there until the death of Prince Nicholas Joseph in 1790. 'Father went for walks with Haydn almost every day,' Liszt said many years later to August Göllerich, one of his closest friends and pupils. From 1804 to 1811 Johann Nepomuk Hummel, the greatest pianist of his day and a pupil of Mozart's, was Kapellmeister at Eisenstadt, and he too was a frequent visitor to Adam's bachelor quarters for evenings of chamber music. Small wonder that his promotion to the senior post in Raiding, which meant giving up these musical links, came as less than an unqualified pleasure.

Music at the Esterházy court had come into its own when Prince Nicholas Joseph took the site of a hunting lodge at the southern end of the Neusiedlersee, which today, as then, nestles against the border between Austria and Hungary, and built there a magnificent Renaissance-style palace. He called it simply Esterháza. The principal family seat, built in the seventeenth century and only a few miles away, was at Eisenstadt, and the administration of the vast complex of industrial and agricultural enterprises was still carried on from there. Esterháza, on the other hand, with its elaborate formal gardens and its 126 rooms, its air of improbability and grandiose fantasy, stood as a temple to the arts and to the joys of cultured living. It was to Prince Nicholas Joseph what Neuschwanstein was to King Ludwig II of Bavaria. Already in the eighteenth century it became known as 'le petit Versailles de l'Hongrie', an embodiment of the French taste and the French values that dominated aristocratic culture and intellectual fashion in Europe in the eighteenth century.

With Nicholas Joseph's death and Haydn's departure the cultural momentum began to slacken. Prince Nicholas II, who inherited the title in 1794, added greatly to the family art collection, which he valued in financial rather than artistic terms, but did little else for the cultural life of his kingdom. 'As the Prince has not been particularly fortunate either in a military or in a diplomatic career, having failed in both,' wrote Lady Frances Shelley, friend of royalty and aristocracy, in her diary of a visit to Esterháza in 1816, 'he is not liked; and his low intrigues prevent his being respected. As a consequence he hates Vienna, abuses his fellow-countrymen and passes his time in rambling from one fine estate to another.' The principal drain on his energies lay apparently in another direction: 'The Prince is a perfect Sultan and possesses ten or twelve houses, inhabited by different ladies, who share his favours and diminish his faculties.'

The buildings and grounds were left to deteriorate in the course of the nineteenth century, and although the estate remained in the family's hands until 1938, the extravagances of Prince Paul Anton and the neglect of his successors had left it virtually bankrupt long before. It was almost destroyed in the fighting between German and Russian troops during the last months of the war in 1945 and, like all other such estates, became Hungarian state property in 1946. Haydn's opera house, together with most of the summer houses and temples, has disappeared but the palace itself still stands as a monument to the magnates and their one-time power. Now called Fertöd, after the nearby village of that name, it has been restored and the once-ravaged 400-acre park redesigned and replanted.

The present-day Burgenland, the Austrian province in which the Esterházys ruled, was created in 1919 out of Hungarian territory. Eisenstadt, its capital, is today in Austria. But the palaces of Esterháza and Forchtenstein, the cradle of the dynasty, were returned to Hungary in 1921, when the *Komitat* of Sopron stubbornly asserted its Magyar identity in a plebiscite. It is a dualism that symbolizes the Esterházys' origin and their history. It is also the ethnic and national background against which Franz Liszt lived his life.

The European historical scene as a whole at this time was still dominated by the figure of Napoleon, who discovered for himself, like many before and after him, not only the vigour of the Hungarian national spirit but also the doggedness with which the country's rulers pursued policies which they saw as vital to the national interest. By attempting to Germanize Hungary in the 1780s from his Habsburg throne in Vienna, for example, Joseph II succeeded only in strengthening the Magyars' pride in their independence and it was left to his successors to realize that this was nothing but a recipe for perpetual unrest and instability. Yet when, playing on this tension and posing as a liberator from the yoke of Austria, as he did in his dealings with the estates of northern Italy, Napoleon set out to alienate the Hungarians from Austria, he found it impossible to do so. Their fate, in its wider context, was inseparable from that of the Habsburgs, and when revolutionary France declared war on Austria in 1792, the Magyar nation was drawn even more firmly into the pattern of Austrian interests.

Politically speaking, these interests were conservative, not to say reactionary. Secure on his throne after Napoleon's defeat at Waterloo, the Emperor Francis II consolidated his position with little heed to the needs or wishes of his Hungarian subjects, and the stirrings of liberalism were held down by the iron hand of Metternich until they broke out in the Revolution of 1848 and the declaration of a virtually independent state of Hungary.

From the court and the aristocracy downward, educated Hungarians spoke mainly German. This was in any case Anna Liszt's native tongue and, since she did not know Hungarian, the language in the little household was, and remained, German. With the exception of a few quaint missives in English, a language which he later made an effort to learn, the thousands of Liszt's letters extant are all in German or French, and sometimes in a mixture of the two.

In the course of his life Liszt had little cause for complaint about the strength of his constitution, and he made light of any temporary ailments that afflicted him. (In the very last days of his life, as he lay in the clutches of pneumonia, the one question he could not tolerate was 'How are you?') But as an infant his condition more than once made his parents tremble for his survival, and on one occasion, shortly before his third birthday, they even ordered a coffin in anticipation of the seemingly inevitable.

Young Franz's first piano lessons came from his father, who was quick to realize what exceptional gifts his son had, and that the world must be made aware of them. 'Every day at lunch,' Liszt told his pupils in Weimar many years later, 'while my parents were eating their dessert, I was made to play six Bach fugues and then transpose them.' At seven, he informed his biographer Lina Ramann in answer to her question, he could read and write, but he also taught himself to write music, and 'wrote more notes than letters'. He was nine when he performed in public for the first time. It was in the nearby town of Sopron, capital of the province, and he played the E flat major Concerto by Ferdinand Ries and an improvisation of his own. Shortly afterwards his father took him to the Esterházy Palace in Eisenstadt to play before Prince Nicholas Joseph, and towards the end of this same year, 1820, to Pressburg, an important provincial capital in which all the leading Hungarian magnates had a palatial residence.

The concert in Pressburg determined the direction of his life from then on. Adam's promotional shrewdness achieved precisely what it was meant to achieve. So impressed were the assembled aristocrats – Count Thadé Amadé, Count Antal Apponyi, Count Michael Esterházy (brother of the reigning prince), Count Gyula Szapary and others – that they decided to establish a fund which would guarantee the young prodigy the sum of 600 gulden* a year for six years, so that he could study with a leading musician. Of the concert itself the local newspaper wrote:

Last Sunday afternoon the nine-year-old virtuoso Franz Liszt had the honour to perform on the pianoforte in the residence of His Excellency Count Michael Esterházy before a numerous company of the highest nobility of our land and of a number of patrons of the arts. The player's extraordinary dexterity, together with the speed and skill which he brought to bear when performing from sight anything, however difficult, that was put

---

* It is impossible to convert nineteenth-century monetary values into realistic modern equivalents, but readers may find it helpful to have a rough idea of the purchasing power of money at this time, together with a conversion table for the currencies that need to be quoted in the course of the book:
  1 thaler = 1.75 gulden or 3 marks or 3.75 francs (French)
  1 Louis d'or = 5 thalers or 24 francs
  1 ducat = 2.85 thalers
800 thalers was held to be a good salary in Germany for a civil servant; a spacious family apartment could be rented for twelve thalers per month, and two furnished rooms for four thalers per month. According to Schiller, a single man of his class could live on 270 thalers a month in Jena and 400 thalers a month in Dresden at the turn of the eighteenth century. Liszt mentions in a letter that a grand piano on which he played at a concert in Budapest in the 1870s cost 1,000 gulden.

before him, gave rise to universal admiration and justifies us in expecting the most wonderful achievements from him.

Overjoyed by the magnates' generous support, Adam Liszt first approached Johann Nepomuk Hummel, whom he had known at Eisenstadt, and who had recently been appointed Kapellmeister to the court at Weimar. Hummel agreed to take on the boy but required a fee of one ducat per lesson, which Adam decided he could not afford. Daily lessons, or at least on three or four days a week, were a matter of course in the nineteenth century. Although the fund provided by the magnates would have covered this expense, the nine-year-old Franz could not have been sent away on his own; Adam would have had to give up his secure job and the family move to Weimar, living on their savings in the hope that he could find fresh employment there.

Adam's thoughts then turned to Carl Czerny in Vienna, who had himself been something of a child prodigy and studied as a boy with Beethoven. Czerny, composer of an enormous number of exercises and studies for piano and a teacher who accepted as pupils only the most gifted of the many young hopefuls who approached him, had already met Adam and his remarkable son two years previously. 'In 1819', he wrote in his autobiography:

a man came to me one morning with a little boy some eight years old and asked me to allow him to play to me on the pianoforte. He was a frail-looking child with pale features, and he swayed to and fro on his stool like one inebriated, so that I repeatedly expected him to fall off. His playing, too, was uneven, blurred, confused; he had no idea of fingering and moved his fingers over the keys entirely at random. Yet notwithstanding this I was amazed at the amount of talent that nature had bestowed on him. When I put a few pieces in front of him, he played them from sight without affectation yet in such a way that one could see that here was a pianist formed by nature herself. It was the same when, in response to his father's request, I gave him a theme on which to improvise, for without the slightest knowledge of harmony he succeeded in bringing a sense of inspiration to what he played.

Adam Liszt had clearly not been able to instil much technical discipline into his extraordinary son, but Czerny unhesitatingly accepted him without asking for a fee. He even paid for the music that his pupil needed, and a year later he recorded with satisfaction: 'Never had I had so enthusiastic, so inspired and so hardworking a pupil.' Posterity has tended to hold Czerny in somewhat disparaging memory as a ruthless peddler of soul-destroying studies and finger-breaking technical exercises. But Liszt, who came to admire him as the champion of Beethoven at a time when the public at large still felt unsettled and uneasy in the consuming presence of this giant, never disguised his respect for his old teacher, however quickly he outstripped him. 'I would do for you whatever I would do for my father,' he wrote to him a few years later.

For Franz to be able to study with Czerny, Adam Liszt had to give up his position on the Esterházy estates and take the family to Vienna. In one sense it involved a sacrifice. But in another it brought him the satisfaction of opening for his son a career in music which he himself, gifted though he was, had been denied, and what he did, he did with his full heart. Anna knew what the sacrifice had meant, and many years later her son showed that he too realized the extent of his debt. 'You are indeed right,' he wrote to her in 1862, 'when you say that not one father in a thousand would have shown such devotion and determination. They are qualities given only to exceptional characters.'

While in Vienna with Czerny, the ten-year-old Franz also had lessons in the use of clefs, key signatures and other technical conventions from the elderly Antonio Salieri – remembered in the popular musical imagination less for his compositions than for his rivalry with Mozart, whom he was at one time believed to have poisoned. A few years earlier, from 1813 to 1817, Schubert had also been a pupil of Salieri's, but although Franz and his father lived close to Schubert during their time in Vienna and might be expected to have come across him at some musical occasion or other, Liszt many years later confessed, sadly, that he had never met either Schubert, or Weber or Goethe – who were also there – personally. He also remembered having composed under Salieri a setting of the liturgical text 'Tantum ergo' – his earliest composition of which we know, but which is no longer extant.

His first piece to have survived also dates from these years with Czerny and Salieri. In 1821 the composer and publisher Anton Diabelli sent a waltz theme of his own invention to fifty composers, among them Beethoven, Schubert, Czerny and Hummel, inviting each of them to write a variation on it (Beethoven declined but later used the theme for his own piano Variations Op. 120). That young Franz should have been one of the fifty was a remarkable honour, an honour not diminished by the conventional, Czerny-like variation that he submitted as No.

9

24 in the collection. The contents describe it as being the work of 'Liszt, Franz (a boy of 11 years of age), born in Hungary'.

As the news of his genius spread, so did the demand for his services at musical soirées in the residences of the Viennese aristocracy, and towards the end of 1822 he performed a Hummel concerto and a free improvisation at a public concert in which the famous soprano Karoline Unger, a soloist in the first performance of Beethoven's Ninth Symphony and at one time fiancée of the poet Lenau, also took part. This led to further engagements, culminating in a solo recital on 13 April 1823, to which he invited Beethoven, in a note entered, probably by his father on his behalf, in Beethoven's Conversation Book the previous day: 'I have so often expressed the wish to Herr von Schindler [Beethoven's factotum] to make your eminent acquaintance and am delighted to be able to do so now, since I shall be giving a recital on Sunday the 13th and most humbly beg you to grace the occasion with your eminent presence.'

As well as being the object of this uninhibited invitation Beethoven was urged, presumably at the suggestion of Adam and Czerny, to provide young Franz with a theme on which to improvise for the occasion. Beethoven's deafness made it impossible for him to hold a conversation, and when visitors came, it was Anton Schindler's task to write down their message and pass it to the master. His verbal responses were not recorded word for word and our only information about them comes from Schindler. Liszt's visit, Schindler implies in his biography of Beethoven, was rather less than a success, probably because both the invitation to the recital and the request for a theme for improvisation – 'a request as indiscreet as it was unreasonable', said Schindler, although he did pass it on to Beethoven – seemed somewhat impertinent.

Yet to everybody's surprise Beethoven did attend the recital. Not only that, but at the end he went impulsively up to the boy and kissed him on the forehead – an act which many were quick to interpret as the bequest of the apostolic succession.

A school of sceptical biographers, going back to Liszt's own day, has maintained that Beethoven was not in fact present at the concert, and that the whole story of the kiss is a romantic fabrication. In the first (1840) and second (1845) editions of his biography, Schindler says that Beethoven was conscious of having acted somewhat brusquely towards young Franz when he presented his request, and decided to make amends by accepting the invitation to the concert on 13 April 1823. By the time of his third edition (1860), however, Schindler had changed his mind. 'Beethoven did *not* attend the concert', he wrote, 'nor any private concert after 1816.' The Conversation Books begin in 1818, and from the following year Beethoven was totally deaf. Lina Ramann recalls having asked Liszt during his last years whether or not the story was true, since doubt had already been cast on it. 'What?' he exclaimed. 'They want to take my kiss away from me?' 'They can't,' replied Lina Ramann, 'because you received it.' 'Of course I did,' he said. Lina Ramann personally presented a copy of the first volume of her biography, published in 1880, to Liszt, who corrected numerous points of detail and wrote copious comments in the margin on matters which he considered especially important or with which he did not agree. But he queries nothing about her account of this episode. And even if, as a different set of sources suggests, Liszt received the kiss in Beethoven's house, not in the concert hall, the reality of the gesture remains. The matter may be trivial in itself. It shows, however, how wary a biographer must be of repeating an argument merely because it reinforces a scepticism that reflects his own inclination and how necessary it is to pursue an investigation as far back as the often less readily accessible documentary sources allow.

However, the success of 'little Liszt' did not rest on whether Beethoven did or did not hear him play. These two years in Vienna had proven financially as well as musically profitable, and, sensing that his son now needed stimuli of a different kind, Adam took the characteristically bold decision that his musical education should be continued in Paris, musical capital of Europe. So on 20 September 1823 the family set out on the long journey westwards. Franz's fame preceded him, and the astute Adam saw to it that some of the towns and cities en route should have the opportunity to hear him, and pay appropriately for the privilege. He gave three concerts in Munich, attended by King Ludwig I and the entire Bavarian court, three more in Augsburg, two in Stuttgart and two in Strasbourg. Paris, where he finally arrived two weeks before Christmas, had also had news that he was coming, and by the following March, Adam wrote in a letter to a friend, he had given two public concerts and played at no fewer than thirty-eight soirées in the residences of the Parisian *haute volée*. One concert brought in 2,000 francs, the other, held in the Italian Opera, 4,700 francs, while for each of the soirées he received between 100 and 150 francs – 'we would never go for less'. 'People simply call him the prodigy,' said his proud father, 'Mozart *redivivus*'. True, accommodation and the cost of living in general were more expensive in Paris than in Vienna but, as Adam finally tells his correspondent with undisguised satisfaction, they have already accumulated a sum of 6,000 gulden to invest.

Adam's plan had been to enrol Franz at the Paris Conservatoire. But on presenting themselves to the director, Luigi Cherubini, they were told that the regulations did not permit the enrolment of foreigners, however gifted, and that Cherubini – himself an Italian – had no power to make exceptions, despite the fact that Franz brought with him a personal letter of recommendation from Prince Klemens von Metternich. It was an incident important enough for him to pencil in his own reference to Metternich's letter when he came to read Lina Ramann's biography over fifty years later.

Downcast as Franz and his father were at the time, this display of cultural chauvinism was probably a blessing in disguise. He needed no piano teacher – his lessons with Czerny turned out to be his last – and the basic knowledge of music theory and composition technique that he still lacked he gained in private tuition outside the Conservatoire, first with the operatic composer Fernando Paer, then with Anton Reicha, who had studied with Joseph Haydn's brother Michael. These were the last two men from whom he had any formal musical instruction.

His round of concerts continued, the enthusiasm of his audiences unflagging. In May 1824, accompanied by his father, who acted the role of impresario-cum-chaperon, he paid the first of his many visits to England. At the Argyll Rooms in London he played to an audience that included Clementi, Ries, Cramer and many of the other distinguished composers living in London at the time, and at Drury Lane he performed a concerto by Hummel on what was billed as 'the new Grand Piano Forte invented by Sebastian Erard'. The climax of the tour was a command performance before King George IV at Carlton House. He then returned to Paris and followed his English triumphs with a similarly dazzling round of the French provinces.

Liszt's remarkable powers of transposition, already stimulated under his father's guidance, were displayed at one of the private soirées he attended in London. A flautist called Alfred Nicholson was to play a composition of his own in C major. The piano, however, was found to be tuned a semitone lower than the pitch of the flute, and the nonplussed pianist declared it impossible to perform the work. Young Franz immediately took his place at the piano and transposed the piece at sight from C to C sharp, to the incredulity of most and the admiration of all.

But he still had the natural instincts of the unspoilt adolescent. 'Just before Liszt's morning concert, for which we had purchased tickets from his father,' recalled the pianist and composer Charles Salaman, 'we became acquainted. I visited him and his father at their lodgings in Frith Street, Soho, and young Liszt came to early dinner at my home. He was a very charmingly natural and unaffected boy, and I have never forgotten his joyful exclamation: "Oh, good! Gooseberry pie!" when his favourite dish was put upon the table.'

Adam Liszt proved highly resourceful in marketing his son's gifts, and presented his terms in a take-it-or-leave-it tone which reflected his total confidence that the response would be: 'We take it.' For two appearances in Manchester in August 1824 he demanded, and got, an enormous fee of £100, plus board and lodging for the two of them. He also laid down the pieces he proposed that his brilliant young son should perform – for the first occasion works by Hummel and Moscheles, for the second a set of variations for piano and orchestra by Czerny and a free improvisation on a theme provided by a member of the audience.

Congenial, albeit strenuous, as this mode of life may have been for father and son, revelling in the adulation and wonderment that attended his every appearance, for Anna Liszt it meant loneliness and neglect in the two hotel rooms that Adam had rented. When she returned to Paris with her son after Adam's death a few years later, her role changed and she eventually acquired her own circle of acquaintances, but as yet she spoke no French, and now, after a year of this isolation, she returned to her native Austria.

Natural and unspoiled though Franz remained in this heady atmosphere of praise, he later looked back on his whole career as a virtuoso with a mixture of irony and disillusionment, in which the noble art of music had been 'reduced to little more than a means of making money' and turned into a source of entertainment for the upper classes. 'There is nothing that I would rather have not done than become a musician in the employ of the rich, who patronized me and paid me like an itinerant entertainer.' A concern with the tensions between the social classes, primarily as they affected the arts but also in their wider human significance, remained with Liszt throughout his life. Like Wagner, he became particularly indignant at the underprivileged position of the musician, who, though the mediator of the divine values of art, had the status of a mere domestic servant. Not for nothing does his first critical essay, published in 1835, bear the title 'On the Social Status of the Musician'.

As though the demands of the performing artist's career were not enough, the thirteen-year-old Franz already had an astonishing collection of compositions to his name, which the gratified yet commercially conscious Adam catalogued to Czerny as: 'two bravura Rondos – which publishers here want to buy but which I am not going to release for a while – another Rondo, a Fantasia, Variations on a number of themes and a Quodlibet on themes from Rossini and Spontini, which he performed to great acclaim before His Majesty the King of England.' A year later, also from England, he told Czerny:

> Franzi has written two respectable Concertos . . . His real passion is composing – the only thing that gives him real joy and happiness. You would be very pleased with his Sonata for Piano Duet, a Trio and a Quintet. His Concertos are somewhat too demanding, and the difficulties they hold for the performer are immense. I always considered Hummel's Concertos difficult enough, but compared with Franzi's they are child's play.

Most of the works that Adam names, including the two concertos, are no longer extant, though two sets of variations (the first bearing the designation Op. 1),* the bravura Rondo, a bravura Allegro and the 'Impromptu on themes from Rossini and Spontini' (what Adam calls a 'Quodlibet') were published 1824–5, most of them by Erard in Paris. Far more significant, however, among the compositions of Liszt the teenager were a one-act opera called *Don Sanche ou le Château d'Amour* and a set of Twelve Studies for Pianoforte (the only ones completed of a projected forty-eight, in all the major and minor keys), which later became the starting-point for the *Grandes Études* of 1839 and the *Études d'exécution transcendante* of 1851.

The little one-act opera *Don Sanche*, with a libretto based on a tale by the eighteenth-century poet and romance writer Claris de Florian, had the first of its four performances at the Paris Opéra on 17 October 1825. It is a fairy-tale work, an episodic love story with a happy ending engineered by a magician in the role of *deus ex machina*, and the episodes were strung together by the

---

* It is difficult to know how Liszt himself numbered these early works. Competing publishers designated them in their own differing ways. For instance, Erard issued the 'Huit Variations' as Op. 1, whereas Hofmeister also called his reissue of the Twelve Studies ('Études pour le piano en douze exercices') Op. 1, which the original French publisher Boisselot had numbered Op. 6. Liszt very soon stopped giving his works opus numbers, and it has been a major problem in Liszt studies to devise an acceptable scheme for cataloguing his works.

librettists, Théaulon and Rancé, with the express purpose, as they wrote in their preface, 'of providing the young prodigy Liszt with a series of varied scenes which would afford his gifts every opportunity to display themselves from numerous different angles'. The musical result is pleasant but undistinguished, to judge from the Overture and other excerpts that have been made (the complete score has never been published) – although it hardly behoves us to talk condescendingly about a composer of fourteen who has a work performed at the Paris Opéra.

As Liszt's music has been doing ever since, *Don Sanche* divided critical opinion into two rival camps. A spokesman for the one reviewed the piece in the *Journal des Débats*: 'The audience listened in chilly silence to this cold, humourless, lifeless and quite unoriginal composition, in which a mere handful of charming motifs are to be found, testifying more to our memory than to the composer's ability. There was not a single number that aroused genuine applause.'

The *Gazette de France* saw the work differently: 'The opera contains several numbers that our most popular composers would not disown . . . Reasonable people, i.e. those who do not demand the impossible, were highly gratified by the remarkable skills of our little green Mozart [*notre petit Mozart en herbe*].'

Perhaps the most generous and most perceptive comment came in a later review, also in the *Gazette de France*: 'As regards the future we venture to believe that *le petit Litz* will not fail to live up to the great expectations that such a début has aroused.' Indeed, as long as six months before the Paris première of the opera, Czerny wrote to Adam Liszt from Vienna: 'A few days ago the theatre bulletin here carried the news that a march from Franz's opera *Don Sanche*, which was already known and rehearsed, has become so popular that it is now being played by every regiment in Paris.' Like the eagerness with which potential librettists pressed their texts on him in the hope of achieving operatic fame for themselves, this no doubt reflected a desire to be seen to be associated with the young genius rather than a critical commitment to the quality of his music – a statement of social celebrity rather than of musical eminence. Yet the fame and the wonder remain.

But there was a price to be paid for this celebrity. From the moment when he left Raiding at the age of ten, Franz never again attended school. Others of his generation, like Schumann, Chopin and Wagner enjoyed – 'survived' might be a better word – a formal primary and grammar school education, while Mendelssohn, of a somewhat higher social estate, had a private tutor for general subjects as well as his music teachers. As one of the fifty or so boys at the village school Liszt was taught the three Rs – in German – but little else. Yet from a comparison of the essays he wrote in the 1830s with Schumann's articles in the *Neue Zeitschrift für Musik* over the same decade, or with Wagner's first essays of the 1840s, one could have no inkling that these were the first critical steps of a young man who had acquired his knowledge of culture through his own virtually untutored reading and a grateful acceptance of external stimuli. Yet more than once in later years he remarked how conscious he had been of the disadvantages left by this lack of a firm educational background, especially since his fame brought him repeatedly into the company of the educated upper classes. In a revealing letter, written in 1854 to his son Daniel, he said:

> Those who have not had a systematic school education always lack a basic reservoir of knowledge on which they can draw, and I frequently regret today that I failed to embark on a strict series of educational courses after my father's death. But on the one hand I knew nobody with that degree of superiority and understanding which a lively mind needs when it is seeking counsel, while on the other hand I was forced from the age of twelve onwards to provide both for my own and my parents' livelihood. Besides this there were my music studies, which occupied my whole time until I was sixteen, when I even began to give lessons in harmony and counterpoint, as well as in pianoforte, and to perform in salons and concert halls.
>
> I succeeded fairly quickly in gaining an artistic reputation and making a respectable living but it would have been of greater value had I seriously developed my mind and sought to bring my knowledge up to that of the outstanding people with whom, in spite of being so young, I came into contact – some of whom deemed me worthy of their friendship. This caused me to turn over a great number of questions in my mind and to make good my lack of formal education, as far as I could, by my own reading.

At the age of fifty-seven he still felt embarrassed by this shortcoming and was seized by the urge to rectify it once and for all. 'So compelling has this urge become,' he wrote to Princess Carolyne von Sayn-Wittgenstein, 'that I dream of nothing but how to satisfy it. I shall therefore withdraw from the world and go to live in the country, there to read, learn and work in peace and tranquillity until the end of my days.' He never did so, of course, for 'withdrawal from the world' was an indulgence that his nature allowed him only in very brief, albeit sincere, moments. But the characteristic honesty with which he unaffectedly admits his deficiency, like the equally open and persistent desire to remedy it – almost as a social obligation, not merely as the private pursuit of self-melioration – both have their place in the anatomy of his psychology.

Soon after the performances of *Don Sanche* in Paris, Adam Liszt and his son set out on another tour of the French provinces, followed by Switzerland, then, in May 1827, paid their third visit to England where one of Franz's sponsors was the Philharmonic Society. Here he played a composition of his own for piano and strings described by Moscheles, who heard it, as a Concerto in A minor which exhibited 'chaotic beauties'. Liszt told Lina Ramann half a century later that he could no longer remember the piece clearly, but manuscripts in the Weimar Liszt Archive show it to be an early version of what was posthumously published as *Malédiction* – the name Liszt gave to the opening theme. Pianistically it already belongs to the characteristic world of his maturity, while the 'chaotic beauties' of some of the complex chromatic writing foreshadow the harmonic originality that was to distinguish his fully developed musical personality.

When he got back to Paris, Franz was far from well. Doctors found that the strain of constant travel, and the demands made by the growing number of concerts, soirées, receptions and other social occasions he was called upon to grace, were undermining his health. They prescribed a respite from these rigours and a course of saline baths at the seaside resort of Boulogne.

A few weeks after they arrived, Adam himself fell sick. The doctor diagnosed typhoid fever. Only days later, on 28 August, he died at the age of fifty-one, and was buried in the town cemetery.

Liszt owed a great deal to the father who had shown such unhesitating and unqualified confidence in him, sacrificed his own career and homeland, given a sense of direction to his earliest musical education and at the end lived for nothing but the promotion of his son's interests. Adam Liszt had cast himself in the role of a Leopold Mozart – and Liszt's early years do have a tenor and a thrust that permit a comparison with the boyhood of Mozart. When Lina Ramann asked Liszt later how he identified the successive phases of his life, he told her that the first came to an end with the death of his father.

For the moment his career as a virtuoso jerked to a halt. Writing to his mother of Adam's death, he suggested that she should come from Austria to Paris and set up house with him there. On her arrival he settled upon her the princely sum of 100,000 francs, his savings from his public and private appearances, which guaranteed her financial security for years to come. He rented a small flat for the two of them on the second floor of rue Montholon No. 7, off the rue Lafayette, at 200 francs a month, where he spent almost all his time practising the piano with no thought of returning to the hectic life he had left, a life rich in material reward but also riddled with disappointment and frustration. It was a time of uncertainty, of loneliness. 'I was depressed by the obstacles being continually put in the way of my attempts to follow the directions in which my thoughts led me,' he later told George Sand. 'I received not a word of sympathy or understanding and could find nobody of like mind – no one among the public at large, let alone from the ranks of artists and intellectuals.'

For a brief moment a strange person of like mind did flit across his path. This was one Chrétien Urhan, organist, composer, rediscoverer of the viola d'amore and one-time leader of the orchestra at the Opéra. Whatever specific musical influences may have passed from the thirty-eight-year-old Urhan to his seventeen-year-old friend – it was he who introduced Liszt to Beethoven's late quartets – his real attraction for Liszt lay in the devout yet romantic and highly subjective Catholicism which governed his personality. Urhan saw all moral, intellectual and artistic life *sub specie aeternitatis*, imposing an almost ascetic discipline of self-denial on his everyday life while allowing his musical fantasy to run free in pieces whose whimsical titles alone – *Elle et moi, La salutation angélique* – stimulated Liszt's sensitive imagination. An air of total eccentricity issued from his presence, an aura of utter self-assurance and self-commitment to which, for a time, his impressionable young friend joyfully surrendered.

But life also made its practical demands and, in order to support himself, he took to giving music lessons – an activity to which he happily returned to the very end of his life. Since his début in Paris three years before, he had come to know many cultured upper-class families in the capital who were delighted, whether from a love of music or merely with an eye on the enhancement of their social prestige, to engage him as a tutor, and he moved freely, and profitably, among them.

One of his pupils was the sixteen-year-old Caroline de Saint-Cricq, daughter of a minister in the cabinet of King Charles X.

They fell passionately in love. But when Liszt was discovered prolonging a music lesson until after midnight, the irate father, on grounds less of sexual morality than of social class, ordered him to leave the house and never return. Shortly afterwards Caroline was married off to an acceptable suitor with whom she lived an unhappy, unfulfilled life which offered nothing that could surpass the memory of this young love. And he, powerful though his commitment to other women became, always held her in fond memory, an adolescent ideal of perfect love made the more perfect by its cruel destruction. They corresponded over the years; he saw her again after his break with Countess Marie d'Agoult in 1844, and bequeathed a ring to her in his will of 1860, but she died many years before him. On the news of her death in 1872 he wrote: 'She was one of the purest revelations on earth of the blessing of God.' But at the time the frustration of his love, and the rough manner in which he, one of the prodigies of the age and the toast of the Paris salons, had been turned out of the Saint-Cricq house like a servant caught stealing the silver, brought him to a state of near collapse. He cancelled his commitments and did not show himself in public. The rumour went around that he had died, and a long obituary appeared in the newspaper *Étoile*, comparing him with Mozart and concluding: 'We mourn his passing and join with his family in lamenting his premature loss.'

The 'lost one' read of his passing with apathy. He had been engrossed in Chateaubriand's novel *René*, and its portrayal of the dissonance between the individual and society, its sentimentalized cult of suffering, and its ultimate conquest of passion by religion combined both to intensify and to justify the *Weltschmerz* of his situation. 'The only motive in my life – its motto, so to say – was the renunciation of all earthly values,' he later recalled. He gave himself over to religious observances, to asceticism and self-denial, and envisaged himself following in the footsteps of St Vincent de Paul, founder of the Roman Catholic Order of Mission Priests, or Lazarite Fathers. It was only the entreaties of his mother that prevented him from entering a seminary – a moment on which he looked back more than once when, at fifty-four, he received minor orders in the Roman Catholic Church and became an Abbé. 'Because of my mother,' he once remarked, 'I remained a layman, and lived all too secular a life.' This was not a pose. Such thoughts would have passed between him and his father, who had himself flirted with the contemplative life, and his self-characterization as 'half-gypsy, half-Franciscan' has too much truth in it to be shrugged off as a whimsical *obiter dictum*. The practical expression of this union of artistic creativity with religious commitment was to come with his grandiose plans in the 1860s for the total renewal of the spirit of Church music.

For almost two years he persisted in this role of anchorite. A sketchbook in the Weimar archive suggests that his musical imagination was far from dormant during this time, but the only composition he seems to have managed to complete alongside his religious exercises and devotional reading was a *Grande Fantaisie sur la Tyrolienne* from Auber's opera *La Fiancée*, dedicated to Chopin and published in 1829.

It was not music, however, that rescued him from his mood of melancholic resignation, nor the private joy of a new personal encounter, but a political event in the world outside – the July Revolution of 1830.

TWO

The Galley Slave of Love

The world of politics impinged on Liszt's life, albeit sporadically, to a greater extent than it did, say, on Mendelssohn's or Schumann's, though far less insistently than on Wagner's. Liszt made no secret of where his sympathies lay, and many were the occasions when he gave recitals in aid of refugees and victims of political turmoil. His own background had made him aware of the conflicts between ethnic and national interests in the conglomerate world of the Habsburg Empire, and he never abjured his oath of spiritual allegiance to his native Hungary – though equally he always knew that his art would suffocate if he were ever to confine it to a Magyar ambience. But such feelings did not find expression in a political *engagement*, still less in a physical involvement in the pursuit of a political aim. One cannot imagine that a warrant would ever have been issued for his arrest on political grounds, as it was for Wagner's, or that his name would have become a rallying-cry for the forces of national liberation, like Verdi's.

The Liszt of 1830, however, impressionable, quick of response, at this moment withdrawn and low in spirit, now faced an encounter with objective reality that forced him to transcend his private miseries. 'It was the sound of the cannon that cured him,' remarked his mother slyly. The cannon he heard were those fired during the three days of fighting at the end of July – '*les Trois Glorieuses*', as they were called – that put an end to the reign of Charles X. The traditionalism that rested on the aristocracy and the Church fell to the forces of bourgeois liberalism: the sovereignty of the people was reasserted, censorship abolished and the principles of democratic control stridently proclaimed. From beneath, but only just beneath, the surface of French political life came the rumbling of the growing strength of the proletarian masses, a strength that would not long be denied its public employment. For the moment, however, bourgeois values prevailed and Louis Philippe, the 'Citizen King', the monarch who

21

walked the streets of his capital with his wife on his arm instead of thundering through them in a coach-and-six, took his place on the throne.

Behind these events lay a body of ideas with a special appeal to the young, to the student generation, and these ideas now penetrated the unusual and unnatural isolation in which Liszt had been trapped since his rough separation from Caroline de Saint-Cricq. Various thinkers of influence had their contribution to make to this intellectual movement, but none was more exciting, more piquantly persuasive than Saint-Simon, a man whose lines of thought were to find their way into Liszt's attitudes at many moments in his life.

Claude Henri Saint-Simon, aristocrat by birth, bourgeois democrat by inclination, preached a kind of humanistic liberalism, both personal and socio-political in relevance. Pantheist and anti-clerical in tendency, libertarian in implication, it disseminated a mood of idealism, tinged with utopian notions of social reform and the defence of the rights of the rising proletariat, that captured the hearts and minds of Christians and sceptics alike and bequeathed to posterity many of the thoughts and principles soon to be codified in the doctrine of scientific socialism. It was a message of self-expression and liberation, personal, social and political. And if it was not quite the moment to inform the workers that they had nothing to lose but their chains, the name of Saint-Simon was not forgotten when that rallying-cry swept through Europe some years later.

His mind enthralled by this idealism, Liszt planned a 'Revolution Symphony', with Beethoven's 'Battle Symphony', *Die Schlacht bei Vittoria*, as his immediate model. Woven into the work, as symbolic of the natural self-expression that is the birthright of all peoples, were to be three national songs – a fifteenth-century Hussite melody in honour of the Slavs, the Lutheran chorale 'Ein feste Burg ist unser Gott' and the Marseillaise. They compose a trinity of national voices – allowing that the Hungarians are not Slavs but also remembering that from the seventeenth century Bohemia was ruled by the Habsburgs as part of their Austro-Hungarian empire – that symbolizes in an uncannily prophetic way the three cultural centres of gravity to which he was drawn throughout his life.

The scrawled four-page sketch, headed '27, 28, 29 Juillet – Paris', and with descriptive, commentative notes scribbled in the margin, reveals very little of the musical content that Liszt had in mind, though some of it later found its way into his symphonic poem *Héroïde funèbre*. But it has a unique place in his biography in that it is the first, and remarkably early, written evidence of his concern with that thrust of musical innovation with which his name is most immediately associated, that is, programme music. He made a few desultory returns to the work in the course of his life, *inter alia* at the time of the 1848 Revolution, but made no sustained attempt to finish it, and it remains a statement of intent.

That everything in the sketch is written in French shows how quickly he had become absorbed into the culture of his newly adopted homeland. Indeed, the few early letters that we have, beginning in 1825, show a remarkable command of French in a boy who had encountered the language for the first time only a year or so earlier. So completely did it oust his native German at this time that by 1828 he was writing in French to his old teacher Carl Czerny in Vienna. The bulk of his thousands of extant letters, and all his essays and critical writings, were written in French, and the instincts and values of his three 'official', albeit illegitimate, children – including his daughter Cosima, wife of Richard Wagner – were those of the French environment in which they were raised. Yet as he never called himself Ferenc, so he never signed himself François but remained faithful to Franz. His letters, other than those in which he uses one of his nicknames, are signed 'F. Liszt', or simply 'F.L.'

Grateful as Liszt needed to be to the political events that startled him out of a not uncharacteristic mood of withdrawal, a series of sudden revolutions in his musical experience, the one following breathlessly on the other, now gripped his mind even more tenaciously. Three encounters, irresistible revelations, each unique in its appeal, together dramatic in their impact, opened new vistas to him and stimulated new energies. The first was with Berlioz, the unpredictable genius who broke every rule in the musical book. The second was with Paganini, an overpowering Mephistophelian character who produced from his violin sounds that no one had thought possible. The third – a greater contrast could scarcely be imagined – was with Chopin, creator of a refined, ordered, introvert world of delicate yet passionate beauty.

Liszt first met Berlioz on the evening before the first performance of the *Symphonie fantastique* on 5 December 1830, at which, Berlioz recalled, the young man attracted the not entirely approving attention of the audience by the wildness of his applause. Berlioz was twenty-seven, eight years older than Liszt. The *King Lear* and *Francs juges* Overtures lay behind him, and much of *La Damnation de Faust* had already been written, but the revolutionary *Symphonie fantastique*, with its unashamedly auto-biographical programme and its startling novelty of musical means, confronted a shocked and uncomprehending audience even more violently with the demands of his wayward genius. He had no musical ancestry that could be reassuringly traced, no context of tradition into which his originality could be absorbed. 'A gigantic nightingale,' the poet Heinrich Heine called him, 'a lark the size of an eagle, such as is said to have existed in primitive times.' His personality, too, and the impetuous, often ill-pondered way in which he thrust his works before the public, had much of the primitive about it. He was an uncomfortable phenomenon, a force for non-conformism and non-compromise, and has remained so ever since.

This was what set Liszt's mind alight. Not that there is any question of specific musical influence – for as Berlioz turned his back on the past and on his contemporaries, so also he founded no school, no dynasty, and has, except in minor technical matters, no successors. But he exuded a spirit of rebellious independence, of subjective self, of confident faith in the creation of a new music, to which the young, impressionable Liszt eagerly responded. 'We felt an immediate affinity,' wrote Berlioz in his memoirs, 'and from that moment our friendship grew stronger and stronger . . . He literally dragged me off to dinner at his house and overwhelmed me with the force of his enthusiasm.' Over the next few years Liszt played at a number of Berlioz's Paris concerts, made an extraordinary piano transcription of the *Symphonie fantastique* – one of the earliest of his many extraordinary exercises in this genre – and never ceased to promote the cause of Berlioz's music. Twenty-five years later, in 1855, he made *Harold in Italy* – a work commissioned by Paganini – the point of departure for one of his most important critical essays on the subject of programme music. The closeness of the two men's personal relationship received public symbolic expression in Berlioz's wish to have Liszt as one of the witnesses at his wedding to Harriet Smithson in October 1833.

In terms of musical temperament, too, history has properly seen them as birds of a feather – unpredictable, unruly spirits with a taste for the grandiose, thorns in the side of the artistic establishment, moments of striking originality in their work lying side by side with banalities and stretches of near-tedium. An awkward fluctuation of response to Berlioz's music, as to Liszt's, on the part of many listeners reflects this ambivalence – a recognition of striking new beauties but also a frustration or irritation at the commonplaces into which these beauties often seem fated to dissolve.

What Berlioz heralded in the realm of composition, the phenomenal Niccolò Paganini revealed in execution. Stories of a strange, unnerving Italian genius of the violin had been spreading across Europe since the beginning of the century, and when, already in his late forties, the mysterious figure finally stalked out from behind his legend and presented himself to audiences in Vienna, Germany, Paris and London, the effect was indescribable – a demonic new music performed with a savage abandon that shattered the composure of all who heard it. His gaunt features, shrivelled and emaciated, and his wild expression were the frightening complement of the music he played – his own music, for he performed hardly any other. Small wonder that people said he had been taught by the devil. So paranoiac was he that he gave out the orchestral parts of his concertos only at rehearsal and gathered them in again immediately after the concert, lest anyone should copy them. As a result none of them – indeed, very little of his music at all – was published during his lifetime.

Paganini gave the first of his Paris concerts on 9 March 1831 in the opera house, and Liszt was among the audience. He never recovered from the experience. 'For two weeks my mind and my hands have been like those of a man possessed,' he wrote to his pupil Pierre Wolff in Geneva. 'I am practising four and five hours a day . . . If I don't go mad, you'll find me a real artist when we meet again – an artist such as you demand to see, and such as one has to be in the world of today. God, what suffering, what misery, what agony there is in those four strings!'

Paganini's sheer technical wizardry, Paganini the musical acrobat, took Liszt's breath away and fired him to make himself, both as composer and performer, the Paganini of the keyboard. He immersed himself in Paganini's 24 Caprices for unaccompanied violin and emerged in 1838 with five of them translated into the *Études d'exécution transcendante d'après Paganini* – 'unplayable as they are,' commented George Bernard Shaw, 'to people who attack a pianoforte with stiff wrists and clenched teeth.'

Much of Liszt's characteristic piano style, of his approach to the art of transcription, and, above all, of his philosophy of the sensuous appeal and spiritual impact of music, lies open to our perception in these early pieces. The title itself, launching a Promethean claim to push back the frontiers of conventional experience and skills – for it is the execution that is to be transcendental, not the music – symbolizes the fire that was in his belly, the exhilarating impetuosity of his assault on accepted limits and proprieties. Thus with a commitment to the spirit, not the letter, of an attitude to the music of the masters that he retained throughout his life, he did not shrink from adding his personal embellishments to the substance of Paganini's original text. Out of the middle section of Paganini's first Caprice, an exercise in arpeggios:

(Paganini, Capriccio No. 1)

Liszt created in the second of his three versions (1838), the following, with a melody of his own added in the tenor:

(Liszt, Paganini Study No. 4)

By the third version of 1851, when he published a revised edition of the complete studies under the new title *Grandes Études de Paganini*, Liszt was in the throes of simplifying his pianistic manner, and such accretions were removed. But at this moment we are in a younger, more passionate world, in which 'transcendental-ism' governed not only these transcriptions but also the original preludes published in 1839 as *24 Grandes Études pour le Piano* (only twelve were composed: they are reworkings of the Twelve Studies of 1826 and the forerunners of the *Études d'exécution transcendante* of 1851. (Liszt incessantly returned to his earlier works, whether in order to modify their content or to transcribe them for a different medium, and this is one of the reasons why the satisfactory compilation of a systematic index of his composi-tions is so difficult.) The only contemporary 'transcendental' piano music comparable to this is that of Alkan, a strange, neurotic man who crossed Liszt's path in Paris a few times in the 1830s and once shared a concert platform with him. Liszt wrote a short piece on Alkan for the *Gazette musicale de Paris* in 1837 but there was no deeper contact, personal or musical, between them.

Beyond the purely technical connotation of Liszt's words to Pierre Wolff – 'What suffering, what misery, what agony there is in those four strings!' – lies an awareness of the power of music to penetrate to the deepest recesses of the human soul. What he sensed in the presence of Paganini's frenzied genius he recognized to be, not a perversion, not the importation into music of alien, potentially destructive non-musical qualities, but a manifestation of the true ethos of music, its innermost nature and ineluctable power. And as one caught in the wake of this irresistible force, one drawn to this extent into the line of the Paganinian succession, Liszt joyfully submitted his own creative activity to the same metaphysical ordinance.

Such are the sentiments that underlie Liszt's essay in the *Gazette musicale de Paris*, mourning Paganini's death nine years later:

> An artist who deems himself strong enough to accept the heritage of Paganini can only set himself a single task, namely, to view art, not as an easy means of promoting his own self-interest and achieving empty fame but as a divine power which unites the whole of mankind. He must make artists realize what they can and must become; and he must arouse and sustain in men's souls a love of the beautiful, which is so close to a love of the good.

Liszt's encounter with the intoxicating art of Paganini occurred only four months after he had been overwhelmed by Berlioz and the *Symphonie fantastique*. Before the end of 1831, still not yet of age, self-possessed yet readily swayed, he had met a third musical genius of this age embarrassingly rich in geniuses, a man only eighteen months older than himself, of similarly humble eastern European origin, also a pianist fêted in aristocratic circles and a willing prey to women but in other, deeper regards his very opposite – Frédéric Chopin.

When Chopin arrived in Paris from Vienna at the end of 1831, his musical personality, both as pianist and composer, was already formed, and although the colours in his musical world became more intense over the mere eighteen years that remained to him, they never changed. He inhabited an intimate, individual world and shrank from the public gaze as instinctively as Liszt courted it, while his health was as fragile as Liszt's was robust. Where Chopin remained a Pole throughout his life, constantly refreshing his sense of national allegiance by seeking the company of his compatriots, Liszt became a cosmopolitan, as at home in France, Germany, and Italy – perhaps even more – as he was in Hungary. To the end of his life Liszt pressed upwards and outwards, in avid search of new experience, responding eagerly to whatever life laid in his path, whereas Chopin's world was closed, private, spiritually as well as musically. Trespassers would not be prosecuted but they would be ignored. On Liszt's spiritual and musical domain they would be welcomed.

Inevitably, therefore, Liszt gained more from Chopin than Chopin was willing to receive from him. Liszt, as he always did, set the tempo, and as time went on Chopin showed less and less inclination to keep pace with it. To begin with, however, at the time of Chopin's first Paris concert in February 1832, the two men were frequently to be found in each other's company and appear to have struck up a cordial friendship. In his monograph on Chopin, written in 1850–1, Liszt describes the salon life in which Chopin felt most at home, sitting by candlelight at the Pleyel grand in his apartment, surrounded by artists and intellectuals – George Sand, Heine, Meyerbeer, Ferdinand Hiller, the Polish poet Julian Niemcewicz, the painter Delacroix, Liszt himself and many others.

Chopin may, as has sometimes been suggested, have come to feel jealous of Liszt's growing fame through the 1830s, and a number of his alleged remarks on Liszt's comprehensive flamboyance have a tartness about them that comes close to sarcasm. He was greatly offended when Liszt, learning that Chopin was out of Paris for a few days, moved into his apartment in the Chaussée d'Antin in order to pursue a love affair in greater comfort, and a letter to Countess Delphine Potocka contains a remarkable outburst behind which there seems to lurk a smouldering resentment:

> When I think of Liszt as a creative artist, I imagine him heavily made up, raising himself on stilts, blowing hard into the trumpets of Jericho *fortissimo* and *prestissimo* . . . He used to bore everybody stiff with his endless talk of literature, religion, philosophy, astronomy. He wants to reach the summit of Parnassus on the back of someone else's Pegasus.

Yet for all this Chopin insisted on preserving for the outside world a firm façade of amicability on the many occasions when they found themselves in each other's company, and there is un-dissembled admiration behind his remark to a friend: 'I should like to steal from him the way to play my Études.'

Nowhere did the community of spirit that the two men could feel find more charming expression than in an anecdote which the Hungarian statesman Count Albert Apponyi said in his memoirs had been told to him by Liszt himself. Chopin and Liszt had been invited to a musical soirée in Paris, and Liszt felt that Chopin had so far put him in the shade. So while Chopin was playing, Liszt went up to the hostess and whispered to her to put out the lights – it would be a delightful experience, he said, to listen to Chopin in the dark. The lights were extinguished, and as Chopin went on playing, Liszt slipped into the chair next to him and, with Chopin entering into the joke, took over from him without a break. When the lights went up, people were amazed to see Liszt sitting at the piano instead of Chopin. Liszt then stood up and said: 'My dear Frédéric, now please do me the favour of sitting down at the piano and playing so as to make people believe it's Liszt!'

'Hats off, gentlemen! A genius!' had been Schumann's famous cry on the publication of Chopin's 'Là ci darem' Variations in 1831. Liszt had his own experience of Chopin's genius, a genius more perfectly formed than his own and for which, frankly and unpatronizingly, he always found unstinting admiration. Envy was not a word in Liszt's vocabulary. And as he absorbed certain elements of Chopin's piano style into his own, so his com-memorative monograph embodies his discursive tribute to the uniqueness of Chopin's nature:

> The genius reveals himself through the emotions that he allows his art to express, through the nobility of his created work,

through so perfect a union of concept and form that one could not envisage the one without the other, since the one appears as the natural embodiment, the free, spontaneous emanation, of the other.

Just such a genius, to Liszt, was Chopin.

His mood of withdrawal cast aside, liberated in artistic spirit, and shortly to become equally liberated in his pursuit of emotional fulfilment, Liszt now stood on the threshold of a new phase in his life, a phase he characterized as 'a tentative period of study and creativity in Paris, then, for a while, in Geneva and Italy'. His mother kept house for him in a new and bigger apartment at rue de Provence No. 61, where he received the handful of well-to-do pupils to whom, with a dignified awareness of the independence to which his reputation entitled him, he deigned to give instruction. This reputation, allied to the elegance and irresistible charm of the slim, handsome young man portrayed in the drawing by Ingres, ensured that Parisian society never let him out of its sight for long.

Among the favoured few – who included Hermine, the sister of the French Romantic poet and dramatist Alfred de Musset – was Valérie, daughter of a cultured Genevan lady called Auguste Boissier. After each two-hour lesson Madame Boissier wrote a detailed chronicle of what had gone on, and the result, the observations of a highly perceptive and intelligent woman, leads us directly into the heart and mind of the twenty-one-year-old Liszt, as well as into his teaching methods and the circumstances of his domestic life. We learn, for instance, that his mother used to sit in on these lessons, and while he was making intense efforts to put his meaning across to Valérie, said Madame Boissier,

Frau Liszt would sigh sadly and make signs to me that he was mad; then she kept on going over to him with sweetmeats and little pills of one kind or another, which he refused. One cannot imagine two people less like each other, yet they make their way together through life in mutual affection, and the little household presents a picture of harmony and happiness.

Madame Boissier was impressed by the fact that in spite of his fame, of his familiarity with the adulation of high society, and of the intensity of the ideals which were forming in his mind, Liszt was always modest, almost humble in his manner, never overbearing, impatient or intolerant. Since he conceived music, not

30

as an end in itself but, like the other arts, a medium through which man gains access to the deep spiritual realities of the world, his lessons did not stop at the solution of technical problems:

> To make his explanations clearer, he would read aloud whole pages from one of his favourite authors, expounding the relationship between music and literature . . . He has read a great deal and absorbed it all, offering his views in the most attractive and interesting manner, without arrogance or that peculiar affectation to which many artists are prone.

Before going through with Valérie a study by Moscheles, for example, he read out a gentle, reflective poem by Victor Hugo, 'À Jeanne', to induce the mood that he wished the performance of the music to convey.

There was more to his modesty of manner than met the eye. Such had been the adulation which surrounded him that it could well have warped his power of sober judgement and his sense of values, and if others remarked on an occasional almost involuntary lapse from these standards, he would unhesitatingly and unresentfully concede his guilt, begging them only to realize how oppressive the weight of his past was. When Ary Scheffer, who painted a striking portrait of him in 1838, reacted tartly to what he called Liszt's 'airs of a man of genius' during a sitting in his Paris studio, Liszt quietly replied: 'You are perfectly right, my friend, but you must try to forgive me. You cannot imagine how it spoils one to have been a child prodigy.'

Liszt set great store by mechanical exercises, Madame Boissier went on – octaves, arpeggios, broken chords and the like – as a path to technical perfection. Valérie was told to practise such exercises for two hours a day. 'Be patient with yourself,' he said. 'You will ruin everything if you try to get on too fast. Nature herself works slowly – follow her example.' He recommended the use of a mahogany rod fastened to the piano, on which the arm could lie motionless, leaving the hand and fingers free to practise trills, rapidly repeated notes and chords going from very soft to very loud and back again – a particularly important technique to him – and similar exercises. This device is in essence the so-called chiroplast, patented by Johann Bernhard Logier in 1814 and perfected by Friedrich Kalkbrenner, one of the leading pianists and composers of the day.

Madame Boissier also paints a colourful picture of Liszt at the piano:

His fingers are very long, his hands small and narrow. He does not hold them in a rounded position, saying that such a posture makes for dry playing, which is something he detests. At the same time he does not hold them flat – they are in fact so flexible that they have no fixed position . . . He never plays with his arm or with his shoulders. He wants the body to be held upright, with the head inclined backwards rather than forwards – this he demands most emphatically . . . He is resolutely opposed to any affected, pretentious, forced style of playing, and his principal concern is with authenticity of musical feeling . . . Moreover he is not easily satisfied with himself either, and often jumps up from the piano in despair because he cannot realize his ideal of perfection.

Sometimes Liszt was so full of his experiences in the French capital that much of a lesson would be given over to enthusiastic storytelling. He had recently dined with a number of famous authors, he said, had been invited to society balls, at one of which he had gazed in fascination from midnight till three in the morning at a young woman married to a man many years her senior, had met a certain Mademoiselle de Barre again, with whom he had gone on a trip to Savoy the previous year, and so on and so on. 'All this', noted Madame Boissier, 'he related with just a *soupçon* of smugness, slowly and deliberately, quite relaxed and without the slightest air of excitement.' On other occasions he would fill almost the entire two hours of the lesson by playing himself, above all Mozart, for whom, as for Schubert, he reserved a special affection until the end of his life. Haydn, on the other hand, he found at this time 'old-fashioned and over-ripe.'

But what impressed Madame Boissier and her daughter as much as Liszt's colourful social life and sense of artistic vocation was his willingness to put himself at the disposal of others, particularly of those less privileged than himself. In the course of his career he played at innumerable charity concerts, presented sums of money to aspiring young musicians, and at the end of his life, to the frequent impatience of his friends, was prepared to give free music lessons to almost everyone who asked him, whether others considered them 'worthy' of the honour or not. Indeed, from Madame Boissier's account he seems almost to have played the role of a social worker. 'He used to visit hospitals, gambling dens and mental asylums,' she recalled, 'going down into the deepest dungeons and even talking to the men in the condemned cells.' The special beneficiaries of his humanitarian instincts in 1832 were the victims of the cholera epidemic that ravaged Paris that year; like a present-day collector for charitable causes, he went from salon to salon, taking a collection from his well-heeled audience at the end of the evening's music and devoting it to the care of the *cholériques*.

'Had he not been a musician of genius,' Madame Boissier concluded, 'he would have become an important philosopher and writer.' The corpus of Liszt's writings will hardly sustain the assertion that here the world has lost a philosopher, though he can lay fair claim to joining the ranks of significant nineteenth-century thinkers on music and culture – a more substantial claim, arguably, than Schumann or Berlioz, though certainly not than Wagner.

The tide of experiences, personal and artistic, continued to swell. As Madame Boissier recounted, he led a hectic social life, and the charm that he exerted on women was beginning to make its strenuous presence felt. The winter of 1832 he spent with the Countess Adèle de la Prunarède, later Duchesse de Fleury, at a lonely, romantic château in the Alps, after meeting her in a Paris salon. Then there was Countess Pauline Plater, one of the many Polish aristocrats resident in the French capital and evidently something of a connoisseur in musicians. 'I would take Hiller as my man around the house, Chopin as my husband and Liszt as my lover,' was her judgement on the relative domestic merits of her three distinguished friends. Yet although it needs two for a love affair, Liszt was, irrespective of how quickly or how willingly he cooperated – and sometimes 'capitulated' would be a more appropriate word – more often the chased than the chaser. It seems somehow appropriate, given his temperament and the course his life followed, that he never married.

Apart from their aristocratic clientèle, he also met in the Paris salons, almost on equal terms, many of the leading French poets, artists and intellectuals of the day. Their names read like a roll-call of potential Nobel prize-winners: Lamartine, Victor Hugo, Alfred de Musset, George Sand, Balzac, Sainte-Beuve, Alexandre Dumas *père*, Edgar Quinet. And, of course, the leading musicians in the city – Cherubini, Meyerbeer, Alkan, Rossini, Bellini – together with any foreigners who chanced to be staying there.

One such was the young Charles Hallé, who later, after his emigration to England, founded the famous Manchester orchestra that bears his name. Hallé tells in his autobiography of an extraordinary concert at which Berlioz conducted the orchestra in a performance of the 'March to the Scaffold' from his *Symphonie fantastique*. When the movement was over, Liszt sat down at the piano and played his own transcription of the piece, 'with an effect', says Hallé, 'even surpassing that of the full orchestra, and creating an indescribable furore'.

The poet Heinrich Heine, who had gone into exile in Paris in 1831 to escape persecution both as a Jew and as a liberal-progressive publicist whom the Metternich regime was determined to silence, regarded Berlioz and Liszt as by far the most remarkable figures in the city's musical life in the 1830s. Heine had slipped easily and gratefully into the milieu of the Paris salons and was himself, as a man of liberal philosophical and political views, a much sought-after figure in these progressive circles. In his *Florentinische Nächte* Heine describes a soirée where, admiringly but not without the heavily sardonic touch that he could never keep out of his voice, he observed and described Liszt at close quarters:

> The evening began with music. Franz Liszt was urged to sit down at the pianoforte, and he allowed himself to be persuaded. Running his hands through his hair and laying bare his inspired brow, he treated us to one of his most dazzling displays of combat. Blood seemed to be oozing out of the keys. If I am not mistaken, he played a passage from Ballanche's *Palingénésie*, translating its ideas into music, which is very helpful for those who cannot read the works of this famous writer in the original. Then he played Berlioz's 'Marche au supplice', a splendid piece written by that young composer, I believe, on the morning of his wedding day. The faces of all those in the room grew pale and ashen, bosoms heaved, with bated breath during the silences, and finally deafening applause. Women become almost intoxicated whenever Liszt plays to them.

Not surprisingly, the mature Liszt, who believed in total commitment, and lived out his belief, had little time for the ironical, satirical Heine, though in the course of the 1840s and 1850s he did set seven poems from Heine's *Buch der Lieder* to music, including the famous 'Lorelei' and 'Du bist wie eine Blume'. Wagner relates that at his forty-fifth birthday party in 1856 Liszt waxed scornful over the shallowness of Heine's verse until challenged by one of the ladies present to admit that 'Heine's name would nevertheless be inscribed on the tablets of immortality'. 'Undoubtedly it will,' Liszt quickly replied, 'but in mud.'

The effect on women of Liszt's playing – which Heine elsewhere puts down to skilful stage-managing – is described by one writer after another. He would lift his eyes from the keyboard and fix his gaze on a particular lady in the audience, holding her in his spell for as long as he chose and making her feel that he was playing to her alone. The American critic James Huneker, who heard the master play towards the end of his life, said wickedly that he could inspect the chairs after a recital by Liszt and tell where the women had been sitting.

Less frivolously, however, Heine also recognized that here was a musician who made music do things, sometimes uncomfortable things, that no one else, not even Paganini, could. As, later, with Wagner, one could be overwhelmed by Liszt's musical personality or repelled by it: one could not be neutral. 'He is no pianist for respectable, law-abiding citizens or drowsy stick-in-the-muds,' said Heine. 'It is highly significant that nobody talks about him with indifference. And what testifies most eloquently to his stature is the unqualified respect which even his opponents have for his importance.' Heine, like everyone else, observed that Liszt was increasingly becoming the centre of his own world, making himself not *an* attraction wherever he appeared, but *the* attraction, until a whole evening's music came from his piano – in other words, the solo recital was born. At the same time he was sharpening his claws as a composer by making piano transcriptions and writing fantasias on other composers' melodies (*Grande Fantaisie symphonique* for piano and orchestra on themes from Berlioz's *Lélio*, performed in Paris in 1835 but never published; a *Grosses Konzertstück* for two pianos based on a number of Mendelssohn's *Lieder ohne Worte*, also unpublished). The year 1835 also saw the publication of the first version of 'Pensée des morts', which subsequently became No. 4 of the *Harmonies poétiques et religieuses*.

But whatever the consummate artistry and self-confidence of his public persona, intellectually and spiritually he was still seeking inspiration and guidance from the great amount of literature that he continued to devour. 'He read an encyclopedia at the same furious pace and with the same insatiability as he read the works of a poet,' wrote Lina Ramann in her biography, and in the margin of his copy Liszt scribbled 'Correct!' A controversial thinker now crossed his path who was to leave an influence that persisted until the end of his life, a man whose thought led at times in the direction of Saint-Simonism but also invoked an interpretation of Roman Catholicism and the Church to which Liszt, with one side of his nature, spontaneously and passionately responded. This man was the Abbé Félicité de Lamennais.

Lamennais had raised a stir in 1817 with the first volume of his *Essai sur l'indifférence*, in which he denounced toleration and expounded, in three subsequent volumes, the revival of ecclesiastical authority as a means of regenerating European society. Subsequently, however, with all the impatience and intolerance of a prophet who knew himself to be on the fringes of heresy, he completely changed his message and identified the cause of Christ with the cause of liberty and democracy, preaching that the regeneration of which society stood in need should be launched on a process of liberalization. 'I believe in the social mission of the Church' was now the heart of his credo.

As he had risen to the message of the Saint-Simonists, so Liszt now found in Lamennais a congenial blend of Catholic reference and social reform, a religious framework within which the legitimate claims of a new and fairer society could find fulfilment. Although his acceptance of the authority of the Church of Rome assumed its explicit public form only when he took minor orders in 1865, he had implicitly conceded its power in personal doctrinal matters from his childhood onwards. At the same time he retained in matters of social thought, particularly because of the impingement of society on the activities of the musician and other artists, a liberal independence not always welcomed by the guardians of Vatican orthodoxy, and it was to these tendencies that Lamennais ministered. In his copy of Lina Ramann's biography the seventy-year-old Liszt has added at this point a sentiment which many a politician, liberal-democratic and not-so-liberal democratic, has used as the starting-point for a programme of social reform: 'The aim of all social institutions must be to improve the lot, material and moral, of the largest and poorest class. To each according to his capabilities, to each capability according to its achievements. Idleness must be banished.'

After Lamennais withdrew from public life to La Chênaie, in Brittany, in 1826, Liszt made proud pilgrimage there to be among the young disciples seeking inspiration and guidance. In a letter written in January 1835 he tells Lamennais he has dedicated to him a recently composed work for piano and orchestra with the title 'De profundis', but the surviving manuscript, held in the archives in Weimar, is fragmentary and has never been published.

From this world of ideals and reforms came one of the first of Liszt's critical essays, published over five numbers of the *Revue et Gazette musicale* in 1835, under the title 'De la situation des artistes et de leur condition dans la société'. This remarkably assured piece of thinking goes well beyond the general statement of theories and ideals that the title leads us to expect. The familiar Romantic rhapsodies, reminiscent of the writings of Jean Paul, Tieck and E.T.A. Hoffmann, on the 'omnipotence and magic power of music' are there, likewise the elevation of Art to the company of God and Mankind in the creation of a divine trinity. Furthermore: 'We believe in infinite progress, in a future for musicians that shall be free and unconfined. This is the faith that we hold, with all the trust and love at our command.'

But Liszt does not leave the matter in this land of effusive enthusiasm and pious hope. Since the education of the concert-going public, he argues, is one of the prime needs of the moment, but since at the same time most writers and critics who should be the agents of this education have no proper sense of standards and values, these critics should be made to undergo an examination to test their suitability for the profession to which they have elected themselves. (To the question 'Quis custodiet ipsos custodes?' Liszt would doubtless have answered: 'I myself'.) Another step towards putting the musical life of the country on a sound footing was to be the establishment of Philharmonic Societies based on the model of that in London. These should plan respectable series of concerts, help to found conservatoires and music libraries and organize periodical competitions, with suitable prizes, in order to attract potential talent and raise standards. It is a set of proposals akin to those which he formulated in 1850, at greater length, for the establishment of a Goethe Foundation in Weimar. Important too, he emphasized, was to raise the social standing of the musician, making to his French audience the same point that Wagner was to make to the King of Saxony eight years later, when he discovered the inadequacies of the Dresden orchestra he had been appointed to conduct.

Committed and earnest though its proposals are, presented with the interminable discursive sentences and persistent rhetorical questions which Liszt's style never shed, 'On the Position of the Artist' is lightened by many a charming satirical touch. Indeed, behind the glossiness and relentless efficiency of his public career lurked a ready wit, often self-deprecatory in tone, which showed his sometimes surprised entourage that he acknowledged the reality of the relationship between subject and object, between artist and created art, and was not merely the centre of his own world. One cannot fail to sense Liszt's delight as he mischievously describes an imaginary conversation in which a conductor reveals the ludicrous nature of the orchestral forces at his command. 'The first violins,' he says, in answer to Liszt's question, consist of myself, my son and Herr M; the seconds, of a retired army surgeon and a lawyer. We have no violas, and the cellist is an old naval officer. No double basses – this instrument never really acclimatized itself to our conditions.

The wind, I'm afraid, is rather our Achilles' heel. We do have a flautist but he's always unwell; we have a clarinettist too, but at the moment his instrument is in Paris, being repaired. The horn, however, is first class – that young man will go a long way. We give him all the other parts that haven't been taken.

These 'other parts', Liszt sardonically concludes, amount to some twelve or fifteen (oboe, trumpet, trombone, etc.), 'all of which this poor, wretched horn-player had to fill in as best he could'.

The orchestra that Liszt later took over in Weimar was fortunately rather better equipped than this, but the raising of standards, and the consequent education of public taste, was a dominant concern of his Weimar years. The same spirit inspired the establishment of Schumann's pioneering musical journal *Neue Zeitschrift für Musik* in 1834, the year before Liszt's 'On the Position of the Artist', and Liszt himself returned a few years later to the subject of the parlous condition of public taste in the essays collected as *Lettres d'un bachelier ès musique* (1835-40).

'I am afraid of what women will do to you,' Adam Liszt had murmured on his deathbed to his sixteen-year-old son. Hitherto, perhaps, there had been little to 'fear' from the amorous encounters that can be laid to his credit. But now there entered his life the first of the two women who influenced, in very different ways and over very different periods of time, the course of his existence, a woman who bore him three children and, for this reason alone, could never vanish completely from his mind. Her name was Countess Marie d'Agoult.

Marie Catherine Sophie de Flavigny was born in Frankfurt-am-Main on 31 December 1805. Her father was the Vicomte Alexandre de Flavigny; her mother was descended from the Frankfurt banking family of the Bethmanns. Raised in an atmosphere of economic prosperity and aristocratic mores – the two were not always found together – she spent her childhood and early adolescence in elegance and freedom, enjoying the mild form of education considered appropriate to fill the few years before a suitable husband was found for her. Most of these years, until the Vicomte died in 1819, were spent at Château Mortier, in Touraine, which he had bought on his retirement from the army. Marie had been baptized in Frankfurt as a Protestant but became a Catholic at her father's bidding, and shortly after his death she entered the convent of Sacré Coeur de Marie in Paris to complete her education.

The thirty-seven-year-old Count Charles d'Agoult, with whom a marriage was arranged in 1827, when she was twenty-two, had had a distinguished military career in Germany, Poland and Spain before being wounded while fighting the Russians at the Battle of Nangis and being left lame by the injury. He now held a minor appointment at the Paris court. But these few words say almost all that there was to say about him. 'Anyone who has seen me for a week knows me by heart,' he admitted. And it was this predictability, this absence of surprise and mystery, that quickly stifled any possibility that his marriage to the impressionable, romantically inclined, intellectually ambitious Marie de Flavigny could be other than a sterile contract. She went her independent way, attaching herself to the ardent intellectuals of the Parisian salons and surrendering to the appeal of fashionable progressive views in matters of religion, philosophy and literature – the works of Saint-Simon, Chateaubriand and Benjamin Constant, Goethe's *Faust*, Sainte-Beuve's *Volupté* and Senancour's *Obermann*, the last-named an epistolary novel that blended Rousseau, Byron and Goethe's *Werther* into an idiosyncratic piece of cultural pessimism which cut deep into the consciousness of the French intelligentsia in the nineteenth century. She also read Shakespeare, Sir Walter Scott, Thomas Moore and the wild, Romantic novels of Mrs Radcliffe, which lead directly to Byron's *Childe Harold* and *Manfred*, English cousins of the handsome, passionate yet gloomy Obermann.

The physical frame that sheltered this animated personality and its power of emotional involvement had a deceptively sedate appearance. Slim, blonde, Marie d'Agoult had well-formed features with a classical poise which betrayed little of her inner discontent, her restlessness, her vulnerability. It was the face of one who found it hard to relax, even harder to regard herself and her situation in other than intensely personal terms, and virtually impossible to display, or even recognize, the quality of humour – though she could be ironic to the point of spitefulness when talking of, or to, a person she did not like. Perhaps one may see it as a face, a mind, in which the elegant rationalism of her father's national culture lay side by side with the earnest idealism of her mother's. 'You have a German expression and a French smile,' her friend Princess Belgiojoso once said to her. The two cultures continue to inform the literary works that she later wrote under the name of Daniel Stern – itself a symbolic hybrid pseudonym.

One evening towards the end of 1833 Marie d'Agoult was among the guests at a party given in the Paris residence of the Marquise Le Vayer. Suddenly there appeared 'the most extraordinary person I had ever seen', she said:

> Tall, extremely thin, pale, with large, sea-green eyes flashing with sudden brilliance like waves glinting in the sun, strong features shot through with suffering, hesitant in his movements and seeming to glide rather than walk, seemingly preoccupied yet at the same time restless, like a ghost waiting for the clock to strike and summon him back to the shades . . .
>
> Franz talked emotionally, breathlessly; with passion he uttered thoughts and opinions totally strange to ears like mine, accustomed as they were to hearing only banal, conventional views. I recall his shining eyes, his gestures and the way he smiled – sometimes earnestly and with a profound gentleness, sometimes ironically, caustically.

These are Marie d'Agoult's first words about the man whose hold over her she could never break – words that capture something of the complexity of the Liszt who never changed. 'A ghost waiting for the clock to strike and summon him back to the shades' – is this not the Liszt who shared his life with Faust and Mephistopheles, the world of his Faust Symphony, of the Mephisto Waltzes, of the 'Inferno' in his Dante Symphony? 'Thoughts and opinions totally strange' – was not a passionate unconventionality central to his nature, the instinctive conviction of a compulsive originality as performer and composer, sustained and objectified by the force of the solipsistic personality? And his smile: no one, neither his sceptical rivals nor his implacable adversaries, could ever gainsay his kindness, his honesty, his humanity – yet he could appear unaffectedly ironical at his own expense, self-deprecatory, refusing to lend himself to a cult of personality or be cast in the role of Messiah.

Countess Marie d'Agoult was twenty-eight, a proud and attractive aristocrat, with two young daughters, a focus of admiring attention in Parisian high society. George Sand, apostle of liberated womanhood, described her as 'beautiful, charming, witty and above all endowed with the advantages of a higher intelligence'. Liszt was twenty-two, of lower middle-class origins, a paid servant of the society into which the Countess had been born and which had engaged him to play to them that evening when they first set eyes on each other. As it had already been with Caroline de Saint-Cricq and the Countess de la Prunarède, and as it was to be many times again in his life, a social gulf lay between him and the women to whom he was attracted. The more famous he became, and the lower the class barriers grew as the century progressed, the less such a distinction came to matter. But at this moment it could have crushed the life out of all but the most ardent and determined liaisons.

Just such a liaison, immediate, passionate, defying the raised eyebrows and frowns of offended orthodoxy, this now became. For Marie, frustrated, trapped in a marriage that was already dead, the brilliance and impulsive originality of the handsome young Franz Liszt flooded the world with a dazzling new light, a light directed at those very ideals – freedom, love, the wonder of art, the brotherhood of man – that informed her own vision of the true life. Here was a promise of liberation and new meaning, enshrined in a figure who conquered her the moment she set eyes on him, a man for whom, against all rational argument, she was prepared to sacrifice family, privilege, position.

And Liszt? The sudden, total affection of an enchanting lady of rank overwhelmed him. He had no family whose contrary interests might have held him back, no one who needed to be considered or consulted. Above all, despite the ponderable discrepancies there for all to see, the Countess's wealth and maturity held a twofold promise – the peace of mind encouraged by economic security, and the sympathy, intellectual and spiritual, that her years brought with them. For with one side of his nature Liszt, for all his extroversion and his unshakeable need of a public with which to surround his activities, hankered after a life of peace and tranquillity, a haven of rest to which he could withdraw in serenity and creative contemplation. It was that longing which had beckoned him as a youth to enter a monastery, which a dozen or so years later was to lead him to abandon his career as the greatest pianist in Europe, which drew him into the arms of Princess Carolyne von Sayn-Wittgenstein and which finally made him, as the Abbé Liszt, a servant of the Roman Catholic Church. Inspired by the love and the passionate understanding with which the eager Marie d'Agoult suddenly flooded his life, he now saw such a glorious prospect opening up before him.

From the beginning the relationship between Franz Liszt and Countess Marie d'Agoult was indeed true love, and from the beginning, by Shakespearean definition, it did not run smooth.

41

The implications for Marie were by far the more serious. By eloping with him, she would be turning her back on her family; to desert her husband would mean liberation but to forfeit her children would cause her deep sorrow. When, towards the end of 1834, her elder daughter Louise died of meningitis at the age of six, her anxiety over the step she was contemplating cut still deeper. Liszt later learned from her chambermaid that she had been on the point of drowning herself, and throughout that year, as her memoirs recall, both she and Liszt made almost despairing attempts to free themselves from each other's clutches. For three months he sought refuge with Lamennais at La Chênaie, trying to forget her.

To no avail. What they had to offer each other was too exciting to ignore, too precious to reject. Marie's pangs of conscience over what she was leaving behind could not outweigh the joys that a beckoning future promised. 'From the first moment I loved you,' he said when they were reunited, 'and felt what that love was and what it was going to demand. I trembled for you. I decided to leave you. But now I see what I have done . . . I shall not let you languish and perish in this misery. I too have a thirst for life!' To stay in Paris – even in France – was impossible, and in the spring of 1835 they travelled south to Switzerland, first to Basel, then to Geneva, where at least the breath of things French could still be felt. 'We are both in reasonably high spirits,' wrote Liszt to his mother in Paris, 'and have not the slightest intention of being unhappy.'

It was an idyllic beginning. They took an apartment with a glorious view in what was then the rue Tabazan (now rue Étienne Dumont No. 22), for which Marie paid, as for practically everything else at this time. It was simply furnished – she mentions an Erard piano, a few books on a shelf and a basket of Alpine flowers – and she had brought just one maid with her, a Swiss girl from Bern. Blissfully happy alone, surrounded by the dramatic beauties of the Alpine landscape, they walked and read together, studying the progressive philosophical and political literature – Lamennais, Saint-Simon, the French Romantic poets – to which they had already been drawn. He gave her, not, perhaps, entirely innocently, a copy of George Sand's recently published novel *Lélia*, an attack on the marriage bond and the society that upholds it, in which the heroine dares to demand physical fulfilment in love and the right to leave her husband if he cannot give it to her.

Music belonged to Marie's world along with the other realms of the cultured mind, although she could not follow him, she confessed, into the theoretical and technical areas of experiment about which he would excitedly talk. But Liszt was not looking for a partner with whom to play duets. The companionship he sought – and he was both the most gregarious and most dependent of men – was that of the complete soul and body, the warmth that spreads from the unconditional surrender of two beings to each other in a moment of ideal beauty.

Intellectually she brought to bear on their relationship an influence both broadening and steadying, sharing with him the joys of a classical education he had not known and helping him to give precision to the thoughts teeming through his mind. Indeed, she even had a hand in the actual writing of some of the essays that he sent to the *Revue et Gazette musicale* between 1835 and 1840. There are passages in her diaries which recur almost word for word in his *Lettres d'un bachelier ès musique*; when he left Venice for his concerts in Vienna at the end of 1839, he expressly asked her to finish his 'letter' on La Scala for him, and there is in the archive left by Daniel Ollivier, Liszt's grandson, a file of Marie's manuscripts with the heading 'Articles Gazette Musicale'. Later in his life the hand of Princess Carolyne von Sayn-Wittgenstein also shows itself in his writings, but neither there nor here can his personal responsibility for the views published in his name be called in question. How often did the Old Masters, having stamped their authority on a painting, delegate to their students the task of completing the work?

The serenity of this new life also stimulated in Liszt a surge of creative musical energy, to which Marie's presence contributed its own magic. She wrote in her memoirs:

> He started to compose, and while he was working, my presence was far from unwelcome to him. On the contrary, when I tried discreetly to withdraw, he held me back, saying that he found it more difficult to collect his thoughts, and that his ideas were much less coherent, when he did not feel me close to him. For me, pretending to read but actually not missing a single movement of his pen or his lips, it was a source of profound joy to watch him thus totally committed to his art, to the radiant spirit which shone in his eyes and which I worshipped in silence.

With this retreat from the metropolis went a liberation of his musical thoughts and desires, as he had sensed it would, and personal happiness joined hands with creative *élan*. Most of his efforts went into the composition of piano fantasias – on themes from Halévy's *La Juive*, Bellini's *I Puritani*, Meyerbeer's *Les Huguenots* and Donizetti's *Lucia di Lammermoor* – and piano transcriptions (Rossini's *Soirées musicales*; Schubert's 'Die Rose', the first of over fifty Schubert transcriptions made between 1838 and 1847); and a duo for violin and piano on Charles Philippe Lafont's romance 'Le Marin.' But he also wrote original piano pieces, chief among them those collected in the *Album d'un voyageur*, most of which found their revised, ultimate form in the first book of the *Années de pèlerinage*, published in 1855.

Every title tells a story, and the names of the pieces in this anthology of moods and impressions, like the successive titles of the collections themselves, reveal the stimuli that worked upon Liszt's mind during these years and the terms in which he saw his life. The 'traveller' responds to the natural beauties of the Swiss countryside – 'Le Lac de Wallenstadt', 'Au bord d'une source', 'Les cloches de Genève' – and to its legendary and literary associations – 'La chapelle de Guillaume Tell', 'Vallée d'Obermann'. A concern with social conditions also continues to exercise his thoughts – the piece 'Lyon' owes its existence to the social unrest in that city which Liszt had seen for himself on the journey from Paris to Switzerland. That twenty years later what had been scenes from a journey to personal happiness became episodes in 'a year of pilgrimage' is a rueful comment on how Liszt later came to see this period in his life.

He wrote considerably more works than have survived, subsequently destroying some and losing others, but we are not likely to have been deprived of a masterpiece. Indeed, he frequently displayed a disarming reserve, not to say scepticism, about the value of his early compositions in general. Asked about them by Lina Ramann, who subjected him to a barrage of such questions while at work on his biography in the 1870s, he replied that if any of them were still lying around unpublished, 'it would be better if they remained quietly lost'.

As well as working on his own compositions, he took over, without fee, a piano class at the newly founded Conservatoire in Geneva. Unlike Wagner, who had no desire to take pupils, or Schumann, whose few months at the Leipzig Conservatoire were a disaster, Liszt was a born teacher, and to the very end of his life pupils were coming from all over Europe and from the United States to his master classes in Weimar, Rome and Budapest. Not only did the opportunity in Geneva satisfy his urge for artistic communication, like the charity concert he gave there at the end of 1835 for the Italian refugees from the war against the Austrians; it also helped to make him and his mistress *personae gratae* in a town not famed for its tolerance of such irregular and improper relationships as theirs.

'The number of people coming to see us gradually grew,' wrote Marie d'Agoult in her memoirs, 'and soon a small circle gathered, first round Franz, then round me, after I had overcome my reluctance to allow them to get to know me. This group showed me great respect, and some of them discreetly expressed to me their sympathy for my situation.' Among visitors who came from Paris, bringing news of the salon life that they had left behind, were the Polish Countess Delphine Potocka and the Italian-born Princess Cristina Belgiojoso (Cristina's estranged husband Emilio was living in Geneva at this time and had his own friendly relationship with the Liszts). Countess Potocka and the Belgiojosos were particular friends of Berlioz and Chopin – for whose liaison with George Sand they had the same sympathy as for that between Liszt and his Countess. Princess Belgiojoso, friend of Garibaldi and Mazzini, famed for her social conscience and her vigorous commitment to the struggle for Italian independence, had already cultivated Liszt the young prodigy in her Paris salon in the company of Rossini, Meyerbeer, Bellini and prominent men of letters. Although only three years older than he, she acted towards him like a mother – 'strict', he considered her – calling him to order when she considered his life-style too extravagant and chaotic but sharing with him a conviction in the primacy of passion as the true agent of thought and action, in politics as in art. 'She said I lived as though I thought I were immortal,' he once remarked of 'Principessa', as he called her.

The botanist Pyrame de Candolle, the orientalist Alphonse Denis, the politician James Fazy, the historian Sismonde de Sismondi, all distinguished members of the Geneva intelligentsia, also became regular callers. So too did the philologist Adolphe Pictet, who described in a delightful, highly-coloured account of a ten-day ramble that he, Liszt, Marie, George Sand – recently divorced – and two other friends made together from Geneva to Chamonix, how Liszt improvised on Mozart's *Dies Irae* on the organ of St Nicolas Cathedral in Fribourg. As his friends listened in amazement, Liszt embarked on an extended Adagio, followed by a double fugue, and left them at the end in a state of exaltation bordering on fear, which led Pictet to wonder what it could be in music that wielded such overwhelming and irresistible power, a power so irrational, so absolute, that one could only tremble at the emotional havoc it could wreak. For George Sand the experience was like that of entering the world of Dante.

When the Bohemian party finally arrived at the Hôtel de l'Union in Geneva, Liszt provocatively asked for Room 13 and entered in the hotel register:

Place of birth:	Parnassus
Occupation:	Musician-philosopher
Arriving from:	Doubt
En route for:	Truth

George Sand, always looking for ways to shock society, who had made the excursion accompanied by her two children, a maid and a mass of luggage, countered with:

Place of birth:	Europe
Residence:	Nature
Arriving from:	God
En route for:	Heaven
Date of passport:	Infinity
Issued by:	Public opinion

In the tenth of her *Lettres d'un voyageur* George Sand gives her own account of this sentimental, almost fantastic journey, made by a group of characters who at times seem larger than life, their feet barely touching the ground. She had turned from a passion for love to a passion for politics, and it was the latter rather than the former that had brought her and Liszt together in Paris a few years earlier, when they had been introduced at her request by her then lover, the poet and dramatist Alfred de Musset. They shared democratic opinions and a sense of compassion for the unfortunates of this life – the poor, the under-privileged, the exiled – and Liszt admired her novels and approved of her ideas on free, romantic love. They also enjoyed a penchant for the flamboyant and for the mischievous pleasure of *épater le bourgeois*. When Lina Ramann wrote in her biography: 'In the depths of his heart he felt little personal attraction to her,' Liszt crossed the whole sentence out. But there is little reason to believe that they were lovers. 'Liszt', she wrote in her *Journal intime*, 'loves no one but God and the Virgin Mary, who does not resemble me in the slightest.'

Not that the prospect did not occur to the cigar-smoking, scandal-loving George. 'If I could have loved Monsieur Liszt,' she said, 'I would have done so out of sheer spite, but I could not.' The spite would have been directed principally at Musset, although he had already moved out of her life, but Marie, whom she met for the first time in Geneva, was a secondary target, an attractive

46

potential victim of the seemingly insatiable and sometimes vindictive desire for conquest of this extraordinary woman. Where Marie d'Agoult remained the perfect aristocrat – she never really felt at her ease unless wearing a gown that had cost a thousand francs, Liszt once remarked – George Sand, though born into an aristocratic family, sought freedom from convention and propriety, held liberal reformist views, and roamed through life as the spirit took her. An on-and-off relationship between the two women lasted until 1838, the year before Liszt and Marie parted, but resumed in 1850 after Marie had herself moved towards a republican position in her *Essai sur la liberté* and *Lettres républicaines*, published under the pseudonym of Daniel Stern.

On 18 December 1835 Marie gave birth to the first of their three children, a girl baptized Blandine Rachel and described in the register by a gullible official who merely wrote down what he was told, as 'the natural daughter of François Liszt, teacher of music, aged 24 years, 1 month, born in Raiding in Hungary, and Catherine-Adelaide Méran, woman of property, aged 24 years, born in Paris, both not married and resident in Geneva. Liszt has freely and voluntarily admitted that he is the father of the said child.' By giving a false name, a false age and a false birthplace, Marie deceived only the record. She was not prepared, as George Sand would have been, to make proud, defiant affirmation of the truth. Liszt remained devoted to all his children and made their education his lasting concern but Blandine was especially precious to him, and her death in childbirth at the age of twenty-six, five years after her marriage, caused him profound grief.

Partly for financial reasons, but more urgently, one feels, in response to an inner voice with an insistent and unmistakeable message, Liszt found his thoughts returning to the concert hall, to the thrill of confrontation with the public. From Lyon, where he played in 1836, he wrote that he could earn between 500 and 750 francs for each recital in a large town, and 300 in smaller places. As with Clara Schumann, when the need arose, he only had to hint that he would be willing to accept an invitation to give a concert or two for his flagging finances to be immediately rejuvenated.

The confidence engendered by this knowledge complemented the assurance, the sense of maturity and independence, that his new life with Marie d'Agoult and the burgeoning of his intellectual powers brought with them, and the subtle change in him struck Madame Boissier, for one, who had observed him closely in Paris five years earlier. 'He is amiable and good-natured,' she noted, but a poor young man, horribly spoiled by society and by his successes . . . It has been his misfortune to live among literary people of the day who have stuffed him with their dangerous doctrines and false notions. He rejects accepted principles and beliefs but I cannot discover what he wishes to put in their place . . . He shrugs his shoulders at the sanctity of marriage and similar bagatelles, and abandons himself to his passions with utter freedom and unconcern.

As he faced the world in this spirit of self-confidence, strengthened by his awareness of his powers and by his commitment to his art, news reached Geneva of the emergence in Paris of a new keyboard virtuoso, a twenty-four-year-old Austrian named Sigismund Thalberg, whose appeal seemed about to eclipse his own. A performing artist has constantly to refresh the public's memory of his skills, and Liszt had been away from Paris, musical capital of the world, for too long. The leading writer on music of the day, François Joseph Fétis, author of the *Biographie universelle des musiciens* and founder of the *Revue musicale de Paris*, called Thalberg an 'epoch-shattering genius', a phrase which stung Liszt into investigating Thalberg's claim for himself.

Much, probably too much, has been made of the fascinating but short-lived 'rivalry' between Liszt and Thalberg by writers who have turned it into a kind of pianistic minstrels' contest on the Wartburg. Lina Ramann recorded that the news of Thalberg's successes 'greatly disturbed and agitated Liszt' and that 'his agitation drove him to go to Paris'. On the relevant page of her biography Liszt deleted 'greatly disturbed and agitated' and substituted 'annoyed', while far from being so worked up that he was 'driven' to go to Paris, he crossed out Ramann's whole sentence and put: 'Curious, he chanced to make his way to Paris.' He seems to have later been at pains to play the whole episode down, and at the time fascinated onlookers no doubt revelled in the contrived theatricality with which the two men were forced to confront each other like the victims in a cock fight. But equally there was more at stake than mere 'curiosity' on Liszt's part, and his fame, for all his self-confidence, was far from a matter of indifference to him.

At all events, whether 'agitated' or just 'curious', Liszt did go to Paris in the summer of 1836, avoiding Thalberg on this occasion but giving recitals of his own, including in his programmes Beethoven's Sonata Op. 106 and his own 'La Juive' and 'I Puritani' Fantasias. 'This is the great new school of pianists!' exclaimed

Berlioz, enraptured. 'From this day onwards we can be prepared for anything and everything from Liszt the composer!' Fétis, on the other hand, now distinguished himself by backing the wrong horse. 'You are the progeny of a school that has outlived itself and has nothing left to do!' he cried to Liszt, 'and certainly not the founder of a new movement. That is what Thalberg is – and this is where the whole difference between you lies!' Liszt now took a look at Thalberg's compositions, decided they were 'empty and mediocre' and published an article saying so. Chopin, whose works had also been unfavourably compared with Thalberg's, entered the fray on Liszt's side, conceding that Thalberg was a splendid performer 'but not the man for me – he plays fortes and pianos with the pedal, not with the hand.' Like Liszt, the aristocratic Thalberg apparently made a particular impression on the ladies, and to criticize his playing or his pieces was a risk not everyone was prepared to take. 'If one were to venture a word of disapproval,' wrote Schumann in a review of Thalberg's recent compositions, 'one would have all the maidens of Germany and the rest of the world on one's back in no time at all.'

In March 1837 Liszt returned to Paris to find Thalberg in residence again after a tour abroad. Two concerts were arranged. Thalberg played two of his Fantasias – on 'God Save the King' and Rossini's *Moïse* – to an audience of 400 in the concert hall of the Conservatoire; Liszt chose to perform before over 3,000 in the opera house, playing his 'Niobe' Fantasia and Weber's *Konzertstück*. The size of audience alone virtually settled the issue of their relative merits.

A few weeks later Princess Belgiojoso organized a fund-raising event in her house for the benefit of the political refugees from her native country, at which both men were to appear. Distinguished figures from public life were invited, and above all the Princess's friends from the Parisian *haute volée*, for the 'feud' between the two men had long since broken the artificial mould of an international piano competition and become a lip-smacking item in the social calendar for that season.

Thalberg played first – his 'Moïse' Fantasia, a show-piece of the kind for which the public clamoured and on which the keyboard gymnasts of the time exuberantly let themselves loose. His reward was the expected enthusiastic applause. Then came Liszt. He had selected his own rival Fantasia, that on the Cavatina from Pacini's *Niobe*, no less spectacular in its acrobatic wizardry and its demands on stamina. His performance was given a tumultuous reception, overshadowing Thalberg's. A simple adjudication in his favour would have been too primitive, and offensive to both men. Princess Belgiojoso's somewhat embarrassed verdict-to-end-all-verdicts ran: 'Thalberg is the best pianist in Paris but there is only one Liszt in the world!'

So the puerilities – the word is Liszt's – of the 'contest', rather, 'non-contest', came thankfully to an end. Like the literary 'Querelle des anciens et des modernes' in seventeenth-century France, or the operatic skirmishes between Gluckists and Piccinnists in eighteenth-century Paris, it had been an artificially fomented crisis, here involving two men who had no desire to become rivals. 'How can people say,' asked Liszt crossly, 'that we have now become reconciled, when we were never enemies?' A creeping contempt for the role played by the public in the conduct of the culture industry as a whole – he had voiced similar views in his social essay 'On the Position of the Artist' – was the dominant impression left by the whole affair. In May 1837 he thankfully turned his back on Paris, making his way to George Sand's house in Nohant, near Chateauroux, where Marie had been staying during the Thalberg episode.

This separation, forced on them by circumstance and leaving no apparent scar, yet gave point to a fear, or semi-fear, that had come over Marie during their first blissful days together in Geneva. For although she could feel her way to a considerable degree into Liszt's musical world, to realize the full nature of his ideals and of the impulses behind his compositions was beyond her, and in this she sensed a danger. 'Perhaps,' she wrote in her memoirs, 'unbeknown to me – and I would never have dared to say anything – a secret instinct was warning me that there was something working against me and threatening our love.' The instinct did not err.

For the moment, however, the surface of their happiness seemed unruffled. After three months in Nohant, where he began work on his piano transcriptions of Beethoven's symphonies and made the first sketches for the Dante Sonata, they set off back to Geneva, stopping first in Lyon, where Liszt gave a few concerts in aid of the unemployed weavers in the city. Barthélémy Prosper Enfantin, socialist writer and leader of the Saint-Simonian school, lived nearby, symbolizing in his presence the union of practical reform and crusading idealism to which Liszt, and later through him Marie d'Agoult, had been drawn since the days of the 1830 Paris Revolution. From Lyon they then visited the poet Lamartine at his retreat by the lake of Saint-Point, near Pontarlier, and finally reached Geneva in August. A special joy awaiting them was their little daughter Blandine, now eighteen months old.

But their wanderlust, the delight of shared discoveries and experiences, urged them to seek out new beauties and explore new cultures, this time, mainly at Marie's urging, in northern Italy. A few days by Lago Maggiore were followed by a visit to Milan, where Liszt gave a recital which earned him the title 'The Paganini of the Keyboard', after which they went back to the lakes and rented the Villa Melzi at Bellagio, on Lake Como. Here, between the oleanders and magnolias, all was solitude and beauty, and no tiresome discord disturbed the private idyll. The moral ambience too, as Marie took grateful note in her diary, helped to make their life 'feel' right, and she quotes, with a blend of relief and defiance, other distinguished adulterous couples who have made their home in Italy. 'Personal behaviour here strikes me as far freer than in France', she noted gratefully. 'Free liaisons do not cause a scandal, and people have no hesitation in using the word lover.'

On Christmas Eve 1837, in the little town of Como, their second daughter was born. She was christened Francesca Gaetana Cosima – the last being a name symbolically derived from Saint Cosmas (in Italian Cosimo; in French Côme) and Como – a woman destined to become, as Cosima Wagner, one of the most dominating and controversial figures in the cultural history of nineteenth-century Europe. Her illegitimacy was expressly recorded in the church baptismal register, while her parents were described as 'both Catholic, the father a professor of music and landowner, the mother of noble birth'.

Liszt continued work on the pianoforte pieces that later comprised the Italian impressions of the *Années de pèlerinage* (*Deuxième Année*), among them the three Petrarch Sonnets and the Dante Sonata. The working-out of this Sonata seems to date only from a period twelve or more years hence, when it received its final title – *Après une lecture de Dante*, with the musical explanation *Fantasia quasi Sonata*. It is the title of a poem by Victor Hugo; Liszt's piece is thus not so much a direct response to Dante – who was something of a cult figure in France in the early nineteenth century – as an experience of Dante filtered through the mind of Hugo. But the seed of the experience was sown during these months in Italy, where, in the 'right' surroundings, he had a vision of the world of Dante and Beatrice as an idealized reflection of the world of Franz Liszt and Marie d'Agoult.

The Swiss pieces of the 'Première Année' had been impressions of nature, responses to places seen; sometimes literary associations formed part of the scene but generally the lake, the spring, the meadow spoke directly through the music, the visual seeking its aural correlative. The Italian pilgrimage, taking Liszt for the first time across the Alps to the 'land where the lemon-trees blossom', as Goethe called it, is sustained by the experiences of art. In spirit, as in subject and thus in form, these piano pieces are like miniature symphonic poems, forerunners of the orchestral works which he composed in Weimar in the 1850s.

Yet his vision was not, as it had been for so many before him, the Italy of Classical tradition, the 'grandeur that was Rome', the pagan world of the Colosseum and the Baths of Caracalla, but the Christian Italy of the Middle Ages and Renaissance, the civilization of Michelangelo, of Raphael, of Petrarch, of Dante. Petrarch's text stands at the head of Liszt's three Sonnets and is meant to be absorbed before the music is played or listened to (he later set the three sonnets as solo songs). Not that it constitutes a detailed programme which he pledges himself to 'illustrate', thought by thought, bar by bar, following the poetic imagery hither and thither. But notwithstanding the autonomy of the music, which has to stand or fall by the criteria proper to music, it is the poem that has released the composer's imagination, and it is from the poem that the player has to begin his performance. Likewise the Dante Sonata, by far the most substantial of the seven numbers of the 'Deuxième Année', presupposes in its structure alone at least an awareness of the existence of the Dantean vision of Inferno, Purgatorio and Paradiso.

Like the 'Première Année', the collection of Italian pieces was later revised during Liszt's years in Weimar and published in the 1850s – the revisions are often so far-reaching that they result in a virtually new piece – but the characteristic qualities of his piano style already command attention. His particular indebtedness to Chopin, above all in the exploitation of chromatic melody and harmony and in the art of decoration, of melodic embroidery, needs no labouring. But Liszt's uniqueness is as absolute as Chopin's uniqueness, and the distance between the two worlds is immense – far greater than that between, say, Schubert and Schumann, or Schumann and Chopin, or Schumann, Chopin and Brahms. Every world has its conventions and mannerisms, features of the artist's handwriting, so to speak, and Liszt's may sometimes be more obtrusive than others': his penchant for remote keys, his sophisticated chromaticism, his glittering passage-work over all seven octaves of the keyboard (and the daunting difficulty of performing it), a heavy reliance on the dramatic qualities of the chord of the diminished seventh, the progressions of octaves, the straining for an orchestral volume and variety of tone and so on. At the end, however, it is the welding together of these and a thousand other characteristics that constitutes his inimitable musical personality. The tenderness is *his* tenderness, the intensity *his* intensity, the theatricality the product of *his* theatre. Here reside the originality and authenticity of his art.

To the totality of Liszt's spiritual world belong also the philosophical and religious impulses that issue from literature – the thought-content, one might call it, of the musical works whose titles reveal their extra-musical *points de départ* and associations. Where the pictorial programme music of Schumann has before it a scene, a mood or a symbolic object which we are invited to observe – a carnival, a dream, a forest, a bird – Liszt immerses us in an intense and total experience of what his chosen subject means to him, an experience compounded of the sensuous and the intellectual, the situational and the visionary, the expressed and the implied, the real and the ideal. And although the form that he gives to his experience is a musical form, there lie behind the music thoughts, emotions, even judgements, proper to other areas of his reflective and creative personality, which cannot be dissociated either from the musical utterance itself or from our understanding of it. What we are facing, in a word, is a *Gesamtkunstwerk*, a union of the arts – and one not so different from Wagner's as one might at first think. *Tasso*, *Macbeth*, *Les Préludes* and the other symphonic poems of Liszt's Weimar years, like the Dante and Faust Symphonies, embody this 'total work of art' in its fullest form.

If Liszt the composer revelled in the tranquillity of Lake Como, Liszt the pianist could not live without the city lights. The city in question, only some thirty miles away, was the provincial capital of Milan, which had been returned to Austrian rule after the defeat of Napoleon. Rossini, who knew Liszt from Paris in the 1820s, had taken up residence here, and although his career as a composer of opera, the foundation of his fame, now lay behind him, his influence on musical life in Italy remained uncontested. It needed only a word from him for Liszt to be invited to give a number of concerts in the city, at which he played his recently completed transcription of the Overture to Rossini's *William Tell*. Such pieces were much to the taste of contemporary audiences, partly because of the bravura content of the performance, partly because of the familiarity of the tunes, which, far from listening to in hushed admiration, they would sing and whistle in chorus with the player.

The Italian journey of Liszt and Marie d'Agoult, sketched in his *Lettres d'un bachelier ès musique*, led to Venice, then back to the Italian lakes, this time to Lugano. While in Venice Liszt read in a newspaper that as a result of the spring rains the Danube had burst its banks and flooded large areas of the Hungarian countryside, as well as the town of Pest, much of which was under water. Immediately he set out for Vienna, alone, to raise money for the flood victims by giving recitals, both public and private. The enthusiasm he aroused was enormous, and the appeal fund swelled not only through the takings at the concerts themselves – some 30,000 florins in all – but also, in the promotional style that accompanies the career of modern popular idols, through the sale of personal mementos. 'I am the man of the moment,' he wrote to Marie. 'Fifty copies of my portrait were sold in the space of twenty-four hours.'

It was an emotional moment – his first return to Vienna since the time, sixteen years before, of his arrival in the Austrian capital from his native Hungary, of his first public appearance as a pianist, of his encounter with Beethoven. The discernment of the audiences before whom he played created an atmosphere to which he responded with programmes of a variety and quality that would have baffled his listeners in Italy. The mandatory operatic pot-pourris were still there, but also Beethoven, Weber, Scarlatti, his own *Grandes Études,* Chopin and some of Schumann's early pieces, including *Carnaval.* This latter he had just come across and immediately put into his repertoire.

At this moment the nineteen-year-old Clara Wieck, soon to become Robert Schumann's wife, chanced to be in Vienna on one of her many European tours. It would be hard to imagine a greater contrast than that between these two artists, seen by audiences as making up, together with Thalberg, the trinity of the greatest piano virtuosi of the day. On the one hand the petite, withdrawn, almost fragile Clara, trained from early childhood by a relentless father driven by the single compulsion to turn his daughter into the prodigy to end all prodigies; she had been deprived of a free, ingenuous childhood in her Dresden home, had had virtually no general education and, cocooned in an unnatural protective shell, knew little of the 'real' world outside – indeed, although in her heart she had already given herself to Schumann, in her day-to-day life she was still tied to her father's apron-strings. And on the other hand the tall, elegant, handsome, self-assured Liszt, well-read, well-connected, man of the world, a born conqueror who was carving his own destiny.

Yet for all their differences they found a level of mutual respect from the moment of their first meeting, which was sought in fact by Liszt, who had heard of Clara's achievements through Chopin. Liszt's 'Niobe' Fantasia was already in Clara's repertoire, and she later added some of his transcriptions of Schubert's songs, 'Ständchen' and 'Erlkönig' among them, but this was the first time she had heard him play. 'Since hearing and watching Liszt's technique,' she wrote in her diary, 'I feel like a beginner.' Yet she plucked up enough courage to play *Carnaval* to him, and he remained unfailingly well-disposed to both Schumann the man and Schumann the composer – a cordiality that Schumann, a gloomy and inaccessible individual for much of the time, found difficulty in returning. Liszt later went so far as to rank *Carnaval* as the equal of Beethoven's Diabelli Variations.

As usual he relished the company of the *haute volée*. To repay their hospitality, he wrote to Marie with thinly-veiled pride, he gave an 'aristocratic soirée', his invitations being accepted by Prince Pückler-Muskau, Prince Fritz Schwarzenberg, his former Hungarian sponsor Count Apponyi, Count Hartig, Count Waldstein, Baron Reischach, Count Paul Esterházy and many other worthies. He was equally frank, to Marie's no great pleasure, about his continued successes among the ladies, reports of which also reached her from other sources.

Yet during these absences in Vienna, Milan and elsewhere we also find him solicitous about her uncertain health since the birth of Cosima and assuring – or reassuring – her, in the somewhat florid style characteristic of all his writing, how much he needed her love:

My dear, good Marie, you are indeed an angel and I am scarcely worthy of you. So do not tell me to come to your aid – it is for you to come to mine. It is for you to make me less unworthy of you day by day. Love me – let us love each other. That is all we need. And let us have hope. The Lord will not fail us.

But at other times a less passionate, less insistent tone creeps into his voice, a hint, not of coolness or uneasiness but at least of distance, of a gentle withdrawal from the intensity of supreme commitment. The word 'love' gives way to 'affection', the use of religious vocabulary grows, as though he were seeking a higher, supra-personal plane on which to set their relationship. He is gripped, he writes, by 'an ineffable affection like that of a brother and friend', and seems to be edging slowly away from the mood of heady excitement in which, as impulsive lovers, they had run away from Paris. Perhaps he was beginning to realize that Marie needed him more than he needed her, and that what she needed was more than he could give. She had had more to sacrifice, more to lose, than he; and the self-reliance which he hoped would accompany her independence, and which would have been the natural expression of the values, intellectual and moral, by which she had chosen to live, seemed hesitant to emerge. It was becoming easier for him to love her at a distance. In this way that part of him which sought the world outside, the world with which he needed to communicate through his art, could find the fulfilment without which he could not in the end survive.

During his absence from Venice, where they had no close friends or acquaintances, he had encouraged her to seek the company of a certain Count Theodoro. When she wrote to him how lonely she was, 'he advised me to take Theodoro as a lover', she recalled in her memoirs. And when they met again, 'I found him hard, dry, ironical', pretending not to understand what she felt and what she needed.

Less willingly, but ultimately no less clearly, Marie too recognized that a blissful episode, a moment of brilliance which had brought new meaning to her life but which she was powerless to prolong, was slowly, inexorably slipping past. The ordeal of separation had to be faced: pretence was idle. She remembered what he had said to her back in the carefree summer of 1833: 'You are not the woman I need but the woman I want.' Now, bitter yet resigned, she wrote to him from Venice in June 1838:

> My love is draining the life out of you. I believe you could love *happily* – but me you have loved *strongly* . . . As for me, I shall never be able to love anyone again, but why should I deprive you of another love which could be the source of a new life for you? I have a deep respect for your freedom.

It all came true. Countess Marie d'Agoult never loved with such intensity again. Franz Liszt did. And his freedom survived this too.

Unequivocal though the looming truth had become, casting its long shadow over their lives, both still affected the occasional gesture proper to a past that would never return – she in forlorn hope, fearing the void that lay before her and her children, he secure in the knowledge of his vocation, yet anxious that feelings should not be hurt, that harsh reality should be tempered with compassion, with patience. Whatever else Liszt's contemporaries found in him to criticize and resent, 'unkindness' was a word never uttered. Until the final break between them his letters continue to express solicitude, understanding, tenderness – love in its passage from ἔρος to ἀγάπη, erotic to brotherly love. The bitter arguments that later broke out between them, above all over the custody and education of their children, and the recriminatory manner in which she then chose to present the nature of their relationship, left him sad and bewildered. If one lives the present fully and honestly, was his philosophy, there will be no cause to deny the past.

The present that they still for the moment shared, 1838 to 1839, led from Venice and Lugano to Geneva, to Florence and eventually, in January 1839, to Rome. In all these towns and cities he gave recitals, public and private, to the by now traditional acclaim. The world lay at his feet. Any concert hall was put at his disposal, and he moved freely in and out of the *palazzi* of the aristocracy as though it were his birthright. Surrounded by the works of art that adorned these palaces, living in the land of Michelangelo and Raphael, of Dante and Petrarch, of Palestrina and Monteverdi, he felt his spirit rise, his aesthetic awareness expand. Inspired by a new friendship with the painter Ingres, at that time director of the École de France in Rome, he began to seek parallels between music and painting, music and architecture – indeed, not merely parallels but the common fount of creativity and spiritual energy from which all art springs.

Yet all this was rather the beginning of the future than a reality of the present. It symbolized where his life was going, not what it had at that moment become. And it was no longer a life in which Marie d'Agoult had a part to play. She chronicled in her diary the sour way in which he had put it one evening in Florence:

> I suffer as I watch a period in my existence coming to an end. Nothing can bring these last three years to life again – there is nothing left for me to learn or to desire; a free, spontaneous life has given way to plans and projects. I am at an age when one feels that nothing is adequate. I feel bitter that I am not what I would wish to be. When one breaks with everything around one, one also breaks something in oneself.

In this moment of strain and disillusion, of imminent disintegration, the third of their children was born in Rome on 9 May 1839. He was christened Daniel, after Marie's favourite Biblical character, and he died tragically at the age of only twenty, three years before his elder sister Blandine. At the time of Daniel's birth Cosima, one of nature's survivors, was two. 'Mademoiselle

Cosima looks feature for feature very much like the lovable Mouche [i.e. Blandine]', wrote her mother to Liszt a few months later, with uninhibited candour, 'except that she is far less beautiful and less striking.' Her lanky form later earned her the unflattering nickname 'The Stork'.

With Rome as his centre, like Venice and Milan earlier, Liszt continued his conquests of the Italian public in nearby towns. From Albano he wrote to Princess Belgiojoso that, as a new venture, instead of playing a collection of pieces by different composers, he had given recitals consisting entirely of his own works, as if to make clear to the audience – to adapt the saying of Louis XIV – 'Le concert, c'est moi!'

To show you what I mean, here is one of the programmes:
1. Overture, *William Tell*, performed by M. Liszt.
2. *Reminiscences of 'I Puritani'*: Fantasia composed and performed by the said M. Liszt.
3. Etudes and short pieces by the same.
4. Improvisation on themes submitted – also by the same.

When this last item formed part of his programme, he would place a box at the entrance to the hall and invite the audience to put envelopes in it containing their themes. A certain irreverence crept into the proceedings when he found that, as well as the popular melodies of the day, 'themes' such as 'Milan Cathedral' and 'Railways' had been put forward. 'For an improvisation on this latter,' he wrote to the Paris violinist Lambert Massard in his *Lettres d'un bachelier ès musique,* 'the only procedure that occurred to me was an uninterrupted series of scales *glissando*, but because I was afraid that, if I tried to compete with the swiftly advancing steam locomotive, I would only break my wrist, I opened another envelope.' In this he found the subject: 'Is it better to get married or remain a bachelor?' 'To which I replied from the platform,' he wrote, 'by reminding the audience of the words of the sage: "Whatever decision one makes about marrying or remaining single, one will live to regret it." '

By gradually edging out, through sensational talent and force of personality, all the others – the minor characters, so to speak – who had originally shared the concert platform with him, Liszt had already made himself the originator of the solo recital. He now, it seems, also initiated the public concert devoted to a single composer – himself, as it happened. The Bayreuth Festival of his future son-in-law was to become the *ne plus ultra* of this artistic self-centredness.

In November 1839 Liszt and the Countess went their separate ways. Leaving the seven-month-old Daniel in the care of a nanny in the town of Palestrina, near Rome, Marie travelled to Paris with Blandine and Cosima and considered sharing a house for a few months with Liszt's mother, who later, against Marie's fruitless resistance, took over the responsibility for her grand-children's education. But in the end she elected to retain her independence. She was facing a vast emptiness, a numb semi-existence. 'I had no plan, no sense of purpose,' she wrote, 'and had formed not the slightest idea of what sort of life I was going to lead.' Those she had regarded as her friends in former days, before she had left the capital with Liszt, pretended to have forgotten her, and she was forced to find a new, inward-looking *modus vivendi*, reading a great deal and finding a new identity as a writer.

She had little doubt that her husband would have taken her back – they never in fact divorced – but this would have meant denying a past which she was pledged, in conviction and self-respect, to preserve. 'My love had been too great,' she wrote in her memoirs, 'too pure in its romantic glory, I would dare to say, for me ever to disown it.' Eventually, greatly sustained by the moral support of the Abbé Lamennais, she established her own salon, as of old, where Delacroix, Alfred de Vigny, Ingres, Bulwer Lytton, Sainte-Beuve – and, in 1859, Wagner – were to be found.

Liszt, by contrast, stood on the threshold of a career which over the next nine years brought him greater fame than ever, a career of furious activity which, ironically, was to leave him unfulfilled and sceptical while the public clapped and cheered. He continued to correspond with Marie – the question of their children's education alone would have made it necessary – but the tone of his letters moves in time from cool to critical, then from critical to resentful. The few planned meetings they later had were attended by neither warmth nor sympathy. Not a single line did he write to her when first Daniel, then Blandine died, and no one informed him of her death in 1876. He merely chanced upon the obituary in a newspaper.

Most of his truly characteristic and most deeply pondered music was yet to come. Apart, possibly, from a few songs – disregarding juvenilia such as the opera *Don Sanche* – his output had consisted entirely of piano works, whether original compositions, operatic paraphrases and fantasias, or transcriptions – *partitions de piano*, as he called them. In this he belongs, with Thalberg, Moscheles, Henri Herz and other keyboard virtuosi, and also with Paganini, to that clan of composer-performers which was a characteristic

product of musical conditions and values in nineteenth-century
Europe. Indeed, he could say through the medium of the piano all
that he wished to say at this moment. Asked by his Geneva friend
Adolphe Pictet whether he did not intend to turn his mind to, say,
the symphonic form, he replied:

> You must realize that my piano is for me what a boat is to a
> sailor, or a horse to an Arab – even more, for it has been my
> language, my life, my very self. It is the guardian of all that
> stirred me most deeply in the passionate days of my youth, and
> I confide to it all my desires, my dreams, my joys and sorrows
> . . . I shall give up studying and extending the world of the
> piano only when I have achieved everything in it that it is
> possible for me to achieve.

Yet leaving aside the obtrusive technical glitter of Liszt's piano
writing which these early pieces already joyously display, one can
find in them solemn moments of an uncannily assured and
penetrative originality, such as the opening of 'Il Pensieroso',
from the 'Deuxième Année' of the *Années de pèlerinage*:

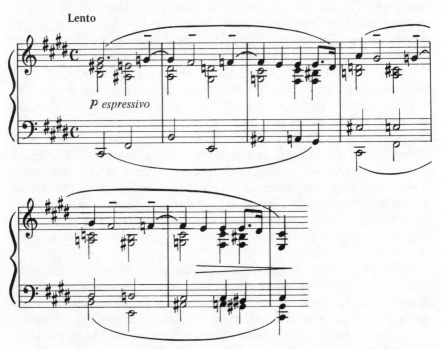

It is the world of *Tristan und Isolde*, of the Twilight of the Gods
motif from the *Ring*, of *Parsifal*. Liszt sowed the seed, saw that

there was a new psychology, a new realm of expression concealed in such brooding, disturbing chromaticism. But the nurturing of the seed, and the harvest, were to be Wagner's.

The story of Franz Liszt and Countess Marie d'Agoult breathes the true air of romance. It has been told and told again, with sympathy, scorn, condescension or offended morality, successive versions merely swelling the stocks of literary ephemera. But there are two contemporary treatments of the story which stand in a quite different relationship to the characters whose fate they describe – two novels, sad, mocking postscripts to the chronicle of events.

One is Balzac's novel, *Béatrix*, written in 1839, the year the lovers separated, with a sequel published six years later. When Balzac visited George Sand at Nohant in February 1838, she told him, with a mixture of relish and spite, the details of the affair between Liszt and Marie, not disguising her own ambiguous interest in the former and mischievous envy of the latter. On this triangular relationship Balzac built a *roman à clef* involving the plight of two lovers, an aristocratic lady and a vain, moderately-gifted musician, who, having scandalized society by their affair, find themselves forced by their pride to carry on with it before the public gaze, although they no longer feel the romantic love they profess and dearly desire to separate. Balzac's ironical verdict on the relationship comes in the subtitle of the novel – *Les galériens*, 'the galley-slaves', captives of a self-induced passion that has lost the power to command.

But Marie d'Agoult saw things differently. In 1846, as 'Daniel Stern', she published a pseudo-autobiographical novel called *Nélida*, reliving for the benefit of the world her years in the company of Liszt. Her heroine, Nélida (an anagram of Daniel), is presented as the daughter of an aristocratic family who, in the manner of the time, is pressed into an unwelcome marriage for dynastic reasons. She makes the acquaintance of a vain, self-centred painter called Guermann Regnier – even the Christian name is a laboured symbol of the juxtaposed French and German worlds; they fall passionately in love, and Nélida deserts her husband. Like Liszt and Marie, Guermann and Nélida elope to Geneva, but Guermann, who has a great artistic following, is lured back to the social life of Paris and leaves Nélida alone. A series of envies and jealousies follows, and they finally part company. Guermann is appointed to paint a number of murals in a German duchy – a thinly disguised reference to Liszt's recent appointment to Weimar – where he discovers that his talents are unequal to the task. His morale is broken; his health deteriorates, and as he lies dying, the faithful Nélida is summoned to his bedside. The two are finally reconciled and he dies in her arms.

The sentimental ending is merely a concession to bad taste, a tear-jerking ruse to ensure that the reader retains to the end the image of a loving and eternally loyal Nélida. Throughout the rest of the novel, however, the author loses no opportunity to portray her thinly-disguised lover, Guermann-Liszt, as a charlatan and a heartless egoist, and herself as his abused, long-suffering yet ever-faithful victim. Not only the framework but also individual episodes in the story were immediately recognized by contemporaries and referred to the life of Marie and Liszt – even his 'contest' with Thalberg in Paris has its counterpart in the novel. The style has a florid fulsomeness which recalls a tart remark made by Liszt on Marie's death in 1876: 'Countess d'Agoult does not believe what she says, so she says it all the more eloquently.'

When *Nélida* first appeared, Liszt received it with remarkable tolerance. Many close to him, including his mother, saw it as a hurtful attack on him, but he took a loftier view. 'Not for a moment did I feel wounded', he wrote to Marie; he even praised the 'aristocratic charm' of her style and congratulated her on the book's success. He was rarely driven to anger, and it was not in his nature to harbour a grudge. In the early years of their separation, moreover, the many letters that passed between them still flicker, even glow, with a concern for each other's well-being; he describes to her in detail his experiences on his concert tours throughout Europe, including his encounters with various women, and when the Hungarian national Diet intimated at the end of 1839 that they proposed to confer a title on him, he asks Marie to design the coat of arms he will need – it should include an owl, he says. The petulant character assassination in which her novel indulged can hardly have left him wholly unmoved, but he had the imagination and the magnanimity to interpret it as the repercussion of a strain and a suffering that had been greater for her than for him.

Twenty years later, in a decision for which charitable reasons do not readily come to mind, Marie republished the novel unchanged and informed him – it was the last time they saw each other – that she also intended to publish her memoirs. 'To this I retorted,' he wrote at the time to Princess Carolyne von Sayn-Wittgenstein, 'that I did not see how she could possibly do anything of such a kind, since whatever she called "memoirs" would be nothing more than lies and pretences. This was the first time I spoke my mind plainly about what was true and what was false.'

Perhaps the smouldering resentment in Marie d'Agoult's mind was her punishment for having loved 'not wisely but too well'. For her love cost her everything: her lover, the care and education of her children, the affection of the one daughter – Cosima – who was still living when her mother died. Love had indeed been, in Byron's phrase, this woman's 'whole existence'; for Liszt, the man, it was 'of man's life a thing apart'. He could not live on love alone, and that life now had to follow its own, new course.

THREE

Conqueror of Europe

In one sense the next eight years in Liszt's life could be accounted for in a single paragraph, the greater part of which would comprise a chronicle of his musical conquests the length and breadth of Europe, from Scotland to Turkey, from Spain to Russia. In city after city the same scenes were repeated: halls filled to over-flowing, whatever the prices, the master's unfailing brilliance and magic, the extraordinary atmosphere, the delirious applause. No less invariable was Liszt's honesty towards his public, his total commitment to his art, his awareness of being a *rara avis*, true, but equally his natural sincerity and generosity. With rare bureaucratic discernment a passport issued to him by the Hungarian authorities in 1846 dispenses with the customary descriptive details of the holder and replaces them with the peremptory statement '*Celebritate sua sat notus!*' ('Sufficiently well-known through his fame').

Apart from the mental effort demanded by a ceaseless round of recitals and the physical strain of hours of bone-shaking travel from one town to the next, the practical arrangements for the concerts were, to start with, also left largely in the hands of the artist himself in all but the largest cities, like Vienna and Paris. Few performers had the good fortune to be attended, like Clara Wieck, by one who made it his life's work to act the role of agent and impresario and the 'assistants' who had pressed their services on Liszt in a not always selfless spirit tended to do his personal cause more harm than good.

Liszt remained throughout his life utterly ignorant of financial matters and became increasingly inept at handling his business affairs with anything resembling efficiency. It was therefore something of a relief when early in 1841, after more than a year of help-cum-hindrance from outsiders with hall bookings, press releases, public announcements and other tiresome practicalities, he met one Gaëtano Belloni in Paris and engaged him as regular secretary and business manager. Given the considerable sums of money that passed through Belloni's hands over the following years and Liszt's unconcern over such matters, it is not surprising that spiteful tales were busily peddled about Belloni quietly re-routing some of the master's fees into his own pocket. But in his will of 1860 Liszt called him 'my faithful and obedient servant and friend' and instructed that he should not go unrewarded.

The emergence at this time of the agent or manager as a new breed in the world of the arts was a concomitant of the growth of the culture industry in general and worked to mutual advantage, especially when a performer had a horror of the mundane minutiae of practical organization. But that third parties should thrust themselves between the artist and his public also displeased many, who saw it as an interference with the precious unity of the musical occasion, a unity already prepared before the moment of public performance. Mendelssohn, for one, resented the presence of these parasites when Liszt played in Leipzig in 1840. 'He is set round,' Mendelssohn wrote to Moscheles,

> by a manager and secretary who administers his affairs so abominably that the public was incensed. It cost us a great amount of trouble to smooth things out before his second recital. The publicity, the changes, the prices, the programmes – in fact, everything that Liszt had not attended to personally, was wrong, and the normally placid Leipzigers were furious. In the meantime they have calmed down, I think, and Hiller, Härtel [of the publishing house of Breitkopf and Härtel], Schumann and I have done our best to counteract the effects of these busybodies' behaviour.

The odyssey that was to last until the autumn of 1847 began in November 1839 in Vienna, where Liszt had arrived after parting from Marie d'Agoult in Italy. The coach delivered him in the Austrian capital at four in the morning; at eight the music publisher Haslinger presented himself at his hotel to discuss details of the six recitals he was due to give. He had already announced his characteristic intention to donate the entire proceeds from these recitals to the Beethoven Memorial Fund. An appeal had been launched in 1835 for a monument to Beethoven in his native town of Bonn, but the response had been pitiful. When Liszt read that the contributions from France amounted to an insulting 424 francs, 90 centimes, he impulsively took the matter into his own hands, offering to raise the necessary money himself, unaided, with the sole proviso that the commission for the statue be given to Lorenzo Bartolini, one-time protégé of Napoleon and the leading Italian sculptor of the day. The appeal committee, realizing that to accept Liszt's offer would publicly set the seal on their responsibility for the whole ignominious episode, instead entrusted the task to the German sculptor Ernst Hähnel. But they were not too proud to accept considerable sums from Liszt between now and 1845, when the memorial was finally unveiled. For his part Liszt had special cause to remember these concerts, for during his stay in Vienna he acquired what he regarded all his life as one of his more precious possessions – the death mask of Beethoven.

Wherever he appeared, Liszt was the man of the moment, the man who made people forget that there were also other pianists to be heard. There was little hope for the likes of Herz, Pixis and Moscheles in a town where Liszt had already played that season. Not without a certain self-satisfaction – and who will grudge him that? – he wrote to Marie d'Agoult from Vienna: 'You can have no idea of how my popularity continues to grow in this promised land.'

His recital programmes would raise the modern concert-goer's incredulous eyebrow: a transcription of a Beethoven symphony, then of a Schubert song, then of an orchestral overture (that to *William Tell* was in great demand), followed by a selection of his own original compositions – a number of the Transcendental Studies, perhaps, or some items from the *Années de pèlerinage* – and, of course, a lavish donation of encores. Or he would make a dismembered Beethoven symphony the framework of the evening, opening with the first movement, followed by one or two pieces of his own, continuing with the second movement, also followed by other pieces, and so on to the finale.

But both the volume and the range of his repertoire were extraordinary. In 1848 August Conradi, a young composer who was helping him with the orchestration of his first symphonic poems at that time, compiled a catalogue, corrected and supplemented by Liszt himself, of all the pieces he had played over his tours of the previous ten years. It runs to almost 300 items. They range from Bach (the Chromatic Fantasia and Fugue, the Goldberg Variations, transcriptions of organ fugues), Beethoven (Concertos 3 and 5, various sonatas including Op. 109, Op. 110 and Op. 111, the Diabelli Variations), Weber (*Konzertstück* and solo pieces), Mendelssohn (the G minor and D minor concertos, sundry fugues and scherzi), Chopin (virtually the complete works, including the two concertos) and Schumann (the F sharp minor Sonata, *Carnaval*, the *Fantaisie* Op. 17) to his own transcriptions and original compositions and some of the more brazenly bravura exercises by lesser rivals and contemporaries such as Moscheles and Czerny. The most striking, but perhaps not surprising, absentee from this company is Mozart: Liszt played none of his sonatas, and apart from his own *Don Giovanni* Fantasia, only the overture to *The Magic Flute* appears in the list.

As to the manner of his playing, the world had already heard and seen for itself, before he left Paris with his Countess, what totally new technical effects he produced and overwhelming emotional sensations he created. In his report in the *Revue et Gazette musicale* in 1836 Berlioz distinguished 'a full, flowing *cantabile*, long and evenly sustained notes, punctuated by sudden clusters of notes played with the utmost brilliance yet without harshness and without sacrificing harmonic richness, together with sequences in minor thirds and octave passages in the middle and bass registers performed *staccato* at incredible speed.' In this extraordinary range, indeed, a range not only of musical weapons but also of *Gesamtkunstwerk* demands in the Wagnerian mould, lay a large part of the secret of his uniqueness. Henry F. Chorley, music critic of the *Athenaeum*, discovered this for himself when he heard Liszt in Paris in 1840: 'The school in which M. Liszt has been trained – the literary and artistic associations of which he has embraced so eagerly – encourages violent contrasts. Passion, according to its canons, must be allowed free way, a momentary distortion being better than a chilling restraint.'

The total musical experience that Liszt had to offer, moreover, required that he be seen as well as heard. 'One has to watch him,' wrote the Paris critic Joseph d'Ortigue ecstatically,

> with his flowing locks, as his fingers flit from one end of the keyboard to the other over a single, ringing note that reverberates like the silver sound of a bell struck by a metal hammer. His fingers seem to stretch and grow longer, as though they were attached to springs, and at times even seem to detach themselves from his hands altogether. One must see him raise his wonderful eyes to the heavens in search of inspiration, then lower his gaze sadly to the floor; his radiant expression is like that of a martyr caught between supreme joy and suffering, and he sends out terrifying darting glances at the audience, frightening, mesmerising and enrapturing them . . . O, one must watch the man, listen to him, then be silent, for we feel all too clearly how feeble our powers of expression become under the intensity of our admiration.

In the popular imagination, reinforced by the spectacular difficulty of some of his own pieces and by contemporary cartoons that thrived on spiteful exaggeration, Liszt lives as the unchallenged chieftain of the tribe of muscular keyboard gymnasts who stunned their audiences into submission by relentless brilliance. Nothing could be less true. The testimony of fellow-musicians like Berlioz and Clara Schumann would alone show how total was his mastery of all registers of expression, the delicate and lyrical as well as the luscious and the heroic. Nor did even the most physically demanding music destroy his composure. 'I may inform my readers,' the pianist Anton Strelezki wrote in his memoirs,

> that, hearing him once play his transcription of Schubert's 'Erlkönig', I was surprised to notice that when he left the piano, not a trace of fatigue or perspiration was to be seen on his face or hands. Only a few weeks after this I heard the same piece played by Anton Rubinstein, and from his appearance at the end you would think he had just come out of a shower with his clothes on. Yet Liszt's rendition was just as vivid as Rubinstein's and his fortissimo had the same tremendous power.

But his fortissimo did take its toll of a piano. Describing him as one who mercilessly destroyed his instruments, a Viennese newspaper compared him to 'a victorious hero on the battlefield', surrounded by the havoc he had wrought. In the margin of the review Liszt added, unabashed: 'At my first concert a *third* piano had to be fetched.'

From Vienna Liszt went to Budapest – more accurately, to Pest, for the twin cities of Buda and Pest were not amalgamated until 1872. It was the first time he had set foot in his native Hungary since the age of ten, when his father had taken him to study under Czerny in Vienna.

His fame had preceded him. The Hungarians, riding on a ground-swell of patriotic pride which, impelled by the oratory of their passionate leader Lajos Kossuth, was to issue in the declaration of a triumphant but short-lived independence from Austria in 1849, hailed him as a national hero who had travelled throughout Europe to bring glory to the name of Hungary. Shortly after arriving in Pest, he went to a performance of *Fidelio* in the national opera house. 'As I appeared in the box,' he wrote to Marie d'Agoult, 'the entire audience began to clap and shout "*Eljen! Eljen!*" [Hail!] I acknowledged the applause three times in regal style. It is something totally unheard-of in this country, I believe – or anywhere else.'

His first four recitals earned him a total of between 10,000 and 11,000 francs, most of which he sent to his mother in Paris for the upkeep and education of his children; he spent very little on himself. His only extravagances while in Pest were two social occasions: he gave a dinner party in the Hotel du Palatin de l'Hongrie for sixty distinguished citizens, which cost him 600 francs, then a supper for thirty men and fifteen of the most attractive women in the city, which included entertainment provided by a Magyar choir, and for which he laid out 900 francs. Three further recitals brought in another 10,000 to 12,000 francs, which he distributed between the Pest Music Society, the Hungarian National Theatre and the Conservatoire.

In response to this generosity the civic authorities arranged a ceremony which profoundly moved him. At the end of his concert in the National Theatre on 4 January 1840, which he had given dressed in Hungarian national costume and rounded off with his Rákóczy March – 'a kind of aristocratic Hungarian Marseillaise', he called it – a group of magnates entered the hall, also resplendent in national livery. Count Leo Festitics delivered a laudatio in Hungarian and presented Liszt in the name of the nation with a magnificent ceremonial sabre set with turquoises, rubies and other precious stones. Liszt, deeply touched by the honour, expressed his gratitude in a short but fulsome speech in French, which Baron Antal Augusz took down as he spoke and then read out in Hungarian. The sabre was among the personal possessions – a gold goblet presented to him by a group of Hungarian ladies later the same year, the Broadwood grand that had belonged to Beethoven, a silver desk given to him in Vienna in 1846 and a solid gold baton set with precious stones, a present from Princess Carolyne von Sayn-Wittgenstein – that he bequeathed to the National Museum in Budapest.

When he left the hall with his hosts to join the coach, he found a crowd of young people thronging the square and carrying flaming torches, while a military band played to shouts of 'Eljen! Eljen!' He managed to push his way through the crowd to his coach but after a few laborious yards he turned to Augusz and said: 'I can't stand this any longer. Let's get out and stop behaving like aristocrats in our coach!' With this they descended and walked in the midst of the cheering throng to Festitics' house, where Liszt was staying. The band played on. Augusz conveyed Liszt's thanks to his compatriots but not until the hero had appeared twice on the balcony and it was well after midnight did the rejoicing multitude finally go home.

Shortly after this triumph he went back to Sopron, scene of his first public performance as a lad of ten, and to his birthplace at Raiding. Here the same enthusiastic welcome awaited him, spiced this time by the appearance of a colourful group of gypsies, who sang and danced their way back into the affectionate memory in which he had held them since his boyhood days. Moments such as these informed the descriptive framework of the book *The Gypsies and their Music in Hungary* which he published in 1859.

March 1840 found him for the first time in Germany – in Leipzig. Among German cultural centres at this time pride of place belonged to Berlin, which, as the capital of Prussia, the largest and most progressive of the states of the German Confederation, both politically and intellectually, had gradually but irresistibly been working itself to the fore since the beginning of the century. The cultural tradition of Leipzig, however, whose university had been paramount in the eighteenth century and whose famous Gewandhaus concerts had been founded as far back as 1781, was still a force to be reckoned with, and its public had a far more sophisticated appreciation of music than those of most other cities of the time. At the same time this appreciation had its roots in solid, conventional values with an in-built conservatism suspicious of novelty and pledged to an institutional status quo. The epithet 'Leipzigerisch' circulated in more forward-looking circles to connote their somewhat disdainful frustration at the heavy-handed mediocrity which this conservatism perpetuated.

Liszt, however, after meeting an initial resistance stemming in part from his reputation as an *enfant terrible* but also from the over-pricing of tickets for his recitals – an inexperienced agent's miscalculation – quickly carried all before him. In a shrewd act of public relations he devoted the last of his three concerts to works by the three leading composers at that time living in Leipzig – Mendelssohn, Schumann and Ferdinand Hiller – and donated his fee to the musicians' benevolent fund. The refined and cultivated Mendelssohn, ever gentlemanly, ever helpful, one of the few major composers – or minor composers, for that matter – against whom scarcely any man of good will had a bad word to say, was at pains to use his position as director of the Gewandhaus concerts to get Liszt the hearing he deserved, far apart though the spiritual and artistic worlds of the two men were. Liszt especially admired the breadth of Mendelssohn's culture. 'He draws wonderful sketches,' he wrote to Marie d'Agoult, 'plays the violin and the viola, can read Homer fluently in Greek and speaks four or five languages with ease.'

Mendelssohn, for his part, found that he got on well personally with Liszt and that Liszt carried utter artistic conviction in whatever he did. But he never came to appreciate Liszt's music – perhaps even to understand it. 'Liszt is a true artist whom you can't help liking even if you disagree with him,' he wrote to Moscheles. 'The only thing he seems to me to lack is true talent for composition – I mean really original ideas.' But this was only 1840, and Liszt composed nothing before Mendelssohn's death in 1847 that could have changed his opinion. The works that Liszt wrote at the height of his powers – the symphonic poems, the Piano Sonata, the big organ works, the Esztergom Mass – would, one fears, have remained inscrutable for Mendelssohn but he would scarcely have wished to deny their originality.

Schumann, whose taciturn, almost morose disposition rendered him all the more inaccessible in these final months of his legal battle for the hand of Clara Wieck, was captivated by Liszt the man, as was Clara. But, like almost everyone else, Liszt got little out of Schumann's company. 'He is excessively withdrawn,' he noted, 'and hardly says a word.' Schumann, moreover, utterly failed to recognize the genius of Liszt the composer – as he subsequently failed to sense the greatness of Wagner. And this, curiously enough, from the man who back in 1831 had cried 'Hats off, gentlemen – a genius!' in the presence of the young Chopin, and who in 1853 apostrophized Brahms as 'a new force that is entering music', the man who 'would suddenly emerge to epitomize the new age'. When Schumann proudly pointed out to Liszt the tangible testimony of Leipzig's intellectual eminence – its university, its publishing houses, its cultural journals – Liszt found it all very bourgeois. 'There are no princesses or duchesses,' he grumbled.

When he visited the Schumanns again in Düsseldorf eleven years later, his music had still not got through to them. He played to them from his *Harmonies poétiques et religieuses*, which caused them considerable discomfort, as Clara recorded in her diary:

> He played with a demonic brilliance, as always, with a mastery like that of the devil himself – I can think of no other way to put it. But oh, what terrible compositions! If a youngster were to write such stuff, one might forgive him, but what can one say when a full-grown man is so deluded? We both felt very sad – it is so depressing.

*

71

In the two extended critiques, 1839 and 1840, that he devoted to Liszt in his *Neue Zeitschrift für Musik*, Schumann gave it as his opinion that, as a composer, Liszt did not take enough trouble over his work: 'Given his outstanding musical nature, I believe that, if he devoted the same time to his compositions as he does to his playing, he could become a significant composer.' Elsewhere, he refers uneasily to Liszt's 'murky flights of fancy' alongside his 'extravagant displays of virtuosity'. For Schumann, as for Mendelssohn, Liszt was too perplexing for comfort.

From Germany Liszt now went back to Paris. His main aim was to see his children, but although he and their mother had gone their independent ways, their affection lingered – on his side a compassionate, almost paternal concern with her well-being, on hers an unmistakeable desire to have him back as her lover. It was on this basis, as uneven and unstable as it was unsatisfactory and unnatural, that their relationship stumbled along until the final break in April 1844. That their lives and careers were growing ever further apart throughout these years made it something of a perverse miracle that the intolerability of any form of association between them should not have forced itself upon them sooner.

On the contrary, the letters that pass between them in the early 1840s have the character of a sustained bout of emotional shadow-boxing between a man and a woman locked in a love contest from which neither – but especially the woman – wishes to be extricated. One of Marie's ploys was to mount a transparent incitement to jealousy by telling him of men who were paying court to her. The diplomat and writer Henry Bulwer Lytton, brother of the author of *Rienzi* and other historical romances, was one such. Coyly yet calculatedly – more accurately, miscalculatedly – she wrote to Liszt telling him of her attachment in the tones of a schoolgirl confession. Tolerantly, good-humouredly, almost indifferently, in the confident tone of one who holds the decision to make or break – and has already decided – he replied:

> How can you thus ask me for permission to be unfaithful?! You know my attitude to events of this kind: you know that facts and deeds are nothing as far as I am concerned, whereas emotions, thoughts and shades of meaning are everything – especially shades of meaning. I wish you always to retain your freedom, for I am convinced that you will use it with nobility and delicacy until the day when you tell me that there is another man who feels more intensely than I, and understands more profoundly than I, what you are and what you can become.

Until this day comes there will be no unfaithfulness and nothing at all will change between us.

Quite consistently he encouraged her to surround herself with as many male admirers as she wished. 'I am delighted to hear of your friendship with Lamartine,' he once told her, 'and very much wish that you would form a union with him. It would be good for both of you.' He would have said the same of the Polish Count Bernard Potocki, the young dramatist Francis Ponsard, the poet Louis de Ronchaud and any of the other eligible beaux in her entourage.

In May 1840, after a month in Paris, Liszt paid a further visit to England, where the memory of the sixteen-year-old prodigy who had played before King George IV had not faded. Then it had been Carlton House; now, before Queen Victoria, the Prince Consort and other members of the Royal Family, it was Buckingham Palace. From this eminence he worked his way steadily, and at times, it seems, rather reluctantly, down the social scale, ending with a series of concerts in the provinces. To his rather hurt surprise, however, the enthusiasm he commanded was far from universal. In part this may reflect the preconceived verdict of Victorian morality on a self-centred, irresponsible philanderer who had sired three children by a noble, devoted woman of whom he had now tired. More tangibly, and within the immediate experience of those who saw and heard him, his whole manner as man and artist, the larger-than-life image that his personality projected, invoked the instinctive disapproval of large sections of a reserved, undemonstrative British bourgeoisie dismissive of the ostentations of 'the Continentals'. His unconventional, dictatorial ambience unsettled the audience and provoked only resentment. The pianist Charles Salaman, who knew him from his first visit, recalled that the uneasiness already set in when Liszt puzzled the public by announcing 'Pianoforte Recitals':

This now commonly accepted term had never previously been used, and people asked, 'What does he mean? How can anyone *recite* upon the pianoforte?' At these recitals, Liszt, after performing a piece set down in his programme, would leave the platform and, descending into the body of the room, where the benches were so arranged as to allow free locomotion, would move about among his auditors and converse with his friends with the gracious condescension of a prince, until he felt disposed to return to the piano.

Salaman was one of the first to observe a feature of Liszt's playing which became increasingly obtrusive and, in the eyes of many, offensive over the coming years, namely, his habit of embellishing through his own cosmetic imagination the pieces of other composers that he played. 'He was rarely content with the simple work of art,' complained Salaman; 'he must elaborate it and "arrange" it, often indeed to extravagance. Even a fugue of Bach became more complex in his hands.'

Nor did the style of his pianism escape withering disparagement. 'Liszt', wrote the *Musical Journal* after his Royal Philharmonic concerts, 'has been presented by the Royal Philharmonic Society with an elegant silver breakfast service for doing that which would cause every young student to receive a severe reprimand, viz., thumping and partially destroying two very fine pianofortes.' By contrast, at a London concert where he played his *Niobe* Fantasia, his Fantasia on *Lucia di Lammermoor*, his *Galop chromatique* and a concerto by Weber, the *Revue et Gazette musicale de Paris* emphasized an aspect of his playing which the popular image has more difficulty in accommodating:

> In spite of his frequent use of *rubato*, which the romantic style requires, no artist has a securer sense of tempo, with the result that he remains in full control of his fantasy and can hold the wildest flights of imagination in check at his will.

Extreme characters must expect to provoke extreme reactions. The most wounding mark of failure is apathy, and the flaccid interest shown by audiences in Manchester and Glasgow confused and depressed him in a new and unwelcome manner. But, as he wrote to Marie d'Agoult, 'The only thought in my mind is to make money. That is why I'm here and that is all I think of.' He earned thirty guineas per concert – 'an unheard-of sum here,' he adds proudly (Thalberg received only twenty guineas) – 'and for twenty-five guineas one can rent a country house in a village outside London, such as Hampstead.' The 10,000 francs he earned from his British recitals he donated to the Beethoven Memorial Fund in Bonn.

However offended the critics affected to be, and however unappreciative the philistine provincials, his success in the aristocratic circles where he felt in his element had the same ring as on the continent of Europe. The Duke of Beaufort opened his doors to him, so did Lady Louise Beresford, wife of Viscount William Beresford, Wellington's leading general in the Peninsular War. Above all it was at the home of the attractive and stimulating

Marguerite, Countess of Blessington, that he enjoyed the lionizing attention to which he had grown accustomed. Lady Blessington and her late husband had led a life of quixotic extravagance in England and abroad, including a period in Genoa in the company of Byron. After her husband's death in 1829 she returned to England and set up house in Kensington with the dashing French dandy and wit Count Alfred d'Orsay, who, as well as possessed of great generosity and charm, was an accomplished painter and sculptor. Turning their home into a centre of attraction for whoever and whatever was novel and stimulating in the worlds of learning, art, science and fashion, they presided over a salon life not unworthy of its Parisian counterpart: Prince Louis Napoleon was a frequent guest, so were Lord Chesterfield, Canning, Palmerston and Lord Castlereagh, while from the world of arts and letters came Bulwer Lytton, Macaulay and Thomas Moore.

When he returned to the continent in the spring of 1841, Liszt again took up the cause of the Beethoven Memorial, playing chiefly in German towns but also returning on one memorable occasion to Paris – memorable because at this moment he met for the first time the man from whom in private life, in public career, in the unfolding of their art and in the history of music, he was henceforth never to be separated. That man was Richard Wagner.

Where close friendships have developed between great artists, based on personal sympathy and a community of cultural interest, the mutuality inherent in any worthwhile relationship is taken for granted. That between Goethe and Schiller, for example, which never reached the point of intimacy at which they exchanged the formal 'Sie' form of address for the familiar 'Du', nevertheless assumed a total frankness, an urge both to influence and be influenced, an undisguised assumption of shared purposes and values, which issued from a sense of reciprocal generosity, of an open concern of the one for the other. Without Goethe, Schiller would not have grasped the living meaning of Classical antiquity; without Schiller, Goethe would not have written his ballads or finished his Faust. Likewise Wordsworth and Coleridge, their companionship sealed from the moment of their first meeting, achieved a meeting of minds which led not only to their joint composition of Lyrical Ballads but to a mutual stimulation of interests and faculties that enriched in intangible and unpredictable ways the quality of their personal and creative lives.

But the relationship between Liszt and Wagner, which ran an erratic and sometimes stormy course for almost forty years, does not meet such a criterion. It was one-sided from the outset – Liszt was the giver, Wagner the taker. That it should have been so at the beginning is no wonder. Liszt was the greatest pianist of the age, prosperous, a man renowned throughout Europe; Wagner, only two years younger, well-nigh penniless, was almost unheard-of and could only approach his famous contemporary in awe, as though mounting the steps of a throne. Years later, when Liszt had retired from the public stage and Wagner had become the greatest and most controversial composer of the day, Wagner was still the taker, now in the intellectual, musical sphere. It is a relationship too biased, except in rare, isolated moments, to be graced with the description of true, intimate, generous friendship. But it is no less vital a relationship for that.

As Wagner relates it, the first encounter between them, the suave, handsome, cosmopolitan virtuoso and his stocky, inelegant, provincial German petitioner, was a non-committal and unpromising affair. Wagner had recently completed the score of *Rienzi*, but there was no immediate prospect of seeing it performed, and he was eking out a penurious existence with his first wife Minna, chiefly through music-copying and other hack-work for the publisher Maurice Schlesinger. Liszt, he had been told, was a generous supporter of worthy causes, and since Wagner never knew a worthier cause than himself, he made his way to Liszt's hotel with hopes high:

I was admitted, and first observed a number of strangers in the salon, who were shortly afterwards joined by Liszt himself, friendly and affable, wearing a house-coat. Unable to take part in the conversation – since it was in French – which was concerned with Liszt's experiences during his recent concert tour of Hungary, I listened for a while with considerable boredom, until he asked in a friendly tone what he could do for me. All I could reply was that I desired to make his acquaintance, to which he appeared to have no objection, adding that he would not forget to send me a ticket for his next matinée. My attempt to broach a conversation on matters of art began and ended with my asking him whether he knew Loewe's setting of 'Erlkönig' as well as Schubert's. His answer 'No' put a stop to my clumsy efforts, and the visit ended by my leaving my address.

When the promised ticket arrived from Belloni, Wagner joined the audience in the Salle Érard:

Entering the crowded hall, I saw that the platform on which the

grand piano stood was under intense siege from the pick of
Parisian female society. I witnessed the enthusiastic ovations
accorded to the revered, world-famed virtuoso, listened to a
number of his bravura pieces such as the Fantasia on *Robert le
Diable*, and came away in a helpless daze.

It was to be a year before their paths crossed again.

In the course of his visits to towns and cities along the
Rhine – Cologne, Bonn, Coblence – Liszt had noticed among the
many romantic little islands, with their ruined castles and their
aura of myth and legend, a tiny eyot called Nonnenwerth, near
Honef. Apart from the disused convent from which it received its
name – there is today a convent school on the island – its only
buildings were a few fishermen's cottages. With the impulsive
thought of turning it into a summer retreat where he could both
work and be together with his children, he leased the island in
1841 and spent this and the following summer there in the
company of Marie and the family. The piano fantasies on *Norma*,
Don Giovanni and Meyerbeer's *Robert le Diable* belong to 1841,
together with transcriptions of Beethoven's Septet and of songs by
Schubert and Mendelssohn, and a 'Paraphrase' on 'God Save the
Queen'. He also made a number of song-settings of his own,
including, for the first time, German texts – Heine's 'Lorelei', two
poems by the patriotic poet Georg Herwegh, Goethe's 'Wandrers
Nachtlied' and the students' song from *Faust*.

Of slight importance in themselves, these settings have a
symbolic interest in that they intimate an extension of Liszt's
thought from the Romance to the Germanic world. Paris had been
his spiritual home: the salon atmosphere, his life with Marie
d'Agoult, his sojourns in French Switzerland and in Italy, his
readings in Lamennais, Saint-Simon and the French Romantics, in
Dante and Petrarch – all this had cocooned him in Romance
values, values consolidated by the pervasive presence of the Roman
Catholic Church. Partly, perhaps, through having put down roots,
however slender, in German soil by choosing the abode of
Nonnenwerth, partly as a result of the remorselessly widening
spiritual gap between him and his mistress, partly also because of
his awareness that Germany offered many challenging cultural
centres yet to conquer, he began to turn his gaze elsewhere.

For Germany was not, like France or Britain, a single political
entity ruled from the centre but a collection of separate and
independent states, each with its own ruler, its own confession, its
own set of social responsibilities and its own cultural policy. A

bigoted, unenlightened prince could condemn his kingdom to intellectual and cultural darkness; he could be artistically conscious and politically backward, like the Grand Duke Ludwig I of Hessen and his son, or whimsical and unpredictable in both spheres, like Karl Eugen of Württemberg, as the young Schiller knew to his cost. Yet he might set great store by art and the things of the mind, like the Grand Duke Karl August and his succession in Weimar, or the Wittelsbach Kings of Bavaria, to whom we owe the magnificent museums and art collections in Munich. Artists and intellectuals would gather at the courts of such men in anxious quest of patronage; theatre, opera and music were given the chance to flourish, men of distinction were sought who would raise the standard and the public status of the arts, and the ensuing success invested the ruler himself with added kudos in the company of his fellow-princes. Thus whereas in a metropolitan country the capital stretches out its tentacles and sucks in the life-blood of the whole nation, draining life from what is then left with the condescending designation of 'the provinces', particularist Germany had a cultural diversity which, whatever the social and political shortcomings on which it rested, was a source of strength – and has remained so, in both East and West.

As Austria and Prussia were by far the largest and most powerful of the German states – the former Catholic, the latter Protestant – so their respective capitals offered the greatest challenge to the prospective artistic conqueror. Liszt had already gained the affection and approval of Vienna. He now set out, at the end of 1841, after concerts in Weimar, Jena, Dresden and Leipzig, to add Berlin to his collection of trophies.

From the early nineteenth century, in particular association with the foundation of the University of Berlin in 1810, Prussia had set the pace in the cultivation of the liberal values that found expression in the Revolution of 1848 and of the nationalistic urges that led to the political unification of Germany in 1871. Minds were open to new ideas, and what had long been a sophisticated public gave an eager welcome to whatever savoured of liberation and novelty, in the sciences as in the humanities. On his accession to the throne in 1840, Friedrich Wilhelm IV proclaimed an idealistic intention to rule in this same spirit, and whatever the disillusionment attendant on his behaviour during the events of 1848, and the mental instability that clouded the last years of his life, he presided over a capital whose cultural discernment demanded, and was accorded, the highest standards.

And since such were the standards that Liszt embodied,

unsurpassed by Thalberg, Moscheles, Kalkbrenner, Clara Schumann or any other of the top-drawer artists who had already submitted their talents for scrutiny, his victory over Berlin was a foregone conclusion. He stayed there for almost three months, from Christmas 1841 until March 1842, and gave twenty-one concerts, playing Bach, Handel, Scarlatti, Beethoven, Schubert and Chopin and also conducting a performance of Beethoven's Fifth Symphony. Nine of these concerts were for charity – the fund for the completion of Cologne Cathedral, the University of Berlin appeal fund, a children's home, and three recitals for the benefit of young musicians whose careers he wished to promote. In addition, as had been his custom in Paris, Vienna, London and Budapest, he played in private before royalty and aristocracy, to the special pleasure of the King and Queen and of the King's brother, later Kaiser Wilhelm I.

Indeed, so total was his victory that for the ten weeks of his stay – it had the feel of an occupation – the name of the King of Prussia seemed to be not Friedrich Wilhelm IV von Hohenzollern but Franz Liszt. His portrait was displayed all over the city and cameos bearing his likeness were to be seen on the dresses of elegant ladies in salons and concert halls, where a rampant hero-worship raged, forerunner of the modern fan-club and hysterical cult of the pop-star idol. He himself entered joyously into the spirit of the act by wearing his flamboyant Hungarian cloaks, his cravats and the remainder of the panoply of his luxuriant wardrobe. It needs only an irreverent flicker of the anachronistic imagination to picture 'I Love Franz' badges being proudly distributed among his female camp-followers, and even more proudly worn.

As well as a dalliance with the beautiful actress Charlotte Hagn, these days in Berlin brought his first encounter with the Romantic writer Bettina von Arnim. Ten years a widow, a woman now almost sixty who had known Goethe and Beethoven and had established her literary reputation in 1835 with the charming blend of fact and fiction called *Goethe's Correspondence with a Child*, Bettina was a perfect Lisztian *femme fatale* – experienced, well-to-do, cultured and sensitive, romantic yet realistic, socially and politically progressive, unashamedly non-conformist, emotionally full-blooded. 'Whatever it is in you that stirs me,' (he uses the intimate form of address, '*Du*') he wrote to her in February 1842, at the pinnacle of his success, 'it arouses in me an urge to make something better of myself, a desire to exert myself as though captivated by the charm of life for the first time.' His letters to her through the 1840s read almost like those of an excited adolescent who is just beginning to understand what life and love are all about. She was among the throng of distinguished guests at his première of *Lohengrin* in Weimar in 1850 and became a regular, vivacious guest at the Villa Altenburg during the reign of Liszt and Princess Carolyne von Sayn-Wittgenstein.

When he made his final departure from Berlin, crowds thronged the streets and the King and Queen drove out from their palace in order to experience the remarkable scenes for themselves, though some members of the court were heard to mutter their disapproval that a mere musician should enjoy such regal homage. When Liszt emerged from his hotel, wrote the critic Ludwig Rellstab, a thousand voices were raised in acclamation:

A carriage pulled up, drawn by six white horses. Amid the shouting and cheering Liszt was practically carried down the steps and into the carriage, where he took his place beside the dignitaries of the university. Thirty coaches-and-four packed with students, and a number of riders on horseback, wearing their academic finery, accompanied his departure, and many other coaches also joined the cavalcade, while thousands swarmed around the scene on foot. The procession moved off in the direction of Unter den Linden avenue, traversed the square where the statue of Frederick the Great is due to be erected, then turned back past the royal palace in the direction of the Frankfurt Gate. Not only were the streets and squares crowded with people but all the windows along the way were filled with spectators.

His journey eastwards from Berlin took him first to Königsberg (today Kaliningrad), where the university awarded him an honorary doctorate in *artis musicae*, then through the Baltic towns of Mitau, Riga and Dorpat (now Tartu), and finally to St Petersburg, where he arrived in the spring of 1842. Travelling with him was Prince Felix von Lichnovsky, a young aristocrat whom he had met in 1841 and who attended his initiation into the Freemasons' 'zur Einigkeit' lodge that year in Frankfurt.

The nebulous half-secular, half-religious origins of free-masonry, in particular its mystic ceremonies and rituals reminiscent of the Dionysian and other ancient mysteries, could not but appeal to Liszt. What others scornfully dismissed as cabalistic élitism and obscurantism was for him an inexhaustible repository of quasi-religious fascination, a kind of secular correlative to his religious *Weltbild*. When, as the lodges developed in nineteenth-century Germany, these aspects of the cult were fused with ideals of humanitarianism and principles of social *engagement*, Liszt found even more in the masonic image to attract him, seeing an identity of purpose in the activities of masonic lodges and of Catholic Orders such as the Mission Priests of Saint Vincent de Paul. In the course of the 1840s he was received into lodges in Berlin and Zurich, and thirty years later renewed his commitment in national terms by joining the lodge in Pest.

For the few years left to him before his assassination, Felix von Lichnovsky was Liszt's closest friend. Three years younger than Liszt, he was the grandson of the Prince Karl von Lichnovsky who had provided Beethoven with his first lodgings in Vienna. Handsome, dashing, with a trail of broken female hearts behind him but also with a reputation for generosity and witty conversation, he cut a figure not unlike Liszt himself. After leaving the army in 1839, he devoted his energies to literature and politics, identifying himself uncompromisingly, sometimes provocatively, with the interests of his class and becoming a right-wing deputy to the National Assembly in 1848. In September of that year, while riding through the streets of Frankfurt with a friend, he was recognized by a group of revolutionaries, dragged from the cellar in which he tried to hide, and killed. At the end of his book on Chopin, written in 1850, Liszt mourned Lichnovsky and Chopin as his dearest friends during these years as an itinerant virtuoso, though whether the friendship between the two men would have survived the arrival in Liszt's life of Princess Carolyne von Sayn-Wittgenstein and the conversion of Liszt the virtuoso into the Abbé Liszt, is a question perhaps better left unasked.

St Petersburg was not to be outdone by Berlin in the scale of its welcome. His visit stood under the patronage of the Empress herself, to whom he had played privately in Germany two years earlier, and the entire imperial court was present when he gave his first recital before an audience of 3,000, proudly displaying on the lapels of his jacket the orders and decorations that he had so far received in the course of his career. 'But what struck the Russians most,' wrote Vladimir Vassilevich Stasov, later the great champion of the Russian nationalist school of composers and the first biographer of Mussorgsky and Borodin,

> was his great mane of blond hair, reaching almost down to his shoulders. No Russian would have dared to wear his hair in such a style; it was strictly forbidden . . . He was very thin and had a marked stoop, and although I had read a great deal about

his 'Florentine profile', which was supposed to give him a resemblance to Dante, I did not find him handsome. Nor was I greatly taken by his mania for decorations or by the rather affected manner in which he behaved towards everyone he met . . .

Just at that moment Liszt, noting the time, walked down from the gallery, elbowed his way through the crowd and moved quickly towards the stage. But instead of mounting the steps, he leapt on to the platform, tore off his white kid gloves and tossed them nonchalantly on to the floor, under the piano. Then, acknowledging the deafening applause, the like of which had not been heard for a century and more, he sat down. A hush fell over the hall. Without further ado he embarked on the opening cello phrase of the overture to *William Tell*. As soon as he had finished this piece, he moved quickly over to another grand piano on the other side of the stage, and throughout the recital he used these two pianos alternately for each piece, facing first one half of the hall, then the other.

The remainder of the all-Liszt programme consisted of *Réminiscences de 'Lucia di Lammermoor'*, the Fantasia on *Don Giovanni*, three song-transcriptions – Beethoven's 'Adelaïde', Schubert's 'Ständchen' and 'Erlkönig' – and the *Galop Chromatique*, a bravura piece written in 1838, for which audiences clamoured at the end of his recitals.

The public in St Petersburg, and indeed in Russia as a whole at this time, had an immense appetite for cultural offerings. The development of the export trade after Peter the Great's foundation of the city at the beginning of the eighteenth century ensured a cosmopolitan outlook, and with it came an eagerness to savour the latest intellectual and artistic novelties from the world of western European culture. Their geographical situation at the eastern extremity of Europe was attended by a sense of cultural isolation, but all the greater was their receptivity, the welcome they offered to those who came bearing new experiences and new ideas. A national artistic consciousness was stirring. Pushkin had been dead a mere five years; Glinka's *A Life for the Tsar* had been first heard in 1836 and his *Russlan and Ludmila*, based on Pushkin's poem, was to be produced in St Petersburg later in the year of Liszt's visit. The world was forming in which the generation of Mussorgsky, Borodin, Balakirev and Cui, all still children at this time, emerged in proud possession of a truly national music, and whatever enriched and enlivened this atmosphere elicited a rare warmth and enthusiasm. So Liszt appeared as a plenipotentiary, a bringer of musical good tidings from Paris, Vienna, Berlin and other corners of the European scene to a public anxious to see its own country become part of that scene. The same expectations attended Clara Schumann's visit two years later, and were as joyfully fulfilled as those that accompanied Liszt's.

One little episode reveals how sovereign was the rule that Liszt exercised over every occasion at which he appeared, whatever the distinction of the company. He was giving a private recital for Tsar Nicholas I and his entourage in the imperial palace. In the course of his playing the Tsar turned to his companions and began to hold a conversation with them, heedless of the music. After a few moments Liszt stopped. Surprised, the Tsar asked him why he had interrupted the piece. 'When the Emperor speaks,' answered Liszt calmly, 'all others must be silent.' Far from indignantly admonishing him for an insolent remark, the Tsar was somewhat taken aback, and Liszt continued his recital in the reverential silence which both he and the music demanded. 'I am the servant of princes,' he once conceded, 'but not their slave.'

Glinka, who was among Liszt's audience in St Petersburg, had a good deal to criticize in his playing, finding his Chopin charming but exaggerated in manner and describing his performance of classical music in general as not what it should have been. 'He struck the keys as though he were chopping meat,' he observed caustically. But Glinka was full of admiration when, at a private soirée given by Count Odoevsky, Liszt played from the autograph score several numbers from *Russlan and Ludmila*, 'which no one knew at that time, and to the amazement of everybody he did not miss a note'. Liszt's ability to feel his way into the world of this totally different music proved to Glinka, and to any others with an initial scepticism to overcome, how comprehensive the nature of his musical genius was.

However dazzling his technical wizardry, and fully conscious of the attendant danger that the masses would not see beyond the brilliance of the surface, Liszt constantly insisted that such skills were merely a means to an end, not an end in themselves. 'The sole purpose of virtuosity,' he wrote in an essay on the singer Pauline Viardot-Garcia in 1859, 'is to enable the artist to reproduce everything that is expressed in the music. For this purpose it is indispensable, and one cannot cultivate it too assiduously.' And in an article on Clara Schumann in 1855: 'Virtuosity is not an excrescence but an integral part of music . . . It is not just a passive servant of the work in question, for either it will breathe life into the work entrusted to it or the work will die.' Nor does he shrink from the corollary that the virtuoso has also the right – who can take his gifts from him? – to lavish his art on a mere trinket and bequeath to it 'his poetic touch'.

This unity of conception and technique had for Liszt a wider reference than that just of performance, for the unity has its origin in the composition of the musical work itself. In all true art, substance and style, the What and the How, fuse into a single whole and create an impregnable unity, but music, by the very fact of its independence of values derived from empirical experiences and thoughts – its abstractness and 'unreality', in other words – enters our consciousness in total, all-embracing terms whose absoluteness and directness give it its unique position among the arts. For whereas one may fairly admit the question 'What is *Hamlet* about?' or 'What is "The Last Judgement" about?', to ask 'What is Beethoven's Fifth Symphony about?' is meaningless. The meaning lies in the music, and words cannot reach it. It is its own world, and that world is inseparable from its expression. Schopenhauer, in *Die Welt als Wille und Vorstellung*, couched it thus, in terms which invest music with the ultimate cosmic meaning, the power to transmit the ethos of nature with an intensity denied to other media of creative expression:

> In that it by-passes ideas, Music is independent of the physical world – in fact, is completely ignorant of the physical world and could exist, in a sense, even if there were no world. This cannot be said of the other arts. Music is as direct an objectification and reflection of the entire Will [= world purpose] as is the World itself and as are the ideas whose manifold forms make up the world of individual objects. Thus far from being, like the other arts, the reflection of these ideas, Music is a reflection of the Will itself, with the same objectivity as that possessed by ideas. This is the reason why the effect of Music is so much more powerful and penetrating than that of the other arts. For while these latter deal only with the shadow, Music deals with the substance.

This is the spirit of absolute demand and total commitment in which Liszt pursued his musical aims, both as executant and as composer, and we, as the beneficiaries of his art, must receive it in like spirit. We cannot approve a lyricism and a dramatic content in his music yet take exception to an alleged sentimentality in the lyricism or a breast-beating exhibitionism in the drama. The sentimentality and the exhibitionism, if such they be, are woven into the warp and woof of the musical texture: seek to ignore them, and one's understanding of the work is partial, distorted; attempt to remove them, and the work disintegrates. To a lesser extent, probably, than Wagner, but no less openly, Liszt makes total demands upon us still today, as he did upon the audiences to whom he played. The totality of these demands is not a pose – whatever Liszt's faults, insincerity was not one of them. We must therefore accept him *in toto*, 'warts and all' – or reject him equally totally, if our aesthetic judgement so inclines.

After a further predictable success in Moscow, Liszt returned briefly to Paris, then spent a second summer on his romantic island of Nonnenwerth with Marie d'Agoult, the three children and Felix von Lichnovsky, a ménage that did not fail to provoke a good deal of tut-tutting among the curious locals. In the autumn Marie went back to the new home and literary career she was making for herself in Paris; the children were returned to the care of their paternal grandmother, who had gained esteem and affection in the French capital in her own right. Liszt, setting out on a journey that a few years hence was to change the entire face of his life, made his way to Weimar for the wedding of the Crown Prince, later Grand Duke Carl Alexander of Sachsen-Weimar-Eisenach, to Princess Sophie, daughter of King William II of the Netherlands.

Weimar had been one of Liszt's ports of call on his German tour the previous year. It was a small, unexciting town living on the memory of a glorious cultural past, but that past was recent enough to stir a desire to recapture it, breathe new life into it, through the accession of men worthy to assume the mantle of Goethe, Schiller and Herder. The young Carl Alexander, grandson of the great Karl August, had grown up under the shadow of Goethe and received the intellectual glories of the Weimar court as his birthright. Seven years younger than Liszt, he set the carefree enthusiasm of his years as heir apparent to the task of reanimating the values that had made Weimar great, and Liszt's visit to the town in 1841, though brief, had fired his imagination. His father, Karl Friedrich, took less interest in the arts than in the practical administration of his estates but his mother, Maria Pavlovna, sister of Tsar Nicholas I of Russia, was a keen singer and even composed a little. She was also very rich, and her son knew that she would put her money where her heart was.

So when Liszt returned to Weimar in October 1842 for Carl

Alexander's wedding, the young Crown Prince had little difficulty in persuading his father to create a special appointment for him as Kapellmeister-at-large, with the responsibility of spending a few months in the dukedom each year and conducting a number of concerts there. Still caught up in the whirl of European recitals, and with as yet no thought of renouncing the pleasure of the limelight, he was in no position at that moment to do what was expected of him, and not until 1844 did he conduct his first concert in Weimar. In Carl Alexander he found a worthy partner for his artistic plans, and the correspondence between them, on cultural policy, on musical works and events, on Goethe, on Wagner – whom Liszt later introduced to the ducal court – lasted to the year of Liszt's death. Among the many scholars and writers with whom Carl Alexander corresponded were Bettina von Arnim, the German novelists Gutzkow, Gustav Freytag and Paul Heyse, the French novelists and poets Chateaubriand and Victor Hugo, Thackeray, and the historians Macaulay and Thiers. It is an interesting comment on cultural relations at the time that all the letters which passed between him and Liszt are written in French.

Brussels, The Hague, Breslau, again St Petersburg and Moscow, Hamburg, Munich, Nuremberg – the catalogue of towns and cities where he played is endless, and the enthusiasm he aroused, invariable. The only variation between one place and another lay in the degree of uncontrollability displayed by the ecstatic women in the audience. 'There was something demonic about him,' wrote Karl Schorn, sober and level-headed President of the district court in Cologne, after Liszt had given a recital there. 'His gaze had the power of a hypnotist – there is no other way of explaining the intoxicating effect that he had on the audience.' And as for the women: 'When he asked for a glass of water and put it down without draining it, the delirious beauties in the hall rushed forward at the end of the recital, picked up the glass and pressed it to their lips so as to quell their passion by taking a sip of the water he had left.'

Outside the hall their behaviour became even more bizarre: 'On one occasion a lady had retrieved a half-smoked cigar that Liszt had thrown away, and in spite of retching several times, she managed to go on smoking it, pretending to find it a ravishing experience.'

Berlin again – where he met Wagner for a second, more agreeable time and received from the King of Prussia the prestigious decoration 'Pour le mérite'. The King later wrote to Liszt in glowing terms: 'What We respect in you, Monsieur, is not only the inspired composer, the skilled artist blessed with the most outstanding gifts, but also the man, by virtue of the charitable causes that you have ceaselessly supported, undeniable proof of which you have given in the course of your journeys through Our lands.' Then Warsaw, Cracow, Stuttgart, Karlsruhe, Marseilles, Madrid, Lisbon: on and on it went through 1843, 1844, 1845, recital after recital, celebration after celebration – and mistress after mistress. For Liszt was a man of flesh and blood, consumed, to be sure, by his art and by his sense of prophetic mission but far from insensitive to the emotions that his personality aroused.

This aspect of his life has polarized opinion about Liszt the man, not least among his biographers. On the one hand, there are the would-be offended moralizers, leering at his libidinous excursions and looking down their noses at his shallow, egotistical immoralities. So much for the 'great man's' strength of character, they sneer – and this in a man who talked of high moral and artistic purpose, and was later to make public testimony of his commitment to the Roman Catholic Church by becoming an Abbé. At the other extreme stand the worshippers and admirers, hesitant to pass judgement on their hero's peccadilloes yet uneasy at the embarrassment that they provoke, trying to look the other way and pretend that such matters are too trivial to dwell on, petty irrelevancies in the face of the true, deeper values for which the master stands.

The superior scorn of the sceptics is as sterile as the evasive apologetics of the disciples are misplaced. Liszt *had* unresolved discords in his character, and such paradoxes must be held in the mind, unexplained yet real, if he is to be understood in the round. One cannot have the one Liszt without the other, the deeply committed artist without the flamboyant, publicity-seeking showman, the hedonistic connoisseur of aristocratic company without the contemplative, deeply religious seeker after humility and truth – or, using his own terms, the gypsy without the Franciscan. An unspoken expectation seems often to creep into the mind of the beholder that the artist, the man who lives for, and by, beauty, must needs have a psychology and a life-style of a purity that will match his high aesthetic ideals. It can shock and disturb us – though it ought not to – when we discover that the greatest of artists is as fallible as the rest of us, faces the same moral pressures and can submit to the same base instincts. And with this discovery comes the uncomfortable awareness that life is not art, that impeccability of aesthetic intention and genius of artistic expression are no guarantee of inner goodness or proof of moral stature.

Life is lived on many levels, and the creative artist, however great, no more disposes of his entire energy on the highest of these levels than do lesser mortals.

Thus Liszt, while seeking a deep companionship, a true marriage of minds, such as he found briefly with Marie d'Agoult and later, more durably, but also more problematically, with Carolyne von Sayn-Wittgenstein, had nothing with which to reproach himself when he also gave way to the attractions of more casual liaisons. *Grandes dames* like Countess Potocka and actresses like Charlotte Hagn, singers like Karoline Unger and Pauline Viardot, courtesans like Marie Duplessis (Dumas's 'dame aux camélias') and the colourful 'Spanish dancer' Lola Montez. Leporello would have been in his element had Liszt been his master. And indeed, there is much in Liszt to remind us of Don Juan – not Don Juan the philanderer, the unscrupulous breaker of hearts, but as Kierkegaard portrayed him in his essay on *Don Giovanni*, the restless idealist in search of perfect fulfilment, a Wandering Jew of the emotions, arousing sympathy rather than censure.

The very same paradoxes govern the world of Liszt the composer. And again, any attempt at reductionism, at 'averaging out', will lead away from his musical world, not towards it. Compelling, highly original and influential works rub shoulders with pieces of a distressing vacuity and banality, even vulgarity. That he returned time and again to his earlier compositions, making second and third versions of them, turning his songs into piano pieces, rearranging piano solos for piano duet or piano and orchestra, transcribing his orchestral works now for piano solo, now for piano duet, and so on and so on – this predilection alone suggests a narcissistic preoccupation with the creatures of his own world. But it also implies a lack of creative stamina, a repeated drying-up of the wells of inventiveness. The visions rise before him but they fade too soon and reappear too rarely. In between lie the wastes of frustration, of discontent, stretches filled with unrelated and often unfulfilling activity. Yet these stretches, Liszt being the man he was, he also lived out to the full, without hesitation or shame. His 'Hungarian' compositions, tributes to the homeland to which he never truly belonged, are similarly remote from the mainstream of his creative energy, excursions into the exotic world of the gypsies in whose nomadic rootlessness he saw a reflection of his own restless life of pilgrimage.

That restless life, the vagrant wanderings of the itinerant virtuoso, had not yet run full course. Apart from the financial rewards it brought him, apart too from the deep satisfaction he drew from playing for charity, he needed to explore to its utmost limits the world he had created, a world that dazzled all who came to see it, a world over which he reigned supreme. But at the same time moments of doubt were creeping in. The glamour seems to mask a condition of the spirit in which all is not well, as though applause and adulation merely distract attention from an inner malaise. In a letter to Lichnovsky in May 1844 he blurts out the poignant sentence: 'As for me, poor devil that I am, what people call my immense success is little consolation for my inner sadness.' All the hectic journeyings were beginning to seem like the flight of a fugitive, a man both escaping and seeking, but not yet finding.

In the summer of 1845, after his tour of Spain and Portugal and further recitals in France and Switzerland, Liszt travelled to Bonn for the crowning of an enterprise which had long been dear to his heart – the final unveiling of the memorial to Beethoven. He conducted Beethoven's Fifth Symphony, played the Emperor Concerto and gave the first performance of a specially composed Festival Cantata for choir and orchestra. The occasion was graced by the presence of King Friedrich Wilhelm IV and his Queen, together with that of their royal guests, Queen Victoria and the Prince Consort. Louis Spohr conducted the Ninth Symphony and the Missa Solemnis, while among the many musicians present were Berlioz and Charles Hallé – who had both come from Paris – Meyerbeer and Moscheles.

A less welcome guest was the notorious Lola Montez, into whose clutches Liszt had fallen the previous year and who now pursued him to Bonn. She was between monarchs, so to speak. A few years earlier she had ministered to the fancies of the Tsar, and the following year found her in the service of King Ludwig I of Bavaria, but between these summits lay many lesser, albeit equally distinguished and attractive peaks of the social and cultural scene, Alexandre Dumas *père* and Liszt among them. At the leading hotel in Bonn, the Gasthof zum Stern, she told the manager that Liszt had invited her to stay with him there but a member of the chorus recognized her and the manager refused to let her in. At the banquet that concluded the festivities, however, she succeeded in wheedling her way into the hall on the arm of a gullible and hopeful elderly citizen. After the toasts had been drunk, she jumped on to a table and, to the general horror, began one of her 'Spanish dances'. Pandemonium broke out and the dignitaries, among them Liszt, hastily left before the situation could get worse. 'Fortunately,' wrote Karl Schorn, who was one of the guests, 'the moment after we left, a storm broke out, with heavy thunder and lightning, which served to cool the heated tempers.'

Such episodes provided grist for the mill of the shrivelled, petty bourgeois provincials for whom a man of Liszt's stature offered an uncomfortable challenge. Berlioz, for one, observed with mystification and sorrow their small-minded jealousy of the man who had done more than any other to make the events of those days possible:

> Some were angry with Liszt because of his phenomenal gifts and extraordinary success; others, because he composed a too attractive cantata, while the other choral works written for the occasion and performed the previous day had been failures, and because he wore his own hair instead of a wig, and because he speaks French too well, and because his German is too good, and because he has not enough enemies, and so on and so on.

'Tear at your chains as you will!' cried Kleist to his fellow-countrymen under the heel of Napoleon. 'You will never break them! The man is too big for you!' 'For not always, indeed, can a feeble vessel contain them,/Only now and again can Man bear the weight of the Gods,' sighed Hölderlin in his ode 'Brod und Wein'. To be larger than life may evoke admiration and worship. But it may also fan envy, fear, which is only a step from distrust, even hate. Liszt experienced the whole gamut of responses during his lifetime.

A spiritual bond of rare power linked Liszt to Beethoven. The moment when the deaf and ailing Beethoven kissed the brow of the eleven-year-old prodigy had faded to little more than a sentimental memory, but the grip that Beethoven's music had on his mind was very real and present, and utterly unshakeable. He had the same breadth of emotional sympathy, the same bigness of soul, the same urge to discovery and novelty, the same sense of powerful commitment; in his recitals he persistently included Beethoven's late piano sonatas, which audiences of the day still found baffling and therefore resented, while his transcriptions for solo piano of the Septet and of all nine symphonies, and, for two pianos, of the third, fourth and fifth pianoforte concertos offered the musical public an immediate experience of this music in the intimacy of their own homes, an experience that could be relived at will.

Liszt left Bonn in low spirits. In nearby Cologne his disenchantment and the strain of his mode of life laid him low, and for the moment he could not go on. Then, after a few weeks, the old round returned – Alsace, Lorraine, the French provinces,

Vienna, Prague, Hungary, Romania, southern Russia – taking him into the winter of 1846–7. Towards the end of 1846 he was taken aback by the appearance of Marie d'Agoult's novel *Nélida*. But the caricature of him in her novel was too crude, too unlifelike – too untrue, he would have said – for it to offend him. It merely symbolized the passage from love to near-hate in Marie d'Agoult's emotions. 'To be quite frank,' he wrote to his friend Lichnovsky, 'if I were not firmly and rationally convinced that I am in fact a very different person from that which people here and there try to make me out to be, I should have long ago flung my whole boring and toilsome nuisance of a career [*die ganze Wurst meiner langweilig–mühseligen Karriere*] out of the window.'

Nélida slammed the door on a part of his past. The blissful solitude of Switzerland and Italy, like the lingering summers on the island of Nonnenwerth, belonged inseparably to this past, the past he had shared with the author of *Nélida*. But the children born of that past were very much part of his present. Convinced that only his plans would meet their needs, and concerned to keep them away from the influence of their mother, he made all decisions on their education his own preserve, relying on his mother to put them into effect. Blandine was already in a Paris boarding school; shortly before her eighth birthday Cosima joined her there after begging her grandmother to be allowed to go. Her father insisted that she be given piano lessons, sent her music that he considered appropriate for her to study and wrote affectionately to all three children. 'Blandine and Cosima were beside themselves with joy when they received your letter,' Anna Liszt once wrote to her son. 'Little Daniel also takes much more interest now when I hear from you, so the next time you write, add a few lines especially for him.'

Throughout his years as a vagrant virtuoso Liszt took great pains to see that what he called 'my Parisian household' was conducted in a suitably genteel style, a task entrusted to his secretary Gaëtano Belloni. As far as his own life and career were concerned, Paris had already taken its place in the past, but it was where his mother had made her home and where his children were being brought up, and the links would never be completely severed.

Cosima wrote eagerly to him as a child, though the awareness seemed slowly to creep over her, starting, perhaps, when he failed to come to her confirmation and first communion in 1847, that his mode of life would often deprive her of his presence when she most desired it. She saw her parents only as separate visitors, and the insecurity wrought by her illegitimacy and her isolation conditioned her for the disastrous marriage to her music teacher Hans von Bülow, into which she was drawn at nineteen. When her brother Daniel died of consumption in her arms at the age of twenty, she blamed her parents, and whatever the influence of Wagner in her hardness towards her father in his old age, its seeds had been sown, as he knew and grieved, in her childhood and youth.

Although the compositions which he completed in occasional moments of tranquillity during these years are generally brief and have little of the sustained originality of his greatest works, they have their flashes of characteristic harmony:

Piano introduction to the *Second Petrarch Sonnet for Tenor and Piano* (1847)

Among these items are a number of short piano pieces, including a 'Feuille d'album' written in St Petersburg in 1843 for Marie von Mouchanov-Kalergis, who later became one of Wagner's most ardent patrons, and more of the inevitable piano transcriptions – the overtures to Weber's *Freischütz* and *Oberon*, some Schubert marches originally written for piano duet, and the Overture to Berlioz's *Les Francs juges*. Most of the pieces from these years, however, are vocal in inspiration – on the one hand original songs, on the other piano transcriptions of Schubert Lieder.

Liszt wrote some eighty songs in the course of his life, many of them taken up for two, three and even four subsequent revisions; about half have their origins in the 1840s, the majority of the remainder coming in his last fifteen or so years.

His vocal works in general constitute a side of his musical activity which is all but totally ignored. Yet because they are not responses to external pressure and have nothing to do with the extroversion of his career in the public limelight, his songs admit us, in both personal and musical terms, into the heart of his private world. They reveal the motifs and experiences that moved him, the values he cherished, the poets in whose utterances he found these values enshrined, and the intimate musical means, free of any suspicion of public affectation, by which he sought to reproduce them in his own terms. Settings of German poets predominate in the 1840s – Heine, Goethe, Uhland, Freiligrath ('O lieb, so lang du lieben kannst', the melody best known from his adaptation of it as the third 'Liebestraum' for piano), Lenau – but there are also poems in French (Victor Hugo, Dumas *père*) and Italian (three sonnets by Petrarch – the three inscribed at the head of the corresponding piano pieces in the 'Deuxième Année' of the *Années de pèlerinage*).

His free, rhapsodical, sometimes theatrical approach to the art of song-writing leads to a curious diffuseness: recitative-like sections for the voice, treating the poetic text, not surprisingly, with a great deal of licence, are set against passages where the interest is carried by the accompaniment. This is not the fusion of voice and piano which distinguishes Schubert's Lieder but an ensemble in which the piano part is in danger of being overloaded with meaning, flawing the unity of the song. In 1850 he wrote to the Austrian composer Joseph Dessauer: 'My early songs are generally too ostentatiously sentimental, and their accompaniments frequently too choc-a-bloc.' If he returned to some of these songs many years later, it was to remove their Baroque exuberances and excesses, and create firmer contours and structures – as in his later revision of the Paganini Studies. But in that the voice does not rule throughout, as in true songs it must, whatever the integration of melody and accompaniment, Liszt's songs have a strange insubstantiality and carry less than full conviction. Heretical as it may sound, there is a firmer unity, hence a greater aesthetic satisfaction, in the third pianoforte 'Liebestraum' than in the song of which it is a transcription.

Characteristically, his approach to the poetic texts that he set is cavalier to the point of recklessness. Arbitrary repetition of individual words and phrases in response to melodic stimulus, dramatic urge or considerations of musical form, belongs to the prerogatives of the song-writer, but Liszt sometimes strains a legitimate freedom to breaking-point. Take the second of Goethe's 'Wandrers Nachtlied' poems:

> Über allen Gipfeln
> Ist Ruh,
> In allen Wipfeln
> Spürest du
> Kaum einen Hauch.
> Die Vöglein schweigen im Walde;
> Warte nur, balde
> Ruhest du auch.

In Liszt's hands these eight beautiful lines are manhandled to produce a text of grotesque proportions that would have made Goethe writhe in his grave:

> Über allen Gipfeln ist Ruh.
> In allen Wipfeln spürest du
> Kaum einen Hauch.
> Die Vöglein schweigen im Walde,
> Warte nur!
> Warte nur!
> Balde,
> Balde,
> Balde ruhest du auch.
> Balde ruhest du auch.
> Du auch.
> Warte nur, warte nur,
> Balde ruhest du auch, du auch!

And for how to make a melodramatic monologue out of an unaffected ballad strophe, one need look only at his setting of Heine's 'Lorelei' (see opposite).

For a musician so sensitive to literary values Liszt was strangely indiscriminate in the poetic texts he set. Unusual too is that, although French was his preferred medium of communication, and

thus the language in which he thought and felt most intensely, the overwhelming majority of his songs are settings of German poems. Goethe, Uhland, Heine, Rückert – these are among his chosen poets. But so too are versifiers such as Freiligrath, Hoffmann von Fallersleben and Rellstab, to say nothing of embarrassing doggerel by his friends Lichnovsky and Peter Cornelius. Rather than seek out poetry of distinction, as Schumann, Brahms or Hugo Wolf did, Liszt set what happened to come his way or was laid in front of him, leaving to works in other, grander formats the demonstration of his commitment to the literary worlds of the great – of Dante, of Goethe, of Shakespeare, of the Bible.

Liszt's piano versions of Schubert songs were among the most popular items in his concert repertoire of the 1840s. But they did not only resound, through their skilfulness and their pianistic effectiveness, to the greater glory of Liszt. Many of the songs themselves – those of the so-called 'Schwanengesang', for instance – had as yet been little heard, and audiences encountered them for the first time through Liszt's transcriptions. Once interest in the originals was aroused, the transcriptions, sadly but inevitably, declined into little more than museum pieces, leaving Liszt in the role of a missionary who, having performed his service on behalf of Schubert, could now only withdraw from the scene. Yet at their best – 'Der Atlas', 'Erlkönig', 'Auf dem Wasser zu singen' – they have more pleasure to offer than contemporary fashion allows.

In both personal and musical character Liszt and Schubert inhabited totally different worlds, but Liszt made no secret of an affection, albeit not uncritical, for the work of 'le musicien le plus poète que jamais', as he called him, whose passionate imagination sought the dramatic potential of the individual moment and thus rapidly burned itself out. 'An extended work caused Schubert difficulties,' he wrote in 1855 in his essay on the song-writer Robert Franz, 'because he could not manage to consolidate his energy and husband his powers.' It is a diagnosis which, with different points of reference, could be turned against Liszt himself.

Many years later he made an attractive little reassertion of his 'special relationship' to Schubert. In 1883 an article on him appeared in the *Biographie des Contemporains* in Paris, in which the author had written that on his concert tours Liszt had concentrated on Bach, Handel, Beethoven and Weber. In his annotations to the article Liszt crossed out the names of Bach and Handel and substituted that of Schubert.

In the winter of 1846–7 Liszt travelled eastwards through the Danube states, reaching the Ukraine in February. He gave a series of concerts in Kiev, the colourful, multi-racial capital of the area, the last of which, with his resolute sense of social obligation and true to his generous nature, he announced as being for charity. '*Génie oblige*' was his answer to those who asked why he drove himself so hard.

On the day of this recital in February 1847 he received a letter containing a substantial donation to the charity fund from a wealthy aristocrat living on an estate in the region of Podolia, south-west of the town. The following day he drove out to pay his respects to the benefactor and convey his personal thanks. It was a meeting that brought a new set of values into his life and changed

TOP LEFT Anna Liszt, *née* Lager, Franz's mother.
Pastel by L. Demarey, 1832.

TOP RIGHT Adam Liszt, Franz's father. Gouache
by an unknown artist, 1819

ABOVE Liszt's birthplace in the village of
Raiding, in the Austrian province of Burgenland.
19th-century oil painting by an unknown artist.

ABOVE The fourteen-year-old Franz Liszt in Paris. Lithograph by Charles Motte, 1825, the year Liszt's *Don Sanche* was produced at the Paris Opéra.

RIGHT Liszt in Rome, 1839. Signed sketch by Ingres, given to Marie d'Agoult, with whom Liszt was living at this time.

BELOW RIGHT Countess Marie d'Agoult. Oil painting by Henri Lehmann, 1839.

BELOW Liszt's three children by Marie d'Agoult: Blandine (1835–62), Cosima (1837–1930) and (centre) Daniel (1839–59). From a painting by Amélie de Lacépède, 1843. Cosima, who married Richard Wagner in 1870 after her divorce from Hans von Bülow, was the only one to survive her parents.

TOP Liszt at the piano. Fictitious but evocative scene in a Paris drawing-room, painted by Josef Danhauser, 1840. From left to right: Alexander Dumas *père*, Victor Hugo, George Sand (seated), Paganini, Rossini, Liszt, Marie d' Agoult (at Liszt's feet). On the piano is a bust of Beethoven.

ABOVE A recital by Liszt in Berlin, 1842. Cartoon by Adolf Brennglas (i.e. Glasbrenner) of the wild scenes that accompanied Liszt's concert performances.

TOP View of Weimar, *ca.* 1810. Etching by
G. M. Kraus. In the centre is the spire of the
Stadtkirche, where the philosopher Herder
preached, and on the left the palace of the Grand
Dukes, built at the end of the 18th century.

ABOVE The Villa Altenburg, Weimar.
Watercolour by Carl Hoffmann, 1859. Liszt lived
here with Princess Carolyne von Sayn-Wittgenstein
from 1848 to 1860.

the course of his entire career, making the thirty-five-year-old hero from the little Hungarian village of Raiding, the world's greatest pianist, seem like a different person. The benefactor's name was Princess Jeanne Elisabeth Carolyne von Sayn-Wittgenstein. She had attended the first of his recitals in Kiev and been so fascinated by his personality that she determined to make his closer acquaintance.

At the time of their first meeting the Princess was twenty-eight, Liszt close on thirty-six. The Princess's father, Peter von Ivanovsky, was a wealthy Polish landowner who had died some years earlier, leaving her in possession of an immense fortune, the majority of it in real estate, over the administration of which, with its 30,000 peasants and other employees, she exercised her own control. At seventeen she was pressed into a marriage with Prince Nicholas von Sayn-Wittgenstein, an aristocrat of German lineage who was serving in the Tsar's army, but separated from him soon afterwards and retired to her country seat at Woronince, taking her young daughter Marie with her. She was short and stocky, pale, with clear blue eyes, a prominent nose and dark hair; she almost invariably wore a simple black gown with a loose jacket and a black lace bonnet tied under the chin, which made her look like the grandmother in a Grimms' fairy tale. Pictures of her hardly evoke the epithet beautiful, nor did her contemporaries – or she herself, for that matter – make such a claim; certainly she could only be at a disadvantage if compared to the fresh, elegant, fine-featured Marie d'Agoult. But Liszt saw her otherwise. 'I pride myself on being a connoisseur of beauty,' he wrote to his mother, 'and I maintain that Princess Wittgenstein is beautiful, even very beautiful, for her soul imparts supreme beauty to her features.' The eye of the beholder prevails.

As a person, the Princess had a determination about her to which Liszt, compliant and generous, fell a ready victim; and she was driven – almost possessed – by a religious conviction to whose appeal he willingly succumbed, now and for the remainder of his life. She became his prompter, his counsellor, his conscience, penetrating every corner of his being.

A few days after his courtesy visit to Woronince Liszt received an invitation from the Princess to return to the house for the birthday celebrations of the ten-year-old Marie. The weeks he spent there sealed their relationship, and only the promises he had made of further recitals in southern Russia forced him to leave. A flood of letters passed between them, passionate testimony to their yearning to be together. In the summer they met in Odessa, then, in September 1847, in the town of Elisavetgrad – known since the Revolution as Kirovograd – he gave what was to be the final concert of his career as a professional pianist. The thought of giving up his profitable itinerant life – '*Saus und Braus*' (in the lap of luxury), he called it – had latterly returned to his mind time and again but the cup of fame and success had first to be drained to the last. Even now, in Elisavetgrad, he did not know that this recital was to mark his farewell. But the moment he arrived back at Woronince, the path before him became clear. 'The solution to the problem of my life is now at hand,' he wrote to his mother:

> An event as unexpected as it was decisive now seems to be tilting the balance of fate in favour of happiness and setting me a task to which I feel equal. It would have to be an unforeseen and very unfortunate series of events that would prevent my hopes from being fulfilled. 1847 will bring me luck. So celebrate my birthday and pray for me – let the children pray for me too.

When she learned what 'the balance of fate' had in store for her son, Anna Liszt, well aware of the trail of aristocratic married women that lay behind him, and uneasily mindful of her husband's worried prophecy of the harm to which Franz would come in their clutches, did not disguise her anxiety. 'My dear child,' she replied to him in a letter sent to Woronince,

> do not consort too much with noble ladies – you have already paid for your experience. Forgive me for putting it this way, but as your mother I have a right to speak frankly. It would cause me great pain if you were to suffer again as the result of an *amour* linked with an excess of ambition . . . You are now thirty-six, which is some consolation to me, for you know the world with all its witchcraft, and it will not seduce you. Dearly as I would have you happy in the possession of a noble and virtuous woman as your wife, your legal wife, it is equally important that you do what is fitting for you. God be with you.

Her fears were laid to rest when she received letters from the Princess herself, assuring her of the sincerity of her relationship to her son and of her determination to triumph over the obstacles that stood in the way of their legal union. In the end it was the obstacles that triumphed.

Back in 1842 Liszt had been appointed Kapellmeister-at-large to the Grand Duke of Sachsen-Weimar-Eisenach; he had conducted a few concerts in Weimar in 1844 but had not taken up the post in earnest. Since the categorical imperative in his life was now to share every moment with the Princess, the thought that they might make their home in Weimar, at least for the time being, came naturally to the fore. And there was another consideration that pointed to Weimar. The Grand Duchess Maria Pavlovna, an admirer of Liszt's, was the sister of Tsar Nicholas I of Russia. Immense difficulties were to be anticipated, first, for the Princess to leave Russia with the intentions that were by now no secret; second, for her to retain unimpeded control of her possessions there; and third – by far the most agonizing problem – for her to achieve a divorce from her husband. In Weimar, so they reasoned, they would be able to persuade the Grand Duchess to influence her brother to help bring about what they both so desperately desired.

So at the beginning of 1848, in a spirit of adventure and optimism, Liszt travelled to Weimar to announce his intention of taking the musical life of the duchy under his wing and to pave the way for a life of happiness with his Princess. In April, having filed a divorce suit against her husband and carrying the proceeds of the sale of some of her property, Princess Carolyne left Russia with her daughter and made for Prince Felix Lichnovsky's castle of Krzyzanovitz, in Silesia, where Liszt had arranged to meet her. Here they spent two happy, blissful weeks before journeying onwards together, passing through Vienna and making a detour to visit Liszt's birthplace in the Burgenland (the house is now a museum devoted to his memory). In June they finally reached the small German town where they were to share each other's lives for the next thirteen years and where Liszt reached the zenith of his powers as a composer. '48 to 61 – serenity and work in Weimar' – such was the autobiographical chapter-heading under which he summarized these years. Of work, as composer, conductor and writer, there was indeed a great deal. The serenity proved more elusive.

FOUR

The Prince and Princess of the Altenburg

Weimar is a hallowed name. Nestling in a hollow surrounded by the wooded hills of Thuringia, the River Ilm wandering gently towards its union with the Saale, the town has a history that can be traced back to the fifth century, yet it never acquired an economic importance that was other than local. The emergence of an urban middle class from the agriculturalism of the Middle Ages was slow; the Peasants' War of 1524–5 and the Thirty Years' War a century later both passed the town by, to the citizens' obvious relief but also with the consequence of further delaying the development of that lively awareness of self and circumstance which they needed, and which the experience of war, perversely, would have brought.

But what was stunted, backward in economic and social terms had its counterpart in a dazzling tradition of intellectual and artistic activity emanating from the court of the Dukes of Sachsen-Weimar-Eisenach, who had made the town their residence from the latter half of the sixteenth century. The painter Lucas Cranach is the first great name on record. A court orchestra was founded in the mid-seventeenth century, while in the palace of Duke Wilhelm Ernst one of the earliest German operatic stages was set up in 1696; in the same age many of the paintings were acquired – Dürer, Cranach, Tintoretto, Rubens, Guido Reni – which form the core of the fine collection still on display there today. Johann Sebastian Bach was court organist and a member of the court orchestra from 1708 to 1717, and his sons Wilhelm Friedemann and Carl Philipp Emmanuel were born here.

It was under the regime of the Dowager Duchess Anna Amalia, however, during the last quarter of the eighteenth century, that the name Weimar became synonymous with the cultivation of supreme philosophical and aesthetic values, the expression of humanistic ideals at their most noble. First Anna Amalia brought Christoph Martin Wieland, novelist and Professor of Philosophy at the nearby University of Erfurt, to become tutor to her fifteen-year-old son, the Crown Prince Karl August. Three years later, in 1775, Goethe arrived in the town at the invitation of Karl August, who had now inherited his father's title, and rapidly became the most brilliant star in the intellectual firmament. At Goethe's suggestion Karl August then summoned to his court the Protestant preacher and humanist Johann Gottfried Herder – philosopher of the Enlightenment, historian of world culture, anthropologist, student of comparative folklore, a universal mind in the mould of the Renaissance – whose church still dominates the skyline with its lofty spire. Finally, towards the end of the century, also drawn by the presence of Goethe, came Schiller, Germany's greatest dramatist, the two establishing a creative friendship unique in the wealth of literary works that it brought forth.

For half a century these four men, and the culture they had founded, brought a ceaseless pilgrimage of intellectuals to Weimar from all over Germany and beyond. Classical German literature was born here and remained centred here, a town with a population then numbering a mere 8,000 or so but with the claim to be, in Otto Grotewohl's words, 'the birthplace of the moral life of our nation'. With Goethe's death in 1832 this era came to an end. The Grand Duke Karl Friedrich and his son Carl Alexander sought to raise music and the visual arts to the eminence hitherto held by literature, but the Weimar that greeted Liszt in 1848 had sunk into a comfortable staidness and was living off the glories of the past. 'How little remains of the grandeur of yesteryear!' mourned the *Leipziger Illustrierte Zeitung* in 1846, the year the railway came to the town:

> Only dead memories are left . . . What can poor Weimar, with its population of barely 14,000, do about it? It has little by way of trade and manufacture, and, in a word, lacks life. When the Duke and his family are away and the schools are on holiday, the streets are empty and deserted, and the life-blood of the town, namely its citizenry, trickles only sluggishly, in dribs and drabs, through its veins, the streets, as through the body of a weary old man.
>
> A town such as this must surely be worried about nutrition, for people have little money to spend, wealth is a rarity and prosperity something quite exceptional; the only ones to be at all well-off are tradesmen such as bakers, butchers and purveyors to the Court.
>
> Furthermore Weimar is no place to attract a visitor from the

city out to make a holiday excursion by train: the sights of the place can easily be disposed of in one day by a leisurely German connoisseur, while a culture-hungry Englishman can finish them off in a matter of hours. If a man decides to stay longer, he will find himself at his wits' end and unredeemably delivered into the hands of the biggest tormenter among all the demons on earth, viz. boredom. With its peculiar conglomeration of features Weimar has all the unpleasant qualities of a small town and none of the pleasant ones.

This piece of jaundiced journalism conveys the view of one whose experience of Weimar began and ended in the streets he walked, one who was an outsider to the ducal court from which, then as for decades in the past, the cultural life of the town issued. For court and town, aristocracy and commonalty still lived in largely separate worlds, and if they were present on the same occasion, the public etiquette of class distinction applied: in the theatre the members of the court sat on the right, the townspeople on the left. Not until after the revolutionary year of 1848 did such divisive conventions lose their authority. Plans for a Goethe Foundation, put forward in the centennial year of 1849, came to naught; so did the historian Leopold Ranke's project of 1867 for the establishment of a German Academy to take its place alongside the Académie française. Carl Alexander did, however, succeed in presiding over a number of notable cultural successes – the creation of an academy of art and a museum, the foundation of the German Shakespeare Society and the Goethe Society, and the restoration of Wartburg Castle – the oldest continuously inhabited castle in the whole of Germany – to mark its 800th anniversary in 1867.

It was the memory of this humanist tradition that led the newly-elected National Assembly to convene in Weimar after the Great War to found what came to be called the Weimar Republic – the Weimar that stood for the ideals of tolerance, moral freedom and human dignity on which the Kaiser's imperial capital of Berlin had trampled. After Hitler had set the Nazi seal on the final disintegration of the Republic in 1933, he cast his own hideous insult at these values by setting up a concentration camp on a hill overlooking the town – the camp with the unforgettable name of Buchenwald.

'We are dealing with three men in one, each at odds with the others,' remarked a Frenchman of his friend Liszt: 'the convivial society *beau*, the virtuoso and the creative composer.' Liszt was not in ignorance of the obstructive game these three creatures were playing. 'This much is certain,' he wrote to Franz Brendel, editor of the *Neue Zeitschrift für Musik*, 'that few have to struggle so laboriously over the tiresome business of self-correction as I, for the whole process of my intellectual development was rendered the more difficult, if not positively impeded, by a multitude of incidents and events.' Now, his personal life given a new inspiration and a new stability, he eagerly grasped the promise of creative serenity that the Weimar court offered, a new seriousness of purpose before him, both as man and artist.

Liszt arrived in Weimar in January 1848 and took up residence in the historic Erbprinz Hotel. Napoleon stayed here in 1807, Alexander von Humboldt in 1827, Weber, Paganini, Mendelssohn, Berlioz and Hebbel were only a few of its other distinguished guests in the course of the century. Even though Liszt went to live with Princess Carolyne in the Villa Altenburg a few months later, communications from the court continued to be addressed to him at the Erbprinz throughout the thirteen years of his stay, for protocol could not allow official cognizance to be taken of the cohabitation of their famous new Kapellmeister with the estranged wife of a Russian aristocrat.

Impatiently he waited for Princess Carolyne to make her final departure from Woronince. Her motives for leaving had become known, and movement beyond the Russian borders, even for an aristocrat, was not without restriction, especially as the scent of revolution was spreading across Europe. He makes mention in his letters to her of the revolutionary movements in Paris, Vienna and elsewhere but turns quickly to personal matters. 'In all the political confusion of the moment,' he writes to her in March, 'the only conviction that remains immovable in my mind is that we must come together again at the earliest possible moment.'

That moment arrived in June. The Princess had managed to get out of Russia on the pretext of needing to go to Carlsbad to take the waters; once here, on Austrian soil, as it then was, she was safe and could make her way the remaining hundred miles in the joy of anticipation. In Weimar, through Liszt's agency, she rented for herself, her eleven-year-old daughter Marie, Marie's Scottish governess, Miss Anderson, and the old servant Kostenecka a villa situated on rising ground above the river, the palace and the historic houses of the town.

A plain, square, three-storey family house built in 1811, the Villa

Altenburg has little architectural interest. Its virtue was spacious-
ness rather than charm. But during the decade that now followed it
became a centre of attraction for musicians from far and wide,
especially those of the progressive younger generation – a kind of
half salon, half private conservatoire where men and women
gathered for inspiration and instruction. Shortly after the Princess
took up residence there, Liszt made part of the house his own and
gradually spent more and more of each day there until, by the end of
the following year, their joint ménage was complete and undisguised.

It was a step as inevitable for the two characters concerned, and
as predictable to informed and observant onlookers, as it was
provocative, unsettling, fraught with tensions and uncertainties.
The social gulf between them ensured a raising of eyebrows and a
vigorous clucking of tongues among the offended members of a
stratified society. Liszt's reputation as a connoisseur of ladies of
rank, and the undisguised knowledge that the Princess had run
away from her husband in order to share her life with her lover,
made the situation no easier.

As befitted her station, the Princess was received at court by
Maria Pavlovna, her compatriot, and hoped, as did Liszt, that the
Grand Duchess would intercede with her brother the Tsar to have
her marriage to Prince Nicholas von Sayn-Wittgenstein annulled,
so that she would be free to marry Liszt. But instead a document
was delivered to her from the Tsar, ordering her to return to
Russia on pain of banishment and the sequestration of her estates.
She refused, and from this moment on the Weimar court no longer
recognized her. She received no more invitations to court
functions and was cold-shouldered on the public occasions she
chose to attend. Adelheid von Schorn, daughter of one of the
Grand Duchess's ladies-in-waiting, described in her memoirs a
characteristic incident that occurred during the unveiling of the
statues of Goethe and Schiller in front of the Weimar theatre in
1857:

> So that people could watch the ceremony, one of our friends
> had made his house in the square available to his acquaintances.
> My mother asked him for seats for the Princess and her
> daughter. We were there in good time. I received Liszt and the
> two ladies at the front door. My mother was upstairs and led
> them towards the window that had been reserved for them;
> there was a throng of well-known people in the room, most of
> them ladies. As soon as they caught sight of the Princess, they
> all withdrew ostentatiously, leaving us suddenly alone.

The Grand Duke Karl Friedrich himself accepted his new Kapellmeister as he found him, while to Carl Alexander, at whose instigation Liszt had been engaged and who succeeded to his father's title in 1853, Liszt symbolized his aspirations to restore Weimar to the cultural eminence it had held in the days of Goethe. Likewise the artistic community was moved more by the fame and inspiration of Liszt the musician than by the foibles and emotional tangles of Liszt the man. The figure at the centre was no stranger to critical, sometimes hostile scrutiny and had the magnanimity of spirit to live through it without blustering indignation or surly rancour. But he would have been less than human – and he could well have set the motto *nihil humani a me alienum puto* on his crest – had he not suffered under the indignities which the Princess was made to bear and from which he was powerless to protect her. Frau von Schwendler, a lady of the court, was one of the few women of the time to see the implacable situation in frankly human terms.

> We must never forget, [she said] that it is not just for pleasure that a person takes such steps which deviate from the customary path of morality, for everybody knows in advance that such actions are bound to lead to conflict with the people around him and with all the circumstances in which he lives. One must have a very strong inner conviction and be subject to very powerful external contingencies to follow such a course. I grieve for the Princess and I grieve also for Liszt – for whether they will be happy together, they themselves can scarcely tell, whereas the suffering brought by the conflict is something they can never escape.

The relationship of Liszt and Princess Carolyne to those around them was not helped by their ostentatious Catholicism in a firmly Protestant state. Liszt attended Mass in the little chapel in the Marienstrasse, 'repeating the words of the liturgy in so loud a voice,' said the poet Karl Linzen, remembering the days when he acted as server at eucharist,

> as though he himself were the celebrant. The chaplain tolerated this patiently, perhaps thereby silently conceding that it was the privilege of genius to behave thus. If my memory serves me correctly, Liszt did not keep strictly to the form of the chant but intoned the phrases of the liturgy with a peculiar impulsiveness and intensity, often with sudden outbursts of passion. Especially the words '*mea culpa, mea maxima culpa*', expressing the

enormity of man's original sin, he would roll round his tongue with an ardour that we boys found utterly new and strange but also at times rather frightening.

Although the occupancy of the Villa Altenburg stood in the name of the Princess Carolyne von Sayn-Wittgenstein, who understood little about music and neither sang nor played, the house was dominated from the beginning by Franz Liszt and given over almost entirely to music performance and composition teaching. There were three large salons used for music-making. The one on the ground floor contained a Viennese grand piano, stacks of music and a number of music desks, and had on the walls medallions of Berlioz, Wagner, Schumann and his wife Clara, a portrait of Liszt's friend Prince Felix Lichnovsky, and Beethoven's death mask. Here Liszt gave his lessons. The salon on the first floor housed an impressive library and two grands, facing each other as for duet playing, one an Erard, the other a Broadwood which had belonged to Beethoven and been presented to Liszt after Beethoven's death by the Viennese publisher Spina. In the largest of the music rooms, on the second floor, stood another Erard grand, a spinet which had for many years belonged to Mozart, and from 1854 onwards, a huge instrument, a strange combination of pedal piano and harmonium, which had been built to Liszt's specification by the firm of Alexandre et fils in Paris.

All these rooms had the character, in one way or another, of public places, where finished or semi-finished products were put on display, sometimes for admiration, sometimes for criticism. The power-house of the Villa Altenburg, the private quarters where Liszt had his study and his rooms for meditation, and which only he and the Princess were allowed to enter, were in a wing built out into the garden behind the house, with direct access both to the courtyard below and to the Princess's apartments in the main building. Here was the famous 'Blue Room', with its floral upholstery, its blue-white drapes and its blue-gold wall covering, where Liszt worked. In one corner stood a birchwood grand by Boisselot of Marseilles, at its side a desk and a little table with an hour-glass on it; there were two sofas, a long bookcase in which he also kept music scores, and a large writing-desk close to the window. On this desk stood a drawing by Edward Steinle, 'St Francis of Paola Walking on the Water'; the only decoration on the walls was a print of Dürer's 'Melancholia'. Apart from the doors that led across to the Princess's rooms and down to the courtyard, a third door opened into his bedroom and a fourth into a chamber cast as a tiny chapel with room only for an icon, a gold crucifix brought by the Princess from Woronince, and two prie-dieus.

But far from being confined to the rooms in which, so to speak, he went about his professional career, Liszt's presence was carried by Princess Carolyne to every corner of the house. An ante-room on the ground floor, adjoining that in which he gave his lessons, housed some of the personal gifts that had been showered on him during his European tours – as a constant smoker of cigars he was especially proud of his valuable collection of pipes and cigar-holders. He and the Princess spent inordinate sums of money on cigars, many of which they presented to their friends, who were made to join in the habit. 'If you are going to spend any considerable time in my company,' he once said jocularly to Alexander Wilhelm Gottschalg, the Weimar court organist, 'you'll have to learn to smoke.'

In the Princess's blue drawing-room on the first floor there hung three paintings by Ary Scheffer – a glamorous oil portrait of Liszt done in 1837, a portrait of the Princess's daughter Marie, and 'The Three Wise Men', the central figure in which bears the transfigured features of Liszt. This picture held for the Princess the status of a shrine, a cult-object symbolizing the two merciless forces which both inspired her life and tore it apart – her love for the Catholic religion and her love for Franz Liszt.

Finally, passing from this salon through the dining-room, with its chairs, window and door drapes in rich red velvet, and with the Princess's magnificent silverware laid out on shelves along the walls, the visitor came to the 'Green Chamber', a private Liszt museum in all but name. Here the Princess had assembled innumerable portraits, busts, reliefs, commemorative medals, gifts of rings, caskets and watches, documents of one kind and another, and a collection of music manuscripts – an exhibition of both love and hero-worship. And what kind of woman was it who loved and worshipped her hero, this pale, animated, intense Polish-Russian aristocrat who, like the Countess Marie d'Agoult a decade earlier, had turned her back on the soul-destroying security of a 'good' marriage, defied the recriminations and snubs of those who used to call themselves her friends, and sought a life of emotional and spiritual fulfilment in the company of this assured yet vulnerable artist of genius?

At the centre of her personality, hence also of the mesmeric power she exerted over him, lay a religious conviction almost frightening in its earnestness. Liszt loved her, in their first years together, unquestioningly, all-consumingly; she loved him no less intensely but more selectively – for the genius that had drawn her into its orbit, and out of profound gratitude for the love which that genius bore her. As his obligation, his bondage, to her was sealed by her sacrifice of family, wealth, homeland, friends, so her commitment to him lay in inducing in his mind the attitudes and qualities that would bring to fruition the immense creative powers within him. And spanning this complex of love, gratitude and duty was an intensely personal, sometimes unorthodox Catholic faith sustained by mystical experience and prayer, into which all else was subsumed. At the same time she had an insatiable desire to communicate this experience to the world at large, writing one book after another – on the *vita contemplativa*, on Buddhism and Christianity, on religion and women – before immuring herself in Rome for the last twenty-five years of her life with her multi-volume study *Des causes intérieures de la faiblesse extérieure de l'Église*. Faith, rather than Hope and Love, prevailed in her apprehension of the Pauline trinity of values.

So distinctive and determined a personality as the Princess could not but divide opinion, both over the true nature of her character and over the quality of her influence on Liszt. It was him they came to see, whether, like most of the older visitors, to pay their respects to the famous new Kapellmeister, or, like the younger generation, to seek inspiration at the feet of the master. But she, his encourager and adviser, his moral tutor, his conscience, was never absent. Those who found Liszt also found his Princess. She would not have had it otherwise, nor would he.

Adelheid von Schorn described her thus:

> She was fairly slight in build and very quick in her movements, short, and brimming over with energy. Her dark hair and eyes, together with a sallow complexion, gave her a foreign aspect – and she was, indeed, of pure Polish descent. A rather large nose gave a strange air of significance to her face, and an expression of remarkable kindness lay on her lips.

> She was, moreover, an excellent hostess, fully a match for the convivial Liszt who always flourished in company, and presided vivaciously over the gatherings in one or other of the music rooms – part discussion groups, part recitals, and generally concluding with Liszt playing to the guests. Her command of German was highly imperfect, though none the less voluble for that – she and Liszt spoke and corresponded with each other entirely in French – but her heavy Slav accent gave a quaint charm to her conversation.

Not that this had any power to move those who came to the Villa Altenburg already sceptical of the character of its occupants and offended by the affront to conventional morality that their relationship posed. The diplomat and writer Theodor von Bernhardi, for instance, a nephew of the poet Ludwig Tieck, who stayed in Weimar in 1851–2, noted with irritation that although she had brought two million roubles with her on her flight from Russia, she constantly pleaded poverty, always wore the same dowdy clothes and emphasized the sacrifice she had made in order to join Liszt by claiming: 'We were reduced to Liszt's ten fingers.' When she later appeared at dinner bedecked with jewels, Bernhardi went on, her claim to be 'reduced to Liszt's ten fingers' looked suspiciously hollow. Furthermore,

> Carolyne is very indiscreet. She asks a lot of questions 'pour avoir le secret de tout le monde' and establishes a kind of authority on the knowledge thus acquired, so that one does not venture to offend her. It is consistent with this that she should herself be devious and evasive, revealing nothing of her own views on politics, art or literature.

The poet Hoffmann von Fallersleben, on the other hand, made frequent visits to the house after moving to Weimar in 1854 and saw the Princess through very different eyes:

> She dispensed a truly regal hospitality, receiving and waiting upon her guests in sovereign style. She was intelligent, broadly educated, widely read, a connoisseur of art, with an accurate judgement in many matters; she was always ready to encourage noble efforts, showed kindness and sympathy to others, gave assistance to the sick and needy and always paid public tribute to those she loved and respected.

Hans von Bülow, who became Liszt's pupil in Weimar in 1851 and later married his daughter Cosima, also admiringly recalled a far more charming Princess than did the unfriendly Bernhardi:

> She conducted the conversation with a splendid keenness of mind, constantly making original remarks that were never superficial, the whole time smoking the thickest and strongest cigars imaginable and filling the room with dense clouds of smoke . . .
> Alchemy, Rahel von Varnhagen, painting, the German nation – in short, we covered the whole macrocosm and microcosm in our conversation, and once more it was the

Princess who made the most brilliant contribution to the discussion . . . It was so fascinating that I could not tear myself away. When I finally did so, it was high time, for my head had been reeling the whole evening, so overwhelmed was I by the way she talked.

An added charm was brought to such evenings by the Princess's young daughter Marie, a gifted girl – born in the same year as Liszt's Cosima – whose artlessness and beauty captivated the hearts of many of her elders. 'A poetic spirit', Hoffmann von Fallersleben called her, 'who has not yet been confronted with the prose of life.' Her mother, people observed, for all the intellectual breadth of her conversation, had little understanding of music, and her attempts to influence the course of Liszt's work often had an irrelevance about them which bordered on the perverse. 'Like a primitive,' said Wagner to Cosima, 'she is only susceptible to the crudest effects in music, to moments of sudden excitement.'

Mornings Liszt devoted to work in his 'Blue Room' – work on *Ce qu'on entend sur la montagne*, *Tasso* and *Les Préludes*, the first of his symphonic poems, on songs to poems by Goethe, on the two piano concertos, on piano transcriptions of the most varied pieces, on his monograph on Chopin. He began to study Bach and to turn his mind for the first time to writing for the organ. And while his thoughts repeatedly returned to the piano (though he never composed at the keyboard), the visions now crowding into his imagination – symphonies on the figures of Faust and Dante, further symphonic poems and essays into programme music – demanded the dynamics and colours of the orchestra, forcing him to master the subtle discipline of orchestration.

Described in this flat, matter-of-fact tone, as a catalogue of the tasks on which Liszt now embarked in the settled circumstances for which he had longed, the scene might suggest a recluse locked away for hours in his study, eschewing all company while he wrestled with the angel – or demon – of artistic creation. But Carolyne would not leave his side. Partly it was the expression of a love that craved the perpetual presence of the beloved, a love that at times threatened to suffocate the object of its desire. And Liszt responded in the tone she wished to hear – how could he do otherwise? 'When you are not here,' he wrote to her in 1851, when she was away with Marie in the spa of Bad Eilsen, 'I cannot do anything worthwhile. Don't think this is just a facile excuse – I need you with me in order to think and breathe.' It is the lover's cry of loneliness. Its truth was not a literal truth but she eagerly grasped it as such, convincing herself that every moment spent apart paralysed his thoughts and starved his creative being of its life-blood. So, looking back many years later on her time with him in the Villa Altenburg, she was able to write to Adelheid von Schorn:

> For twelve years I looked after him in this way, carrying on my own work in the same room with him, otherwise he would never have composed all those works that distinguish his Weimar period. It was not genius he lacked but persistence, perseverance, the ability to stick at something (not a graceful expression but a great virtue). Unless someone helps him, he is incapable of going on, and when he feels he cannot go on, he resorts to stimulants. This only makes his condition worse, and so the vicious circle closes all the more tightly. One has to sit with him and carry on with one's own work for as long as one wants him to continue with his. Without the quiet, gentle yet constant company of a loving woman he is simply incapable of achieving anything great – he can only revise and refine what he has done already.

Whatever she may have believed at the time, and wanted to believe, by 1882, the date of this letter, she knew full well that it was not so. Many were the months when they had been separated after leaving Weimar, yet he worked unremittingly on some of his largest pieces – religious works such as *The Legend of Saint Elizabeth* and *Christus*, direct expressions of their shared concern with the mystical values of Catholicism and the renewal of Church music. Even at this remove she seemed determined to maintain the fiction of Liszt's dependence on her for the fruition of his creative gifts.

The emotional bondage which they preached and practised during these early years in Weimar was an inevitable attendant of the strains and tensions, in part self-induced but initially and primarily the product of social pressures, to which their irregular union was subjected. From the beginning the Princess tried desperately to secure a divorce, pleading that she had been forced by her family into this early, unhappy marriage to Prince Nicholas von Sayn-Wittgenstein; Maria Pavlovna, she hoped, would intercede with her brother, Tsar Nicholas I. But this desirable end, the only solution both morally, socially and legally right, at once generated its own tension in that as devout Catholics, Liszt and the Princess found themselves imprisoned between their personal emotions and the inexorable dogma of their Church. They were united both through their love and through their shared sense of sin.

Nor did the strains end in the private sphere. Technically and officially Liszt had come to Weimar in order to take up the duties of Kapellmeister extraordinary to the grand-ducal court. True, he had seen it less as a challenge in its own right than as a means of securing a base for the pursuance of his own creative aims with a minimum of interference and uncertainty. And nothing could in theory be more desirable for a composer than to have at his permanent disposal his own musicians and singers, his own facilities for rehearsal and his own resident audience for performing the works he has it in mind to write. But once face to face with his concrete musical tasks, he found the situation dispiriting and alarming. His players were poorly paid, their morale low. Rank-and-file members of the orchestra received annual salaries ranging from 300 thalers down to a mere 100 thalers; even the first violoncellist, one Bernhard Cossmann, who later became a teacher at the Moscow conservatoire, earned only 350 thalers. When one of the musicians, a man with twenty years' experience, approached the comptroller's office and protested that he could not support himself and his six children on a salary of 200 thalers, he was condescendingly given a grant-in-aid of ten thalers 'as an exception', in return for a written promise 'that he refrain from any future importuning on the grounds of his large family and resume living within his former means'.

Liszt tried repeatedly to improve the situation. The legitimacy of the grievances was acknowledged – the players' salaries had not increased in forty years, and after the 1848 Revolution they even lost the free allowances of grain and wood they had formerly received. But only minor improvements were made in their position. 'The Exchequer regrets . . .' came the dismally familiar response. It was only the stimulating prospect of playing under Liszt that attracted players of any calibre to Weimar during these years – men like the violinist Joseph Joachim, who arrived in October 1850 as leader of the orchestra for a salary of 500 thalers.

The orchestra that Liszt inherited totalled thirty-five players; the choir of twenty-nine comprised sixteen women and thirteen men, and there was a *corps de ballet* of six dancers. These were the forces under his command for the first performance of Wagner's *Lohengrin* in August 1850. By the following year he succeeded in engaging three more orchestral players, to produce a complement of thirty-eight: five first violins, six second violins, three violas, four violoncellos, three double basses, two flutes, two oboes, two clarinets, two bassoons, four horns, two trumpets, one trombone, one tuba and one tympanist. That same year he indented for two more trombones, two key bugles, harp, organ and additional percussion (cymbals, triangle, bass drum) but since by the time he left Weimar in 1859 the strength of the orchestra had only risen by one, little heed had apparently been paid to his requests.

As Kapellmeister extraordinary Liszt received his emoluments not, like his unfortunate players, from the exiguous budget of the court theatre but from the Grand Duchess's privy purse – some 1,200 thalers per annum in the first instance, then 1,600 thalers and more, with additional sums for music lessons and other personal services to members of the grand-ducal family. Measured against the salaries of his musicians and, indeed, against professional salaries in general at the time, this provided a very satisfactory income, but the style of life to which he and the Princess laid claim in their villa ensured that a use was found for every cent of it. A ceaseless stream of house guests came and went, parties and musical soirées meant constant entertaining, and the young pupil who found himself in financial difficulties could always expect to be offered a hundred thalers or so to tide him over. Small wonder that debts relentlessly accumulated. By 1855 the Princess owed local merchants an impressive total of 15,600 thalers, and both the Russian ambassador to the Grand Duchy and the court itself had to intervene in order to ward off a public scandal.

A circumstance such as this was grist to the mill of those – and they were legion – who wished to see the back of this troublesome woman. The divorce for which she had hoped had still not materialized, and her sinful posturing with the court's most distinguished servant continued to offend public morality; moreover, the champions of propriety and convention went on, it set a deplorable example to the young Princess Marie and undermined her moral sense. For a while, indeed, under pressure from Prince Nicholas von Sayn-Wittgenstein, Marie was taken away from the Villa Altenburg and placed in the care of the Grand Duchess in the palace, only to find her way back eventually to the company of her mother and of the man who had joyfully but improperly taken over the role of father. There was even talk of arranging a marriage with the French ambassador, Baron Talleyrand, in order to remove her to a respectable and stable environment. Watzdorf, the minister charged with reporting to Maria Pavlovna on the whole embarrassing affair, spoke for many:

I could only regard it as a stroke of good fortune for the town, and especially for the Court, if the Princess were soon to leave. On the last occasion I saw her, her girth struck me as highly suspicious, and if the fears that arose in me were to prove well-founded, it would be a truly lamentable state of affairs; even if I am mistaken, the situation is little better. For a woman who is not yet divorced to live openly with her lover is an affront to morality . . . My advice to Your Highness is to urge the Kaiser to approve a marriage between Princess Marie and Baron Talleyrand at an early date, and to inform her mother that, if she proposes to continue living with Dr Liszt as hitherto, her departure from Weimar would be extremely desirable.

Whether Carolyne was indeed pregnant, as Watzdorf snidely hints, we cannot know. Officially they had no children. But contemporaries in a position to know, and not merely those with a personal or moralistic axe to grind, indicate that children were in fact born to the Princess during these years – not, obviously, in Weimar itself but in small, unobtrusive places which could be relied upon to keep the secret. Possibly her visits to the little spa of Bad Eilsen, near Bückeburg, were not unconnected with this.

Carl Maria Cornelius, for instance, son of Peter Cornelius, who joined Liszt in the Villa Altenburg in 1852 and became one of his closest disciples, records in his biography of his father that Liszt and the Princess had three children who were born in other towns than Weimar and brought up in Brussels. One of these, according to Cornelius, was Franz Servais, adopted son of the Belgian violoncellist Adrien François Servais. On his foster-father's death in 1866, Franz was entrusted to the care of Liszt, and in 1869 Liszt sent him to Bülow in Munich. Cornelius writes: 'A new friend, who had come to Munich to study, was Franz Servais, a son of Liszt's and Princess Wittgenstein's, who had been brought up in Brussels by the excellent cellist Servais. He bore a marked resemblance to Liszt, the gentle side of whose nature was particularly pronounced in him.' Writing to the Princess in 1870, Liszt himself refers to the similarity between Franz Servais and his own son Daniel, who had died tragically in 1859 at the age of twenty, but the letter reveals nothing more intimate. Nor do Liszt's extant letters to Servais read like those of father to son. Carl Maria Cornelius writes as though his information comes from his father – surely an impeccable source. But we have only his word for it.

To the end of his life Liszt faced claims to his paternity, whether by a mother or her child, which were characterized more by pride than by embarrassment, let alone by silent shame. The last case, well within the memory of people living in Weimar today, is that of Frau Ilona Höhnel, daughter of one Ilona von Kovacsis, who allegedly fell in love with Liszt in the 1880s and bore him a daughter, who became a piano teacher in Weimar and later married a hairdresser there called Höhnel. Her parentage was always assumed, no less readily by the world as by herself, it seems, to be that of the legend, and when she died in 1963, the inscription on her grave described her as 'Franz Liszts Tochter'. Perhaps she was. There appears to be no documentary 'proof' of the kind a claim of paternity would require – but in such cases, and in such an age, one would hardly expect there to be. Those who could tell us have long since taken their secret with them.

In the wider historical context, that of the Europe of which Germany was only a part, and of the Germany within which the voice of the Grand Duchy of Sachsen-Weimar-Eisenach carried virtually no political influence, the first years of Liszt's residence in Weimar stood under the shadow of the 1848 Revolution and its aftermath. In the country as a whole at this time two out of every three Germans still made their living from the land. Industrialization came considerably later than in England, and the more hesitant the progress of mechanization, the slower the pace of social change. In the rural Grand Duchy of Weimar the bourgeoisie, divided within itself, could do little to establish an identity vis-à-vis the aristocracy and the court officials; even the construction of the railway line Erfurt–Weimar–Halle in 1846–7 took a long time to have a significant influence on economic development. As the revolutionary wave spread across Germany from France in March 1848, a few demonstrations were called in the Weimar market place and in front of the palace, and the Grand Duke responded by proclaiming an amnesty for political prisoners and introducing a few cosmetic innovations in the constitution of his government. But even after the establishment of a town council in 1850 the citizens at large found little practical change in the location of political power; not until the late 1860s, for instance, did the first signs of an organized working-class movement begin to stir.

Liszt had a keen sense of social justice and a ready sympathy for those whom life had treated unkindly but he had no taste for direct political argument or involvement. At the same time he was far from oblivious to the meaning of political happenings around him. Back in 1830, stimulated by the July Revolution in Paris, he had sketched a 'Revolution Symphony'; five years later he had

115

commemorated the revolt of the French textile workers in 'Lyon', the first item in his *Album d'un voyageur*, and among the first pieces he composed in Weimar was a martial 'Workers' Chorus' to a piece of doggerel by a fortunately anonymous poet, beginning 'Advance, ye workers and peasants all! Soldiers and writers, hear the call!' On hearing of the March Revolution in Hungary in 1848, he wrote to Princess Carolyne: 'My fellow-countrymen have embarked on so decisive, so Hungarian and so unanimous a course that it is impossible not to accord them a legitimate sympathy.'

But his regard for such issues remained basically human and personal. It was not the political system or the social structure that aroused his resentment but the effects on the individual, above all the individual artist, of the wrongs that the system and the structure perpetuated. As in the 1830s he had raised his voice in protest against the humiliating treatment meted out to court musicians, so in his various Weimar essays he returns to the plight of the artist condemned to serve a philistine public. 'All in all,' he wrote in his book on Chopin, 'and with a few exceptions, we must concede that the artist has more to lose than to gain by finding himself at home in the company of high society, for he will become enervated, go into decline and sink to the level of a mere charming entertainer.' But a radical crusade against that high society, or even an open *engagement* to preserve and reform it, did not lie in his nature, as it did in that of his friend Felix von Lichnovsky. And as it did in the life of the man who now forced his way into Liszt's life and never again left it – Richard Wagner.

> Finding myself so shamefully disappointed in my hope of securing a better income, I found myself forced to explore every avenue to better my position. I therefore came upon the idea of discussing the matter with Liszt and asking him for suggestions on how I might improve my difficult situation.

Thus Wagner in his autobiography *Mein Leben*, obsessed, as ever, with his financial situation and assuming, like many, that Liszt was a wealthy man waiting only to sponsor his gifted but less fortunate fellows. Already at the time of their first encounters back in 1841 in Paris the penurious, unknown Wagner had little else in his resentful mind but the injustice that separated his own struggling existence from the hero-worship enjoyed by the rich, brilliantly successful Liszt. 'After putting his financial affairs in order by giving just two highly profitable recitals, Liszt devoted his attention entirely to cultivating his *gloire*': – such was the sour mood in which Wagner recalled those days. They had met again the following year in Berlin, by which time the première of *Rienzi* in Dresden had given Wagner's name some currency, and saw each other in passing a few times in the succeeding years, but this visit to Weimar in August 1848 set their relationship on a quite different footing. To be sure, nothing tangible came out of these few days as far as Wagner's immediate hopes for support were concerned, but as he wrote, in the somewhat pompous style to which he was prone, 'this entire encounter, which was as cordial as it was stimulating, and despite its brevity, did not fail to leave both a felicitous and encouraging impression on me'.

Wagner's sense of encouragement did not err. He now had not only *Rienzi* to his name but also *Der fliegende Holländer* and *Tannhäuser* and was no longer the unheard-of suppliant of ten years ago. Liszt realized that here was a musical and cultural force to be reckoned with, a 'New Music' that lived in a world akin to his own, in a form to which his own powers of expression did not extend. He therefore decided to put *Tannhäuser* into production – it had not been performed in any opera house since its première in Dresden four years earlier – and in February 1849, after the pundits had pronounced it 'unplayable', he conducted it in Weimar with Josef Tichatschek, creator of the part, in the title role. Shortly afterwards Liszt sent a glowing article on the work to the *Journal des débats* in Paris.

Hard on the heels of this service to Wagner the composer came an act of succour towards Wagner the man, Wagner as *homo politicus* – an act which sealed the intensity and the permanence of their relationship.

At the beginning of May a popular revolt had broken out in Dresden. The King of Saxony had arbitrarily dissolved the newly constituted state assembly formed in the process of liberalization and democratization set in train by the National Assembly of 1848. The King may or may not have bargained for the violent protest that followed, but he and his ministers were forced to leave the city, and a provisional government of civic officials was set up. Wagner was among those detailed to report on the movements of the Saxon troops, who, together with Prussian reinforcements, were massing to counter-attack.

When that attack came, it scattered the rebels in a mere two days. The members of the provisional government fled, and with them those known to have been active supporters of the rebellion, among them the Russian anarchist Bakunin, the architect Gottfried Semper, and Wagner. Many, including Bakunin, were captured and brought to trial, but Wagner, with the help of friends, made his way from Dresden to Chemnitz, then took the post-chaise to Weimar and presented himself before an astonished Liszt.

Liszt was in the midst of preparations for a further performance of *Tannhäuser*, so what more natural than to assume that the composer would be eager to discuss matters of interpretation with the conductor? 'I found it hard,' wrote Wagner drily, 'to make it clear to my friend that I had left my position as Royal Kapellmeister in Dresden in a somewhat less than orderly manner.' The Grand Duchy did not fall within the immediate jurisdiction of Saxony, for each of the thirty-five states and four free cities that constituted the German Confederation after the Congress of Vienna in 1815 had its own political autonomy. But once it became known that Wagner was being hunted for his part in the rebellion, other states could hardly profess ignorance if his presence were detected and the Saxon police asked for him to be handed over.

The story that Wagner had to tell compounded in Liszt the feeling of irritation and frustration induced by his own personal circumstances of the moment, and to Wagner's surprise and gratification Liszt, usually so suave, confident and self-controlled, suddenly launched into an angry denunciation of the world and its ways. Wagner confessed that he did not properly understand the context of this outburst, but it was no less revealing for that.

Disturbed by the fate that threatened his new friend – for such Wagner had now, at the latest, become – Liszt hurriedly consulted with a few influential acquaintances he could trust as to how Wagner might best be brought to safety. With a gift of sixty thalers from Princess Carolyne, a false passport supplied by a friend of Liszt's and the knowledge that the cost of his long journey southwards to Switzerland – the only sure haven – had been guaranteed by Liszt in advance, Wagner went into exile. It was to be eleven years and three-and-a-half operas before he was allowed to return.

In spite of the worries and dangers that pursued him, these brief few days in Weimar brought Wagner a moment of deep pleasure – the opportunity to listen to an orchestral rehearsal of *Tannhäuser* under Liszt. The musical delight would have been reward enough in itself – Liszt's interpretation 'emphasized the musical aspect rather than the dramatic', he observed. Even more moving was the joyous awareness of the presence of an adventurous spirit akin to his own, of a mind that lived in the same world. 'For the first time,' he wrote enthusiastically in *Mein Leben*, 'the glowing, flattering feeling came over me that here was someone who understood me and shared my most intimate feelings.'

118

The Liszt that Wagner left behind in May 1849 had a wealth of creative plans in his mind – plans for critical studies on music and musicians, for public events and activities in Weimar, and above all for the direction in which his work as a composer should lead. With an orchestra and choir, however modest, at his disposal, and with only nominal demands made upon him by his court duties, he stood poised to explore new areas of expression, new media, and to achieve a productivity unequalled either before or after this moment.

It is often difficult to ascribe a single date to Liszt's works. A sketch may lie for years in a drawer before being brought out and worked up into a definitive form; a published piece may be reworked, sometimes substantially, then reissued in its new, revalidated guise – or guises, since there may be more than one such revision; a work may be recast for a different medium, with the addition of second and third thoughts. Some pieces may even have a history that embraces all these contingencies. Thus in the *Album d'un voyageur* and the succeeding *Années de pèlerinage*, or in the *Études d'exécution transcendante*, we are faced with rival imprimaturs, and the basic question of when the opus as we have it was conceived may receive no final answer – or several final answers, according to the way we choose to view the evidence.

The question arises in a particularly intriguing form à propos the two piano concertos. The principal themes of the first concerto date back to the 1830s but not until arriving in Weimar does Liszt appear to have worked on the concerto as such, which was essentially complete by 1849, then reworked in 1853. He himself gave the first performance in the ducal palace in 1855, with Berlioz conducting, but made further changes the following year, its final form being published in 1857. The work *qua* concerto can hardly be set earlier than 1849, but his intense concentration on composition in the 1850s, above all in the orchestral sphere, means that the Liszt of 1857 was a very different composer, in range, power and confidence, from the aspirant who had arrived in Weimar ten years earlier. The extraordinary variety of the symphonic poems written during this decade shows how great the difference was. Similarly, the roots of the second piano concerto also lie in the 1830s: again it was given its true concerto form in 1849, revised in 1853, then in 1857, the year Liszt gave its first performance, and published in 1863.

In the fact that for both concertos it should be the year 1849 which is pivotal lies a consideration vital to Liszt's development over the coming years. Hitherto he had ventured only hesitantly into the world of the orchestra; but if the piano concertos were to take proper shape, the claims of the orchestral accompaniment would have to be met, and this need now turned his thoughts in new directions.

I should be delighted for you to have the opportunity of hearing our orchestra play a few things; though still inadequately staffed in the string department, they know these works quite well and bring a considerable verve to their playing. I owe a great deal of useful experience to the frequent rehearsals of my works with them over recent years. I think I can say, without boasting, that I have spared no effort to make my works satisfactory both in form and in instrumentation. As a result of the various changes and revisions I made, especially in tone-colour – an element which has come to acquire a far greater importance for me – I have been forced to make three or four versions of the score of each of the enclosed works [viz., six of his symphonic poems] and try them out. Thanks to my position here I was able to indulge in this somewhat laborious and expensive procedure, which has had the advantage that even if the works should be considered bad, at least they are as good as I can make them.

In these characteristically self-deprecating lines written to Christian Lobe, editor of the *Allgemeine musikalische Zeitung*, in 1856, Liszt confesses how painstaking was the process by which his orchestral works took shape. That he used his orchestra as a kind of guinea-pig, uncertain of what his orchestration actually sounded like until he had put the parts in front of the players, is itself a statement of hesitancy, and although tone-colour, as he says, was a quality that came to matter more and more to him, it seems to have demanded years of concentration before he could confidently 'hear' his orchestral works while he was scoring them. Liszt's musical instincts were basically homophonic, and the constituent parts of the harmonic base on which his melody rested occupied his mind only at a later stage in the proceedings.

For many years, indeed, he left the initial instrumentation of his orchestral works to others. He would first write out a kind of short score on three or four staves, indicating the instrumentation he had in mind, then hand it to a young colleague versed in the technicalities of orchestration to prepare a full score. This he would then revise himself, sometimes seeking the orchestrator's help a second and third time before declaring himself finally satisfied.

His most valuable helper during these early Weimar years was the young Swiss composer Joachim Raff, some of whose compositions had been published a few years earlier on the recommendation of Mendelssohn, and who had already offered his services to Liszt in the course of the Beethoven Festival in Bonn in 1845. Eleven years Liszt's junior, Raff arrived in Weimar in a glow of mingled pride and enthusiasm, an unqualified admirer of Liszt the man and Liszt the musician. At the same time he brought with him a self-confidence born of the knowledge that Liszt's invitation implied that he, Raff, had at that moment something to give to the great man, something Liszt needed for the furtherance of his art. Raff thus arrived with a sense of mission and with a predisposition to pique and resentment if his expectations were thwarted.

At the beginning all went well. 'Liszt accepts my criticisms with the utmost patience,' he wrote, gratified,

> and shows he is prepared to learn . . . I wish to make it quite clear that I have had some influence on his latest works – a modest influence, no doubt, but an influence none the less, thanks to the fact that he sensibly realizes that four eyes can see better than two. So now he willingly accepts a number of my comments against which he would have formerly been disposed to protest.

Liszt also took an interest in Raff's own compositions and arranged for him to conduct the first performance of his opera *König Alfred* in 1851. Raff had a room in the Villa Altenburg, and by copying out scores and parts at Liszt's behest, translating his occasional critical essay from French into German and attending to a host of other practical matters, he worked himself into the role of private secretary, even receiving visitors on Liszt's behalf when he was away.

But as Raff's sense of importance grew, so Liszt's need for his specific help in matters of orchestration receded. He soon exhausted his function, and although Liszt was not the man to 'use' people to his own ends, like Wagner, Raff found the inevitable subordination of his role more and more difficult to tolerate. He had also had from the beginning a tense relationship with Princess Carolyne, whom he suspected of being jealous that he might make inroads on her influence over Liszt. 'The way she pampers him in her blind devotion,' he complained, 'and finds everything he does holy and sublime – she is not in the slightest musical – often proves a considerable obstacle to arriving at the truth.' By 1856 he had become too disgruntled to stay in Weimar any longer and moved to Wiesbaden, where he became a well-known composer and teacher in his own right, ending his days as Principal of the Hoch Conservatoire in Frankfurt.

In a moment of euphoria Raff once claimed that certain orchestral works bearing Liszt's name had more of Raff in them than of Liszt. Liszt was a scrupulous corrector of final printed editions, and what left his pen for the last time was his and his alone, but it remains something of a flaw in his orchestral works of the early 1850s that an element of mediacy has crept into the creative act.

The symphonic poem *Tasso*, written in 1849 for the Weimar celebrations of the centennial of Goethe's birth, illustrates his procedure. On the basis of Liszt's sketch August Conradi, a young composer of operettas who had reached Weimar before Raff, prepared an orchestral score in great haste, and the work was performed in this version on the commemorative occasion. Liszt, however, was far from satisfied with the result, made numerous alterations, and conducted it in its new form the following year. Still not content, he gave the score to Raff with instructions to prepare a new version, which Raff did in 1851. Rehearsals revealed still further shortcomings, and Liszt continued to change this and that until finally losing interest and laying the piece aside. Some three years later, now versed in the craft of orchestration and confident of his powers, he made his final modifications to Raff's score and gave the work its definitive form. It is idle to speculate whether, without Raff's spadework, *Tasso* would have the form it has, or would even have been written at all. His share in its composition cannot be gainsaid. But the work we have is Liszt's.

In *Tasso*, as in all his other twelve symphonic poems, Liszt set out, not to portray a series of events or to reproduce the biography of an individual character, a kind of spiritual pilgrim's progress, but to convey a poetic idea, a mood for the under-standing of basic spiritual realities – 'the renewal of music through the spirit of poetry', as he put it. There is very little purely descriptive music to be found in his *oeuvre*. Often he explicitly stated the underlying idea or induced the relevant mood of the work in a preface to the score, so that, in a sense, the work begins not with the first notes but with the initiatory, sometimes almost incantatory words of this preface.

Thus he tells us that *Tasso* presents a picture of the Italian Renaissance poet as seen in Goethe's drama and Byron's poem, the artist who suffered neglect and misunderstanding in his lifetime but received triumphant rehabilitation after his death – hence the sub-title 'Lamento e trionfo'. *Prometheus* (1850) was written for the unveiling in Weimar of a statue to the great thinker Johann Gottfried Herder and has as its starting-point Herder's dramatic poem 'Der entfesselte Prometheus': Liszt's 'message' blends the noble humanistic values of Herder's thought with the legend of the unbound Titan, symbolizing the release of the powers of man and the advent of the new age of human freedom, aspiration and happiness. Also Classical in association, *Orpheus* (1854), the progeny of Liszt's performance of Gluck's *Orfeo* that year to celebrate the birthday of the Grand Duchess Maria Pavlovna, rests on a broad cantilena representing Orpheus' magical singing and the power of art to open the gates of Orcus; at the end of a hymn-like coda the music sinks serenely to rest in a spirit of peace and reconciliation. *Mazeppa* (1851) and the poem of that name by Victor Hugo, *Les Préludes* (1854) and Lamartine's 'Méditations poétiques', *Die Hunnenschlacht* (1857) and Kaulbach's painting of the victory of Christian virtue over barbarian passion – so the images and concepts from art and literature continued to give the breath of life to his music.

Liszt set his symphonic poems – he frequently called them simply Overtures – in line of descent from Berlioz's programme symphony, a form which he regarded as expressive of modern ideals, as oratorio and cantata had codified the ideals of earlier ages (the term *symphonische Dichtung* itself first appears as the sub-title of *Tasso* in the programme of a concert given in Weimar in April 1854). Of the nature of programme music itself he had an equally firm conception which he expressed in 1855 in his essay 'Berlioz und seine "Harold-Symphonie" ', in a convoluted, Baroque style unfortunately characteristic of his literary manner:

A programme has no other purpose than to draw attention in advance to the impulses which led the composer to create his work, the thoughts which he strove to embody in it. Although it is childish and pointless, indeed generally a mistake, to construct a programme after the event and to try and explain the emotional content of an instrumental piece, since the word will destroy the magic, profane the emotions, destroy the delicate web of spiritual values which was only cast in this form because it could not have been encompassed in words, pictures or ideas, the composer himself has control of his work and may have created it under the influence of particular impulses of which he desires to make his listeners fully and completely aware.

The peculiar abstractness of this 'delicate web of spiritual values', its disengagement from the world of substantial physical realities, led Liszt to characterize music vis-à-vis the other arts in the same metaphysical terms as other Romantic thinkers of the nineteenth century. In his essay on Schumann, also published in the *Neue Zeitschrift für Musik* in 1855, he writes:

It would appear that the other arts are more intimately linked to the necessities of life than is music.

And he quotes from Hegel's *Aesthetics*:

Music is soul, spirit, producing sounds which are absolute and meant for itself alone, and content in its perception of itself . . . The peculiar power of music over us is an elemental power, that is, it derives solely from the world of sound, in which the art of music lives.

E.T.A. Hoffmann, author of the famous 'Tales', expresses the same thought in his essay on Beethoven: 'Music unfolds before us a new kingdom, a world which has nothing in common with the world of sensuous reality around us . . .' while the formulation of Schopenhauer, who brings to its culmination the Romantic conception of a cosmos ordered by, hence ultimately to be understood through, music, runs:

In that it by-passes ideas, music is independent of the physical world – in fact, is completely ignorant of the physical world and could exist, in a sense, even if there were no world . . . This is the reason why the effect of music is so much more powerful and penetrating than that of the other arts. For while these latter deal only with the shadow, music deals with the substance.

And it is ultimately to the context of this substance, this metaphysical experience *sui generis*, that Liszt's programme music addresses itself. It responds to basic, unconditional and supra-personal psychological realities, and through such outward symbols as the 'Lamento e trionfo' pattern of so many of his symphonic poems, reflects – even becomes, at such moments – a profound existential reality.

In the realm of programme music, the music with which his name is most immediately associated, Liszt the composer and Liszt the writer find their common home. And in feeling compelled to write about music as well as compose it, he joins a distinguished company in his age – Berlioz, Weber, Schumann, Wagner – the first age of composers seized with the need to explore, explain, justify their creative activity in writing. But there were also other issues that occupied his mind, other personalities and principles on which he wished to make his voice heard. One such personality was Chopin, on whom he wrote a monograph in 1850–1 under the shadow of Chopin's recent death, reworking it in 1879 with the addition of liberal splashes of Polish local colour provided by Princess Carolyne.

From the moment of their first encounter in Paris in 1832 Liszt never lost his affection for Chopin the man and his admiration of Chopin the musician. They were of the same age, had both made their careers outside their native land, moved gladly and elegantly in upper-crust society and been the idols of the cultured élite, especially its adoring women. In temperament and artistic personality, however, an immense gulf lay between the spectacular, adventurous, extrovert life pursued by the one and the private, withdrawn, almost secret world sought by the other, and a spiritual intimacy between them, let alone an identity of aesthetic purpose, could hardly take life. Chopin, moreover, found it more difficult to come to terms with his ebullient Hungarian contemporary than did Liszt with the reserved, delicate Pole.

Liszt, of course, knew this better than anyone else. But his *Frédéric Chopin* is a sincere, unreserved tribute to the man whom he regarded as one of his closest friends of recent years. Heine, Meyerbeer, Hiller, Delacroix, Niemcewicz, George Sand – all the luminaries of Parisian salon life in the 1830s act out their roles in Liszt's narrative as he describes Chopin's playing in the intimate, subdued setting in which he felt most at home. Schumann, who greeted Chopin's début as a composer with an enthusiasm equal to Liszt's, later became cooler in his attitude, complaining that Chopin had failed to develop and that an air of sameness surrounded his music. Liszt, on the other hand, saw in the ostensible restrictedness and concentratedness of Chopin's *oeuvre* a source of strength, the recognition and acceptance by the composer of the true nature of his gifts. 'By confining himself to writing exclusively for the piano,' he observed, 'Chopin displayed one of the most valuable characteristics that a composer can possess – the realization of the true form in which he has been called upon to achieve his pre-eminence.'

The praise of Chopin was not the only activity to occupy the mind of Liszt the writer in these energetic and productive years. In July 1849, above the signatures of the explorer and scientist Alexander von Humboldt, writers and scholars like Varnhagen von Ense, Ludwig Rellstab and Hans Ferdinand Massmann, the sculptor Christian Daniel Rauch and others, an appeal was published for the establishment of a foundation to promote the creation of works of art 'which should exercise a beneficial influence on the moral progress of the nation'. Liszt had long concerned himself with how to raise the level of aesthetic appreciation in the public, and therefore with the status of art and artists in the community. Rising to this proposal for a Goethe Foundation, he put forward a detailed plan for competitions to be held in literature, painting, sculpture and music in cycle, each year's competition being devoted to one of the four; the winning paintings and sculptures would be exhibited in a special Goethe Museum in Weimar, dramas and musical works would be performed in festival, and special editions printed of the successful novels, poetry and essays. The whole enterprise could be financed, he calculated, on a capital of 100,000 thalers.

It was a characteristically adventurous vision which caught the imagination of the Grand Duke Carl Alexander and would have made Weimar the cultural capital of Germany almost overnight. Princess Carolyne told him from the beginning that a little duchy like that of Sachsen-Weimar-Eisenach could not possibly afford to mount such an undertaking, besides which not all those with an opinion to express accepted that Liszt's proposals represented the ideal form to impose on such a Foundation. Wagner, for example, wrote from his exile in Zurich that he considered it unwise to dissipate the available energies over four different arts, and that the tradition of Goethe and Schiller would be better served with a competition for drama alone, from which that particular art-form could expect to gain some substantial advantage.

So vexed was Liszt over the frustration of the project that he seems to have considered giving up his post in small-time Weimar altogether and going to Paris. Ten years later, after he really had resigned, the matter still rankled, less out of injured pride than from a sense of a missed opportunity of restoring to Weimar some of its former cultural kudos and making it, as he put it in a letter to Carl Alexander in February 1860, 'a centralizing influence in the field of art and literature, a force for German unity'. To the objection that the Grand Duchy could not afford so ambitious a programme, Liszt made a blunt observation familiar to reluctant sponsors in all ages: 'The growth of their private wealth is very important to the members of the aristocracy but that does not relieve them of the need to consolidate their family line and their rule by means of donations which will earn them respect and devotion at home and praise and esteem outside.' This praise and esteem, however, remained too expensive.

For the annual Goethe celebrations in August 1850, which

coincided with the unveiling of the statue of Herder, Liszt committed himself, under the exiled composer's enthusiastic urging, to give the first performance of *Lohengrin*. He had at first resigned himself to the belief that such a revolutionary work made demands far beyond the capabilities of the forces at his command, but Wagner was determined that his new-found friend should be the one to introduce the work to the world. Once convinced, Liszt tolerated no half-measures. 'The authorities are going to invest almost 2,000 thalers in the production,' he wrote to Wagner in delight, 'a greater sum than anybody can remember ever being spent in Weimar.'

Distinguished figures came from many parts of Europe – the critic Jules Janin and the poet Gérard de Nerval from Paris, Joseph Fétis from Brussels, Henry Chorley, music critic of the *Athenaeum*, from London – and from the length and breadth of the German-speaking world: Meyerbeer, Robert Franz, Bettina von Arnim, Karl Gutzkow and a host of others. The success of the work, like that of *Tannhäuser* the previous year, was immediate, and a highly gratified Wagner lost no time in expressing his gratitude to the man behind it:

> As far as I can judge from the reports reaching me about the performance of my *Lohengrin* in Weimar, one thing stands out as firm and beyond all doubt: that is, the immense unselfish effort that you have made on behalf of my opera, the moving affection that you have shown towards me, and your genius for making the impossible, possible. Only subsequently have I come to see clearly what a gigantic task you took upon yourself and brought to a triumphant conclusion.

Wagner owed an immense debt to Liszt at this time. Lonely and isolated in Switzerland, unable to promote the cause of his operas in the country to which they belonged, a country in which he had more enemies than friends, he was thrown upon the grace and service of a handful of men who sensed that in these works lay the seeds of the music of the future. Paramount among these men was Franz Liszt. 'It was he who made me feel an artist again,' wrote Wagner, 'a new and complete artist, lifting me out of my depression and assuring me with all the earnestness and enthusiasm at his command that I was not alone but was truly and profoundly understood, even by those who seemed farthest away from me.'

Now, after his first two years of exile had reduced him to a state of almost complete inertia, Wagner picked up the fragmentary text of *Der Ring des Nibelungen* again, a new confidence surging through him as he returned to face the challenge of his vision. When Liszt went to see him in Zurich in 1853 – their first meeting since Liszt had helped the fugitive revolutionary to evade the clutches of the Saxon police four years before – the joy of reunion opened the flood-gates of Wagner's musical invention. 'My delight over Liszt's visit was as great as it was sincere,' he recalled in *Mein Leben*, 'but above all it was stimulating, making me return to musical composition after so long an interruption.' That interruption had lasted almost five years. It was ended by the long, rolling E flat major chord that opens the Prelude to *Das Rheingold* – which is at the same time the prelude to the Wagner of the whole *Ring*, of *Tristan und Isolde*, of *Die Meistersinger von Nürnberg*, of *Parsifal*.

Throughout his life, even in the face of an egoism which was at times heartless and callous, Liszt never wavered in his commitment to Wagner's music. In 1853 he added *Der fliegende Holländer* to *Tannhäuser* and *Lohengrin* at Weimar; he published essays on all three of these and on *Das Rheingold*; he made piano transcriptions of overtures, arias and individual scenes from most of Wagner's music dramas, right down to *Parsifal*; and he never refused the counsel and comfort for which Wagner so often turned to him. Had Liszt had his way, Wagner would have been offered the chance to make of Weimar what he later made of Bayreuth. 'It seems to me not merely appropriate but essential, virtually imperative,' wrote Liszt to the Grand Duke Carl Alexander from a visit to Wagner in Zurich in 1856, 'that Wagner's *Nibelungen* should be performed in the first instance in Weimar.' All this was an expression, not of admiration for the attractions of an individual work, or for particular conceptions and skills, but of an overwhelming conviction that here was an utterly new art-form, a revolutionary new ideal cast as a holy grail to be sought through a revolutionary new music which made total demands upon its listeners.

Liszt's conviction did not err. It is not difficult to point to the use of the *Leitmotif* by earlier composers; or to trace, through Berlioz, Chopin and Liszt himself, the antecedents of the chromaticism which Wagner exploited in ways hitherto undreamt of; or to show where 'endless melody' might have had its roots. And there are striking parallels between phrases in Liszt and in Wagner – though not as many, perhaps, as some musical Hercule Poirots have claimed to detect. The conclusion of 'Il Pensieroso' from Book II of the *Années de pèlerinage*, the reprise and final cadence of the famous third 'Liebestraum', page after page of the

Piano Sonata, of the Dante Symphony, of the Faust Symphony – a chromatic idiom of astonishing and beautiful originality descends upon us time and again, leaving in us the sense of a mind looking outward and upward in its quest for self-expression. In 1859 Wagner wrote to Bülow: 'There are many matters on which Liszt and I are quite frank between us – for instance, that since I have become acquainted with his compositions, I have become a completely different man in matters of harmony' – which is as close as Wagner would ever come to admitting that his music owed anything to anyone else.

Yet what matters, and what Liszt both knew and was too honest to wish to conceal, was that, unlike himself, Wagner had created a total and all-consuming new world with its own laws, its own logic, its own self-generated and self-contoured meaning. Where the constituent parts of that world and that meaning came from has only passing interest; central is the vital originality of the whole, of the new created reality, and the magnitude of that creation. The originality of Liszt is beyond dispute. But we do not establish his greatness as a composer by pointing to the isolated innovations and stimuli that he gave to others. He has to be seen within the world that he himself created. And when Liszt's world is compared to Wagner's it appears restricted, eclectic, somehow not quite complete – a world rather stocked with brilliant, striking, beautiful things than itself a brilliant, striking, beautiful creation. Perhaps Liszt was a victim of his own originality. Perhaps he lacked the ultimate perception, or the perseverance, to explore what lay beyond the foothills and minor peaks that he had scaled – the vast, overwhelming landscape charted by Richard Wagner. But the view from the foothills has its own glories.

In a letter of November 1852, consoling Wagner over his joyless existence in Zurich, Liszt wrote: 'One single chord will bring us closer together than all the verbal utterances in the world,' and bade his friend farewell with a melancholy chromatic sequence:

Notes can indeed go where words can not.

*

Tannhäuser, Lohengrin and *Der fliegende Holländer* were far from being the only substantial operas that Liszt introduced to the Weimar public during the 1850s. Sustained by the search for quality, not content to pander to the undemanding tastes of the conventional audience, he developed a repertory of forty-four operas, no fewer than twenty-five of them by contemporary composers. *Don Giovanni, Die Zauberflöte;* Gluck's *Iphigénie en Aulide, Armide* and *Alceste; Fidelio;* Rossini's *Guillaume Tell;* Weber's *Euryanthe;* Bellini's *Norma* – these were some of the 'classics' he kept in stock. This body of established operas he then spiced with modern works of as yet unproven durability but in which he had confidence, a confidence on some occasions misplaced, on others triumphantly vindicated. Who today remembers Flotow's *Indra* or Anton Rubinstein's *Die sibirischen Jäger?* But he also gave Berlioz's *Benvenuto Cellini,* Meyerbeer's *Les Huguenots* and Verdi's *Ernani.* And in 1855 he broke a lance for Schumann by performing his *Genoveva;* that the undramatic work made little impact was Schumann's fault, not Liszt's.

In his concert programmes he set similar store by modern works. This meant above all his own symphonic poems and the orchestral and choral works of Berlioz – the *Symphonie fantastique, L'enfance du Christ, Harold in Italy* and most of the overtures. He also used the concert hall to give Wagner's music further currency, conducting the Overture to *Tannhäuser* and the Faust Overture. But again as in his operatic policy, he looked eagerly for works by little-known composers who might have in them that urge to experiment, that zeal to push back the frontiers of experience and expression, which was the driving power in his own musical consciousness. 'Make new things, children!' cried Wagner to those who had resigned themselves to a sterile routine of repetition and imitation. The call is for the 'Music of the Future', for the promotion of the values of the 'New German School', at its head Liszt and Wagner. Like any challenge to the status quo, the call provoked opposition. But it also quickly brought young musicians to Weimar from all parts, to learn from the brilliant, inspiring yet always approachable and generous genius in the Villa Altenburg where the values of the new art lay. The poet and dramatist Friedrich Hebbel, who visited the Altenburg in 1858, declared that, while he could pass no judgement on Liszt's music, he 'had gathered round him a circle the like of which I had seen nowhere else on earth, with the most original of ideas and emotions'.

A year after Raff's arrival, the twenty-one-year-old Hans von

Bülow took up residence in the Villa Altenburg, where the magic of Liszt's personality overwhelmed him. 'He is the complete man,' he wrote excitedly to his mother. 'Yesterday morning I attended his rehearsal of *Fidelio* and was swept off my feet by the way he conducted.' Bülow had already embraced Wagner's music with enthusiasm, and had been among the select group to whom Wagner read the poem of *Siegfrieds Tod* in Dresden in November 1848. What more natural than that he should make his way to the 'future capital of the world', as he called Weimar, where the High Priest of the Wagnerian cause held sway? And as for Liszt: 'I regard myself as his father,' he wrote to Bülow's mother, 'and in ten years' time it will be just the same as it is today.'

Well before those ten years were up, it was more than just the same. Bülow, nervous and highly-strung, of a well-to-do Protestant family, had married the Catholic, strong-willed Cosima Liszt, and his idol had become his father-in-law. It was only one of the triangular relationships into which Bülow, the archetypal man in the middle, one of nature's losers, was fated to be drawn. His commitment to Wagner had led him to Liszt, and he never escaped their shadow. Then, after only six years with Cosima, he lost her irrevocably to the composer of *Tristan und Isolde*, who took her as his mistress, then as his wife, leaving the unhappy Bülow with the ironic consolation of a pianist's career inspired by Liszt and a conductor's career whose initiation he owed to Wagner.

Even closer to Liszt at this time than either Raff or Bülow was the young musician Peter Cornelius, nephew of the well-known German painter of that name. Like many others, the twenty-eight-year-old Cornelius first came to Weimar thinking merely of a deferential call at the court of Franz Liszt, only to find himself drawn into the ranks of the monarch's vassals, yielding him rare and faithful service over many years. 'You have no idea how great and good a man Liszt is!' he wrote excitedly to his brother Carl. 'He combines the most consummate technical mastery in every respect with a young man's ability to learn.' Liszt offered to lend Cornelius 100 thalers to set up as a music teacher – 'though I am not a banker or anything like that', he added with a smile.

When he arrived in Weimar from Berlin, Cornelius was withdrawn, unsure of himself, a very different character from Liszt, with whom he shared, however, a deep though undogmatic Roman Catholicism. 'Our friendship rests on our identical convictions in art and religion,' he wrote to his mother. Impressionable young musicians caught up in the wake of the maestro's dominating personality faced the hazard of losing their individuality, of being unable to survive in the crushing presence of genius. Cornelius too knew this fear, the fear, as the haunted poet Rilke put it, that even if an angel were to hear his cry and come down to comfort him in his despair, 'he would perish under its stronger being'. But the stronger being of Liszt strengthened Cornelius, fostered his independence, making his aesthetic judgements surer and more cogent than those of either the fawning worshippers at the Altenburg or of the scornful detractors outside.

Nor was he afraid to contradict Princess Carolyne, whom he admired and to whose inspiration he attributed Liszt's industry and sense of purpose. When the Princess maintained that Liszt's orchestration was better than Berlioz's, he told her flatly that it was not (he was right). And of Liszt's symphonic poem *Festklänge*, which drew from the Princess the ecstatic utterance 'If only you knew how much I love that piece!', Cornelius wrote in his diary, playing sarcastically on the words forming the compound title of the work: 'Liszt's *Festklänge* left an embarrassing impression on me. One senses a restless, noble spirit in the piece, yearning for festive [*Fest*] joy but unable to find adequate sounds [*Klänge*] to express it' (he was right again).

Yet for Cornelius, as for virtually all the acolytes at the Villa Altenburg, the moment had to come when personal interest, the need to expand and explore, asserted itself over loyalty to the master, whose needs and preoccupations became increasingly constricting. After the ill-received première of his opera *Der Barbier von Bagdad* – the overture to which is the only music of his generally played today – under Liszt in 1858, and a visit to Wagner in Switzerland the same year, Cornelius left Weimar and joined the Wagnerian entourage, becoming one of the few in whom, over the years, Wagner placed willing and grateful trust. But he never allowed himself to be swamped by the powerful personalities whose world he elected to share. 'It is a strange thing,' he wrote in 1867 to his fiancée Bertha Jung:

Liszt was a really kind person, yet despite all his ravings and unpredictable moods, I prefer Wagner. With Liszt one always had an uneasy feeling that he was wearing a public mask, yet it is himself, and only himself, that he is after – let there be no mistake about that. Is the same true of Wagner, and of Berlioz? If so, then God preserve us from geniuses, and let us be content with the status of little men.

What Cornelius enjoyed, or endured, for almost a decade,

Joseph Joachim, 'the King of Violinists', tolerated for only two years. Called by Liszt to lead the Weimar orchestra, he found himself growing more and more uneasy over the direction Liszt's music was taking. To Liszt the man he remained unshakeably loyal, and all knew it. It was he who was charged by Clara Schumann with the sad task of conveying the news of her husband's death to Liszt and the other friends who had supported the cause of Schumann's music. What he discovered he was unable to do – though at the time he could not bring himself to disclose – was to make common cause with those who had pledged their lives to the promotion of Liszt's 'New German Music'. Four years after resigning his post, he summoned the courage to confess, regretfully yet defiantly, what had burdened his mind: 'Your music is completely alien to me: it conflicts with everything in the spirit of the great masters of the past from whom I have drawn sustenance since my youth . . . How could I feel myself a comrade-in-arms of those who assembled behind your banner and made the dissemination of your works their life purpose?'

The young Johannes Brahms sized up the situation even more peremptorily than Joachim. He came to Weimar in June 1853 in the company of the Hungarian gypsy violinist Ede Reményi, with whom he was on a recital tour. Barely twenty years old and totally unknown, with only a handful of unpublished piano pieces and songs to his name, Brahms made his pilgrimage to the Villa Altenburg with much the same thoughts in mind as the many others of his generation who had trodden the path before him. Liszt stood for a new direction in music: some sought with enthusiasm to follow him in that direction, more turned their backs on it in disapproval or scorn, but the rising generation wanted to see for itself what it had to offer, young composers carrying in their baggage their latest compositions in the hope that the master would set his seal of approval on them. Brahms had brought with him his Scherzo in E flat minor, Op. 4. An American pianist called William Mason, who had joined the Altenburg circle earlier that year, sat with him, Raff and Reményi as they waited for Liszt to appear, and glanced at the manuscript as it lay on the table. He found it almost totally illegible and wondered how Brahms would decipher it. When Liszt finally arrived, Brahms was too nervous to play and the others could not persuade him. Whereupon Liszt good-humouredly picked up the manuscript, sat down at the piano and began to play Brahms's piece himself. 'He read it off in such a marvellous way,' wrote the incredulous Mason in his memoirs, 'at the same time carrying on a running accompaniment of audible criticism of the music – that Brahms was amazed and delighted.'

But the Altenburg did not hold what Brahms sought. A short while after he left and was soon found in the company of Robert and Clara Schumann in Düsseldorf, led there by the music of the man who was to hail him as the composer who 'would suddenly emerge to epitomize the new age, as Athena sprang fully armed from the head of Zeus'. It was a sad moment of aberration when in 1860 Brahms and Joachim put their names to the public statement declaring opposition to the 'New German School' – meaning Liszt and Wagner and their followers, though they do not name names – as embodying tendencies 'abhorrent to the innermost nature of music', tendencies which the signatories to the declaration 'could only deplore and condemn'. One had, it seemed, to take sides – to be a Lisztian-Wagnerian, or a Brahmsian, either from birth, like Hugo Wolf and the critic Eduard Hanslick, or in undergoing a conversion from the one faith to the other, like Bülow, Cornelius and Joachim: one could not just be an innocent music-lover. Liszt later came to have a high regard for Brahms, seeing him as a spiritual descendant of Schumann, 'except that he lacks Schumann's spontaneity'. 'But,' he added, 'he is the worst pianist I ever heard, and a most unequal, unpredictable conductor.' Brahms, for his part, did his best to avoid Liszt in future.

A visitor of a totally different kind who arrived at the Villa Altenburg in the same year, 1853, accompanied by her two young sons, was an attractive young widow called Agnes Street, née Klindworth, daughter of a journalist and sometime Prussian-cum-Austrian secret agent. She came as one of Liszt's many pupils and would-be pupils; she left, two years later, having become very much more. He fell in love with her, and until the end of his life she claimed a place in his heart – one might even say, in his soul – that no one else, not even Princess Carolyne, could fill. She was the very opposite of the Princess – quiet, withdrawn, given to spending her time in her own company, with a commitment to music equal to the Princess's surrender to religion. Liszt was accustomed to an entourage of hero-worshipping women, whose presence he did not invite but whom he would not turn away. With Agnes Street he was the seeker as much as the sought, and his letters to her over a span of thirty years, published simply as 'Letters to a Friend', reveal many of the secrets of Liszt the private citizen, captured in moments when he could let drop the public persona and the need to take account of how his thoughts and feelings would be received. After completing a major composition, or beset with worries over the course of his relationship with the Princess, he would confide to her the thoughts uppermost in his mind, and she was among the first with whom he shared the news, in May 1865, that he had taken minor orders in the Roman Catholic Church.

Yet his commitment to the Princess remained unchallengeable, invulnerable, and marriage was its only proper consummation. Back in 1850 he already confidently spoke in a letter to his mother of 'Madame la Princesse, whom I soon hope to have the pleasure of calling my wife', adding: 'I shall have a wife after my own heart, a woman far beyond my dreams, my desires and my ambitions . . . a woman whose love and devotion are boundless, without compare . . . She will become the mother of my children, for their actual mother has been nothing but a wicked stepmother to them.'

The cruel charge of the 'wicked stepmother' shows how bitter his attitude towards Marie d'Agoult had become. But the prospect of a new family alignment, with the Princess playing the role of mother, was what now dominated his thoughts, a prospect which his own mother did her anxious best to help realize. The two women had developed a cordial understanding. When, on her way from Paris to visit her son in 1853, Anna Liszt broke her leg in Erfurt, a few miles short of Weimar, Princess Carolyne regularly visited her until she had recovered sufficiently to travel on to the Villa Altenburg, bringing with her an atmosphere of reassurance and practical encouragement which meant a great deal to Liszt and his consort. His children by Countess Marie d'Agoult, particularly his two daughters, acquired a symbolical role in the consolidation of his new union, the more so since he had from the beginning claimed the exclusive right to determine the manner of their upbringing and schooling. 'I alone met the not inconsiderable costs of their education,' he told Lina Ramann. 'Princess Wittgenstein generously helped me during the years [1848–54] when they were in the charge of Madame Patersi and again later when the two girls stayed in Berlin with Madame von Bülow.' He also paid the fees for his son Daniel to attend the Lycée Bonaparte in Paris.

Sadly, the two girls did not cherish the same warmth and concern for their father as he for them. Cosima, in particular, resented her illegitimacy and her cosmopolitan rootlessness, suffering under the realization that neither of her parents was prepared to do more than care for her at a distance, her father having meanwhile allied himself with a new mistress, set his sights on new artistic goals and left his daughters to the mercies of a succession of elderly governesses. His occasional visits to Paris, like that in the autumn of 1853 with Princess Carolyne and her daughter Marie, were no substitute for an intact and ordered family life. And when the children came to stay at the Villa Altenburg in the summer of 1855, the agitated and unconventional ménage that confronted them would scarcely have exuded a security and serenity that might have stabilized the foundation of their lives. Small wonder that, only nineteen, and after knowing him for a mere six weeks, Cosima should have thrown herself into the arms of Hans von Bülow, in whose mother's house she was staying.

Meanwhile Liszt's relationship with the Princess was sluggishly following its doom-laden course. As marriage so often had the character of a business transaction, so also had divorce. Prince Nicholas von Sayn-Wittgenstein, while realizing the hopelessness of ever reclaiming his lost wife, and though bearing Liszt no personal ill-will, would not agree to a divorce without making sure that his economic interests did not suffer. He therefore came personally to Weimar in 1852 with a document proposing divorce on condition a) that his daughter Marie be entrusted to the guardianship of the Dowager Grand Duchess Maria Pavlovna, and b) that in the event of the Princess's remarriage all fourteen of her estates in Russia revert to Marie as the child of her first marriage, except that one-seventh of them should be given to Prince Nicholas 'by way of compensation'. The Princess would receive 200,000 roubles in cash but nothing further. Prince Nicholas, Princess Carolyne and Crown Princess Marie signed the agreement, with Liszt and Baron von Vitzthum, Comptroller of the Grand Ducal Estates, as witnesses.

Weimar tongues had plenty to wag about – a Russian aristocrat visiting his daughter in the house where his wife was living openly with her morganatic lover. The Prince had even been heard to murmur to the cantor at the Grand Duke's villa of Tiefurt, outside Weimar: 'She was too good for me and I was too insignificant for her.' Liszt was filled with a new confidence. From his 'Blue Room' in the Villa Altenburg came the joyful sound of a new E flat major Polonaise he had just finished, as his mind dwelt on the folk art of the Princess's native land. An even more insistent optimism sprang from his symphonic poem *Festklänge*, composed in proud anticipation of the nuptial festivities that would soon put the triumphant public seal on his union with his beloved.

The festivities never took place. The confidence was without foundation, the optimism disintegrated and the *Festklänge*, a sadly inferior effusion, was eventually put to the celebration of a very different event – the thirtieth anniversary, in 1854, of the accession of Maria Pavlovna. For although Princess Carolyne had received a document establishing her divorce, its validity was only secular. Without a guarantee of the blessing of the Church neither she nor Liszt, both of them devout Catholics, could contemplate the step they desperately longed to take. She had defiled the sacrament of matrimony, while the Church saw the indissolubility of marriage as a cornerstone of its social dogma. Circumstances could, however, lead to the granting of a Papal dispensation, and their hope focused on this, especially after Prince Nicholas von Sayn-Wittgenstein remarried in Russia in 1857. But their many enemies saw to it that the Holy See received as unfavourable reports as possible of the goings-on in the Altenburg.

The only ground on which she could legitimately claim a divorce was that she had been forced into marriage against her will, but although she put this contention forward, it convinced no one. Nor did she help her case by offering money to strategically placed officials. 'She even tried to bribe *me*,' complained Baron Apolonius von Maltitz, Russian ambassador to the Grand Duchy. While prepared, in the face of his eminence, to turn a blind eye to the culpability of its Kapellmeister, the Weimar court saw no reason to conceal its displeasure at the brazen immorality of his mistress.

Princess Carolyne took refuge in prayer and in the religiosity to which her nature so readily responded. There were moments when she came close to going out of her mind. Once, in the middle of the night, she woke up and began to rush around the house in such distraction that her daughter went to Liszt's room to seek his help in calming her. Only after Marie had read aloud to her long passages from the Bible, bringing the assurance of God's mercy to those who truly repent, did she regain her peace of mind.

Inwardly Liszt followed her into this realm, seeking the same consolation. Answering a question many years later from Lina Ramann, he said: 'My mystical tendencies have always been based on the Bible – chiefly the New Testament – the biographies of certain saints (in particular that of Francis of Assisi) and the book variously ascribed to Gerson or Thomas à Kempis – the *Imitatio Christi*.' Not only the nature of Liszt's beliefs can be gleaned from this confession but also an insight into what lies behind the allusive religious titles of many of his pieces.

Outwardly he sublimated his cares and frustrations in a sustained thrust of creative activity such as he had never before experienced. As well as the twelve symphonic poems, whose originality would alone give him his place in the history of music, he wrote some of his finest piano music, his two greatest organ works, the Esztergom Mass and other religious music, and two symphonies – the Dante Symphony and the Faust Symphony – together with the *Two Episodes from Lenau's Faust*.

Liszt was at the zenith of his powers. He had come to Weimar with thoughts of concentration, of composure, of consolidation. In one sense the public fulfilment had followed: he had made the Villa Altenburg a centre of the 'New Music', had attracted young musicians there from all over Europe, had sent men down the revolutionary trail blazed by Berlioz and Wagner, had found himself as thinker and composer. In another sense his eager expectations had run aground on the rocks of frustration, of stultification: a legitimate union with the woman he loved was being denied him, and with it the settled prospects which, in his eyes, would assure the continuity of his creative achievement.

Yet who can penetrate the mystery of artistic creation? Who can say that the hindrances to personal happiness did not provide just that spur which drove him cruelly forward to the heights of originality and beauty which are now there for all to see? The joy of the Princess's presence remained, so too her influence on the course of his thoughts and emotions, but the paths charted by his intellectual energies could only be his own, and a mere inventory of the titles of his works of the 1850s reveals the worlds in which his mind dwelt, the worlds in which he found both inspiration and spiritual sustenance.

> Whither comes this peace, O Lord, that floods my being?
> Whither comes this faith with which my heart o'erflows?
> I was abandoned, anxious, filled with fear,
> Assailed by doubts and battered by the winds.
> But truth and goodness soughtst thou in the dreams of sages,
> And peace among the hearts of mortals rent by strife.

So begins the poem by Lamartine which Liszt set at the head of 'Bénédiction de Dieu dans la solitude', the sixth of the ten piano pieces collected under the Lamartinian title *Harmonies poétiques et religieuses* and published in 1853. It is from faith that he now draws strength to survive, and only in the contemplation of faith can he find true peace, the peace that passes all understanding. Other pieces in the collection – 'Ave Maria', 'Pater Noster', 'Miserere d'après Palestrina' – are cast in a liturgical mould, embracing in its turn the secular realities of love ('Cantique d'amour') and death ('Funérailles' – an elegy in memory of fallen heroes in the liberal-democratic reform movement of 1848–9, including his dear friend Prince Felix von Lichnovsky). The titles tell all. Likewise the dedication to 'Jeanne Elisabeth Carolyne', the Christian names of Princess von Sayn-Wittgenstein, leaves nothing – or everything, if one chooses to see it that way – to the imagination.

No less explicit, but in a demonstrative, extrovert way, are the other piano works prepared for definitive publication at this time. These include the first fifteen Hungarian Rhapsodies – built on melodies he had earlier heard or come across and published in the 1840s – the six gentle *Consolations* (Liszt took the word from a collection of poems by Sainte-Beuve), a number of the inevitable piano transcriptions – Beethoven's 'An die ferne Geliebte', Hummel's Septet, individual items from Mendelssohn, Berlioz, Meyerbeer – and, perhaps supreme among all his piano works, the Sonata in B minor, completed in 1853 and dedicated to Schumann.

'Klindworth has just played me your grand Sonata. It is of incomparable beauty, magnificent, charming, profound and noble – as sublime as you yourself. I am profoundly moved.' Thus Wagner to Liszt in April 1855. It is the archetypal statement of the polarizing impact of Liszt's music. For the whole man is here, in his flamboyance and his introspection, his heroism and his tenderness, his guileless spontaneity and his mysterious allusiveness. A music of extremes – to be received as such or not at all. The showmanship is there, but so is the grandeur: one cannot choose some parts and reject the others. And as the extremes are palpably present, coexistent, so they are resiliently irreconcilable. The half-Franciscan which Liszt recognized in himself cannot be secularized into the half-gypsy, nor the latter, in its turn, beatified as the half-Franciscan. As recipients of his B minor Sonata, as of his *oeuvre* in the round, we must carry the total reality in our minds, whatever its paradoxes and strains. His music demands from us something akin to the 'negative capability' in which Keats found the source of Shakespeare's power – the willingness to give up the 'irritable reaching after fact and reason' and to remain 'in uncertainties, mysteries, doubts'.

The uncertainties and mysteries beset the very opening bars of the Sonata, when, in a work announced as being in B minor, the argument is launched on the premiss set out in the extract overleaf, murmured 'under the breath'.

Throughout the unbroken web of themes and their transformations that reaches to the glorious harmonies of the final *pianissimo* chords – 'I attach the greatest value to my harmonies,'

he once said to Marie d'Agoult – runs the power of an emotional unity, a unity in diversity. The logic of the classical sonata, the controlled interplay of themes within a balanced key-structure, could not contain his vision; he needed a new logic, the logic of emotional argument, which created its own form in the course of its self-expression. The structural principle is now unitary, the argument being conducted through the development of a series of points of reference – in other words, through the studied exploitation, throughout the piece, of a number of individual motifs. The principle is the same as that underlying the symphonic poem: there the unity derives in the first instance from the singularity of the character, event or scene which is the spiritual origin of the work, but in musical terms it is conveyed by thematic means, subtleties of characterization and mood finding expression in the juxtaposition and variation of motifs. This is what holds together, in technical terms, the three sections and coda of Liszt's Sonata. On a grander scale it is the philosophy of composition manifested in the music-dramas of Richard Wagner.

Seen in these terms, Liszt's B minor Sonata is a paradigm of those strivings and inclinations that come together under the generic heading of Romanticism. The unashamed extroversion, the abandonment to strident self-assertion at one moment and to a withdrawn lyricism at the next, the exploration of extremes and an urge towards the infinite, yet the desire to encompass all experience within a defined unity, the unity of subjective expression, of self – in such phrases one can invoke, but never define or encompass, the world of Liszt the Romantic. For the Romantic vision will not be contained or curbed. It seeks infinity, the distant ideals of Novalis's evocative 'Blue Flower', the eternity that is the proper province of music. 'No art is so complete an expression of the inner human spirit, and employs such utterly spiritual and ethereal means, as music,' wrote E.T.A. Hoffmann in his discourse *Über alte und neue Kirchenmusik*. 'Intimations of the highest and holiest things, of the divine power that kindles the spark of life in the whole of Nature, come to us in sound, in music, in song, the expression of life in its supreme richness and abundance.' Such was the heuristic meaning of music, of all art, to the Romantic imagination. Such also is the spirit that rules over the music of Liszt.

For those unable or unwilling to face the revolutionary significance of what Liszt was doing, the Sonata in B minor could not but remain a thorn in the flesh. Like Beethoven, like Berlioz, like Wagner – but unlike Bach, or Mozart, or Mendelssohn – Liszt was a source of unrest and disquiet in the world of music, an agent of confrontation and challenge. Such men do not make life easy for their conservative contemporaries, and Hanslick spoke not only for himself when, after listening to a performance of the work by Bülow, he spluttered in rage:

> It is impossible to convey the nature of this musical monster in words. Never have I heard a more impudent or brazen concatenation of utterly disparate elements, such savage ravings, so bloody an assault on all that is musical. First taken aback, then left aghast, at the end I felt overcome by an irresistible desire to laugh. There is nothing here to discuss. Anybody who has heard this thing and liked it is beyond hope.

That Brahms fell asleep when Liszt played his Sonata to him in the Altenburg is, one must hope – not least for Brahms's sake – merely a spiteful story. But the Hanslicks of the time were pleased to help it on its way.

That much of what Liszt sowed fell on stony ground was a fate as dispiriting as it was familiar and predictable but it could not divert him from his urge to embrace the world, whether the world responded with love, suspicion or distaste. Cosima knew this as intimately as anyone:

> His works are part of his natural love for mankind, of his need to communicate: he is also speaking to someone through them – going out of himself rather than retreating into himself, if you will. That someone never came forward to listen to him was unjust to the point of cruelty, for the things he had to say were fine and noble.

What Liszt's Sonata is to piano music, the Prelude and Fugue on BACH and the Fantasia and Fugue on 'Ad nos, ad salutarem undam', together with the later Variations on 'Weinen, Klagen', are to organ music. He had no formal tuition in the organ, and only rarely found occasion to play the instrument, the techniques of which were a far cry from those that distinguished his piano music. In Weimar, however, his mind frequently returned to Bach, a number of whose works – the Chromatic Fantasia and Fugue, the Goldberg Variations, some of the *Well-Tempered Clavier* – had figured in the recital programmes of his European tours. The 'Thomas Aquinas of music' was his name for the greatest of all masters of counterpoint and of all composers for the organ, and he cast his tribute in the form of fantasies and fugues sustained by an excitement and a boldness of harmony within a majestic design of Romantic power.

This same majesty, the same expansiveness of outstretched arms seeking to embrace a totality of spiritual and intellectual experience, sustain two of the greatest of all Liszt's works, from this or any other period of his creative life – the Faust Symphony and the Dante Symphony. The foundations of both symphonies had been laid in the 1840s, but it was 1854 before he set his mind to expanding and completing the argument of his Faust material, and 1856, after a year's deliberations over what is in fact a far shorter work, before the Dante Symphony was ready for performance. Both works embody, in triumphant yet utterly different ways, the creative ideal upon which Liszt gazed during these years of supreme power in Weimar, the ideal which he described in a letter to Agnes Street as 'the renewal of music through its inner union with poetry'. This renewal, he went on, would initiate not only 'a new freedom in the development of art' but also a movement 'which would correspond more closely to the spirit of the age'. His words, like the two symphonies themselves, return us to the world of programme music.

Goethe's *Faust* was first brought to Liszt's attention by Berlioz when they met in Paris in December 1830 on the eve of the first performance of the *Symphonie fantastique*. The immediate incentive to compose a work on the subject came also from Berlioz, who in the mid-1840s was at work on his *Damnation de Faust* and had shown his enthusiastic admirer in Paris how he was setting about the task. The contemporary paintings by Ary Scheffer of scenes from the Faust story may also have helped to kindle his imagination. He made a plan for his own work on the subject at this time but the demands of his concert career left him little chance to think the composition through. When he visited Wagner in Zurich in the summer of 1853, however, he had it with him in a sufficiently advanced state to be able to take his friend through the work. In August 1854 he devoted his whole mind to the project, completing it in full score in a mere two months; three years later he added the radiant setting of the final words of Goethe's poem which bring the work to its serene close. He conducted its first public performance in the Weimar Hoftheater in September 1857 at a concert of his music to mark a threefold celebration – the unveiling of the joint memorial to Goethe and Schiller and of the statue of Wieland, and the laying of the foundation stone of the memorial to the Grand Duke Karl August. It demands a large orchestra – three flutes, two oboes, two clarinets, two bassoons, four horns, three trumpets, three trombones, tuba, tympani, cymbals, triangle, harp and organ, with tenor solo and male voice choir – and bears a dedication to Hector Berlioz.

The story of Faust – the craver for knowledge and experience who bequeathes his soul to the devil in return for the devil's services in ministering to his desires over the twenty-four years that the agreement between them shall last – might have been designed for Liszt. How well he knew the destructive tension that tormented Faust's 'two souls', the conflict between man's noblest spiritual aspirations, the service of the ideals of art, life and beauty, and his material ambitions, his pursuit of shallow pleasures, of fickle fame, of the enticements of false gods! And how keenly he felt the Goethean polarity of the good and the evil principles, of the Lord and Mephistopheles, of Faust the seeker after redemption, the legatee of divine grace, and Faust the libertine, the dissolute sinner. Here was a paradigm of man at his most human, fallible yet sublime, a character in whom he could recognize his own dissatisfactions, his own impatient protests at the weight of finite restrictions, the restless perfectionism that drove him to incessant revision of his own compositions. In 1860 he returned to the subject with *Two Episodes from Lenau's Faust* for orchestra (the second being the famous first Mephisto Waltz) and from the last years of his life come three more Mephisto Waltzes and a Mephisto Polka, as the allure of the sinister and destructive Mephisto edged the earnestly striving Faust aside. In the Abbé Liszt too, it seems, the devil often had the best tunes.

Seizing, not on the dramatic action as such, still less on the quality of the story as a Christian morality, but on individual symbolic values and moments, Liszt composed for his Faust Symphony a triptych of expansive movements with the titles 'Faust', 'Gretchen' and 'Mephistopheles', the final chorus '*Alles Vergängliche ist nur ein Gleichnis*' ('All that passes is but a parable') following as a coda. Each panel of the triptych is a

143

character study, a symphonic poem in itself, the themes symbolizing different aspects of the spiritual personality of the three figures in turn – Faust in agony and doubt, his mind a battlefield of warring forces, Gretchen the innocent, consumed by love for her seducer, and Mephistopheles, emissary of Satan, 'the spirit of perpetual negation', whose defeat is certain but without whom the victory of love and goodness would be meaningless. And as though to convey through his own means the Goethean principle that good and evil are recto and verso of a single reality, either taking its meaning from the other – it was with the Lord's consent that Mephisto appeared before Faust as the devil-tempter – Liszt used for his Mephisto scherzo sardonic, mocking forms of the Faust themes. 'Liszt is the first to have expressed irony in music,' said Bartók. The two, Faust and Mephisto, are united as positive and negative poles, the one dependent on the other, but in the assurance of redemption through love, through 'das Ewig-Weibliche' of the final chorus towards which the whole work unflinchingly moves. The pattern is thus the 'Lamento e trionfo' of *Tasso, Prometheus, Hamlet* and most of Liszt's other symphonic poems but with the significant difference that whereas all except three of the symphonic poems proclaim their triumphant conclusions *fortissimo*, the Faust Symphony reaches its culmination in gentle repose and serenity, bathed in the glow of divine salvation and bliss. It is a victory to be whispered, not shouted.

As the Faust Symphony expresses conflicts and concerns that lie at the heart of Liszt's being, so the Dante Symphony – *Eine Symphonie zu Dantes Divina Commedia*, in its published title – does so no less. His readings in Dante with Marie d'Agoult during their idyllic years together in the 1830s had sown the seed from which the Dante Sonata for piano had later grown, and throughout his life he drew from the world of the *Vita Nuova* and the *Divine Comedy* a spiritual sustenance without which his life would have been much the poorer. The *Divine Comedy*, in particular, embodied the values in terms of which he found his own philosophy of the meaning and purpose of the world – Beatrice and the ideal of love, the guidance of the artist through life by the power of philosophy and reason in the person of the poet Virgil, the progress of man through Hell and Purgatory to the Earthly Paradise of temporal felicity and spiritual freedom, and ultimately, led by the divine wisdom incarnated in Beatrice, through Paradise itself – a glimpse of the beatific vision and an intimation of eternity.

In 1847, his religious experience given a fresh intensity by

Princess Carolyne von Sayn-Wittgenstein, Liszt returned to the world of Dante and drafted the main themes for a substantial work on the *Divine Comedy*. His first thought, curious and entertaining in its conception, was to compose a kind of incidental music to a series of illustrations to Dante's epic painted by Buonaventura Genelli, which were to be projected on to a screen by the newly invented device of the diorama. However, this idea came to nothing, and it was to be another eight years before he took up the work again; he completed it one year later, in June 1856, and conducted its miserable first performance in Dresden in November the following year – 'an utter failure owing to insufficient rehearsals,' he told his friend Dr Carl Gille, concert director in Jena. The same large orchestra is required as for the Faust Symphony, with the addition of a harmonium and a second harp but without organ; there is a four-part chorus of women's or boys' voices and a short soprano solo.

It had been Liszt's original and natural intention to follow the tripartite form of the *Divine Comedy* and call his three movements 'Inferno', 'Purgatorio' and 'Paradiso'. The 'Inferno' would be dominated by the line *'Lasciate ogni speranza voi ch'entrate'* ('Abandon hope, all ye that enter here') inscribed above the gate to Hell – words which appear in the score at certain points with their own musical rhythm – and the Finale would contain music for the 'heavenly choirs'. But when Wagner, to whom the work was later dedicated, learned of this plan, he wrote a long letter to Liszt setting out his objections, most of which stemmed from his refusal to accept Dante's Christian world-picture:

I do not doubt for one moment that the Inferno and Purgatorio movements will be a success but I have grave reservations about the Paradiso, confirmed by your intention to use a choir. The weakest part of the Ninth Symphony is the last movement, with its choral Finale: its interest is purely aesthetic, in that it reveals to us in an extremely direct manner the embarrassment of the composer who, having depicted Hell and Purgatory, finds himself expected to portray Paradise. There is a real problem about this Paradise, my dear Franz, and if you need proof, it is most strikingly supplied by Dante himself, for his Paradiso is likewise the weakest part of his Divine Comedy.

Dante never lost his position of supreme eminence in Liszt's spiritual hierarchy; Wagner, by the criteria of art, forced himself ever more insistently into the ranks of this hierarchy, until over twenty years later Liszt arrived at a highly personal equation. 'To me,' he wrote to Baroness Olga von Meyendorff, one of his closest confidantes in later life, 'Wagner is the equal of Dante.' Which is the equivalent of saying: 'Art and Religion are one.'

Wagner's intervention introduced a discordance between the religious claims of the subject matter with which Liszt was grappling and the aesthetic – or seemingly aesthetic – considerations that Wagner now put forward. At this moment the atheist revolutionary in exile, Wagner had his own doctrinal reasons for disliking a specific presentation of the triumphs of a life in paradise. But whatever his motives, his decided opposition to an independent 'Paradiso' movement unsettled Liszt's confidence in his own vision, and the three movements were reduced to two, the 'Purgatorio' being concluded by a Magnificat, an intimation of the paradise beyond. On this reading of the philosophy of the work Liszt properly brought the symphony to a tranquil conclusion, *pianissimo*.

But Princess Carolyne, with a dogmatic religious zeal which usurped the role of the aesthetic judgement that she lacked, insisted that the work called for a triumphant *fortissimo* conclusion, and bound to her will as he was, Liszt obediently composed a new ending, which he played to Wagner on a visit to Zurich in 1856. 'I was appalled,' wrote Wagner in *Mein Leben*, 'to hear the soft and gentle Magnificat suddenly interrupted by a pompous plagal cadence, and I cried: "No! No! Not that! Take it out! No Lord in majesty!" "You're right!" exclaimed Liszt. "That's what I said too. The Princess made me change my mind, but now I'm going to have what you think best." ' Whereupon he restored the original conclusion.

That the Dante Symphony makes a lesser impact, musically, than the Faust Symphony derives principally from the absence of dramatic contrast within the work as a whole. This in turn rests on the nature of the poem. For whatever the gulf between the agonies of Hell and the bliss of Heaven, the Dantesque *Weltbild* is one and indivisible, an all-encompassing vision with a single focus, an allegory moving relentlessly along the predictable path of redemption. Open conflicts are subsumed in a predetermined aura of peace, and the balanced juxtaposition of contrasted forces, the structural principle on which the aesthetic satisfaction of any extended musical work depends, is undermined from the outset. A total contrition and humility, even a faith untouched by anxiety or doubt, may, as in Liszt's work, come to express itself in art in a mood of tensionless homogeneity which denies musical appreciation its full satisfaction. The profoundest truths need not elicit the greatest art, nor need the noblest causes. Princess Carolyne never understood this; Liszt, reluctantly, did, though not too convincingly at the moment of his Dante Symphony.

Yet he could never dissociate his beliefs from his art. Everything he did came from the whole man: had he not been the man he was, he never ceased to insist, he could not have composed the music he did. Back in his twenties, at the time of his encounter with Lamennais, he wrote an essay 'On the Church Music of the Future', envisaging a new art that met the needs of a Church which rested on the shoulders not of priests and theologians but of the people, the masses. This music he called 'musique humanitaire', defined as 'a powerful, fervent and impressive art that should represent a solemn union of Church and theatre in monumental grandeur . . . passionate and unrestrained, reverent and dramatic, intense and serene, direct and sincere'. The Lamennaisian, Saint-Simonian new society in which his 'humanitarian music' was to take its place had not come to pass, but his conception of the social function of art *per se*, as of Church music in particular, did not change.

Indeed, he came to see the innate spirit of music itself as virtually identical with that of the Christian religion. 'One may say,' he wrote to Joseph d'Ortigue, friend of his Paris days, 'that music is religious in essence and, like the human soul, Christian by nature. And when it is united with words, what more natural use could it make of its powers than to sing the glory of God and thus act as a mediator between the two worlds, the finite and the eternal?'

His first score of the Dante Symphony contains an explicit symbol of this union – the initials IND, In Nomine Domini, which stand at the head of the work. At the end of each movement he set a row of capital Bs, which concealed a meaning private to the Princess and himself. He would sometimes refer to the two of them as *'les bons bessons'* (BB) 'the good twins', then incorporate this in the phrase '(*que*) *le bon Dieu bénisse les bons bessons'* (BBBB) and finally, alluding to the Princess's origins, substitute for 'Dieu' the Polish for 'God', 'bŏze', to give *'bon bŏze bénisse les bons bessons'* (BBBBB).

This is the Liszt who embarked in 1855 on the first of the series of works with which he intended to pioneer a reform of Church music – the Esztergom Mass (sometimes called the Gran Mass, Gran being the German name for Esztergom), composed for the reconsecration of Esztergom Cathedral, in Hungary, in August 1856. It is a superb composition, passionate and full-blooded, written with an *élan* and at a speed which, as one who tended rather to ponder and revise over extended periods, he scarcely achieved again in a large-scale work. 'I do not know what the thing will sound like,' he wrote to Wagner, shortly after finishing it, 'but one thing I can say – that I prayed over it more than I composed it.'

Predictably, voices were raised in protest that it should be the ostentatious one-time virtuoso Liszt, now openly flouting the morality of the Catholic Church while professing his allegiance to it, who was charged to write the inaugural Mass. It needed the intercession of influential friends, above all Baron Antal Augusz, to convince Cardinal Szitovski, Primate of Hungary, that the commission had been given to the right man, and the triumphant reception of the work by the congregation of 4,000, led by the Austrian Emperor Franz Joseph, various archdukes, and the magnates of Hungary, forestalled any further carping.

Liszt, always overjoyed to be in his native land, travelled to Hungary to conduct the performance in the cathedral. An unmistakeable figure, he was fêted wherever he went, and when he entered and left any restaurant or public place, he wrote to Princess Carolyne, the guests would rise to their feet and shout *'Eljen! Eljen!'* A further performance of the Mass in Pest was followed by one of his Mass for male voice choir at the consecration of the Hermina Chapel in the town, then by a concert of his music at which he conducted the first performance of the symphonic poem *Hungaria* and *Les Préludes*, which the applauding audience demanded be repeated in its entirety.

Finally, in a gesture which filled him with a profounder happiness than all the acclaim of the world, the Franciscan community in Pest made him an honorary member of their fraternity, an honour which had about it a contentious quality akin to that which has attached to the award of certain Nobel prizes in modern times. On his way back to Weimar he passed through Vienna, where, to honour his presence in the city, Johann Strauss conducted a performance of the final section of his symphonic poem *Mazeppa*. Rarely had a period of so few weeks brought him such deep and lasting happiness.

Not only in Hungary was Liszt the conductor in demand. Nor did he use the Weimar orchestra and choir merely to promote the cause of his own music. In 1853 he organized a music festival at Ballenstedt, in the Harz Mountains, seat of the dukes of Anhalt; later the same year he arranged a similar festival in Karlsruhe. In 1855 he conducted his symphonic poems *Orpheus* and *Prometheus* in Brunswick, and in Berlin the first performance of his setting of Psalm 13 ('How long wilt Thou forget me, O Lord?') for tenor, chorus and orchestra. The following year he was invited to conduct at the Mozart Centenary Festival in Vienna – an occasion at which Clara Schumann, whose always equivocal relationship with Liszt had steadily deteriorated over the years, refused to perform – and in 1857, after appearing in Leipzig, he directed the 35th Music Festival of the Lower Rhine in Aachen, which included music by Berlioz and Wagner as well as his own Pianoforte Concerto No. 1, played by Hans von Bülow. The following year he conducted his Second Piano Concerto (with Tausig as soloist), *Die Ideale* and the Dante Symphony at a concert in Prague.

Of his social, non-professional excursions during these years the most stimulating were those to visit Wagner in Switzerland. He went twice in 1853, on the second occasion at the head of a veritable delegation of Wagnerian admirers including Bülow, Joachim, Peter Cornelius and the Hungarian violinist Ede Reményi. Then, with the Princess and her daughter Marie alone, he went again in the autumn of 1856, celebrating his forty-fifth birthday in the famous Hotel Baur in Zurich in the company of the architect Gottfried Semper, the Swiss novelist Gottfried Keller, the aesthetician Friedrich Theodor Vischer and others. 'Anybody the city could produce was present,' recalled Wagner. The impression made by Liszt the artist on the physiologist and philosopher Jacob Moleschott is interesting in that it comes from a keen and totally unprejudiced observer:

> He evoked great respect, and one hesitated to be so immodest as to ask him to give a sample of his skill, but he did not cut himself off or behave like a man who has come from another world in order just to display his art and then take it away with him again. No – he brought his art with him and wafted it through the room, and nothing gave him greater pleasure than when his own light shone in others and his own warmth was felt in others. His emotion was centred on his art, not calculated just to arouse self-adulation.

A poetic tribute to Liszt telegraphed from Weimar by the poet Hoffmann von Fallersleben was read out to the company by Wagner's fellow-exile Georg Herwegh, then Wagner and Frau Heim, wife of the Zurich music director, accompanied by Liszt at the piano, sang the first act of *Die Walküre*, and excerpts from Liszt's symphonic poems were performed on two pianos. Normally a man of sound health, and impatient of temporary disorders, Liszt contracted a painful rash at this time, which confined him to his bed for a considerable time. But when the condition passed, he became his old irrepressible self. 'I remember an entertaining evening at Herwegh's,' wrote Wagner in *Mein Leben*, 'when a horribly out-of-tune piano elicited the same enthusiasm from Liszt as the frightful cigars which he used to prefer at that time to those of superior quality. It reminded us all not so much of magic as of witchcraft when he played a wonderful improvisation for us on this instrument.'

Back in Weimar he received a visit from George Eliot and her consort George Henry Lewes – 'a remarkably ugly couple,' he remarked. When Lewes told him that he and his companion were not in fact married, Liszt said he attached no importance to such things. Nevertheless, when Liszt came to dine with them at the Erbprinz, Lewes was uneasy, whereas George Eliot behaved with characteristic lack of embarrassment. 'I have often observed,' commented Liszt, 'that the men are the more uncomfortable in such "irregular circumstances".' She was especially struck by Liszt's kindness and hospitality, and wrote:

> Liszt is the first really inspired man I ever saw. His face might serve as a model for a Saint John in its sweetness when he is in repose but seated at the piano he is as grand as one of Michelangelo's prophets . . . He is a glorious creature in every way – a bright genius, with a tender, loving nature, and a face in which this combination is perfectly expressed.

Shortly before he left for Esztergom in August 1856, Liszt received a letter from Joachim, who three years earlier had deserted the 'New Music' of Liszt and Wagner for the Schumann-Brahms circle. After two years of slow, inexorable deterioration, wrote Joachim, Schumann had died in a mental asylum near Bonn. 'Even though fate and both physical and spiritual experience may have shaped your lives very differently,' wrote Joachim in his letter, 'I am certain that no man has a greater desire or capacity than you to understand the full stature of our departed friend in its beauty and purity.'

Liszt had indeed grasped Schumann's originality right from the beginning, and included *Carnaval*, *Kreisleriana* and other pieces in his recitals at a time when few showed any confidence in Schumann's music. In 1855, a year before Schumann's death, he conducted *Genoveva* in Weimar, and had performed his *Manfred* music and part of the *Szenen aus Goethe's Faust* some years earlier. But his reward had been suspicion and resentment from both Schumann and Clara, and Clara's tone became increasingly hostile whenever she had cause to mention him in her diaries. She told the publishers to remove his name from the dedication of Schumann's Fantasie Op. 17, and the day after Liszt's death she wrote in her diary:

> How sad that one cannot mourn him with a full heart: the glitter surrounding him only makes for a sombre image of him both as man and artist. He was an outstanding virtuoso but as such, a dangerous model for the young . . . In addition he was a bad composer, and in this too a disastrous example for many, though the effects have not penetrated so deeply. His compositions are trivial and boring; he used to deceive people by his charm and his virtuosity into performing them but we may expect that with his passing they will soon disappear for ever.

Her words would be risible if they were not so sad.

Superimposed on this welter of musical activity in the middle 1850s were three events in his private life, each of which moved him deeply. Two were occasions for rejoicing – the marriage of his two daughters. The other was the death of his son.

In 1848, at the instance of Princess Carolyne, Blandine and Cosima had been entrusted to the matronly regimen of the Princess's own former governess, the elderly Madame Patersi de Fossombroni. As the years slipped by, this regime became more and more unnatural for the lively teenage girls. The presence in the city of their mother, who had meanwhile established herself in an elegant little Renaissance house at the upper end of the Champs-Elysées and gathered a salon of literary friends around her, was both a delight and a cause of divided loyalty, especially as they could not escape the lurking influence of their father's mistress in the background. In August 1855 Liszt therefore arranged for them to leave Paris and be cared for in Berlin by the mother of Hans von Bülow.

After two years under Liszt's tutelage in Weimar, Bülow, an overwrought young man prone to drive himself into states of near exhaustion, returned to his native Berlin as a formidable pianist and potentially brilliant conductor, and took up a post at the Stern Conservatoire. The arrival of the two Liszt daughters, especially the vivacious, self-willed, if not overly attractive Cosima, threw the impressionable Bülow completely off balance, and his glowing letters to her father about the progress she was making in the piano lessons he was giving her had so unambiguous a tenor that no one was surprised when, after knowing her for a mere three months, he formally asked Liszt for her hand in marriage.

On her side Cosima, unhappy at having been wrenched from the Parisian environment where she felt she belonged, was in a mood to grasp at any invitation that offered a change in her stifling dependence, and in August 1857 the Catholic Cosima Liszt and the Protestant Hans von Bülow were married in the Catholic Hedwigskirche in Berlin. 'She feels the *démon intérieur* and will always sacrifice to it what it demands of her,' said her mother, Countess Marie d'Agoult. 'Circumstances have pushed her into a marriage in which, I fear, there will be happiness for no one.'

There was certainly none for the ill-matched couple. Barely a year later they went to Zurich to visit Wagner. Shortly before they took their leave, Cosima, alone with Wagner for a moment, fell at his feet and covered his hands with tears and kisses. 'Astonished and alarmed,' Wagner afterwards told Mathilde Wesendonk, 'I gazed upon this mystery without being able to unravel it.' It was to be five years before the mystery fully unravelled itself. In 1863 Wagner went to see the Bülows in Berlin and took a ride with Cosima one afternoon in a carriage. 'Weeping and sobbing,' he wrote in his autobiography, 'we pledged ourselves to each other alone.' For Bülow it was the unhappy end of a hopeless adventure, for Cosima, the submission to a power that bound her to one of the most irresistible musical geniuses the world has known. For Liszt, soon to become the less than willing father-in-law of this fellow-genius a mere two years younger than himself, it marked the onset of years of disappointment, of strained relationships with those dear to him, of a sadness which it was not in his power to diffuse.

At the same time it was, in a sense, not in his nature to wish to diffuse it. He had determined to have his daughters raised in his own image, and could therefore hardly be surprised if he felt their growing pains as his own. 'In order to completely satisfy me,' he once wrote to Marie d'Agoult, 'they must not content themselves with merely idling their time away. They must be re-born in the spirit of the best that is in me – only then will they really be mine.' It was a formula for self-imposed suffering.

Blandine, prettier and more charming than her younger sister, caused him less heart-searching. From the many admirers who surrounded her she chose a young lawyer called Émile Ollivier, who later became a minister in the government of Napoleon III, and married him on her father's birthday in the same year as Cosima married Bülow. At the time when Liszt gave his consent to the match he had not even met Ollivier but he accepted

Blandine's choice without demur. After her tragic death in childbirth five years later he continued to visit his son-in-law in his mansion in Paris, in which old Anna Liszt, reduced to hobbling around on crutches but still sound in constitution and as keen of perception as ever, then also lived.

Men like Liszt divide the world into two camps, and the offensive camp shouts the louder. So it was in the days of Liszt the virtuoso pianist; so it was with his liaisons with Countess Marie d'Agoult, Princess Carolyne von Sayn-Wittgenstein and a bevy of other ladies, high and low; and so it was with the music he composed, performed and promoted during his years at the court of Weimar. True, the Dowager Grand Duchess Maria Pavlovna and the Grand Duke Carl Alexander retained their confidence and their loyalty in the face of political hostility and scheming. But Liszt knew that the most he could expect from the Weimar public as a body was a sullen and largely uncomprehending resentment, both over the music he tried to force them to listen to and over his participation in activities which, as they saw it, lay outside his competence.

> If I were to go over to the anti-Liszt camp, [wrote Hans von Bülow to his father from Weimar,] it would bring me immense popularity overnight. Liszt's enemies here are like the jetsam one finds by the sea. He concerns himself with other things besides playing the piano – the Goethe Foundation and so on – and this puts people's backs up, because the only right they are basically prepared to allow him is to entertain them as a pianist, which is something he has given up once and for all.

The ill-will was mutual. 'If your Highness wishes there to be music performed in Weimar,' wrote Liszt to Maria Pavlovna in 1851, after conducting Berlioz's *Harold in Italy* to an almost empty house, 'I shall do so to the best of my ability. But I long ago came to the conclusion that the Weimar public is not worth a brass farthing.'

Matters came to a head in 1858. Throughout that year the funds available for promoting the cause of music in the Grand Duchy were steadily whittled away under the aegis of Franz Dingelstedt, the recently appointed General Director of the Court Theatre and orchestra. Dingelstedt was a man of considerable flair in the conduct of theatrical affairs and had little interest in seeing money diverted from drama into concerts and operas. Then, in December, Liszt announced the première of young Peter Cornelius's comic opera *Der Barbier von Bagdad*, for which Dingelstedt had refused to release funds and against which he had been waging a clandestine campaign from the moment Liszt began rehearsals. At the end of the performance a booing and whistling and trampling erupted with a violence out of all proportion to the gentle demands made by the charming, unpretentious music. And indeed, like the scandalous occasion of the Paris *Tannhäuser* in 1861 the hostility had been deliberately generated in advance and the performance itself used as a convenient moment to mount a comprehensive anti-Liszt demonstration.

Liszt knew full well what this all meant. Turning away from the stage, he stood in silence, facing the pandemonium with arms folded. 'I shall never forget the way he looked at us,' said one of the audience. 'His expression filled me with terror.'

But there was nothing to be accomplished by terror. A tension that had slowly been growing more intolerable had now reached breaking-point. The scenes at the performance of *Der Barbier von Bagdad*, as Liszt put it to Carl Alexander, were merely 'the last drops that caused the bucket, which had long been full, to finally overflow'. What had filled the bucket had been the *Symphonie fantastique, The Damnation of Faust, Harold in Italy, Der fliegende Holländer, Tannhäuser, Lohengrin*; that poor Cornelius had been made to bring it to overflowing is nothing but a cruel quirk of history. A few weeks later Liszt wrote to Carl Alexander to say he could no longer continue to serve the court under the humiliating conditions he had recently had to endure. 'I have never been good for anything but to chart the course for others,' he observed in bitter self-analysis, 'and even at that I had ceased to be successful.'

The Grand Duke did not give up his Kapellmeister extraordinary without a struggle, and for the whole of the following year he tried to find a way of assuring him of the artistic autonomy he demanded. But Liszt had made up his mind. Weimar, and what it stood for, now belonged to the past, not least because it symbolized the relentless frustration of his desire to marry the woman he loved.

One of the areas of experience in which he found a challenge to set against this frustration was the culture of his homeland – specifically, the music of the Hungarian gypsies. That Liszt's career could ever have been confined within national barriers is an unreal notion. To Ödön von Mihalovich, his successor as Director of the Academy of Music in Budapest, he once wrote: 'If you were not chained to Budapest, your career as a composer would develop more freely. You can be certain that in a few years' time no Hungarian composer will make his mark anywhere but in his own country, where progress only proceeds by fits and starts.'

Yet pride in his Hungarian background, an anxiety over the people's well-being and a concern with the political decisions that affected their lives stayed with him to the end of his life. In 1846, caught up in the helter-skelter of his European concert tours, he had found time to write to Baron Majthényi and Count Leo Festitics from Vienna: 'Believe me when I say that my highest and most sincere ambition will always be to serve my great and noble country with all the power at my command.' And almost thirty years later, bequeathing a number of his personal possessions to the National Museum in Budapest: 'I am your fellow-countryman, proud to be able to place my humble artistic talents at the service of Hungary and to encourage all artists to pledge themselves to their native land.'

The playing of gypsy bands, with their cimbaloms and their idiosyncratic rubato violin style, belonged to Liszt's earliest musical experiences as a boy. For him the gypsies created and bore the indigenous tradition of Hungarian music, and there had never been reason to think otherwise. The salient features of this idiom – in melody the 'gypsy' scale, the minor mode with an augmented second between the third and fourth and between the sixth and seventh degrees, and in rhythm the *alla zoppa* inverted dotted figure, or 'Scotch snap', and other syncopations – found their way into his 'Hungarian' compositions, above all the nineteen Hungarian Rhapsodies, the majority of which have their origins in popular melodies which he heard in the 1830s and 1840s. In the mid-1850s, accompanying the publication of the bulk of the Rhapsodies, he turned his mind to the cultural phenomenon of this gypsy music as such and wrote a monograph called *Des Bohémiens et de leur musique en Hongrie*, published in Paris in 1859.

The title arouses expectations of a study analytical and scientific at least in part, a sifting of the historical evidence relevant to a subject of which large areas lay in darkness, and still do. But this was not Liszt's way. Fascinated by the mysterious Eastern origins and nomadic history of the tziganes, and carried along by a conviction, emotional, not rational, that the music of his boyhood experience, the music which flowed through his veins, was music of gypsy provenance, he embraced without further argument the enthusiastic conclusion that Hungarian music was none other than gypsy music. On this conclusion he then built an impressionistic, rhapsodical narrative ranging in characteristically undisciplined manner over all that he had read, heard and personally experienced about the history, culture and customs of the tziganes.

Part One, under the heading 'The Two Wandering Races', compares the gypsies and the Jews as peoples without a homeland – a comparison guaranteed to upset all sides. Unlike Wagner, Liszt was totally free of any taint of anti-Semitism, and the music of the synagogue, indeed the whole Jewish rite, greatly moved him. But in his view of the effects of the tragic rootlessness of the Jews on their art, above all the absence of the quality of genius in the midst of a profusion of talent, he strikes the same position as Wagner in his notorious essay *Music and the Jews* of 1850, and sets Mendelssohn and Meyerbeer against Bach and Beethoven in a sense similar to that in which Wagner excludes the Jews from his conception of the *Volk* as the only true source of spiritual community. Part Two, called 'Gypsy Life in Relation to Art', describes the life of the gypsies in various parts of the world, and derives on the one hand from Liszt's own experience of the Magyar world, on the other from recently published articles on the subject; the experiences and opinions of Princess Carolyne also seem to have found their way into this section. Part Three then turns specifically to Hungarian 'gypsy' music.

Liszt did not research in the field, nor did he approach the subject as a scholar. He knew that the gypsies came from Hindustan to Hungary, where, partly on the basis of their black magic rituals, they were taken to be Egyptians – hence their name in English. What he did not know, and did not stop to ponder, was that, although the so-called gypsy scale is probably of Indian origin, the gypsies were the interpreters of the music they played rather than its creators. And the music they performed was not what people called, and still call, 'gypsy music,' nor is it traditional Magyar folk music but 'a comparatively recent type of Hungarian popular art music,' as Béla Bartók put it, 'composed, almost without exception, by Hungarians of the upper middle class.' Liszt had no knowledge of Hungarian peasant folk melodies in their authentic form, since revealed through the work of Vikár, Bartók, Kódaly and others, and simply drew on his own experience to propose the equation Hungarian = Gypsy. But rather than that the Hungarians lacked an aboriginal folk music tradition and owed everything to the immigrant gypsies, the gypsies' interpretative skill was superimposed upon the particular strain of Hungarian musical culture that they assimilated and propagated. Put this way, the argument returns in a strange way to the comparison between the gypsies and the Jews which Liszt draws in the first part of his book, and what he called 'Hungarian' Rhapsodies – the same is true of Brahms's 'Hungarian' Dances – should really be called 'Gypsy' Rhapsodies.

The publication of *The Gypsies and their Music in Hungary* provoked angry protests from Liszt's patriotic Hungarian readers. Still clamped in the yoke of the Habsburg monarchy, the Hungarians needed all the energy they could command in order to preserve their national identity and self-esteem, and a statement by one supposedly of their own number which seemed tantamount to denying them an indigenous musical culture could be received only as an act of treason. They had as little demonstrable evidence to refute Liszt's thesis as he had to support it, and their indignation was as irrational as his romanticism had been misplaced. Kálmán Simonfly, a well known singer in the 1860s and a generous admirer of Liszt, broke publicly with him over his gypsy book on the ground that it was his patriotic duty to do so. When in 1886 the question arose whether Liszt's remains should properly be returned to Hungary, the Prime Minister of the day, Kálmán Tisza, could still not resist a moment of reprobation. 'At the very time,' he said, 'when Hungary had lost almost everything but her music, Liszt chose to proclaim to the world at large that it was not Magyar music at all but gypsy music.' Contemporary voices were also raised in objection to certain passages on the Jews: some found them anti-Semitic by sheer virtue of the barefaced parallel drawn between Jews and other gypsies, others – later including Hans von Bülow, to his shame – took exception to what they saw as an overly sympathetic view of the plight of the homeless and stateless children of Israel.

Liszt, who was proud of his little book, had not bargained for such reactions and regarded them all as totally misdirected – which they were. But his attempts in private and public letters to make his position clear, particularly after the appearance of a second edition in 1881, only made matters worse. He had touched too many sore spots. It was no longer an argument about music – in a sense it never had been – but about social and political issues which raised the temperature of discussion to white heat, and still does. Wagner underwent the same experience and attracted similar extreme reactions. But he had a broader back than his father-in-law.

As a whole, 1859, the year of *The Gypsies and their Music in Hungary*, brought him more darkness and sadness than joy and light. It opened with a series of rancorous exchanges with Wagner, who, with the tact of a bull in a china shop, chose this moment to launch one of his aggressive campaigns for funds on his own behalf: 'Did I not make it absolutely plain to you that I am desperately trying to get some money together, while all you can do is make fun of me? You are fortunate enough not to know what hardship means. Send me your *Dante* and your Mass – but first send money!' In an unusual fit of pique Liszt drily replied: 'Since the Dante Symphony and the Mass are not negotiable like bank shares, it will scarcely be necessary for me to send you them.' In the weeks that followed the two men returned to something like their former cordiality and nothing would shake Liszt's commitment to Wagner's music, but the scars never completely healed. 'My membership of the Franciscan Brotherhood has sometimes been essential for me to endure a number of unendurable things,' he sighed in mingled weariness and gratitude.

In June his most loyal patron and supporter, the Dowager Grand Duchess Maria Pavlovna, died at the age of seventy-three in the Belvedere Palace outside Weimar. Many had been the occasions when he had laid the difficulties of his position before her, both as Kapellmeister and as consort of Princess Carolyne, and she had done much to draw him back from the brink of despair. In October, however, occurred two events which helped to lift his sagging spirits: one was his elevation to the Austrian peerage, the other, less unequivocal in its effects, was the marriage of Princess Carolyne's daughter Marie.

Despite the temptations, and whatever stories his tireless detractors peddled, Liszt was not a vain man. But from his childhood he had moved in aristocratic circles and come to feel upper-class society as his proper milieu; he also had a sense of his true worth and saw no reason to spurn the honours that were offered him in good faith. Such honours found their irresistible way to him like iron filings to a magnet. In 1842 he was elected a Member of the Royal Prussian Academy of Arts, made an honorary Doctor of the University of Königsberg and awarded the highest Prussian civilian honour, the 'Pour le mérite'; in 1843 he was created a Privy Councillor by Prince Friedrich Wilhelm von Hohenzollern-Hechingen. On an earlier occasion that probably moved him more deeply than any of these, he had been presented with a jewelled sabre in Budapest by the Hungarian magnates on his triumphant return to his native land. The conferral now of the Order of the Iron Crown by the Austrian Emperor Franz Joseph I helped to raise his self-esteem in a dark year of his life, and when asked in 1883 to correct an article on himself for the *Biographie des Contemporains*, he appended a list of more than fifty such honours he had received.

After he took minor orders in the Catholic Church in 1865, any prospect there might have been of his accepting the hereditary peerage that accompanied the award of the Iron Crown vanished and he petitioned the Emperor for the title to pass to his Uncle Eduard – the cherished relative whom, six years younger than himself, he had always addressed as 'cousin'. On 'Uncle' Eduard's death in 1879 the title 'von Liszt' was taken by his son, also called Eduard and also a lawyer, who published in 1938 a collection of reminiscences and items of private information about his great-uncle.

On the other side of the family, so to speak, the surface of life in the Villa Altenburg was more than rippled when the twenty-two-year-old Marie von Sayn-Wittgenstein, the Princess's daughter, married Prince Konstantin von Hohenlohe-Schillingsfürst, major-domo to the Austrian imperial household, and went to live with him in Vienna. When she came to Weimar with her mother in 1848, she was eleven, and since her parents had been separated some six or seven years before that, she knew little of her father, whose role had virtually been assumed by Liszt. Even his letters to her while she was still little more than a child show his devotion to 'Magnolette,' as he called her, and as many visitors noted with pleasure, she brought her own charm to life in the Altenburg. Her departure from Weimar left life in the villa the poorer, with Liszt, in many ways at his most vulnerable in this agitated and uncertain time, feeling that a vital part of his existence had been cut away.

Yet in a way he and Princess Carolyne bore a deep personal responsibility for the loss. It was not a love match. When the dramatist Friedrich Hebbel, who had visited the Altenburg more than once before, came to the house shortly before the wedding, he met a joyless Marie. 'Here was no happy bride with boundless hopes for the future,' he wrote in his diary, 'but a broken woman preparing to sacrifice herself, filled with a fear that she was about to lose a great deal.' The sacrifice, her commitment to an aristocrat who was probably the most elevated among her many suitors, fulfilled on one hand the desire of Liszt and the Princess that through such a match Marie's life should be set on a reassuring foundation which would help to redeem the continued irregularity of their own relationship. But at the same time it cast a new spotlight on this relationship and brought it an unwelcome new prominence at a moment when utter stalemate seemed to have been reached in their efforts to legalize their union.

Then the situation took an unexpected turn. A tenant on the

Princess's Russian estates, a man called Okraszevski, arrived in Weimar with the news that the old Metropolitan of St Petersburg, Bishop Hotonievski, who had consistently refused to countenance the Princess's divorce, had died. His successor, suggested Okraszevski, might prove more amenable, and he undertook to act as broker, asking for a fee of 70,000 roubles should he succeed. Prince Nicholas von Sayn-Wittgenstein had divorced Princess Carolyne in 1855 and remarried two years later; ownership of her estates had been transferred to her daughter, and he had no desire to thwart her plans to marry Liszt. In the spring of 1860 Okraszevski returned from Russia carrying the divorce decree. All that remained was to secure the confirmation of the Pope in Rome, which, they thought in their new-found optimism, should surely be little more than a formality.

While Okraszevski was engaged on his errand, the final blow fell that the black year of 1859 had to deal. Ten days before Christmas, in the house of Hans and Cosima von Bülow in Berlin, Liszt's son Daniel died at the age of twenty. He was a brilliant boy, the most outstanding of his year at the Lycée Bonaparte in Paris, given to philosophical meditation and increasingly drawn to his father since becoming a student in Vienna. In the summer vacation of 1859 he first went to visit some friends in Dresden, then travelled on to see his sister Cosima in Berlin. Here he suddenly contracted consumption, and after a few weeks it became clear that he would not recover. Cosima informed her father, who arrived in Berlin a few days before Daniel died. 'He was breathing with great difficulty,' he wrote to Princess Carolyne, 'and he jerked out his words with an effort, though with no indication that his mind was wandering. Down to his last moment there was not the slightest impediment to his intellectual faculties.' He passed away with barely a sigh. His last words were: 'I go to prepare a place before you.' In the months that followed Liszt transmuted his private grief into 'Les Morts', the first of three orchestral *Odes funèbres* written between now and 1866, which he asked should be played at his own funeral (it was not).

In May 1860 Princess Carolyne, bearing her Russian divorce decree, travelled to Rome for what she confidently expected would be the final scene of the drama. She took quarters first in the Piazza di Spagna, then in the adjacent Via del Babuino No. 89, 'a very modest furnished flat on the third floor', as Malwida von Meysenbug, the aristocratic revolutionary and close friend of Wagner, described it, 'fairly tasteless and devoid of any real elegance, as was usually the case at that time with rented apartments in Rome'. Other visitors complained of the stuffy, smoke-laden atmosphere and that the Princess never opened a window; books lay scattered everywhere, with a large bowl of sweets and chocolates, numerous vases of flowers, a number of busts of Liszt and a grand piano.

Liszt stayed behind in the unnaturally quiet, deserted Altenburg. No longer part of the public musical life of Weimar, he worked with a kind of desultory devotion on a number of religious compositions – the oratorios *Christus* and *Die Legende von der heiligen Elisabeth*, psalm settings, the two *Legends* 'St Francis of Assisi Preaching to the Birds' and 'St Francis of Paola Walking on the Water' – and waited for news of the Princess's mission. Neither of them could know that she would never set foot in the house again.

Through the offices of Gustav von Hohenlohe, brother of her son-in-law and later to become Cardinal, Princess Carolyne was granted an audience of Pope Pius IX and pleaded her case. Months went by in silence. 'She followed the Pope wherever he went,' said her daughter, 'in order to receive his blessing and to remind him of her petition but this importunate behaviour only aroused his disapproval.' Her Polish relatives also made sure that their disapproval of the proposed marriage reached His Holiness's ears, and only after a second audience in September did the Vatican give its consent.

Back in the loneliness of Weimar, waiting for news from Rome, Liszt drew up a will. It was far more than a mere dispensation of earthly possessions. For as well as its bequests to Bülow, Cornelius and others of what he calls 'The Confraternity of the New German School', and its renewed declaration of unreserved confidence in Wagner as the standard-bearer of modern music, it contains the frankest public commitment he ever uttered to the inspiration and solace that he had received from the Princess throughout his years in Weimar:

All my good thoughts and good deeds over the past twelve years I owe to her on whom I so desperately yearn to bestow the sweet name of wife, though human spitefulness and despicable intrigues have hitherto doggedly frustrated it – Jeanne Elisabeth Carolyne, Princess Wittgenstein née Ivanovska. It is only with indescribable emotion that I can write her name. She is firmly, inseparably linked with my career, my worries, my whole existence. I kneel before her to give her my blessing and to express my gratitude to her as my guardian angel and as my mediator before God.

To the guardian angel herself he sent an uninhibited piece of self-analysis at this time:

> My entire life has been nothing but an odyssey of love, if you will permit the phrase. I was fitted only for loving – and so far, alas, I have only succeeded in loving badly . . . There are many vices which, if I am not mistaken, are completely foreign to my nature. When I think back over the many long years during which I have not been to confession, I cannot recall the slightest trace of pride or envy, still less of meanness or hatred. My besetting hazard is this need for a certain emotional intensity which quickly leads me to a state of paradox in intellectual matters and to an excessive indulgence in alcoholic stimulants. I promised that I would reform in this latter respect but it will not be without effort.

On his forty-ninth birthday, 22 October, the civic authorities of Weimar – with some considerable relief, one feels – paid a final tribute to its departing Kapellmeister. They appointed him an honorary citizen, crowning the event in the evening with a torchlight procession that wended its musical way from the market place, across the bridge over the River Ilm and up the hill that led to the Villa Altenburg. Liszt stood by the open window of the salon on the first floor and waved to the applauding crowd below. It was a moment of confused ironies. From the time he had arrived in the town an undercurrent of disapproval and resentment had flowed against him – disapproval of his cohabitation with Princess Carolyne and his life-style in general, resentment at the merciless determination with which he forced the 'New Music' on them. The smouldering feud between the town and the Altenburg was at an end. The town had won. Now, before returning to enjoy the fruits of their victory in peace, the worthy burghers made a public demonstration of affection and respect for the man who had been a thorn in their side for as long as they had known him.

A last achievement did, however, still await him. One of the most cherished projects of his early days in Weimar had been the establishment of an institution for the cultivation of the arts, to be known as the Goethe Foundation. For all the fine words that were spoken, the plan remained in the mind. It was some small consolation to him when, in the summer of 1861, Carl Alexander accepted his proposal that a music festival be held in Weimar at which a 'Universal German Musical Association' – the Allgemeiner Deutscher Musikverein – should be set up. Among the works performed at the inauguration were Liszt's *Prometheus*, his

A major Piano Concerto, played by Tausig, and the complete Faust Symphony, conducted from sight by Bülow. Guest of honour, among a throng of admirers from all over the country, was Richard Wagner, who had been granted an amnesty the previous year and was now free to return to any part of Germany except his native Saxony.

It was a remarkable occasion – a kind of final fling, a triumphant farewell to the house which Liszt had made the temple of a new musical culture and from which he had preached a new set of musical values. His young Swiss pupil Wendelin Weissheimer, later an indefatigable promoter of the Wagnerian cause, described the Bohemian scene in his memoirs:

Liszt had put us up, one and all, in the Altenburg, but as more and more arrived, there were in the end not enough beds to go round. So in a large room in the annexe a great pile of hay was laid across the floor with huge linen cloths over it, and here, in a state of semi-undress, the merry company slept for the few hours given over to rest – if sleep were at all possible, that is. The Master insisted on lying down in the middle of us. Only towards dawn did we grow tired enough to close our eyes.

One morning Liszt was the first to rise, and we heard him going 'Bim, bim, bam, boom, bam, bim', from the *piano* pizzicato double-bass passage in the first movement of his Faust Symphony, which had often had to be repeated at the last rehearsal. We immediately cupped our hands over our mouths and sang the horn entry that followed. This greatly amused Liszt, and he cried: 'Once more!' He started up his pizzicato 'Bim, bim, bam . . .' again, and we came in with our 'Ber, ber-er', like the horns. Among jolly incidents like this we dressed ourselves and sat down to breakfast at the long table in the dining room, where we had to find room for more and more people as time went on. Then after breakfast we split up for our various rehearsals.

The Allgemeiner Deutscher Musikverein survived the chequered course of German history down to 1937, when it was disbanded under the presidency, by a vicious irony, of Peter Raabe, one-time custodian of the Liszt Museum in Weimar.

That the Vatican had decided in Princess Carolyne's favour did not, however, put an end to the agonizing affair of her remarriage. Weimar lay in the diocese of Fulda, and the Bishop of Fulda received via the Papal nuncio in Vienna authority to perform the ceremony. But the Bishop, under renewed pressure from the enemy party, which maintained that the Princess's plea rested on perjured evidence, refused to do so. The case went back to the Vatican. The Princess waited in Rome, Liszt in Weimar, as month after frustrating month went by. Finally, in August 1861, the Cardinals reaffirmed their original decision.

If Princess Carolyne had returned to Germany immediately, the wedding could have taken place. Instead she wrote to Liszt and urged him to join her in Rome so that they could be married in the city which embodied their profoundest beliefs and aspirations. After the last of his guests at the Musikverein celebrations had gone, he made his own plans to leave the house. The valuables were taken by Carl Alexander into his palace for safe keeping, the keys were handed to cousin Eduard, who had come to the Musikverein party from Vienna, and Liszt returned for his last few days to the Erbprinz Hotel, where his sojourn in Weimar had begun in the revolutionary year of 1848. Since then he had enacted his own revolution.

On 10 August Eduard Lassen, a Danish musician who later became music director in Weimar, wrote in his diary:

> The Altenburg is a melancholy sight. Today the rooms have been locked and sealed, tomorrow Liszt moves into the Erbprinz and on the 17th he will say goodbye to the town. He has taken six months' leave, but I do not think he will come back. Life in Weimar has ceased to be enjoyable. Two years ago the young Lady Marie went, then the Princess, and now Liszt. There is nothing left.

Two days later Liszt wrote to Princess Carolyne:

> As I already told you in my telegram, at two o'clock today, in blazing sunshine, I left the house where for twelve years you performed such good works and so passionately pursued the cause of beauty. When I walked through the empty rooms, I could not restrain my tears. But after a final pause at the priedieu where you always knelt with me, I felt a sense of release, which gave me strength. Since you went, the house has seemed to me more like a coffin than anything else. Leaving it seems to bring me closer to you, and I now breathe more freely.

On 17 August, in the heat of the midday sun, Liszt left the Erbprinz and made his way alone to the railway station. After a brief visit to Carl Alexander at his country seat of Wilhelmsthal and a stay in Löwenberg, in Silesia, with Princess Carolyne's daughter Marie and her husband, he travelled to Berlin to see

Cosima and Bülow. From there he went to Paris, partly to be with Wagner after the notorious disaster of the *Tannhäuser* performances earlier in the year, partly to see his daughter Blandine, partly, perhaps, just because Paris was Paris and he had a feeling he would not see it again for a long while. He called on his aristocratic friends again, together with Meyerbeer, Rossini and other leading musicians, and made the acquaintance of Baudelaire, who had recently taken up cudgels on Wagner's behalf, at a breakfast in Gounod's house – in short, as Wagner put it, he 'was back on his old endless round'.

A less relaxed moment in this round, a moment of pain yet also of a joy not wholly forgotten, was a re-encounter, after sixteen years, with the mother of his children. Countess Marie d'Agoult was now fifty-six. When they met, he said, recalling the places they had visited together, and with a flicker of an eye towards the figure of the conceited painter Guermann Regnier in the Countess's novel *Nélida*: 'You never had faith in me but you see now that I have turned into something respectable after all.'

'At this,' as Liszt described the encounter to Princess Carolyne, 'Marie's face became bathed in tears. I kissed her brow – the first time in many years – and said to her: "Marie, let me use the language of a simple countryman. God bless you. Wish me no evil." She was unable to reply and her tears flowed the more copiously.' He bade her a tender farewell. Then, as he was descending the stairs, he suddenly had a vision of his poor son Daniel and an icy realization gripped his mind: 'During the three or four hours I had spent with his mother, we did not refer to him once.' He could cherish the memory of her as a lover and retain an affectionate respect for her as a person but had never admitted her to the role of mother. And that she chose to republish *Nélida* three years later hardly suggests that she wished him well.

Early in the morning of 21 October Liszt arrived in Rome – 'the place where one only half-feels one's pain', Peter Cornelius described it – and took rooms in the Via Felice No. 113 (now Via Sistina). Princess Carolyne, in blissful possession of the document which she trusted to assuage all the pain of the past decade, had planned their wedding for the following day, his fiftieth birthday, and for the past few days she had been decorating the nearby church of San Carlo al Corso in preparation for the occasion. So recklessly was she prepared to tempt fate that she drew up a will, signed it as Carolyne Liszt and post-dated it 23 October 1861, the day after that set aside for the wedding. The sad document now lies in the Library of Congress in Washington.

Late the same evening a messenger from the Vatican knocked at the door of the Princess's apartment in the Via del Babuino and delivered a decree ordering a postponement of the wedding while yet more matters concerning her divorce were investigated. According to her daughter Marie, a cousin of the Princess had chanced to be in Rome and visited the church; struck by the flowers and lavish decorations, he asked what festivities were being prepared, and was told. The old suspicions and animosities returned, and he succeeded – how, we do not know – in convincing the Pope that grave doubts still remained about the honesty of the Princess's deposition and that her documents from St Petersburg should be examined once more. Marie wrote:

This demand at the eleventh hour seemed to her the ultimate blow of fate; even *her* will was now finally broken. She declined to release the documents, and gave up the fight. She had transplanted Liszt to Rome to share in her new ideal and to have him as her champion in her crusade to glorify the Church . . . So the agonizing, attenuated martyrdom of these two souls now began, two souls who had meant everything to each other but who were now perpetually groping after each other like two blind people, without ever finding one another.

Love as non-fulfilment, as resignation – the vanity, the unreality of earthly happiness and submission to the decrees of divine providence. 'Our Church is so strong,' Liszt once said to Adelheid von Schorn, 'because it *compels* obedience. We *must* obey, to the point of being hanged.' And so saying, wrote Adelheid, he drew his finger across his neck. Liszt's acceptance of divine will was swifter, more complete than his lover's in matters of the world as of the self.

And the Altenburg? For five years it stood empty, a lifeless shell. Then in 1867 Liszt received a communication from Minister von Watzdorf that the house was needed for the new commanding officer of the regiment stationed in the town, together with his staff; the 'Blue Room', however, added Watzdorf, was still at Liszt's disposal. But nothing could be more remote, more painful, than the prospect of living there again.

Today the villa, though not the garden wing in which Liszt worked, still stands, divided into flats – grey, drab, with the scent of neglect that hangs over so many of the historic buildings in the country that has inherited it. One wonders how much the residents know of the extraordinary happenings that shelter behind the laconic stone inscription mounted above the door through which they pass in and out: 'Here lived Franz Liszt 1848–1861'.

FIVE

'Mephistopheles in the Guise of an Abbé'

Rome 1861. The opening of the last decade before the Italian government proclaimed a national constitution and made the Eternal City the capital of Italy. In 1849, in the wake of the European revolutions, the temporal power of the Popes had been abrogated and a republic declared, only for France and her allies to besiege the city and restore the reactionary government of Pope Pius IX, who continued to rule as an absolute monarch until the establishment of Italian national unity in 1870. Dogmatic religion reigned; the urban scene was dominated by priests, monks, nuns – and beggars. From the Papal court issued an ethos of celibacy, of denial of the pleasures of the flesh: the demand was for worship, fervent resignation and willing submission to authority.

Princess Carolyne had been living in this incense-laden world for a year and a half, alone, before Liszt arrived to be confronted with the frustration of everything that had given their life its meaning. Like him, with one side of her being she belonged to the world of religious absolutism that surrounded her, the world that denied them the fulfilment of their desire. But, also like him, she had a pattern of subjective urges that claimed their due. The problem was one of reconciliation, and on what, or whose, terms.

Liszt now faced the cruellest of ironies. He had come to Rome to celebrate a victory and had been met by a defeat. He could not return whence he had come, either alone or in company. Hitherto he had assumed his natural place as the focus of attention – first Liszt the lion of European pianists, then Liszt the prophet and promoter of the 'New Music'. Here in Rome, surrounded by the splendours of Antiquity and the Renaissance, aware at every step of the looming dominance of the curia, he felt his stature dwindle, his confidence falter. And if now there was to be no Madame Liszt, how could his life go forward? Or perhaps the prospect of a Madame Liszt in his life had been a chimera, a self-deception, a vision that had long been paling and had now, thankfully, all but evanesced?

Whatever the psychological to-ing and fro-ing within a strained and labile situation, the denial of his marriage to Carolyne von Sayn-Wittgenstein never ceased to be a source of pain and sorrow to him. He never withdrew from his commitment to marry her; had her determination persisted, his loyalty would have held – he was that sort of person. But was he, to use the vulgar phrase, the 'marrying kind'? Peter Cornelius, whose keen eye saw through most of what went on in the Villa Altenburg, regarded the Princess as the driving force, even the inspiration, behind the immense creativity of Liszt's Weimar years. But in his biography of his father, from whom the information presumably came, Carl Maria Cornelius wrote: 'Liszt's nature was not suited to wedlock in the slightest, and he could not be expected to marry an ageing woman. The Princess had once followed him and thrown herself at his feet. He was sufficient of a cavalier to humour her, and to his own surprise the affair grew into a great passion, which then eventually cooled.'

The Princess could not fail to notice the change in him and confided her fears to her friend and helper Adelheid von Schorn, who recorded in her memoirs:

> During the time he had been apart from her Liszt became indifferent: the intention of establishing a legal union with her was no longer a necessity for him . . . He was, of course, prepared at any time to lead her to the altar, but her feminine intuition told her that for him it would only have been a fulfilment of his duty, so she did not speak of it any more, thus sacrificing the whole purpose of her life.

Others who had shared Liszt's last eighteen months in Weimar also sensed that things had changed. Cornelius, who never had much sympathy for Liszt's desire to take minor orders in the Catholic Church and also felt deeply for the Princess during her unhappy struggles, came close to seeing Liszt as deliberately weakening the ties that bound them: on the one hand a disloyalty to the woman who had given up everything for him, on the other a betrayal of the artistic genius whose awakening and burgeoning he owed in large measure to her. Karl Tausig said bluntly: 'Liszt's whole journey to Rome was sheer humbug.' Wagner saw, with disapproval, the same dichotomy. 'Outwardly Liszt was too much of an Abbé, inwardly too little,' he waspishly observed.

Yet if the question of a weakening will on Liszt's part may be raised, so too may the state of mind of Princess Carolyne. When asked to allow her marriage annulment papers from the Russian

Consistory to be examined again in the Vatican, she had refused. A few weeks later she confessed to Eduard von Liszt, 'I have utterly failed.' In 1864, after the death of Prince Nicholas von Sayn-Wittgenstein had removed any possible further obstacle to her marriage with him, Liszt paid a visit to Carl Alexander in Weimar and wrote to her from there: 'The Grand Duke did not hesitate to reiterate his view that, since Prince Wittgenstein had now died, nothing stood in the way of the resolution of our problem, for it was inconceivable that one should give up a struggle that one had been waging for fifteen years when in sight of victory.' The Princess made no response. In a letter to him eight years later she wrote the sentence that summed up her attitude to the whole tortured, confused, unhappy, at times unreal episode: 'Fate did not wish it to be.'

And indeed, if Liszt's desire and need had waned, the Princess's will was now finally broken. The whole world had been against them – why not God also? She saw the hand of God in everything, and this, as so often in people of such propensity, inclined her to a mood of resignation in the face of every setback, large or small, and an accompanying reluctance to believe that providence might on occasion actually wish her well. Like Carl Alexander, both her friends and Liszt's could not fathom why she did not accept her husband's death as an act of divine intervention, as she had hitherto accepted all the 'slings and arrows of outrageous fortune'. Liszt's daughter Cosima commented: 'I have accustomed myself to the thought of understanding nothing about the affair, and feel only a great sense of suffering in the depths of my heart.' Neither Liszt nor Princess Carolyne had any longer the desire, the passion, the will to consummate before God and the world the relationship which for over a decade had given their life its meaning.

There could hardly fail to be times when they returned to these years in their letters, nor could their visions of what was, and what might have been, either be identical or remain static. Looking back in 1872, the Princess wrote to him:

At that moment the need was to seek something better, and providence led you to find that something better, I believe, in art, which took the place of what could not be brought to pass. It would be the greatest of mistakes, emotionally and intellectually, if you were to regret that moment. What failed to eventualize at that time was, in an abstract sense, something beneficial, for, in a concrete sense, the moment when it would have brought you joy had already passed.

It was a diagnosis that did not flinch before blunt reality. He now turned his back on the musical concerns of his Weimar years and looked to Catholic liturgy and legend for new values. She, tireless in prayer and devotional exercises, buried herself in the Byzantine intricacies of her *Inner Causes of the External Weakness of the Church*.

So they lived side by side in Rome, together yet apart, heedless – he for a while, she for ever – of the praises and blandishments of the world, bound in their individual ways to the ethos of the Holy City and servants of its ideology.

Service was indeed now the prevailing thought in Liszt's mind. 'I am firmly resolved to stay here for a considerable time and work energetically, purposefully and without interruption,' he wrote to Dr Franz Brendel, editor of the *Neue Zeitschrift für Musik*. 'Having dealt in Germany with the problem of symphonic form to the best of my ability, I now intend to turn to oratorio and related forms.'

In other words religious choral music now claimed his mind, whether directly for ritual purposes, like the Mass, or for the ennoblement of the religious consciousness – oratorios, motets, psalms. The music of the Church needed a firmer, purer foundation, with Gregorian chant returned to its rightful place, and this confident ambition – originally nurtured in the Princess's mind rather than in his – began to grow in his imagination. Pope Pius IX christened him, to his great delight, 'my Palestrina' and took a benevolent interest in his music.

As the latter-day Palestrina saw himself, it was precisely the coincidence of art and faith, the one sustaining the other, that conferred on him the prerogative to undertake his task and pledged him its blessing. The stronger his faith, he wanted to believe, the greater his art, and this was his answer to those who viewed with dismay the turn that his life had now taken. 'I feel a Christian to the depths of my being,' he wrote to the critic Joseph d'Ortigue, friend of his early days in Paris, shortly after arriving in Rome,

> and I submit my soul with jubilation to the gentle yoke of Christ, our Saviour, seeking in humility to act as His Church commands us in love to do . . . I shall not cease to be a musician by becoming more of a Christian – on the contrary, I hope thereby to acquire a more perfect conscience as a musician and fulfil my artistic calling with all the more strength.

A sense of inspired self-sufficiency came over him in this mood.

As he put it to Brendel: 'At my age what one has to search for is to be found internally not externally.'

Nevertheless, externally the cultured foreigner could feel very much at his ease in Rome. The English, the French and the Scandinavians – the plays of Ibsen were being hotly debated at this time – were all strongly represented but the German artistic community of over two hundred, the majority of them painters, made up by far the largest contingent. A Deutscher Künstlerverein had been founded in 1845 for promoting intellectual discussion, arranging exhibitions and the like, and the Pope himself took notice of their activities. Among those there for at least part of each year during Liszt's time were the literary historian Gervinus, the novelist Fanny Lewald and the sculptor Kaspar von Zumbusch, whose bronze head of King Ludwig II stands in front of the Wagner villa of Wahnfried in Bayreuth.

Die Legende von der heiligen Elisabeth (*The Legend of Saint Elizabeth*), the first of the large-scale products of Liszt's plan for 'energetic and purposeful' work in Rome, shows the direction in which his thoughts were running – and his difficulty, or incapacity, to find forms for their convincing expression. The figure of Elizabeth appealed to him for many reasons. She was a princess from his native Hungary and had come as a child to Thuringia, the province to which Weimar belonged; then she was portrayed in a series of frescos by Moritz von Schwind in Wartburg Castle, which Liszt had often admired and which revived in him his urge to enrich the art of music by drawing upon literary and pictorial stimuli. Above all, the essence of her personality, according to the legend, lay in her surrender to a life of charitable works, of ministrations to the sick and of severe penances, a life of devotion which embraced the values by which Liszt now, and for the rest of his life, set the greatest store. Here he found the same vision as that proclaimed by the *chorus mysticus* at the end of his Faust Symphony – life on earth as a mere fleeting reflection of the eternal and the divine, captured at its most perfect in ideal womanhood. And over the whole work hovers the aura of mystical Catholicism. 'It smells more of incense than of roses,' remarked the cynical Nietzsche.

In a work so permeated by symbolic meaning, explicit presentation must yield to allusion; what in operatic form would be acted out before the eye has to be conveyed through stimulation of the imagination. Since the limits of physical representation are soon reached, the profoundest truths must be transmitted by other means. So despite the readiness with which he responded to the attractions of ostentation and display, and for all the extroversion in which his music abounds, Liszt could never in his maturity write an opera. Not that the thought had not crossed his mind. The Archive in Weimar has a scenario, in French, for an opera based on Byron's historical tragedy *Sardanapalus*, and Liszt mentions the project in various letters written between 1846 and 1851, but only sketches for the music have survived. And not surprisingly. For Liszt's expressed attitude towards opera, in his article on A. B. Marx's book *Die Musik des neunzehnten Jahrhunderts* (1855), does not conceal his uneasy awareness of the limitations of the form. 'It lacks the indescribable magic of perspective, of semi-shadows, of Fata Morgana', he wrote, 'which allows the imagination to behold wonderful images. The inadequate realism of the stage hinders these qualities the moment it seeks to replace the brilliant visions of the imagination by spectacle and display, which acquire the quality of mere parody.' Even Wagner's operas, *qua* operas, could not entirely quell his uneasiness: he saw them as revolutionary music rather than revolutionary operas, works whose greatness resided in the totality of their demands and for which the term opera – or any other term, even Wagner's own 'music drama' – was utterly inadequate.

But in oratorio or dramatic cantata, as he saw it, the imagination would be stimulated, not satiated. The visions created by the individual subjective mind are stronger than any set before it by an external intelligence, and the sung text should be half of an equation, the other half of which is the creative receptivity of the listener. As with the titles of programme music – invocations of a scene or a mood, the associations of a name or an object – words would launch the work, but music would quickly assume its true role of opening the way to the deepest level of understanding. Wagner's scornful dismissal of oratorios as 'sexless operatic embryos' left Liszt untouched. Indeed, it reveals how wide the gulf between the two men could sometimes be.

Like the Faust and Dante Symphonies, therefore, Liszt's *Saint Elizabeth* offers not a continuum of dramatic action but a linked series of scenes, like Schwind's frescos in Wartburg Castle, each evocative of a particular moment – Elizabeth's arrival at the Wartburg, her marriage to Ludwig von Thüringen, Ludwig's departure on crusade to the Holy Land and so on – and each with its own inner musical logic. Part of this logic, and of the logic of *Saint Elizabeth* as a whole, derives from the symbolism of the melodic material that Liszt sought to incorporate in the work. The principal motif, he informs us in his note to the printed score, is taken from an Hungarian antiphon sung on the feast of Saint Elizabeth, embodying both the personal reference to the saint and the ambience of Gregorian chant. Likewise the Crusaders' March uses an old Hungarian melody that he turned up in the course of his searches. Such effective, if eclectic features, taken with the rich colours painted by a lavishly appointed orchestra on a broad canvas, made for an immediate success which no other choral work of Liszt's ever enjoyed. He himself conducted its première at the first Hungarian National Music Festival in Pest in August 1865. The following year it was given in Munich under Hans von Bülow and in Prague under Smetana, then, in 1867, in the Great Hall of the Wartburg itself to commemorate the 800th anniversary of the castle. Liszt dedicated the score of the work to Wagner's saviour, the young King Ludwig II of Bavaria, who had his own relationship to Wartburg Castle through the figure of Tannhäuser and the world of the Minnesinger and enshrined in his castle of Neuschwanstein the same romanticized ideals of religious legend.

Alongside *Saint Elizabeth* stands *Christus*, an oratorio in fourteen scenes to texts from the Bible, the Catholic liturgy and various Latin hymns, assembled by Liszt himself. Most of the music was written between 1862 and 1866; individual parts were performed in Rome in the 1860s and the whole work given for the first time in the Stadtkirche in Weimar in 1873. Like *Saint Elizabeth* it centres on ideals and symbolic values, not on biographical narrative. Inspiration and redemption through Christ's self-sacrifice and resurrection, through the peace and love that He preached – such was the effect that Liszt wished his oratorio to have. But the profundity of an ideal cannot guarantee the profundity of the work of art to which it may give rise. The earnestness of *Christus* does not inspire, the historical drama is not converted into vital dramatic experience in the music, and a solemn sameness droops doggedly over the pious choruses. In the last analysis its significance is rather that of an autobiographical utterance, vividly personal in reference, than of a work that can hold up its head proudly and independently in the company of *Messiah*, *The Creation* and *Elijah*.

In his appearance too the new commitment in Liszt's life showed itself to observers who, remembering Liszt the virtuoso and holding in their mind's eye a vision of Liszt the Grail King of the Altenburg, had expected something different. The historian Ferdinand Gregorovius, one of the German intellectuals and artists living in Rome at the time, noted in his diary for 13 April 1862: 'I made the acquaintance of Liszt, a striking, demonic figure, tall, gaunt, with long grey hair. Frau von Stein maintains that he has virtually burnt himself out and that only the outer shell still stands, out of which a tiny, ghostlike flame flickers up from time to time.' His public image was 'fanatically Catholic', Gregorovius recalled, adding that 'he also seemed to have a deep-seated need for work'.

Like his oratorios, so also the Masses, psalms, hymns and other smaller religious works to which Liszt devoted his mind during these years in Rome are conceived, in one way or another, as direct acts of Christian worship and veneration. This lies in the nature of settings of Biblical, liturgical or other devotional texts – Psalm 13 ('How long wilt Thou forget me, O Lord?'), Psalm 19 ('The heavens declare the glory of God'), Psalm 23 ('The Lord is my shepherd'), the *Legend of Saint Cecilia*, the *Prayer to Saint Francis of Paola*. But the same spirit inspires 'free' works such as the two *Legends* for piano, 'Saint Francis of Assisi Preaching to the Birds' and 'Saint Francis of Paola Walking on the Water', each of which is prefaced by a passage describing the particular incident from the life of the saint. This is evocative programme music in the familiar Lisztian mould, now sustained, however, not so much by spontaneous associations in their own right as by the contemplative purpose they were intended to serve. Experiences of outward reality lead inwards to the private world of the beholder, ministering to his deepest needs – indeed, to use a blunt term coined many years later, it is *Gebrauchsmusik*, art with an ulterior motive. Liszt saw it as music absolute and unconditional, music *ad maiorem Dei gloriam*. But it is a confined, monastic, albeit intense conception of the deity. At this moment Liszt is not merely half but wholly Franciscan.

His daughter Cosima put it in sensitive words after his death:

> He believed in a union of noble minds to build the *civitas Dei*. The loneliness of this task was one of the factors that made him turn away from the world spiritually, without, however, his being able to affect the quality of human kindness which, now devoid of hope, yet continued to shine forth from him, like the little red clouds we see in the sky at dusk as darkness falls.

He was driven still further down the path of religious commitment by the death of his daughter Blandine – 'Moucheron', as he called her – in September 1862. A month earlier she had given joyful birth to a son, christened Daniel in memory of the brother she had lost three years earlier. Suddenly a fever took hold of her: unable to eat or sleep, she gradually wasted away and died in her husband's country house at St Tropez, a mere twenty-seven years old.

To lose his elder daughter so soon after his son, and in the very time when he had finally surrendered his will to personal fulfilment in the company of Princess Carolyne, only intensified in Liszt a resignation to the inscrutability of divine providence. Two of his three children had been taken from him; their mother, once so dear to him, had long ceased to have a place in his life; the woman to whom he had desperately sought an ordered attachment for over a decade was not to become his wife; his work towards the ideal of a 'New Music' had been cut off in full flood. Withdrawal, contemplation, service were all that remained. In a letter to her father the year before she died, Blandine herself looked sadly on the unsettled atmosphere that shrouded the life of the family, with a mother from whom they had been deliberately kept apart and a father who was generally elsewhere:

> One of us [Daniel] was snatched away in his prime, at a moment when so many of his beautiful dreams could have come true. Cosima is in Germany, and I am alone with grandmama as before; you too are distant, as usual, and we shall celebrate the 2nd of April with the certainty that Cosima will be far away and Daniel yet farther away, but all united with us in our thoughts and prayers – especially in our prayer that all blessings may rest upon your head.

Cosima, locked in a marriage which brought her less and less joy, felt Blandine's death as intensely as her father and saw it as the final destruction of whatever family unity the children had managed to salvage from their dislocated upbringing. 'My sister was the most charming person I ever knew,' she wrote to the poet Alfred Meissner –

> beautiful, gentle, heroic, good. The unusual situation that attended our birth forged a bond between us three children which most brothers and sisters are incapable of imagining, and which I am now dragging along behind me like a burdensome chain. I shall never love anyone as I loved these two, and I feel as though my roots have been torn out when my heart reaches out to touch them. I am left only with a sense of emptiness. *Sustine et abstine.*

The last words could have been plucked from a letter of her father's, so careworn, so resigned do they sound.

Whatever Liszt's wish for creative seclusion, his presence in Rome could hardly go unnoticed, and from the moment he arrived his company was eagerly sought after, especially by women. He had lost none of his appeal. As they used to fight with each other to grab a half-smoked cigar that he threw away, so now, Gregorovius reported, an American lady seized the cover of a chair on which he had been sitting, framed it and hung it on her wall. 'If, like Liszt, a man manages to avoid despising the whole of the human race at such moments,' observed Gregorovius sarcastically, 'then he deserves high praise.'

In June 1863 Liszt left the Via Felice and went at the invitation of Father Agostino Theiner, the Pope's archivist, to live in the monastery of Madonna del Rosario at Monte Mario, on the outskirts of the city. 'My sojourn in Rome,' he wrote to his friend Dr Carl Gille in Jena, enclosing a photograph of his monastery,

> marks the third and probably last period of my life, which has always been troubled but always industrious and striving upwards. Thus I need a good deal of time to bring various long works – and my life itself – to a satisfactory conclusion. This need I find fulfilled in my retirement here. My present monastic abode provides me not only with a glorious view over the whole of Rome, the Campagna and the mountains but also what I had longed for – seclusion and peace.

He did not behave in the monastery as one to whom special privileges or luxuries were due. On the contrary, he lived in simple, not to say spartan circumstances, a far cry from the open-handed expansiveness that had filled the Altenburg. His one small room contained a table, a chair and a few books, with pictures of the saints on the walls, a marble cast of Chopin's right hand and – the only concession to his special genius – a battered, out-of-tune piano with a missing D. He also had two cats, which were looked after for him during the times he was away.

But that the man who had turned his back on the world to come and live in this monastic community was someone particular could not be denied when a few days after his arrival he received a special visitor. 'His Holiness Pope Pius IX came to the chapel of Madonna del Rosario', he wrote excitedly to Franz Brendel,

> and hallowed my quarters with His presence. After I had given His Holiness some small proof of my skill on the harmonium and on my poor piano, he spoke a few profound words to me in the most gracious manner, enjoining me to seek things divine in

things earthly, and through my harmonies that echoed and then faded away to prepare myself for those harmonies which would resound for ever . . . The day before yesterday I was granted an audience in the Vatican, and the Pope presented me with a beautiful cameo of the Madonna.

Heavenwards though the eyes of the Church may have been turned, the Vatican was not so preoccupied as to blind itself to the worldly benefits that the presence in their midst of a celebrity such as Liszt could bring. He was prevailed upon to perform again in public after a silence of many years, and in March 1864 played a group of religious pieces at a concert in aid of Peter's Pence, to the enthusiasm of the large audience and the gratification of the organizers. The Papal choir also took part, while to consummate the importance of the occasion four cardinals attended and delivered homilies between the musical items. A few months later he played again before the Pope, this time in the Pontiff's summer residence of Castel Gandolfo, where he laid before His Holiness his conception of the revivification of Church music on the basis of Gregorian chant.

Part of his time he spent completing his piano transcriptions of Beethoven's symphonies for Breitkopf and Härtel, also reliving on his battered little piano the greatest moments in the Church music of the past. 'For all my admiration of Handel, my predilection for Bach remains unshaken,' he wrote to Gille, 'and after I have edified myself sufficiently with Handel's common chords, I long for the wonderful dissonances of the Passion and the B minor Mass.'

Then, in August, came a moment both eagerly and apprehensively awaited, a moment bearing the prospect of a renewal of artistic influence and success but also the fear that a confrontation with the past would open wounds only lately healed. It was the moment of his first return to Germany for three years – a decision induced in part by an invitation to Karlsruhe to attend a meeting of the Allgemeiner Deutscher Musikverein, which he had helped to found, and in part by repeated pleas from the Grand Duke Carl Alexander that he should consider resuming his connection with Weimar in some form or other.

At Karlsruhe he had hoped to meet Bülow and Wagner – it was, after all, largely to promote his and Wagner's 'New Music' that the Musikverein had been brought into existence. But Bülow was suffering from one of his many fits of indisposition and had stayed in Berlin, while the supreme egoist Wagner, consumed by the joys of the newly found patronage of King Ludwig II and by his liaison with Bülow's wife, had his mind on grander things. Cosima, however, already pregnant by Wagner but as yet to nobody else's sure knowledge, joined her father in Karlsruhe and brought him some consolation for the absence of others. Consolation also came with the warm reception given to his *Festklänge* and other works played at the Musikverein meeting. Toasts were drunk to him at banquets and parties, and in the company of Agnes Street, the actor Eduard Devrient and others of Altenburg days, he once again stood in the limelight of praise and flattery.

Although peeved at Wagner's absence from Karlsruhe, Liszt allowed Cosima to persuade him to accompany her back to Bavaria and to the villa on the shores of Lake Starnberg which the King had put at Wagner's disposal. Liszt's ill-humour melted under Wagner's ardent, endless homilies on his 'Work of Art of the Future'; his old passion for 'Richard the Glorious' returned, and after accompanying him to Munich to visit the painter Kaulbach, he left for Weimar with lightness in his heart. Wagner, always one to surround himself with eminent admirers, wanted him to stay in Munich for good and was irritated when Liszt declined. 'Why can't he become one of us?' he wrote tetchily to Bülow.

Liszt arrived at Weimar at three o'clock in the morning, and since the only cab at the station was already full, he walked down through the dark streets into the town, brushing past the shadows of memory, crossed the Kegelbrücke and climbed the short, steep hill to the villa which had once been his life. 'The walls are chanting and wailing. And how many spectres I met on the way!' he wrote to the Princess. 'Schubert's *Doppelgänger* would have been the closest relative to that ghostly family!' More substantial was his meeting with Carl Alexander, from which emerged a gentlemen's agreement that at some time in the future he should return to Weimar for part of each year and give of his musical services in whichever form took his fancy.

Having described this cordial meeting to Princess Carolyne in one of his regular letters, Liszt was shocked to receive a furious reply from her, calling the Grand Duke a 'political harlot' who would promise everything but fulfil nothing. She could hardly contain herself when Liszt honoured his gentlemen's agreement with the Grand Duke a few years later.

After three weeks in Weimar Liszt travelled to Berlin to visit Bülow, who was smarting under the wound of his wife's affair with Wagner – though he apparently said nothing to his father-in-law at this moment. Liszt had never been so absorbed in his own problems that he could not open his heart to the young man he cherished as his own son, but he had had enough of Germany for the present. 'I find the German atmosphere unbearably oppressive,' he wrote to the Princess. So as soon as he could, he left with Cosima for Paris to see his mother. Now seventy-three, as sharp and direct as ever, old Anna Liszt lived in the big house belonging to Émile Ollivier, Blandine's widowed husband, and here Liszt joined her. Princess Carolyne, resolute of will and unyielding of conviction, was also there in spirit, for she had urged Liszt, it seems, to use his visit to persuade his mother to take the sacraments which, with her straightforward and uncomplicated relationship to her Creator, she had always regarded as the superfluous trappings of faith. No less resolute than her son's commander, she continued to refuse, seeing no reason to change her ways at her age and leaving him to confess his failure when he got back to Rome.

One embarrassing ordeal remained for him – a meeting arranged by Cosima at which her two parents were made to sit down side by side. Cosima had her own grudging admiration for Princess Carolyne but she and her sisters resented the influence the Princess had exerted, through Liszt, on the course of their education, and always made clear their loyalty to their real mother. For Cosima the occasion had a natural attraction, the more so, perhaps, because of the uneasiness and insecurity of her own ambiguous emotional situation between a pitied but unloved Bülow and an all-demanding, irresistible Wagner. Liszt related it calmly, almost disinterestedly, to the Princess in Rome. His final port of call in this hectic absence from Rome, which had filled a mere four weeks but had felt like as many years, was St Tropez, to say his own last prayer at the grave of his beloved Blandine.

October 1864 found him back in his monastery. 'It would be more sensible for my German friends to come and visit me here, instead of tempting me to go abroad,' he had written to Brendel at the beginning of the year. And some of his German friends began to take him at his word, especially musicians from Altenburg days, but also others to whom he had already become something of a legend. Kurd von Schlözer, a Secretary of State at the Prussian legation in Rome, observed him from close quarters and recorded in his *Römische Briefe 1864–1869* a number of deferential but not uncritical impressions. 'Everything Liszt says smacks of originality and inspiration,' Schlözer said, 'and one is always aware that he once held a position of immense importance in the world.' He spoke partly in French, partly in German, as Borodin also remarked when he visited Liszt in Weimar some ten years later.

Once the violinist Ede Reményi came, and he and Liszt gave a furious performance together of the Mephisto Waltz from Liszt's music to Lenau's *Faust*. 'When they had finished, there followed a typically English episode,' wrote Schlözer, who was among the guests crowded into the little room:

> A Mr Douglas, British Vice-Consul in Naples, who had come with Reményi, suddenly rushed up to Liszt and said: 'May I beg a favour of you?' 'By all means', replied Liszt. 'May I play just one chord on your instrument?' asked Mr Douglas. 'As many as you like', answered Liszt. Whereupon Mr Douglas strode solemnly over to the piano with the missing D, struck a chord, then took out his notebook and entered in it that on Monday, May 30, 1864 at four o'clock in the afternoon in the monastery of Santa Maria del Rosario, where Liszt was staying, he, Douglas, had played a chord on the great man's piano.

In April 1865 he performed at another concert in aid of Church funds, this time in the hall of the Capitol, playing 'Cantique d'amour', the last of the *Harmonies poétiques et religieuses* – 'and as there was no end to the applause, I added my transcription of Rossini's "La Charité",' he noted with pleasure. A few days later, in the Palazzo Barberini, he played his transcription of Schubert's 'Erlkönig' and Weber's *Invitation to the Waltz* – 'a curious farewell to the world,' wrote Gregorovius. 'No one suspected that he already had his Abbé's stockings in his pocket.'

His Abbé's stockings? The day after this 'farewell' concert, he repaired to the Lazarite monastery in Rome. Rising at half-past six each morning, he began the day with meditation; Mass was celebrated at half-past eight, after which he dedicated himself to the scriptures until the midday meal in the refectory. After a short siesta, more scripture reading, followed by a walk in the monastery garden, an hour's silent meditation and supper at eight o'clock, also taken in complete silence; the day closed with an hour-and-a-half's talk in the room of the Father Superior, and at ten he was back in the darkness of his cell. Then came the moment that consecrated these devotional preparations, a moment whose arrival was kept secret from everybody except Princess Carolyne, Cardinal Hohenlohe and the Pope. Liszt released the story in a letter to his patron Prince Konstantin von Hohenzollern-Hechingen:

On Tuesday the 25th of April, the feast of St Mark the Evangelist, I entered into the ecclesiastical state by receiving minor orders in the Chapel of His Serene Highness Monseigneur Hohenlohe in the Vatican. Convinced, as I was, that this act would strengthen my footsteps along the right path, I performed it without effort, in all simplicity and honesty of intention. It is consistent, moreover, with the early intentions of my youth, as well as with the line of development that my musical work has been following these past four years – work which I now propose to pursue with renewed vigour, since I regard it as the least imperfect manifestation of my nature.

To put it in familiar terms: if 'the habit does not make the monk', neither does it prevent him from being one. And if the monk is already formed inwardly, why should he not assume the outer appearance also? But I am forgetting that I have not the slightest intention of becoming a monk, in the strict sense of the word. I have no vocation for this, and it is sufficient for me to belong to the hierarchy of the Church to the extent that the minor orders assign. It is not the frock that I have donned but the cassock.

And your Highness will, I am sure, permit me the small vanity of mentioning that people pay me the compliment of saying that I wear the cassock as though I had worn it all my life.

In a similar letter to Hans von Bülow, telling him that he had received the tonsure – barely visible under his flowing, grey locks, Kurd von Schlözer rather waggishly observed – he added: 'It is superfluous to point out that this step is not unconsidered or sentimental in any way but rather a consequence of my manner of life over recent years.' At his audience of the Pope immediately after the ceremony Liszt said: 'Holy Father, there is a great harvest to be brought in – here is one more harvester.'

The four minor orders were those of door-keeper, reader, acolyte and exorcist. They made Liszt a cleric but not a priest: he could not celebrate Mass or hear confession, and was free to return to his secular status whenever he desired, even to marry. But he wore the cassock until the end of his life and wished to be known as the 'Abbé Liszt'. 'The Catholic piety of my childhood has taken on regular and regulating shape in my emotional life,' he wrote to Agnes Street; 'it is unnecessary to say that no change has taken place in me.' And although the decision was his, and his alone, the sense of continuity stretched back to his father Adam, who – could it have not been constantly in his mind at this time? – had spent two years of his early manhood as a Franciscan novice.

Yet however often he insisted on the naturalness, even the proper inevitability of his step, it provoked reactions in the world at large which ranged from the astounded to the sceptical, from the appreciative to the scornful. When Gregorovius met the new acolyte and exorcist a week later, he noted acidly in his diary: 'Yesterday I saw Liszt in his clerical vestments. He was alighting from a carriage, his black silk cassock fluttering ironically behind him. Mephistopheles in the guise of an Abbé.' Liszt's former disciple Peter Cornelius, now seemingly out of touch with the real issues in Liszt's mind, was incensed. 'I have no intention of writing to him,' he said to his fiancée Bertha Jung; 'I cannot agree with his becoming a cleric or with his behaviour towards the Princess – that deprives me of all sympathy for him, and when I wrote to her, I did not mention his name.' Some, reported Schlözer, even spread the story that influential circles in the Vatican, led by Cardinal Hohenlohe, had exerted pressure on him in order to forestall any amorous escapade he might be contemplating, since his relationship to Princess Carolyne had now perforce become purely platonic. But the Princess had indignantly denied to him, added Schlözer, that there was any truth in such a tale.

Anna Liszt, back in Paris, was taken aback by her son's action and made no secret either of her astonishment or of her disapproval. But her letter to him is also a moving tribute, a mother's expression of gratitude whose sincerity is not open to question:

People sometimes talk so often about an eventuality that it actually comes to pass, and that is what has happened with this change of status on your part. The papers have frequently reported that you had elected to become a cleric, and I vigorously opposed the idea whenever it was brought up. So your letter of April 27, which I received yesterday, upset me deeply, and I burst into tears. Forgive me – I was not prepared for such news from you. But after reflection – *la nuit porte conseil*, they say – I bowed to your will and His . . . It is a great commitment, but you have been preparing yourself for it on the Monte Mario for a long time. I have noticed it in your letters to me for some time past – they were so beautiful, so pious that I was often deeply moved and shed a few tears for you. And now in this latest one you ask my forgiveness. My child, I have nothing to forgive you. Your good qualities have always far outweighed your youthful shortcomings. You have always done your duty, thereby bringing me peace and happiness. That I can live in contentment and free from worry is something I owe to you.

So live on happily, my dear child. If the blessing of a feeble old mother can achieve anything with the Almighty, then I bless you a thousand times.

Less than a year later, at the age of seventy-eight, this far from 'feeble old mother' – 'a woman rich in emotion and in common sense', her son once described her – was dead. But she died at peace with his decision, as she had lived with self-assurance and good humour through the vicissitudes that his susceptibilities, his prominence and his unpredictability inflicted upon her. It had been a deeply sincere relationship between two very different personalities.

Some of his friends never came to terms with the 'new' Liszt, especially in Weimar, where the tall figure in the black cassock striding through the narrow streets attracted an almost startled attention. To Princess Carolyne, however, the person closest to Liszt and the first victim of his decision, it was a moment both of recalled dissonance and final resolution, a time for rejoicing and for sorrow. 'I feel both proud and sad,' she said. The soutane was a symbol of one side of Liszt's personality, a public testimony to convictions which the Princess had strengthened and made explicit in him – hence her pride at this moment, enhanced by her excited visions of him as the new Palestrina.

Her sadness, the other term in her polarity of emotions, rested on a fear that in bringing him to Rome she had been listening to the voice not of God but of her own selfish desires, however much those desires might embrace the service of others. 'I do not think I have done anything fine in contributing to your decision to take holy orders,' she wrote to him two years later. 'I may even have done something base and mean, sacrificing you because I feel at my ease here. Perhaps I am merely pandering to the egoistic desire of an old woman and cherishing illusory hopes – or am I in reality obeying the Lord by inducing you to undertake a great task in His name and for the edification of the whole world?' So uncertain was she of herself that the horrible thought of Judas Iscariot crossed her mind.

Liszt, who could act no less self-interestedly but had nothing to dissemble, saw no conflict between the call of the spirit and the renewed pursuit of his artistic aims. 'I will show people what music written in a cassock really is,' he said defiantly to his friend Kurd von Schlözer, Prussian minister to the Vatican. The paradox of the man, the coexistence within him, irrepressible and undisguised, of contrary forces that would have torn other minds apart or reduced them to nerveless impotence, again thrust itself before the eyes of his bewildered fellows when he came to dinner at Schlözer's house a few days after receiving the tonsure and, by inevitable request, took his place at the Bechstein grand in the salon.

'He sat at the piano with the air of a Mephistopheles,' Schlözer recorded in his diary, 'and cast his demonic glances exultantly to left and right.' The lure of the keyboard had not left him – indeed, it never did. A few years later Schlözer visited Liszt in the Villa d'Este, where he was then living, and found him sitting at a little dumb keyboard, practising a trill from Beethoven's Sonata Op. 109. He had always played this trill with the second and third fingers, he explained, but was now trying it out with the third and fourth.

Liszt as Mephistopheles – the equation has something perverse about it, and in Schlözer's tone of voice, as in Gregorovius', lies a barely concealed hostility. To be sure, the figure fascinated Liszt throughout his life: he wrote four Mephisto Waltzes and a Mephisto Polka, and no biography will fail to mention his grotesque three-headed walking stick with the heads of Saint Francis, Gretchen and Mephistopheles carved on its handle. But – if we retain the Goethean context – there is much more of Faust about Liszt than there is of Mephistopheles. Liszt was never 'the spirit that constantly negates' of Goethe's drama, the cynical tempter, the brash power-seeker; rather, he stands, like Faust, as the seeker after truth and striver after good, an agent of intellectual and spiritual progress, a man of human, all-too-human frailties but a force for the survival of positive values. 'Such a man,' sing the angels, after Faust's body has been laid to rest, 'we can redeem.' Who, at the end, would deny Liszt that same redemption, prerogative of the same credentials?

In August, four months after receiving the tonsure, he was back in Hungary for the twenty-fifth anniversary of the foundation of the Pest Conservatoire, sunning himself in the applause which his countrymen showered upon him. He conducted the première of Saint Elizabeth and the 'Inferno' from his Dante Symphony, and a few days later played the two St Francis Legends in public for the first time.

1866 took him to Paris for what turned out to be an unhappy performance of the Esztergom Mass in the church of Saint-Eustache. His old friend Joseph d'Ortigue declared himself unable, or unwilling, to give an opinion on the music. Berlioz, who was also present, kept a stony silence. Only Rossini, who had already conveyed his understanding of Liszt's assumption of clerical orders, found appreciative words to say.

Equally unhappy was a meeting, arranged against his instincts but on the prompting of his son-in-law Émile Ollivier, with Marie d'Agoult. Marie had recently seen fit to republish her novel *Nélida*, with its lampoon of Liszt as a mediocre artist impelled by an overweening self-centredness. Now she intended to go further. Liszt wrote to Princess Carolyne from Paris:

> She told me that she proposed to publish her memoirs. I retorted that I considered her incapable of doing anything of such a kind, since what she called 'memoirs' would be nothing more than lies and pretences [*poses et mensonges*]. This was the first time I spoke my mind about what was true and what was false. They were hard words but it was my duty to say them . . . Unfortunately there is no pleasant way of expressing certain things that are bound to offend people. One cannot perform surgical operations by waving a fan.

He never saw her again. And for whatever reason, she did not carry out her intention – or threat. Her memoirs, albeit incomplete, were only published half a century later, in 1927, by her grandson Daniel Ollivier. Inevitably the accounts she gives of highly personal episodes portray a very different set of circumstances and motifs from those that he describes, and much is related in an emotional, high-pitched tone that tempts one to say, with the Queen in *Hamlet*, 'The lady doth protest too much, methinks.' There is no shortage, one suspects, of 'pretences'; about the 'lies' one may need to be a little more reticent.

The following year Liszt attended the annual festival of the Allgemeiner Deutscher Musikverein in Meiningen and a performance of *Saint Elizabeth* in its spiritual home of Wartburg Castle, while Rome itself – more accurately, the Vatican, his spiritual and temporal master – heard him play and conduct from among his copious new works of religious afflatus. Further decorations and honours, mere fugitive symbols of esteem but gestures he delightedly acknowledged, swelled his already considerable cachet – the Bavarian Order of St Michael, the French Order of Guadeloupe and, following the performance of his Coronation

Mass in Budapest in June 1867, Commander of the Order of Franz Joseph, conferred by the Austrian Emperor.

In February 1867 a fourth daughter, christened Eva, was born to Cosima in Tribschen, the villa on the shore of Lake Lucerne where Wagner was living. Hans von Bülow, who had for months been a miserable, helpless spectator to the affair between his wife and Wagner, had no illusions about whose child Eva was (her third daughter, Isolde, was also Wagner's; only her two eldest, Daniela and Blandine, were Bülow's). When he received the news, he went to Tribschen from Basel, where he was then teaching, approached Cosima's bedside and murmured: 'Je pardonne.' 'Il ne faut pas pardonner,' replied Cosima, 'il faut comprendre.'

Liszt could readily understand but found it harder to forgive. He was caught between two sets of conflicting loyalties – to his daughter and his favourite pupil on the one hand, to his artistic idol, the greatest composer of the age, on the other. His often strained but never broken loyalty to Cosima implied both a tolerance of her adultery and an acceptance of Bülow's degradation, yet with neither of these realities could he make his peace. That both he and his daughter were Catholics only heightened the embarrassment, and he felt deeply offended when she renounced her faith two years after marrying Wagner.

So when, in the course of his tour of Germany in the summer of 1867, he raised the question of a visit to Tribschen, a certain uneasiness and trepidation lay over the event. For Liszt it was an act part duty, part pleasure, half feared, half eagerly awaited. Wagner too found the prospect unsettling. 'Visit by Liszt. Dreaded it but proved pleasurable,' he wrote afterwards in his *Annals*. And indeed they did succeed in recapturing much of their earlier spontaneity and rapport. Wagner had almost finished scoring his *Meistersinger*, and the two men performed large parts of the work together, Wagner singing the vocal parts, Liszt accompanying him on the piano. But the irregularity of the domestic situation, and the mortification of Bülow, for which he made Cosima more responsible than her lover, quickly came over him again. He did not attend their wedding in 1870, and for five years father and daughter exchanged nothing but cold formalities. Her apparent hardness towards him persisted right down to his death, showing itself in a form which many at that time called callousness.

One will hardly imagine that the hand of the *éminence grise* cannot be detected in this confusion of emotions. The Princess's relationship to Cosima had barely ever attained cordiality, while for Wagner the man and musician she felt a jealousy and animosity that were warmly reciprocated. For a long while she tried to keep the wound open. But Liszt could not live in an environment of antagonisms. As Wagner's stature grew with the foundation of the Bayreuth Festival, so also did Liszt's sense of awe and wonder, and he brooked no infringement of his conviction of Wagner's greatness. That he died in Wagner's adopted town during a festival of Wagner's works has its own poignant appropriateness.

The *Missa Choralis* for choir and organ, part polyphonic, part hymnic, using Gregorian melodies; the completion of the final numbers of the oratorio *Christus*; a Hymn to the Pope; the Hungarian Coronation Mass for the enthronement of the Emperor Franz Joseph I – 'musically a pretty feeble work', Liszt described it, though it still retains its popularity in Hungary: such were some of the contributions of Liszt's Franciscan half to the interests of the Church. The other half – the gypsy, the showman, Mephistopheles or whatever else it had been christened – occupied itself with the two so-called piano 'Illustrations' to Meyerbeer's *L'Africaine*, the Fantasia on Mosonyi's Hungarian opera *Szep Ilonka*, piano transcriptions from Verdi's *Don Carlos* and of the 'Liebestod' from Wagner's *Tristan und Isolde*, and editions of piano sonatas by Schubert and Weber.

But firm though his professed intentions were, and prodigious his energy, Liszt's years in Rome had a strange diffuseness about them. A driving aesthetic impulse, as distinct from the pressures of religious consciousness and conviction, an urge comparable to that which had underlain the 'transcendentalism' of his early piano music and the philosophy of programme music that had filled his Weimar years, was missing. Liszt never had the single-minded determination of Wagner. But neither had he ever lacked grand causes in which to invest his enthusiasm and his energy. Now the grand cause was missing, the voice of artistic challenge weak. A violin concerto, besought from him successively by Paganini's pupil Sivori, by Reményi and by August Wilhelmj (later leader of the orchestra at the first Bayreuth Festival) in the course of the 1860s, never seriously occupied his thoughts ('I do not know when I shall find time to compose it,' he said airily to Wagner's patron and one-time lover Jessie Laussot in 1886). And an oratorio on the life of St Stanislaus, a project dear to Princess Carolyne's Polish heart, held his attention only in stray moments. Driven by no demon, he trod the same musical paths, secular and religious, as in the past – not from force of habit, for that would contradict his innermost nature, but without proof of irresistible vocation or of insistent creative power.

Indeed, his whole commitment to the art he professed seemed at times to be slipping from him. The American painter George Healy, one of the considerable colony of foreign artists in Rome, recorded in his reminiscences that Liszt confessed to sometimes not touching a piano for two months on end, while the poet Longfellow and his sister, who stayed with Healy on their European tour in 1868, observed that there was a thick layer of dust on the piano in Liszt's new, more spacious quarters in the monastery of Santa Francesca Romana, to which he had moved at the end of the previous year.

But when he did play, it was the old Liszt. He still delighted in embroidering the classics with his own ornaments. While playing duets with the young Princess Marie von Thurn und Taxis during a visit to the family palace in 1869, 'he amused himself by introducing variations while we were playing', wrote the Princess, 'and this threw me into terrible confusion'.

Nor had the cassock diminished his muscular strength, as Princess Marie ruefully remembered. 'He played on our poor little Pleyel the improvisation on Viennese themes that he had played before Napoleon III, and the piano has never quite recovered from having been at the mercy of the lion's claw.' Like many who were fascinated by the lion, Marie found Princess Carolyne von Sayn-Wittgenstein a far from attractive lioness. 'Her face was long and sallow,' she recalled, 'her cheekbones protruded, her nose was long and pointed, her eyes small and very prominent, and her large mouth full of bad teeth. Yet her remarkably ugly face was alive with intelligence.' But for Marie von Thurn und Taxis intelligence, like patriotism, was not enough, and she concluded: 'I must confess that, notwithstanding her extraordinary intelligence and passionate temperament, she always appeared to me singularly lacking in charm. I have never understood how Liszt endured her.'

The generosity for which many had cause to be grateful was as much in evidence now as ever. Before leaving for his habitual daily stroll through the city, Liszt would instruct his servant to fill his right pocket with silver coins, the left with coppers. On his return home his servant would find that he had given away all the silver to children or beggars and kept only the coppers for himself.

Likewise with the rising generation of musicians. When the young pianist Walter Bache, one of the earliest disciples of his music in England, met him in Rome for the first time, he was so overawed that he could hardly stutter a word. Mistaking Bache's nervousness for a prelude to one of the characteristic solicitations for financial assistance that pursued him all his life, Liszt took pity on the young man and immediately asked: 'Is it money you need?' This embarrassed the unfortunate Bache still further, and only with difficulty did he manage to stammer that it was for the inspiration of the great man's presence, not for his money, that he had come. In 1867, shortly after his return to London, Bache joined with Karl Klindworth, the pianist and writer Edward Dannreuther and Bülow's pupil Frits Hartvigson to form 'The Working Men's Society', pledged to propagate the music of the New German School – above all the works of Liszt and Wagner but also those of Schumann, Raff, the Dane Niels Gade and the Russian Anton Rubinstein.

The Abbé Liszt himself, in the *santa indifferenza* of devotional reading and worship, showed scant concern with publicity of this or any other kind on behalf of his music. In the spring of 1865 he had written to Jessie Laussot:

Knowing from experience how little favour my works encounter, I have forced myself to adopt a kind of rigorous disregard of them, a passive resignation. During the years of my activity in Germany I consistently held to the rule of never asking anyone to have my works performed. I even went further and actually dissuaded many people who showed inclinations in this direction, and I shall continue to do so elsewhere.

Three years later, shortly before leaving Rome, he revealed a similar diffidence over a forthcoming meeting of the Allgemeiner Deutscher Musikverein in the Saxon town of Altenburg. 'I have nothing to find fault with in the draft of the Altenburg programme,' he wrote to Dr Franz Brendel, 'save that my name appears too often in it. I am afraid I shall appear too obtrusive if a number of works of mine are performed on every such occasion.' And to Franz Servais in Brussels in 1869, with an undissembled bitterness: 'Will you please tell Monsieur Brassin [the French pianist Louis Brassin] that I thank him very much for not having feared that he would compromise his success as a virtuoso by choosing to play my concerto. Up to now all the best-known French pianists except Saint-Saëns have shrunk from playing anything of mine except transcriptions, since my original compositions are considered ridiculous and intolerable.'

Liszt had come to Rome with the secret hope that his impulse to service and his thoughts on the reconstitution of Church music might be graced with some formal acknowledgement from the Vatican – perhaps an invitation to conduct, or to compose some pieces for the Papal choir. But he received merely benevolent murmurings and a few visits from the Holy Father. No official appointment was ever offered to him, even of a liberal kind like that of Kapellmeister extraordinary at Weimar, leave alone anything approaching the status of 'Master of the Pope's Music'. Abbé or no Abbé, he was known to have arrived in the Holy City filled with the hope of being allowed to marry his mistress of many years standing, and, before this, to have brought three children into the world by one of a number of earlier mistresses. Such characters breed controversy, and controversy breeds enemies. A conservative authority like the Roman Catholic Church was hardly likely to smooth the path of such a man towards a position of representative eminence. Indulgence he could expect, and was granted, but not preferment.

The force of inward-looking monasticism persisted in his consciousness through the presence of Princess Carolyne, who had immured herself in her untidy, stuffy, smoke-filled rooms in the Via del Babuino with no other thought in mind than subordination to the discipline imposed by her gargantuan work *Des Causes intérieures de la faiblesse extérieure de l'Église*. His loyalty to her never faltered. But a sense of claustrophobia was creeping over him, the negative correlative of the wanderlust that belonged to his extrovert nature and which perpetually urged him, restless artist and compulsive actor, to seek the public context for his activities. The Grand Duke Carl Alexander had long cherished the hope that Liszt would one day return to Weimar, however little the opposition there to the man and his music might have moderated, and however persistent Liszt's memory of his disappointment and disillusionment. When the two men met at the Römisches Haus in Weimar in the summer of 1864, they had agreed to a loose association between Liszt and the Grand Duchy from some moment in the future when – or if – his total commitment to Rome should slacken.

When Liszt told her of the arrangement, Princess Carolyne viewed the prospect with horror. 'Not that I see Rome through rose-coloured spectacles,' came her response:

I am well aware of its disorders and imperfections. If the question were asked: 'Of what do you have more here than you would have there?', the answer would be 'Virtually nothing.' But to the question 'Of what do you have less here?' the answer would be 'A great deal.' The lies, the temptations, the subtle disparagements, making things appear what they are not – this, at least, is not to be found here. Sacha does not deserve you, nor can he give you what you deserve.

Liszt, on the contrary, did think that Carl Alexander could give him at least part of what he wanted, and in early January 1869 he took the night train from Rome via Florence, Padua and Verona to Munich, where he arrived two days later at five o'clock in the morning. After a rest in Munich he started out on the final stage of the wearisome journey, reaching a cold, dark Weimar at midnight. It was no longer the Weimar he had once cherished, the Weimar of his romantic 'New Music', of the Villa Altenburg. But it was to offer him a generous refuge for part of every year from now until he died.

SIX

'My Three-pronged Life'

I shall not be able to decide about my proposed stay in Weimar until the end of the year. Till then I shall stay quietly here or nearby, in the area that extends as far as the maritime baths at Ancona. I have had to politely decline a number of other invitations. Next year a considerable change may well take place in my external circumstances and draw me closer to Germany again. But what form this last chapter of my life will take, I cannot yet tell.

That Liszt should feel, when he put this in a letter to Dr Franz Brendel from Rome in June 1868, that his ties with Germany would grow closer in the years to come, had its conscious roots in his dissatisfaction with the conditions of his artistic life in Rome and his awareness of Carl Alexander's beckoning hand in Weimar. But that he was entering 'the last chapter of his life' was an uncanny presentiment. He was fifty-seven, still in grateful possession of reasonably sound health, still able to drive himself hard, still possessed of the magnanimity of temperament that made him eager to give to the world and receive from it.

Yet his creative life at its most compelling and most vital lay behind him. Stagnation was not an estate he knew, nor was lethargy. But a driving sense of irresistible purpose had deserted him, and although many of the younger generation were still to respond to his magnetic appeal as a teacher, a sustained originality of mind never returned to him as a composer, however striking the occasional thought or the fleeting intention. Gone too was the urge to write about the world around him – about the social scene, about his fellow-composers, about his visions of the future, in so far as they had not faded into the light of common day. There is a sad symbolism in the restless wandering of the last fifteen years of his life – Weimar, Budapest, Rome, Bayreuth, Vienna, Berlin, Paris, everywhere welcomed, everywhere fêted, but nowhere

TOP LEFT Princess Carolyne von Sayn-Wittgenstein and her daughter Marie. Photograph by Louis Held of Weimar after a lithograph by C. Fischer, *ca.* 1844. Princess Carolyne, of Polish descent, left her Russian husband in 1848 with her daughter Marie to live with Liszt in Weimar but never married him.

TOP RIGHT Franz Liszt. Portrait by the American artist George Healy, Rome, 1868.

ABOVE View of Buda and Pest, 1854. Lithograph by F. Sandmann. The twin towns, on either side of the Danube, were united in 1872. From that year onwards Liszt spent part of every year here until his death.

TOP Liszt playing in the salon of the Wagner villa of Wahnfried in Bayreuth. Wagner is seated left centre, holding a score; Cosima and her son Siegfried are in the left foreground; in the chair on the left of the table in the centre is the conductor Hermann Levi, and turning over the pages for Liszt is Hans Richter.

ABOVE LEFT Liszt in 1883. Photograph by Nadar.

ABOVE RIGHT Liszt's Bechstein grand piano in the salon of the Hofgärtnerei in Weimar, his principal residence from 1869 until his death in 1886, and now a Liszt Museum. The instrument was presented by the manufacturer to Liszt at the time he took up residence.

Manuscript of the opening of Liszt's Hungarian
Rhapsody No 4 in E flat.

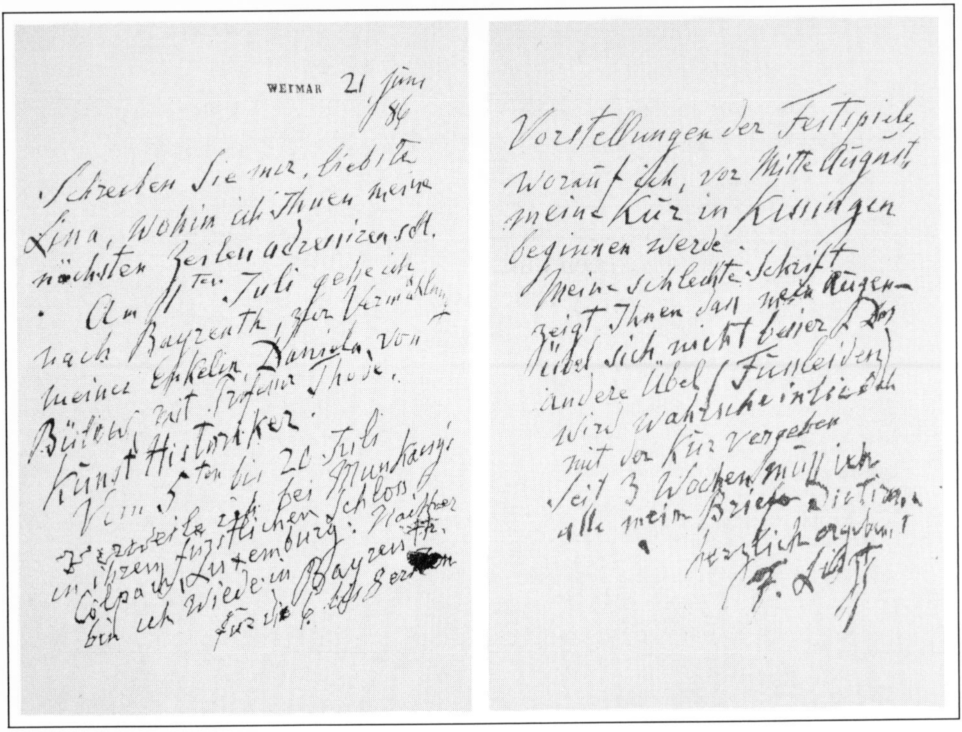

WEIMAR 21 Juni 86

[handwritten letter facsimile, two pages]

ABOVE Letter from Liszt to his young friend Lina Schmalhausen, written a little over a month before his death. The text reads in translation:

Write and tell me, dearest Lina, where to address my next letter. On July 1st I shall go to Bayreuth for the wedding of my granddaughter Daniela von Bülow to the art historian Professor Thode. From July 5th to 20th I shall be with the Munkacsys on their princely estate of Colpach in Luxemburg; after that I shall be back in Bayreuth for the first six to eight performances at the Festival, and shall then, before the middle of August, begin my health cure in Kissingen.

My bad handwriting shows you that my eye complaint is getting no better. The other ailment (my foot condition) will probably pass during my health cure. For the last three weeks I have had to dictate all my letters.

With most sincere devotion
F. Liszt

RIGHT Liszt's funeral procession moving through the streets of Bayreuth, 3 August 1886. Contemporary print.

absolutely, unreservedly at home. It was autumn, the time when fullness had passed, the time which the poet Rilke mourned in black resignation: 'He who has still no home will never build one now.'

But when he arrived in Weimar that winter night in 1869, a home did seem to have been built for him. On the western flank of the park through which the little River Ilm threaded its gentle way stood a two-storeyed, eighteenth-century house, plain and stocky, in which the Grand Duke's head gardener lived – the so-called Hofgärtnerei. The gardener lived on the ground floor: the second floor Carl Alexander had decorated and furnished in an elegance befitting the status of the man he now invited to occupy it for as long as he wished.

Liszt was enchanted. 'People tell me,' he wrote to Princess Carolyne, 'that the Grand Duchess and her daughters went to a great deal of trouble over choosing the carpets, the curtains and so on. Indeed, the whole apartment has a "Wagnerian" luxury about it to which the good citizens of Weimar are quite unaccustomed.' The Princess did not readily make her peace with his desertion, as she saw it, of his vocation in Rome, and while solicitous of his well-being, also felt entitled to be kept informed, like a father-confessor, of every movement in his life. Since she could no longer watch over him herself, she charged young Adelheid von Schorn, daughter of the Henriette von Schorn who had been among the few Weimar courtiers to hold faithfully to Liszt and his Princess during their years in the Villa Altenburg, to observe and report on the minutiae of his daily life. 'Assume your place by his side in my name,' the Princess instructed her, 'lest others assume it . . . And take control of his household little by little.'

His modest apartment in the Hofgärtnerei was a far cry from the mansion on the Altenburg, a mere half-mile away on the other side of the river. Only one of the four rooms had any pretensions to grandeur – the light, spacious salon divisible in the centre by crimson curtains, which served as reception room, study and music room. A concert Bechstein, presented by the famous Berlin manufacturer to Liszt at the time he took up residence, stood by the windows on the east-facing side; to the south, between sofas, armchairs, tables and his writing-desk, the view stretched out across the park towards the Römisches Haus and the Belvedere. On a smaller writing-desk in a corner stood a marble bust of Countess Marie von Mouchanov-Kalergis, a long-standing supporter of both Liszt and Wagner, and on the wall above it hung a chalk sketch of Beethoven. From the salon a door led to the small bedroom, and overlooking the road was the dining-room; finally, with a window facing towards the town, there was a small chamber for his manservant. Liszt had a succession of servants during his latter years, and though increasingly dependent on them for day-to-day services, had his difficulties with each in turn and sometimes wondered whether he would not have been better off alone.

In the settled serenity of the Hofgärtnerei, ran Carl Alexander's secret hope, Liszt would again turn the eyes of the musical world towards Weimar, reviving memories of his reign in the Villa Altenburg in the 1850s and perpetuating the humanistic cultural tradition of Goethe, Schiller and Herder. Liszt himself, indeed, could also see part of his life in such terms. But only part of it. As a comprehensive mode of existence, it left too many vital parts of his nature untouched, too many demands unfulfilled, among them the inspiration and solace of a Catholic environment. By Easter he had returned to the quarters in the Villa d'Este which Cardinal Hohenlohe always kept free for him. 'The days slip by swiftly and peacefully,' he wrote to the Cardinal. 'I have no need to search for my Eldorado – I have found it, here in my tower and on my terrace.' And here he stayed with the occasional excursion to Munich, Vienna and elsewhere for the best part of another year, resuming his mingled life of religious contemplation, of earnest conversation with Princess Carolyne and social gatherings with the German community in Rome, and of desultory work on transcriptions and arrangements of his own music. His occasional recitals for charity were high points in the social calendar. 'The news that Liszt was going to play again spread like wildfire in Rome,' wrote his pupil Nadine Helbig, wife of the archaeologist Wolfgang Helbig, in her memoirs,

> and Englishmen, Americans and all his other friends fell over each other to get tickets. The number of trains on the recently completed railway line from the city was quadrupled and they rolled incessantly past, while a stream of coaches was spread out along the road through the Campagna like a solid black line. Not for centuries had Tivoli been so crowded with people.

During his visit to Munich in September for the first performance of *Das Rheingold* he met the Russian critic Vladimir Stasov, who had last seen him twenty-five years ago and was eager to see how the great virtuoso of those days had changed. 'The Liszt I now saw was an old man of nearly sixty,' wrote Stasov, with the humble air of a monk, attired in the long, sombre cassock of an Abbé. But his head was still crowned by a thick mane, and his eyes had lost none of their sparkle, strength and keenness. When he begins to talk to you, his hands are folded tightly on his chest as if he were about to rub them together – a gesture of humility often observed among Catholic priests. But once he becomes caught up in conversation, his clerical posture vanishes. His movements lose their restraint and pious humility; he raises his head and shedding, as it were, his monkish pose, once again becomes forceful, dynamic. You see before you the old Liszt, the genius, the eagle.

But musically, to Stasov's regret, it was no longer the old Liszt:

In vain I begged him to play at least a few excerpts from his *Danse macabre*, from *Faust in the Tavern*, *Hunnenschlacht*, or *Dante*. He was adamant and replied to all my pleas: 'All these are works of *that* period! No, I don't play them any more!'

He did, however, play a few bars of *Ce qu'on entend sur la montagne:*

Then, as if he had suddenly remembered something, he stopped. He said it recalled too vividly an earlier period, an earlier state of mind, and he began to play his new Mass. I listened with deep interest; after all, it was Liszt playing and a Liszt Mass. But I thought sadly to myself: Why did Liszt have to change so terribly? Why did he have to become an Abbé?

A pleasant breath of cool, Nordic air was wafted into the chambers of the Villa d'Este with the arrival in the winter of 1869 of the twenty-six-year-old Edvard Grieg. Grieg, who had had much of his musical education in Leipzig, and to whom the German 'New Music' was a stimulating reality, had sent his Violin Sonata Op. 8 to Liszt the preceding year and received a characteristically generous response. 'Your piece reveals a pronounced and highly developed creative gift distinguished by a quality of reflection,' Liszt wrote, 'and this gift only needs to follow its natural bent in order to achieve real eminence.'

So when Grieg was given a government scholarship to study for a while in Rome, a personal call on the legendary Abbé in the Villa d'Este stood high on his list of obligations. It was the same kind, sympathetic man he found, the same dazzling, uncanny pianist of whom dozens had recorded their breathless admiration. 'He does not just play,' wrote Grieg to his parents; 'one forgets he is a musician, and he becomes a prophet proclaiming the Last Judgement until all the spirits of the universe vibrate under his fingers. He penetrates the deepest recesses of the mind and his demonic power strikes at one's innermost soul.'

In another letter to his parents a few weeks later, Grieg described a second visit in excited detail:

I had the good fortune to have just received back the manuscript of my piano concerto from Leipzig, so I took it with me. As well as myself there were present Winding, Sgambati [two of Liszt's pupils], a German Lisztian unknown to me and a bevy of the usual young ladies who would have completely devoured the Master if they had been given the chance. They vie with each other to sit at his side and look for opportunities to press his hand . . .

Winding and I eagerly waited to see whether he really would sight-read my concerto. For my part I considered it impossible, but Liszt took a different view. 'Would you like to play it?' he asked me. 'No, I can't,' I replied at once: 'I haven't yet had a chance to practise it.' Picking up the manuscript, he said with his characteristic smile: 'Very well, now I'll show you that I can't either.' With that he began to play.

When he came to the end, he gave the work back to me and said, with unusual warmth: 'You must go on in the same vein – you have all the necessary ability. And don't let anybody put you off!' This last injunction meant a very great deal to me. There was something about the way he spoke that made his words sound like a kind of blessing.

A far less welcome visitor to Rome in 1870 was a woman who contributed a bizarre chapter to the already colourful history of Liszt's relationships with women and made herself a small fortune in the process. Her real name was Olga Zielinska, daughter of a manufacturer of boot polish in the Polish town of Lvov, but she announced to the world that she was the Countess Olga Janina, and it is as the 'Cossack Countess' that she is remembered.

Hardly any other episode in his life, not even from the abandoned days of his adventures with Lola Montez, Marie Duplessis and an impressive cortège of aristocratic conquests, has stimulated so much inventiveness in the community of writers on Liszt. Right from his days as a child prodigy Liszt had been a figure larger than life; for her brief moment of shared exposure in his limelight, so too, in her intolerable, pathological way, was Olga Janina.

Nineteen years old, strikingly beautiful, married for a year to a husband whom she had horse-whipped on her wedding night and then deserted, Olga first invaded Liszt's life in Rome in 1869. Herself a pianist of some talent, she had inflamed her imagination with infatuated visions of the great master and now forced her embarrassing attention upon him, first at Santa Francesca Romana, then in the Villa d'Este, gaining admittance to his quarters disguised as one of the young gardeners on the estate who had been sent to deliver a bouquet of flowers. The whole adventure was made the more piquant by the thought that it was the Abbé Liszt, recipient of the minor orders of the Catholic Church, not merely Franz Liszt, the musician of legendary fame, who was her prey.

She then pursued him to Weimar and, the following year, to Budapest. He had been warned what to expect. 'In the middle of November,' he wrote to Princess Carolyne, having disclosed in earlier letters, bit by embarrassed bit, the course of the preposterous affair,

letters from Schuberth in New York and from Antoine Hébert [Director of the French Academy in Rome] counselled me to be on my guard against the vengeance of an hysterical madwoman. Madame Janina had apparently told her friends that she was determined to come to Budapest to kill herself and me. When she arrived, she came into my room armed with a pistol and several phials of poison, which she had already shown me twice before, the previous winter. Quietly I said to her: 'Madame, it is a wicked thing you are planning to do. I beg you to desist – but I cannot stop you.'

Two hours later Baron Augusz came and found her still with me. She announced to them in a loud voice that her sole purpose in life was to kill me and then commit suicide. I insisted that the police be not asked to intervene – in any case it would have been pointless, since Madame Janina is quite capable of firing her pistol before they have time to put handcuffs on her. The next day she left for Paris.

In fact, she did not simply 'leave' for Paris. Liszt had no wish to make a public scandal of the affair, which would have brought credit on nobody, but after a further attempt to poison herself in his room, she was deported from Hungary as a menace to public order and disappeared from Liszt's life for ever.

Or almost for ever. Two years later there appeared in Paris a book called *Souvenirs d'une cosaque*, bearing the author's name Robert Franz. It unravels a fantastic autobiographical tale of a beautiful young Cossack noblewoman, savage and untamed, a passionate rider of Arab horses, who marries when little more than a child and, after horse-whipping her husband, deserts him on the morning after the wedding. Rescued from a state of despair by the Director of the Kiev Conservatoire and by the beauty of the music of Chopin, she makes the acquaintance of the revolutionary new music of X in Vienna, writes to him in Rome, where he lives as an Abbé, and is invited to become his pupil there. After a few tender meetings he takes her in his arms and declares his love for her: 'Appelle-moi Ferencz, tutoie-moi!' They spend the night together, then go to Weimar, where various flimsily disguised characters from Liszt's entourage make their appearance, including Adelheid von Schorn, Marie von Mouchanov-Kalergis and a certain 'Madame X' who lives in a house opposite Liszt and has installed a telescope with which to see into his dining-room and bedroom. Desperately trying to rid herself of his love, she finally takes two poison capsules in his presence – she had intended one for each of them – but survives, leaves him for ever and concludes her story with the heart-rending cry 'Mon amour était mort!'

The *Souvenirs d'une cosaque* became a *succès de scandale* overnight. The following year the extraordinary Olga Janina – for it was she who nestled behind 'Robert Franz' – made an even more brazen foray into literature by publishing, anonymously, a lurid story called *Mémoires d'une pianiste*, put out as an autobiographical riposte to *Souvenirs d'une cosaque* by the Monsieur X, i.e. Liszt, whom she had presented as her seducer and lover. The whole bizarre story, embellished with racy episodes showing the hero in amorous escapades with other young ladies, is relived, with new distortions and imputations, through the mind of the victim whom Olga makes responsible for it. Finally, still not content, she revamped the entire ludicrous drama in two novels published in 1874 and 1875 under a further pseudonym, Sylvia Zorelli, called *Les amours d'une cosaque, par un ami de l'Abbé X* and *Le roman du pianiste et de la cosaque*. At the age of sixty Liszt had evidently still not lost the charisma to provoke the writer of fiction, as in his younger days he had lent his personality to Balzac for his novel *Béatrix* and to Marie d'Agoult for her pseudo-biographical *Nélida*.

Yet there is a sufficient coincidence of truth between known facts, Liszt's admissions and Olga Janina's technicolour narrative for much of the psychological detail in that narrative to retain its credence. The words put into Liszt's mouth need not have been uttered, and Olga, like Marie d'Agoult, was smarting from the wound of rejection and insult. But an apocryphal story can be true in spirit if not in letter, and the man who could at one moment burn with erotic desire and at the next give himself over to religious contemplation and penitential exercises is the man we know as Franz Liszt. 'Liszt's nature is too tender, too artistic, too impressionable for him to live without the company of women,' said Princess Carolyne to Adelheid von Schorn. 'He needs many of them around him, as in his orchestra he needs many instruments with a variety of rich timbres.' And as each new piece brought a novel orchestral experience, so each new erotic encounter both created and fulfilled a fresh emotional need. Even Olga Janina had intellectual and musical qualities sufficient to arouse Liszt's attention, otherwise he would hardly have written about her in such detail to the Princess or allowed her fate to prey on his mind as persistently as it did:

> It distresses me to see so gifted and intelligent a woman obsessed with pursuing a path that can lead only to her physical and moral ruin. For years she has been feeding her mind exclusively on the most perverted of theories and sophistries. Her staple reading consists of the blasphemies, execrations and absurdities of Proudhon and the new school of atheists, agamists and anarchists. Madame Sand she finds insipid and feeble. And as for poetry, she is mad about Baudelaire's *Fleurs du mal*. What will become of her? The loss of her fortune and a number of attempts at suicide are not the happiest of omens for the future.

There is one more curious episode that temporarily linked the lives of Franz Liszt and the Cossack Countess. In the early 1870s Liszt wrote a three-part piano tutor which, in the presence of the Weimar court organist Alexander Wilhelm Gottschalg, he promised to the Leipzig publisher Julius Schuberth in 1874 for the sum of 5,000 thalers. In a moment of characteristic weakness, recalled Gottschalg in his memoirs, Liszt gave Olga Janina the manuscript to take to New York, where Schuberth was attending to the affairs of his American office, together with a letter of credit for 1,800 thalers, to be paid to her out of the fee due. Schuberth gave her the money but she handed him only two of the three parts, which consisted of technical exercises. Olga intended to use the 1,800 thalers to launch a career as a pianist but her talent did not reach the level of her imagination and she soon returned to

Europe. Schuberth threatened to take Liszt to court over the non-delivery of the third part; Princess Carolyne, in a tit-for-tat, later demanded that Schuberth pay the remainder of the fee. The two sets of technical exercises were published shortly after Liszt's death. The third part, consisting of twelve large-scale studies, has never been found.

While the *bizarreries* of the Olga Janina charade were working their way through Liszt's life, Germany was experiencing one of the most momentous developments of its modern history. Down to the Congress of Vienna in 1815, which redrew the political map of Europe after the defeat of Napoleon Bonaparte, Germany had consisted of three hundred or more sovereign states of the most disparate size and quality. In place of the old Holy Roman Empire, which had survived, on paper at least, for the past thousand years, a loose confederation of thirty-nine sovereign states was established, the largest of them Austria and Prussia, followed by Bavaria and Saxony. But this was still a long way from the national political unity which had for centuries been taken for granted in England or France. The older the nineteenth century became, the stronger became the conviction among the Germans that they too had a right to this unity.

Initially the currents of liberal reform coursing through the country in the early decades of the century also flowed into patriotic channels, for the liberation and political self-fulfilment of the individual could be naturally and effortlessly equated with the quest for a sense of national identity and national destiny. As the century progressed, however, it became sadly evident that German national unity was not going to be achieved by consensus politics, by the free and eager assertion of the public will, but – if at all – could only be imposed by an authority born of necessity, the necessity of establishing a community of interests. What liberal, democratic urges failed to consummate from below was presented to the nation as a *fait accompli* from above – by Bismarck, the Chancellor of 'blood and iron', who used the weapon of war against alleged enemies in order to forge a militant sense of common purpose among Germans of north and south, east and west.

By the end of the third and last of Bismarck's successful wars, that against France in 1870–71, the moment of truth had arrived. Amy Fay, a young American pianist who had recently arrived in Berlin from Chicago, wrote:

The people just gave up everything and stood in the streets all day long on each side of the railroad track. The trains passed every fifteen minutes, packed with the brave fellows who were going off to lose their lives on a mere pretext. Then there would be one continuous cheering all along as they passed, and all the women would cry, and the men would execrate Napoleon. The Prussians don't seem to have any feelings of revenge but regard the French as a set of lunatics whom they are going to bring to reason.

There was universal rejoicing when the German armies, made up of contingents from all the German states, finally blotted out the memory of the collected indignities inflicted by France on Germany since the time of Louis XIV, and national pride ran high. What better moment to proclaim the Second Reich? So on 18 January 1871, in the Hall of Mirrors of the palace of Versailles – the very room in which the French were to exact sweet, spiteful vengeance in 1918 – King Wilhelm I of Prussia assumed the title of German Kaiser, to the triumphant sound of trumpets and drums throughout the German lands.

'The ideal of my art stands and falls with the regeneration and prosperity of Germany,' declared Wagner proudly. Liszt, despite his musical kinship to, and his unwavering support for, Wagner, and however much of his musical life had its focus in Germany, stood in the enemy camp, both as man and artist. The abiding influences on his early intellectual development had been French, Paris was where he had laid the foundations of his musical fame, and French was his preferred language. And by a quirk of circumstance it was Liszt's son-in-law, Emile Ollivier, widowed husband of his daughter Blandine and Prime Minister in the government of Napoleon III, who was called upon to proclaim the French declaration of war on Prussia in July 1870.

Bismarck's Prussia Liszt found brash and unrefined. Instead he lauded Napoleon III, seeing him in a noble trinity with Mazzini and the Pope as 'the wisest, most able and best ruler of the age', and when Napoleon died in 1873, Liszt looked to the time when he would take his rightful place in the Invalides alongside his uncle Bonaparte. 'A noble soul and a man of all-embracing intelligence,' he described him, adding, with more benevolence than political acumen, 'I believed, and still believe, that Napoleon III's rule met the needs and movements of our age more satisfactorily than that of anyone else.' With the defeat of the French at Sedan, a mere two weeks after the outbreak of the Franco-Prussian war, Liszt saw the end of his hopes for the assumption by France of the cultural leadership of Europe. 'Voltaire's prediction has come true,' he wrote to Princess Carolyne, 'the century of Prussian dominance has finally arrived.'

But, again unlike Wagner, Liszt never allowed himself to be consumed by the political issues of the day. He would briefly express a few thoughts in a conversation or in a letter, then return to the personal or musical matter in hand. In the months before the outbreak of the war he was back in Weimar from Rome to conduct Beethoven's Ninth Symphony and the first performance of his own secular cantata for the Beethoven celebrations of the Allgemeiner Deutscher Musikverein. 'As we watch him at work,' reported the *Weimarische Zeitung*, 'perpetually active, selfless, inspired, serene, whether helping and encouraging ambitious young artists or stimulating the cultivation of a new, noble idea, it is a spirit of surrender and love, of true humanity, of unflinching purpose, that distinguishes his every act, his entire nature. Yet at the same time what modesty pervades this dignity, this proud nobility!'

These qualities coalesced in the confusion yet magnanimity of spirit with which he received the news that, on the day before the war between France and Prussia broke out, Hans and Cosima von Bülow had been divorced in Berlin. Cosima was his flesh and blood. But Bülow, the wronged party, victim of the love between Cosima and Wagner that would brook no impediment, had his greater sympathy. He had not seen his daughter or her consort for two years, nor was the passing of the ice age of their relations yet in sight. 'I read some old letters from my father,' wrote Cosima bitterly in her diary in March 1871, 'which made it clear to me once more that I had never had a father or a mother.' When Wagner sent Liszt one of the first printed copies of *Mein Leben*, the manuscript of which had been devotedly written by Cosima from Wagner's dictation, Liszt was pained rather than flattered. He was more isolated than he knew, wrote Countess Mouchanov-Kalergis to Cosima, who added in her diary: 'A person who has always looked outwards and always concentrated on the outside world quickly develops an inner spiritual vacuum, and I do not think that a belief in the infallibility of the Pope can fill this vacuum.'

What Cosima describes, with no particular hint of kindness, is one side of the Lisztian equation. The exploitation of his transcendental pianism, a ceaseless display of his powers, the extrovert kaleidoscope of his personal relations, his constant occupation of the centre of the stage, his reluctance, or inability, to put down roots for more than a short while and, to the very end of his life, a peripatetic existence, the price of a freewheeling cosmopolitanism – all this made for the impoverishment of the contemplative, inward-looking side of his personality, a neglect of those values on which he would have to rely if the public world around him were to collapse. His retreat to Rome had been his way of acknowledging this and of trying to redeem it. 'Truly great men are those who combine contrary qualities within themselves,' he once observed to Baroness Olga von Meyendorff – a restatement of Goethe's concept of polarity, the necessity of complementary opposites, the Hegelian dialectic.

But his restless emergence from this retreat and his return to the old ways make their own statement about his psychology. In June 1871, as a further public gesture designed to draw the bonds between Liszt and his native country tighter, the Hungarian Prime Minister, Count Gyula Andrássy, appointed him a Privy Councillor with an annual stipend of 4,000 florins, in the expectation that a National Academy of Music would be founded in Budapest with Liszt as its director. In the event the Academy did not materialize until 1875, but Liszt felt he could hardly accept the stipend and the honour without offering something in return. Princess Carolyne, moreover, whose voice had to be listened to on this, as on every other subject, viewed Budapest, a 'capital city', with a far more favourable eye than sleepily provincial Weimar, which might, she dared to hope, be gradually pushed out of his life by the new Hungarian appeal. She even contemplated going with him to Budapest herself.

So from the following year, 1872, onwards, he arranged to spend three or four months of each year in Budapest, giving free master classes, as in Weimar, to almost all who presented themselves to him, and advising on the establishment of the new Academy of Music. From now until the end of his life he shared most of his time between the three places – Rome, Weimar, Budapest – which had come to claim their particular part, spiritually and materially, of his personality and his energy. The first three or four months of each year he spent in Budapest; shortly after Easter he moved westwards to Weimar, settling himself in the Hofgärtnerei with his retinue of admiring pupils but also, as in Budapest, paying frequent visits to the country mansions of his aristocratic friends in other parts of the country. Then towards the end of the summer, his teaching year finished so to speak, he retired to the Villa d'Este for the remainder of the year, there to give his mind over to composition and contemplation in the company of the Princess and of his freinds.

He called it his *'vie trifurquée'*, his 'three-pronged life', a description that has a positive, even defiant ring about it. In fact it conceals a rootlessness, a state of permanent migration, an admission that while to the outside world he was the hero everywhere in demand, in reality he was the homeless visitor, the man in permanent transit. In the shadow of the Franciscan tradition he had few worldly possessions and even fewer material aspirations. But it was as much the haplessness of neglect and uncertainty as the modesty of a self-imposed asceticism.

The sense that here lay a path which led into the intimate recesses of Liszt's being conveyed itself irresistibly to many unattached women who found themselves in his company at one point or other of his triangular life. In Budapest there was a certain Mademoiselle Hortense Vogt who followed him everywhere, claiming to be his wife and taking rooms in a hotel under this pretence until being unmasked and turned out. 'The said demoiselle refuses to give up the idea that it is her vocation to bring about my matrimonial happiness in spite of me,' he told Olga von Meyendorff, widow of the one-time Russian ambassador to the Weimar court, 'but I shall avoid calling in the police for as long as possible.' When he adds, 'Fortunately I am entirely blameless in this whole ludicrous and distasteful affair,' we have no reason to doubt it.

The Polish Baroness Olga von Meyendorff, whose husband died suddenly in 1871 when she was thirty-eight, had her own designs on Liszt. 'She makes an impression of icy coldness and at the same time of tropical heat . . . She looks like a woman who "has a history" . . . a type of woman such as the heroines of foreign novels are modelled on' – such was Amy Fay's description of her. A forceful, intellectual woman, not unlike Princess Carolyne von Sayn-Wittgenstein in her urge to dominate, she saw in Liszt a father for her four sons, and in herself a surrogate in Weimar for the absent Carolyne. He spent much time in her company during his months in the Hofgärtnerei, and until the very end of his life wrote to her from Rome and Budapest in great detail about the literary and philosophical issues that exercised his mind, sometimes as often as three or four times a week. We glean that he regularly read the literary journals from Paris, such as the *Revue des deux mondes*, together with Victor Hugo, Merimée, Balzac, Zola, Flaubert's *Tentation de St Antoine* and, years after first being swept off his feet by them, the works of Lamennais. He also struggled with Nietzsche's *Birth of Tragedy*, of which, at Wagner's behest, Nietzsche had sent him a copy immediately it appeared, but its direction of thought and its manner were totally alien to his own. 'I feel too ignorant to understand much of Nietzsche,' he wrote to Olga von Meyendorff, 'who dazzles me with his fine style much more than he enlightens me . . . Let us leave to others more learned than us these perilous paths of thought and remain at one in our hearts with our heavenly Father and His Son, Jesus Christ our Saviour.'

Gone, in these letters to Olga von Meyendorff, is that enthusiastic rambling through the implications of an argument which had filled his critical essays of the 1830s and 1850s. The Byzantine tortuousness of his style in those days imposed its own test of the reader's patience, but a sense of commitment glowed through the whole enterprise, whereas now, for all the undiminished need he has to communicate, a sustained concentration, even the old breadth of interests and sympathies, has left him. There is the occasional passing reference to Bismarck but nothing on the events of 1871 or the emergence of the new German Empire, no mention of Proudhon or Karl Marx, and only a single casual reference to Ferdinand Lassalle.

He received between fifty and sixty letters a week, he told Baroness von Meyendorff, but found letter-writing increasingly laborious. His constant travelling, often in uncomfortable conditions and at all times of the day and night, left no marks on his health: he had few physical ailments to complain of and made light of any temporary discomforts. 'Unusually for me,' he wrote to her from Rome in September 1871, 'I have been suffering from a disorder which forced me to spend a few days in bed for the first time in years.' And in response to a well-meant enquiry, he replied testily: 'I hate people worrying about my state of health, which is always sufficiently good.'

Also 'sufficiently good' – but only just – was his financial situation. When Wagner launched his scheme of Patronage Certificates in 1871 to help finance his Festival Theatre at Bayreuth, Liszt, in spite of his strained personal relationship with Wagner and Cosima at the time, was among the first to come forward. At 300 thalers each the certificates would commend themselves primarily, so Wagner reckoned, to wealthy aristocratic patrons, but Liszt owed it to his unshakeable faith in Wagner's music to join this company. He therefore bought three certificates, which, he admitted, 'given the modesty of my income, was no easy matter for me'.

The patronage scheme totally failed to achieve what Wagner had hoped. But as one of its unexpected by-products, the Bayreuth project proved to be the agent that brought Liszt, his daughter and his son-in-law together again after five years of cold, almost complete silence. On 18 May 1872, in the unpredictable way he could sometimes behave, Wagner sent a fulsome letter to Liszt, heavy with flattery and giving no hint that anything had ever been amiss between them. The 22nd of that month, Wagner's fifty-ninth birthday, was to mark one of the greatest moments in his life – the laying of the foundation stone of his Festival Theatre. He wrote and implored Liszt to come to Bayreuth and join the other distinguished guests. And indeed, had any man a greater moral right to be there than he? 'So if I say "Come!",' Wagner ended his letter, 'I am really saying "Come to yourself!", because here you will find yourself. Take my blessing and my love, whichever way you decide.'

Liszt was deeply moved. They were words he had yearned to hear, words that dissolved at a touch an unhappiness that had etched its way deeply into his life. 'I long for the time', he replied from Weimar,

> when all the unreal obligations that keep me at a distance will cease and we shall see each other again. It will then become clear to you how inseparable my soul is from you and Cosima, and how deeply I share the joys of your 'second' life, a higher life in which you can accomplish what would have otherwise been denied you.

Yet Liszt decided not to go to Bayreuth for the ceremony. Or rather, Princess Carolyne decided for him. She had no idea what Wagner's *Gesamtkunstwerk* was about, and had always been jealous of Liszt's self-sacrifice, as she saw it, to Wagner the man and to the unconditional demands made by his art. She also feared that Liszt's Catholic faith might loosen its hold on his mind under the persistent irritation of Wagner's blatant anti-clericalism and often cynical anti-Christianity, and time and again she taunted him with not living up to the supreme obligations which the soutane, public demonstration of his faith, imposed upon him. And he would not, or could not, assert his instincts, his desires, even his profound convictions against her. 'You seem to believe that the Princess exerts some kind of pressure on me,' he wrote to Olga von Meyendorff from Budapest in 1874. *'This is not so and will never be so . . . I retain my complete independence'* (Liszt's italics). Many observers would have begged to differ.

But although the foundation stone of the Festspielhaus on Bayreuth's Grüner Hügel was laid without Liszt, the strained silence of the last five years had at last been broken, and four months later, in September, Wagner and Cosima travelled to Weimar to visit him. His quarters in the Hofgärtnerei they found charming, and Cosima was relieved that his state of health appeared to be good. His mental state, however, filled her with alarm. 'I was horrified to see how weary he was,' she wrote in her diary for 3 September:

He scarcely spoke the entire evening, while I talked about all manner of things, and Richard, so as to keep the conversation going, engaged in a jocular argument with Baroness Loen [wife of the Intendant of the Weimar Court theatre] about whether his music was really as popular as people said. But the whole time I was haunted by a vision of the whole tragedy of my father's life, and that night I wept a great deal.

The following day Liszt played to them at her request – the 'Liebestod' from Wagner's *Tristan und Isolde*, Chopin Preludes, some Beethoven and his own Mephisto Waltz – but the joy of reunion had already begun to fade. Liszt seemed withdrawn, as though he regretted having shown so much emotion and affection the previous day. 'He played the Adagio from the Hammerklavier Sonata, quite deliberately, and scarcely gave me a glance during lunch but talked the whole time to Baroness von Meyendorff,' wrote Cosima. On the unpleasant twelve-hour train journey back to Bayreuth Wagner broke out in a fit of jealousy against Liszt, which, however, said Cosima, soon passed. As to her own feelings: 'I left in sadness. It was not the parting that caused me pain but the fear that I might have left him for ever.'

In October, accompanied by his valet Miska Sipka, Liszt made the same wearisome journey and paid his first visit to Bayreuth. Here, in fresh surroundings, and in particular away from the lurking image of the Villa Altenburg, he became more relaxed and more confiding, telling Cosima in private how Princess Carolyne constantly sought to drive a wedge between them and keep him away from Wagner's wicked influence. He did not even shrink from revealing that when the Grand Duke Carl Alexander heard of the Patronage Certificates which Wagner was canvassing for Bayreuth, he had snapped: 'I won't give him a penny!' Nor could he refrain from returning to the fate of Hans von Bülow, whom, he said, Cosima and Wagner would for ever have on their consciences, even though they had now been legally married for over two years.

They visited the site of the Festspielhaus, Liszt played from his oratorio *Christus*, and one evening Wagner read aloud the poem of his *Parsifal*. 'Father enjoyed Bayreuth,' wrote his daughter in her diary, 'but he is tired, so tired.' There was even talk of his moving there for good, 'for there was somehow the feeling that he belonged to us'. Two days later was his sixty-first birthday. But he left the day before and spent his birthday quite alone in Regensburg – 'this being the concession he felt he had to make to his relationship with Princess Wittgenstein,' added Cosima sardonically in her diary. 'It makes me very sad.'

Barely had he returned to Weimar than he set out, exceptionally early this year, for Hungary, making his way in the first place to Horpács, near Sopron, country seat of his friend and supporter Count Imre Széchenyi, who later became Austrian ambassador in Berlin. With Széchenyi and the composer Ödön Mihalovich, who was to succeed him as Director of the Academy of Music in Budapest, Liszt drove across to Raiding, the village where he was born. He had last been there in 1848. The Esterházy estate on which his father had worked was now rented to an absentee landlord in Vienna but otherwise, he wrote to his uncle Eduard von Liszt, 'I found no perceptible changes in the house since my last visit twenty-four years ago.' He had hoped to keep his visit a private act of nostalgic piety but 'the peasants recognized me at once, came to pay their respects to me at the inn and rang the church bell as we drove away'. Whether or not this happy occasion helped to rekindle a sentimental thought from the past, he gave earnest, albeit short-lived attention during these months in Budapest to the task of learning Hungarian, visiting a Piarist monk for lessons in the language. It was a gesture true to character, but scarcely more than a gesture, and if the spirit was willing, the flesh was decidedly weak.

During the Budapest season that followed he gave recitals in the Redoute and in the concert hall of the Hotel Hungaria, including one to raise funds for the deaf and ailing composer Robert Franz – the musician whose name Olga Janina had taken in vain for her *Souvenirs d'une cosaque*. Liszt had transcribed twelve of Franz's Lieder for piano back in the 1840s, and even if his essay on him (1855) appears to consist of little more than rephrasings of statements supplied by Franz himself, he remained well-intentioned towards the charming, gentle man and his charming, gentle music.

The year 1873 saw an even larger number of ardent young musicians flock to Weimar for his master classes. He accepted no fee and turned only the totally ungifted away, to the annoyance of those who felt that some of the rich young ladies and gentlemen present were wasting his time and had come only so that they could later boast of having been 'a pupil of Liszt's'. If such there were, it was a small price to pay for the legion of distinguished names – Eugen d'Albert, Moritz Rosenthal, Frederic Lamond, Emil Sauer, Alexander Siloti, August Göllerich and many more – that could trace their musical ancestry back to him.

How did these pupils see the Master? What form did his lessons take? What musical values did he promote? A colourful set of answers – a kind of companion-piece to Madame Auguste Boissier's memoir on his piano lessons in Paris in 1831–2 – emerges from a little book written by Amy Fay, described as 'une blonde et piquante Américaine' by the young Vincent d'Indy, who came from France at this time to join the circle in the Hofgärtnerei. Amy Fay had arrived in Germany from Chicago in 1870 at the age of twenty-six and first studied at the piano school of young Karl Tausig, Liszt's disciple of Villa Altenburg days and a stout supporter of the Wagnerian cause, in Berlin. Tausig died of typhoid in 1871, aged only thirty, and after a period of unsettled wandering, Amy came in May 1873 to Weimar, where she stayed for Liszt's summer season. 'He is the most interesting and striking looking man imaginable,' she wrote:

Tall and slight, with deep-set eyes, shaggy eyebrows and long, iron-grey hair, which he wears parted in the middle.

His mouth turns up at the corners, which gives him a most crafty and Mephistophelian expression when he smiles, and his whole appearance and manner have a sort of Jesuitical elegance and ease. His hands are very narrow, with long and slender fingers that look as if they had twice as many joints as other people's. They are so flexible and supple that it makes you nervous to look at them . . .

But the most extraordinary thing about Liszt is his wonderful variety of expression and play of feature. One moment his face will look dreamy, shadowy, tragic; the next he will be insinuating, amiable, ironical, sardonic, but always with the same captivating grace of manner.

That Liszt was the born teacher, not only the born virtuoso, emerged from the way he liberated his pupils' emotions and powers of understanding, rather than imposing on them his own ideological requirements. One day Miss Fay played the first movement of Chopin's B minor Sonata to him:

You feel so free with him, and he develops the very spirit of music in you. He doesn't keep nagging you all the time but leaves you to your own conception. Now and then he will make a criticism, or play a passage, and with a few words give you enough to think of all the rest of your life.

One day when I was playing, I made too much movement with my hand in a rotatory sort of passage where it was difficult to avoid it. 'Keep your hand still, Fräulein,' he said. 'Don't make an omelette!'

There was no shortage of such lighter moments:

Liszt sometimes strikes wrong notes when he plays, but it does not trouble him in the least. On the contrary, he rather enjoys it. It always amuses him instead of disconcerting him when he comes down squarely wrong, as it affords him an opportunity of displaying his ingenuity and giving things such a turn that the false note will appear simply as a key leading to new and unexpected beauties. So instead of giving you a chance to say, 'He has made a mistake,' he forces you to say, 'He has shown how to get out of a mistake.'

The biggest event in the Weimar musical calendar that summer was the first complete performance of Liszt's oratorio *Christus* – 'the last great victim of this Romano-Latin world', Wagner none too generously called it. He and Cosima came from Bayreuth for the occasion, bringing Cosima's daughter Daniela with them, but left as soon afterwards as they could; the Hungarian magnate Count Albert Apponyi travelled from Budapest, together with Mihalovich and the pianist Kornél Abrányi, Raff came from Wiesbaden and Karl Riedel, president of the Wagner-Verein, from Leipzig. Titled ladies such as Countess Mouchanov-Kalergis and Countess Marie von Schleinitz – names as frequently found in the Wagnerian lists as in the roll of honour of Lisztian supporters – also took their expected places.

After only a few bars of the orchestral introduction Wagner leaned over to Cosima and whispered: 'He's conducting splendidly – it will be a fine performance!' In her diary Cosima described the work in paradoxical terms that recall the influence of Lamennais: 'It is the formulation of a faith in a new order of ecclesiastical affairs established without faith, and the naïve expression of this far from naïve creation: a cultivation of the mass appeal of pomp and circumstance, though in the Church itself this pomp is merely a web in which such minds become fatally entangled.'

It could have been Wagner himself speaking – and probably was.

*

A similar glittering company assembled a few months later for the marriage of the Grand Duke's son Carl August. Liszt conducted Beethoven's Ninth Symphony at the celebrations and played Weber's Polonaise and his own Hungarian Fantasia, accompanied by the Weimar orchestra under Kapellmeister Eduard Lassen. To judge from Amy Fay's breathless account of the rehearsal, however, Lassen's presence could have been dispensed with:

> Liszt scarcely looked at the keys, and it was astounding to see his hands rushing up and down the piano and performing passages of the utmost rapidity and difficulty, while his head was turned all the while towards the orchestra, and he kept up a running fire of remarks with them continually: 'Violins, strike in sharp here!' 'Trumpets, not too loud there!' etc. He did everything with the most immense aplomb and without seeming to pay any attention to his hands, which moved of themselves as though they were independent beings and had their own brain and everything! He never did the same thing twice. If it were a scale the first time, he would do it in double or broken thirds the second, and so on, constantly surprising you with some new turn.

Such ecstatic terms, it might disdainfully be said, are only what one would expect from an infatuated young lady caught in the master's web. A witness of a very different kind, however, a student in Leipzig at the time and certainly not an easy victim of superficial brilliance, found his ambience no less charismatic. Charles Villiers Stanford recollected:

> He was the very reverse of all my anticipations, which inclined me, perhaps from the caricatures familiar to me in my boyhood, to expect to see an inspired acrobat, with high-action arms and wild locks falling on the keys. I saw instead a dignified, composed figure who sat like a rock, never indulging in a theatrical gesture or helping out his amazingly full tone with the splashes and crashes of a charlatan, producing all his effects with the simplest means and giving the impression of such ease that the most difficult passages sounded like child's play.

A quite different experience, Stanford saucily adds, from the playing of a certain young lady to whom Hans von Bülow made a deep bow and said: 'I congratulate you, Mademoiselle, on playing the easiest possible passages with the utmost possible difficulty.'

211

At the end of 1873 Liszt was honoured by the city of Budapest with an individual celebration to mark the fiftieth anniversary of the launching of his public career. *Christus* was again the work chosen as the musical centre-piece; the Order of the Golden Laurel Wreath was bestowed on the composer and a scholarship in his name established at the newly-founded Academy of Music. In place of his provisional quarters in the presbytery of the old church in the Inner Town he was offered a spacious apartment in the Academy building, Hal tér (Fish Market) No. 4.

The intention to entice him, by one means or another, to dedicate himself to the musical interests of the country that claimed him for its own, lay on the surface. And he submitted to the enticement – up to a point. 'I may surely be allowed to claim,' he wrote to his old friend and sponsor Baron Antal Augusz in May 1873, 'that despite my lamentable ignorance of the Hungarian language, in my heart and mind I shall remain a Magyar from the cradle to the grave, and I thus earnestly desire to promote the cultivation of Hungarian music.' But whatever his emotional ties to his Hungarian homeland, he had long since realized that Hungary was too small to hold him. It had been true then and was equally true now.

Yet, again as so often in the recent past, such a swirl of publicity could mask only for short moments the deep loneliness of the man. Acclamations here, honours there only intensified his awareness of the absence of a centre to his life, a single area of devotedness to which all else could be related – in a word, a home. 'I own no house,' he wrote to Cosima, 'and you know that the objects and pictures that I loved are not in the Hofgärtnerei. I have no rooms of my own in Pest and shall have to remain *toujours en vedette* [always in the limelight], as Frederick the Great once said, and as poor in spirit as in possessions.'

Rome too had sunk to the status of a port of call. But only here, he felt, did he enjoy the freedom from commitments which allowed him unbroken periods of composition. 'After arriving here on Sunday evening,' he wrote to Olga von Meyendorff from the Villa d'Este in June 1874, 'I have stayed alone in my rooms without stirring, except to go to the Franciscan chapel adjoining the Villa d'Este. I hope to continue this mode of life, which I greatly enjoy, during the summer and autumn.' And a few days later: 'My existence here suits me very well, thanks to its utter monotony. I scarcely leave my room and see hardly anyone.'

Except, of course, Princess Carolyne. His visits to the Via del Babuino were regular and frequent, especially as the Princess's state of health had become distressingly unstable in recent years, not least as a result of her unnatural, self-imposed confinement within the four walls of her musty apartment. She was plagued with rheumatism, and constant reading and writing in poor light had damaged her eyes. She had not moved outside Rome since arriving there in 1860; she went nowhere on foot – on the few occasions she left the house to pay a call, she travelled by carriage. Assorted infections and ailments confined her to her bed for weeks at a time but she did not raise her eyes for a moment from her gigantic theological treatise. It was a cruel blow when the unorthodoxy of her views, in particular the highly spiritualized and anti-authoritarian tendency that they displayed, led to the nine volumes of the work already circulated being ceremonially placed on the Vatican Index of prohibited books in 1877.

The musical rewards of Liszt's Roman retreat were sadly exiguous. Apart from *Die Glocken des Strassburger Münsters* (1876), a setting for choir and orchestra of a dull religious poem by Longfellow, he undertook little more than hack-work – arrangements of his symphonic poems for four hands, revisions of old transcriptions of songs by Beethoven, Mendelssohn and Robert Franz and of excerpts from Wagner's operas. 'You will consider this work superficial and not very important,' he wrote apologetically to Baroness von Meyendorff. 'I agree. But for want of anything better I am devoting myself to it with a kind of conscientious enthusiasm, and I fancy it is a better way than any other of improving myself musically.' They read like the words of a tired man, a man who sometimes had to convince himself that he was doing what he was not. Malwida von Meysenbug once said to him: 'It is good that you still remain faithful to Rome.' Liszt replied: 'I only come for the sake of one person. Otherwise I would not set foot in the place again.' Perhaps that laconic remark conceals almost the whole truth.

The Bells of Strassburg Cathedral 'tolled' for the first time, as he put it, in March 1875 at a joint Liszt-Wagner concert in Pest designed to raise money for the Festspielhaus in Bayreuth. He also played Beethoven's Emperor Concerto under the young Hans Richter – who conducted the first Bayreuth *Ring* the following year and later became conductor of the Hallé Orchestra in Manchester – while Wagner conducted excerpts from *Die Walküre*, *Siegfried* and *Götterdämmerung*. The usually so communicative Cosima maintains a silence in her diary about the concert itself, noting only that the rehearsal left a great deal to be desired and making clear her dislike of the Hungarians and their

213

country, where she found prices exorbitant and public life corrupt. She had already been nudged in this direction by the news that earlier in the year her father had returned to Budapest from Rome to find that his rooms had been burgled and his silver and linen taken. The thief turned out to be a crony of his manservant Miska Sipka.

Such an episode, distasteful in itself, could barely ruffle the surface of Liszt's blissful confidence in the essential goodness of man. The complete, naïve trust that he himself had in others he assumed they had in each other. He disliked sealing his letters because, he said, it implied dishonesty on the part of postal officials.

Quite apart from Liszt's activity and the final opening of the Academy of Music under his presidency in the autumn of 1875, Budapest offered a vigorous musical life of its own. Symphonies by Mozart, Beethoven and Schumann, Verdi's *Requiem*, various pieces by Saint-Saëns, Goldmark's opera *Die Königin von Saba* and Bizet's *Carmen* – 'music by no means boring, even polished, but of a kind most successful in Paris' was Liszt's verdict on the last-named – all figured in the space of a few weeks. Particularly well represented were the operas and concert works of the Russian composer and pianist Anton Rubinstein, whom Liszt met from time to time both in Budapest and in Rome, and whom he rated among the leading composers of the day. As well as Rubinstein, Paderewski and Wieniawski were to be found among those, professionals and amateurs alike, who filled the room at his private musical soirées in the Academy. 'How many musicians became known through him and owe any recognition they met with to the publicity he gave them!' wrote Count Albert Apponyi in his memoirs.

April 1875 took Liszt back towards Weimar, accompanied by a new manservant, a Montenegrin rogue called Spiridion Knezevics, who spoke German, Italian and Hungarian and brought impeccable references with him from his previous employers but whose overbearing ways caused Liszt considerable irritation over the six years that he tolerated him. He stopped en route first in Vienna, as the ever-welcome guest of his uncle-cum-cousin Eduard von Liszt, then in Munich, where he had hoped to see Wagner and King Ludwig at performances of *Tristan und Isolde* and of excerpts from the *Ring*. But the King was unwell and the performances were cancelled; some consolation for his disappointment came in the person of the painter Franz von Lenbach, whom he had known for a number of years and who did four portraits of him at different times in his life.

This year Weimar itself proved to be more a springboard for visits to other parts of Germany than a base for consolidated activity. At one moment he was en route for Hannover for a performance of his *Saint Elizabeth* and a concert to raise funds for a Bach monument in Eisenach; at another he was at Schloss Wilhelmsthal with the Grand Duke Carl Alexander and his party. Then, early in August, shortly before leaving for his early winter sojourn in Rome, he went to Bayreuth for the first set of full rehearsals of the *Ring*. Up to then rehearsals for separate groups had been held in Wahnfried, Wagner's private villa. Now that the festival theatre itself was complete, the orchestra, led by August Wilhelmj and conducted by Hans Richter, took its place for the first time, somewhat apprehensively, in the sunken pit to which the famous acoustics of the wooden building owe so much. 'There will be two rehearsals each day until August 15', Liszt wrote to Olga von Meyendorff, 'and I shall stay until the final chord.' With Baroness Marie von Schleinitz, the conductor Hermann Levi, the painter Johann Overbeck and other Wagnerites he also stayed on for the lavish garden party that Wagner gave in the grounds of Wahnfried for all his artists and technicians – 140 in all. At Wagner's request Liszt played his 'St Francis of Assisi Preaching to the Birds' – 'for the benefit of those in the orchestra who had never heard him play', wrote Cosima in her diary.

The same generosity and benevolence for which so many had had cause to be grateful impressed itself on those who met him for the first time during the twilight of his life. Susanne Weinert, governess to the Wagner children in Wahnfried, remembered him as 'a delightful old gentleman whose amiability attracted everyone, including the servants'. He at once became absorbed into the family life of the house, and Fräulein Weinert describes a charming occasion when, at the end of a day's rehearsals, she, Grosspapa Liszt in his black cassock, Cosima and the three children – Isolde, Eva and the seven-year-old Siegfried – all danced in the big hall to the waltz from Weber's *Freischütz*, played by Wagner on the piano. 'Liszt's relations with his son-in-law,' observed Fräulein Weinert, 'were cordial and intimate but also respectful. Each recognized the other as a great master.' Wagner was at the height of his powers, brimming with energy, about to experience the triumphant fulfilment of an incredible dream. Liszt, only two years his senior, seemed a generation older, a great figure with a past, not a future, recalling the description of him in Gregorovius's *Roman Journals* twelve years earlier as 'virtually burnt out, with

215

only the outer shell still standing, out of which a tiny, ghostlike flame flickers up from time to time'.

He even seemed to waver in his enthusiasm for the new Academy of Music in Budapest. His hopes of persuading Franz Witt, a church composer from Regensburg (home of the famous 'Domspatzen' choir), and above all his beloved Hans von Bülow to accept the first posts on the teaching staff came to naught but other appointments had been made – the composer Ferenc Erkel as Director, Robert Volkmann as Professor of Composition and Kornél Abrányi as Secretary. He wrote to his Uncle Eduard from Rome in September 1875 that he hoped to be in Budapest by the middle of November to attend to the affairs of the Academy, 'which it is my duty to fashion in the face of somewhat difficult local circumstances'.

Yet a few weeks later this sense of duty capitulated in the face of the allurement of the Villa d'Este and the presence of Princess Carolyne, and sheltering behind the evasive phrase 'all things considered', he wrote to Abrányi that he had decided not to come until the following February. 'By that time,' he added, in an uncharacteristically disingenuous tone, 'work at the Academy ought to be well established.' No less a person than the King enquired disapprovingly of Ágoston Trefort, Minister of Culture, why Liszt had not arrived punctually to take up his duties. His protracted stay in Rome produced the twelve little piano pieces called *Arbre de Noël*, but hardly anything else, save for a thematic catalogue of his published works for which the firm of Breitkopf and Härtel had asked.

A week before his return to Budapest on Ash Wednesday 1876, the countryside up-river from the capital was devastated by floods. The Danube burst its banks and made over 15,000 people homeless in the worst natural disaster for forty years, and the whole country – the King and Queen, the Church, the army and the civic authorities – immediately set about seeing that aid swiftly found its way to the victims. Liszt's characteristic response was to give a recital and donate the proceeds – a princely 8,000 forints – to the relief fund. In his eyes it was an emergence from retirement, a return to the concert platform which had ceased for many years to represent what he saw as the true course of his life. 'I hope never to play the piano in public again,' he said to Baroness von Meyendorff when he told her about the recital.

But he saw it as a perfect termination. 'In the year 1838,' he wrote to Trefort, when I returned to Vienna for the first time, I gave my *first* concert in aid of the victims of the flood disaster at Pest. It will be a comfort to me if I can now *close* my protracted career as a virtuoso by fulfilling a similar duty. I shall remain Hungary's true and grateful son until I die.

The concert tradition now passed to his pupils, and less than a week after his last recital in the Redoute the first concert by students of the new Academy of Music took place. In the first years of its existence Liszt took a master class of nine pupils, most of them women, yet apart from Sophie Menter, who came from Munich to Budapest, and Martha Remmert, who followed him there from Weimar, no woman has joined the famous names of the Lisztian succession.

Beset by the demands of the present and absorbed in the needs of the future as he watched the progress of the young musicians in his charge, Liszt was for a moment wrenched back into the past when he read in a newspaper an announcement of the death, on 5 March 1876, of Countess Marie d'Agoult. She was seventy-one. At her bedside when she died was the poet Louis de Ronchaud, a friend from her days with Liszt in the 1830s and her closest companion during her latter years as Daniel Stern.

No one in Paris had written to tell him of her death. Even Cosima received the news only after the funeral: she saw no cause to write to her father, and her diary gives no hint that he ever mentioned the matter. In a letter to Princess Carolyne on 14 March, his tone was almost callous in its fatalistic detachment:

The newspapers report that Daniel Stern has died. Casting hypocrisy aside, I could not bring myself to weep any more now, after her passing, than during her lifetime. La Rochefoucauld has well said that hypocrisy is homage paid to virtue, but one is still entitled to prefer true homage to false – except at certain moments of ecstasy, which she subsequently could not bear to remember. Moreover at my age condolences are as embarrassing as congratulations. *Il mondo va da sè* – one lives one's life, occupies oneself, grieves, suffers, deceives oneself, changes one's views and dies as best one can. The sacrament to be most desired seems to me to be that of extreme unction.

It was a sad way to say goodbye, a bitter denial of a part of his life which, for all its naïvety and improbability, was as authentic as any other. Perhaps its most tragic aspect had been that, far from lending hope of a reconciliation, the three unhappy children involved had driven the antagonists even further apart. Liszt had always claimed that he had done far more for them than she. Marie, in her turn, took this as a shameless act of selfishness on his part, which she was powerless to counter. To the very end it was the children who were the innocent subjects of their parents' mutual recriminations. Over forty years earlier Marie had concluded one of her last letters to him with the savage words: 'One day your daughters may well ask you: "Where is our mother?" And you will reply: "I did not want you to have one".' Writing to Olga von Meyendorff a few days after Marie's death, he made his own last comment in the same implacable tone: 'The only thing for me to do is to keep quiet and bury in silence the strange behaviour of Madame d'Agoult towards her children.'

But a dynamic event was about to dwarf all personal irritations, an event which symbolized the joyful fulfilment, on one plane, of the artistic ideals Liszt had tirelessly upheld, and sent a formidable shock-wave through the culture of nineteenth-century Europe – the inauguration of Wagner's Festival Theatre at Bayreuth with the first performance of the complete *Ring des Nibelungen*.

Liszt travelled from Weimar to Bayreuth at the end of July. Cosima found him looking well, and Wagner felt 'greatly invigorated by his presence'. But he was just one among the many distinguished personalities who had come to witness the fulfilment of one man's extraordinary dream, and it was that one man, Richard Wagner, who stood in the centre of the stage, commanding, cajoling, dominating. Two emperors were present – Kaiser Wilhelm and Don Pedro II of Brazil – the King of Württemberg, Grand Duke Carl Alexander of Weimar, the Grand Duke of Schwerin and other German princes, together with many of the lesser aristocracy. The contingent of musicians was headed by Bruckner, Tchaikovsky, Saint-Saëns and Grieg; Cosima observed a particularly strong British presence, with Stanford, Hubert Parry and Charles Hallé among those who attended one or other of the three *Ring* cycles that made up the first Festival. The writers Karl Hillebrand and Catulle Mendès, the painters Makart and Adolf Menzel, Nietzsche – who endured only *Das Rheingold*, then crept away from Bayreuth with fear and apprehension in his heart at what the Wagner cult might lead to – Otto and Mathilde Wesendonk, Malwida von Meysenbug, King Ludwig II of Bavaria, who came for the third cycle: such names can stand for them all. In this company Franz Liszt was not the celebrant but just a member of the congregation.

Yet he worshipped with the same gladness in his heart as those around him. Whatever personal issues had wounded their friendship – and Wagner's immense egoism strained any relationship – his conviction of Wagner's greatness and his support for Wagner's ideals never faltered. They were, after all, his own ideals as well, the goals of a 'New German Music' associated as much with his name as with Wagner's.

And Wagner, who considered that the world owed him a living, and who was not always the readiest of men to acknowledge gratitude, made public testimony to his debt. At the end of the first *Ring* cycle he gave a lavish banquet for performers and dignitaries in the restaurant of the Festspielhaus. After a sort of secular sermon, of the kind to which he was addicted, on the final words of Goethe's *Faust* – 'All that passes/Is but a Parable' – Wagner raised his glass and proposed a toast to Liszt. 'If it had not been for this man,' he declared to his guests, 'the world would know nothing about me.' There were not many such moments of unalloyed pleasure left for Liszt to enjoy.

His three-pronged life followed its now familiar path. After a visit to Hannover to see the sickly and lethargic Bülow, whose lowness of spirit, however heavily overstated, always evoked his sympathy, he paid his annual call on his Uncle Eduard in Vienna and reached Budapest in the middle of October. In the course of the winter season he played at two charity concerts and conducted his *Saint Elizabeth*, then returned to Vienna the following March to play the Emperor Concerto and the piano part in Beethoven's Choral Fantasia Op. 80 at a concert for the Beethoven Memorial Fund. Three public appearances in five months may be a far cry from the days of the Liszt of the concert circuit, but neither does it imply an attitude of total withdrawal. Many had heard and seen him play since Gregorovius described as early as 1865 what he called Liszt's farewell concert. Like many other performing artists, he retired more than once.

On his way from Vienna to Weimar for the summer of 1877 he went back to Bayreuth, now quiet and relieved of Festival fever, for another of his periodic bitter-sweet sojourns with his daughter and her family. The sweetness lay in the feeling of belonging, the personal joy of a lonely father in the presence of his only surviving child, and the profound satisfaction of sharing in the achievement of the greatest composer of the age. More than once Cosima and Wagner had begged him to realize how appropriate, how spiritually 'right' it would be if he gave up his triangular wanderings and took his place in their household. The bitterness spread from his knowledge that, despite its flickering sincerity, his relationship both with his daughter and with his son-in-law bore wounds which had never completely healed. An unpredictability of response, the compound product of a resentment of the circumstances of her birth and upbringing, the lurking presence of the first husband for whom her father had never forsworn his affection, and the unconditional demands made on her emotional life by the egocentric genius to whom she had sacrificed herself, corroded the spontaneity of his approaches to Cosima. Nor could he suppress the embarrassed feeling that Wagner was as aware as any unprejudiced observer of the decline of his creative powers over the past fifteen years, and that Wagner had no time for the religious values in whose service most of his music had ostentatiously been cast since he left Weimar for Rome.

Most powerfully of all, perhaps, the Bayreuth ideal for which Wagner lived gradually strangled, like the tentacles of an octopus, the lives of all around him. Freedom of reaction, independence of judgement were crushed in the name of a higher loyalty which knew no ifs and buts. This insistence on unconditional submission was, and is, the source of the opposition to what Wagner's music stands for, the source of the fear that the independent will and the independent judgement will be swept away. The man who set foot over the threshold of Wahnfried sensed the danger. The disciples gladly submitted. Those who would not, stayed away. Liszt could not bring himself to this – it would have meant denying too much that was dear to him. But he came with a step that was less than eager, and with a joy in his heart that was less than unconfined. Cosima too felt the anxious fragility of the future. 'April 3rd: Said goodbye to my father,' she wrote in her diary. 'Went with him to Neumarkt, where I watched his train leave for Meiningen. As I waved for the last time, he hid his face. Shall I ever see him again?'

This year brought two composers to Weimar for whom Liszt had a special admiration. First came Borodin, spokesman for the school of contemporary Russians whose music Liszt did his best to promote. Although Borodin recalled, in his account of his visit, that Liszt suffered frequently from abdominal pains, he was struck by his cheerfulness and lightheartedness as the conversation switched every few sentences from French to German and back. Liszt asked Borodin to play from *Prince Igor*, after which the two men played Borodin's First Symphony together as a piano duet.

The other visitor was Saint-Saëns, who had first heard and met Liszt in Paris in 1852 and been overwhelmed by his personality ever since. For his part Liszt declared that, apart from Rubinstein, he knew 'no one among contemporary artists who, taking everything into account, is his equal in talent, knowledge and diversity of skills'. Saint-Saëns came for his opera *Samson et Dalila*, which, due in no small measure to Liszt's intercession, was to have its first performance in Weimar at the end of the year. He was accompanied by Fauré, who had brought a number of his compositions with him, but after trying a few pages of Fauré's Ballade Op. 19, Liszt handed it back, saying he found it too difficult – not difficult pianistically, he could hardly mean, but conceptually.

The old freewheeling vivacity had not deserted him. An American, Mrs Margaret Chanler, who was at his sixty-sixth birthday party in Rome in October and thrilled to his look of 'penetrating intelligence combined with kindly gaiety', related an episode that took place at one of his piano classes:

A student played one of Liszt's Rhapsodies; it had been practised conscientiously but it did not satisfy the master. There were splashy arpeggios and rockets of rapidly ascending chromatic diminished sevenths.

'Why don't you play it this way?' asked Liszt, sitting at his second piano and playing the passage with careless bravura.

'It is not written like that in my copy,' objected the youth.

'Oh, you don't need to take it so literally,' answered the composer.

Yet this same relaxed, convivial figure could write a month later to Baroness Olga von Meyendorff, in a tone of barely conceivable gloom and depression: 'Let me tell you once again that I am extremely tired of life. But since I believe that God's Fifth Commandment, "Thou shalt not kill", also applies to suicide, I shall go on living, full of penitence and contrition for having publicly broken the Ninth Commandment.'

The pattern of his secluded, comfortable life in the Villa d'Este he described thus:

When Cardinal Hohenlohe is here, we have lunch together at one o'clock, usually tête-a-tête, and meet again for an hour in the evening, also without other company. The rest of the time I stay in my room, except for the morning hour at mass. Supper is served to me alone, and I go to bed a little before ten.

His daily reading consisted of the main Roman newspapers and various devotional works, 'together with a number of cantos of the *Divina Commedia*, which bring me comfort'. Playing for personal pleasure counted for little: 'I have a magnificent Erard piano installed in my sitting-room, which I have hardly opened.' And the small-scale religious compositions that he completed brought him little satisfaction and equally little recognition. When he offered three of them to the publisher Pustet in Regensburg – *Via Crucis*, fourteen short episodes for choir and organ, portraying the stations of the Cross; *Septem Sacramenta*, seven short devotional texts, also for choir and organ; and *Rosario*, a 'rosary' of four similar devotional settings – Pustet turned them down. What a thought – manuscripts from the composer of the Transcendental Studies, of the Hungarian Rhapsodies, of the Faust and Dante Symphonies, of the symphonic poems, rejected by a publisher!

Not rejected were the pianoforte pieces of the 'Troisième Année' of the *Années de pèlerinage*, a latter-day companion to the two sets of forty years earlier and a fleeting return to the secular world of programme music. Here the centre of inspiration is the beauty of the villa where he lived and the spiritual sustenance offered by the Holy City: on the one hand music addressed to the famous cypresses and fountains of the Villa d'Este, on the other meditations entitled 'Sunt lacrimae rerum' and 'Sursum corda', the music of the man honoured in 1879 by being appointed an honorary canon of the Seminary of Saint Albano. 'Les jeux d'eau à la Villa d'Este' takes its impressionistic place alongside 'Au bord d'une source' as Liszt's contribution to water-music – 'the model for all musical fountains that have ever played since that time,' Busoni called it. A more profound musical metaphor of Liszt's spiritual world during these twilight years is the opening of the second of the two pieces that bear the title 'Aux cyprès de la Villa d'Este' (see opposite).

The resemblance to the opening of *Tristan* does not much matter – the harmonic 'feel' is in any case quite different. But in this one phrase lies the loneliness, the starkness, blended with an inner strength, of the man who has defined his purpose, the man prepared to say, for better or for worse, *'alea est jacta'* – 'the die is cast'.

In these pieces of the 'Troisième Année' of Liszt's musical pilgrimage, written between 1867 and 1877, lie some of his last moments of characteristic beauty – the sumptuousness of remote keys, the thrill of rich modulation, brilliance of keyboard writing, originality of peroration and cadence. Yet they remain but moments – fleeting images of colour against an undistinguished, sometimes repetitious grey background bereft of energy and tension, the work of a painter whose desires cannot overcome his weariness and his fading vision.

In Budapest the young Academy of Music was growing at a remarkable rate, and its original site on the Hal tér square quickly became too small to accommodate the profusion of eager students. At the end of 1879 it therefore moved into a large, three-storey house at Sugárút No. 67, in which appropriate quarters were also provided for its President. In addition to the furniture to be expected, such as his Chickering grand and a large desk at which he worked, his bedroom contained a prayer stool beneath a crucifix on the wall, a picture of Beethoven and a photograph of Bülow.

Liszt never regarded his position as merely nominal. He concerned himself with teaching appointments, with curricula, with students' concerts and with all policy matters, seeing his work as a service both to young musicians and to his native country, and often giving grants-in-aid from his own adequate but by no means abundant funds. 'Many a poor, half-starved student was enabled to continue his studies, and keep body and soul together at the same time, through Liszt's unostentatious generosity,' said the Englishman who called himself Anton Strelezki, in his *Personal Recollections of Chats with Liszt*. 'The calls on his pocket were perpetual, and only too often, I fear, he was most outrageously imposed upon.'

But such things mattered little to him. What in Rome, under the shadow of the Church to which he had pledged himself, and of the woman whose will he could never resist, had been subdued, introverted, sublimated, became in Weimar, and especially in Budapest, liberated, externalized, almost ecstatic. Young ladies repeatedly begged him – never in vain – to let them paint his portrait. When his pupil Janka Wohl called on him one day and found him surrounded by seven or eight such budding young artists, he turned to her with a smile and said: 'I feel like Saint Sebastian, with these paint brushes as the arrows.'

The Liszt of society and sociability returned. Many were the musicians who came to Budapest in the late 1870s at times when they knew he would be there – Delibes, Sarasate, Wieniawski, Massenet, Saint-Saëns. In January 1880 the violinist Joseph Joachim, once so close to him but long estranged from both the man and his music, broke a twenty-year silence by calling on him after a concert he had given in the city.

'My happiest pastime in Budapest is whist in excellent company,' he wrote to Baroness Olga von Meyendorff. 'We do not usually play for stakes, and if so, then only for ten florins or so. The faces on the cards – kings, queens, knaves and aces – have something attractive and stable about them, which is not always the case with corresponding faces in real life.' Over a glass of tokay he would relate, in a mixture of French and German, this or that entertaining episode from his iridescent past, impressing the guests with his knowledge of Hungarian politics and the public issues of the day. He had a shining confidence in the advance of human knowledge and saw the virtues of all positive activity – that of scientists, doctors, nurses and engineers, as well as that of artists – in the radiant light of an optimistic Christianity. 'There is, and will always remain, something new under the sun, and the Father of heavenly mercy will eventually reward the long and persevering labour of mankind,' he wrote to Baroness von Meyendorff.

'We were never allowed to ask him to play,' said Polyxena, daughter of Ferenc Pulszky, Director of the National Museum, about the soirées in her father's house,

but when the others round the whist table played badly and Liszt won, he rewarded us handsomely by sitting down at the piano and beginning to improvise or play some Beethoven or Chopin . . .

He could not bear the sight of a closed piano. So we used to lock it secretly and hide the key. Engrossed in earnest conversation and chewing a long Havana cigar (he had a passion for the strongest there were), he would cast sideways glances at the piano and become restless. Finally he would get to his feet and try to open the lid. Then, of course, we had to fetch the key. Flinging the lid open, he sat down and started to play a mixture of things, sometimes improvising for hours and making the strings of the piano sound now like the human voice, now like a full orchestra. We listened in reverent silence and had the feeling that this music had somehow made us better, nobler beings.

The one-armed pianist Count Géza Zichy, for whom Liszt wrote a number of pieces for the left hand alone, admitted slyly in his memoirs that Liszt's partners at the whist table needed little encouragement to lose a succession of hands in return for a private musical treat of this kind.

The summers in Germany – Weimar, Bayreuth, Vienna, an occasional excursion elsewhere for a special musical event, then back to Weimar – were filled with a similar combination of master classes and social engagements, a blend of loving encouragement of the young and a relaxed acceptance of a homage attendant upon his fame. This fame accompanied him to Paris in June 1878, when with his valet Spiridion he travelled to Paris as the Hungarian representative on the international musical jury at the Universal Exhibition. He found such lengthy journeys increasingly unpleasant and had already turned down several private invitations to visit the Paris Exhibition, but when Minister Trefort sent a telegram to Weimar expressing the 'universal wish' that he should attend in the name of Hungary, he could not refuse. 'I shall not be wanting when there is something to be done for Hungary,' he wrote to Eduard von Liszt in Vienna.

Representing Austria at the Exhibition was the feared and formidable Viennese critic Eduard Hanslick, champion of Schumann and Brahms and self-proclaimed enemy of the music of

Liszt and Wagner. Yet Hanslick rose to the occasion and proposed, to general acclamation, that the jury should appoint Liszt their honorary president, for 'no other country had sent a musician of such distinction'. As he walked round the instruments in the exhibition with Hanslick and a group of the other jurors, the crowd around them grew larger and larger, and every few moments Hanslick had to reply to the breathlessly whispered question: 'De grâce, Monsieur, n'est-ce pas Litz?' (the French always had difficulties with his name). 'Liszt was at that time the most famous personality in the whole of Europe,' wrote Hanslick in his autobiography. 'Everyone knew, at least from pictures, the gaunt figure in his Abbé's robe and broad-brimmed hat, with his sharp features and his Jove-like head set around with its snow-white mane.' Such was the weight of his opinion that a word of approval or criticism of one or other of the instruments would have served to make or break the reputation of its manufacturer. So, noted Hanslick admiringly, 'being well aware of this, he tactfully refrained from passing judgement'. Victor Hugo, recently returned from exile to reclaim his throne as the Grand Old Man of French literature, was among those in whose august company he spent some pleasant hours away from the Exhibition.

Successive annual festivals of the Allgemeiner Deutscher Musikverein continued, in spite of Liszt's wishes, to be mini-celebrations of his own music. At Erfurt in 1878 he conducted Hans von Bronsart's Piano Concerto, with Bülow as soloist, and his own symphonic poem *Hungaria*; at Wiesbaden in 1879 Bülow conducted the Faust Symphony; and at Baden-Baden in 1880, with Liszt present, his 'dramatic romance' *Jeanne d'Arc au bûcher*, with the Beatitudes and 'Tu es Petrus' from *Christus* were given. In between these festivals he travelled elsewhere to attend important performances of his works – the Esztergom Mass in Vienna in 1879; the complete *Christus* in Frankfurt-am-Main and *Ce qu'on entend sur la montagne* in Sondershausen later the same year; *Die Glocken des Strassburger Münsters*, the *Missa Choralis* and the symphonic poem *Die Ideale* at a concert in Vienna in 1880.

In this same year, 1880, there appeared the first volume of the first full-scale biography of Liszt. It was the work of Lina Ramann, a middle-aged music teacher in Nuremberg, who had already published a textbook on musical education and a study of Liszt's *Christus*, and had firmly committed herself to the cause of the 'New Music'. Some of her pupils had gone on to study under Liszt, who had no reason to object when it was suggested that she undertake a full-scale study of his life and work, and he unhesitatingly provided the answers to the stream of questions which she put to him about the earlier, less accessible phases of his life.

Lina Ramann worked from the beginning under the eagle eye of Princess Carolyne, whom she visited in Rome in order to receive, as it were, a statement of desired objectives. 'I hope very much she will perform her task well,' wrote the Princess to Adelheid von Schorn. 'But if she does not,' she threatened, 'I can supply what is missing myself.' And this, it seems, is just what she did, ensuring that Lina Ramann left the 'right' impression, especially of some of the more problematical episodes in her narrative, such as Liszt's affair with Marie d'Agoult. Princess Carolyne had not known Marie but she had an immovable jealousy of her memory. From the moment she entered Liszt's life she had thrust herself into the role of the mother of his and Marie's three children and striven in every other conceivable way to make him deny the past. There was no aspect of his life over which, in her possessiveness and tenacity, she did not claim sovereign rights of decision, and his character had a soft centre that invited, almost provoked, the invasion of a strong will such as hers. All first biographies enjoy a privileged status, and Lina Ramann's is no exception. But with Princess Carolyne constantly peering over her shoulder she could hardly be expected to produce the open, unprejudiced document which the world had the wish, and perhaps the right, to be offered.

Liszt himself spoke well of Lina Ramann from the moment in 1873 when he first met her – 'very intelligent, hard-working, with a noble character,' he described her – and saw no cause to withhold his praise of her labours on his behalf. But she did not show him her manuscript before publication, so that he was almost as unprepared as any other reader for the tone and content of her story; the corrections of detail and the spontaneous comments in the margin of his copy would otherwise have been made before the book appeared in print.

When asked by one Commendator von Jägemann whether Lina Ramann's biography was 'classical', he replied: 'To be accounted "classical" one must first be dead, then be seen by the world as immortal. At present I lay claim to neither of these estates.' The self-deprecation is as genuine as the playful smile that accompanies it.

SEVEN

The Weariness of the Nomad

'1880, July 18: Liszt lost consciousness in the park and collapsed.' The laconic entry in his diary by the Weimar court organist Alexander Gottschalg, a friend of long standing, gives almost the first serious indication that all was not well with Liszt's health. He had had a basically strong constitution, and if stricken with an occasional indisposition, he would make as light of it as possible. 'It was Jean-Jacques Rousseau, I think,' he once mused, 'who said that any man past forty who is not his own doctor must be considered an imbecile – a condition in which I see no great benefit.'

But now, on the brink of his seventies, the loneliness and disjointedness of his existence, factors psychological rather than physical, had undermined his powers of resistance. The *vie trifurquée* was losing its impulse and its meaning, the journeyings becoming perfunctory, the sense of achievement and satisfaction dwindling. In Budapest the Academy of Music was taking longer to fulfil his expectations of it than he had hoped, and the frustrations played on his nerves. Weimar, by now oppressively familiar in ambience, had no new challenge to offer and his life there seemed merely to mark time. 'Why am I in Weimar?' runs a depressing letter to Princess Carolyne written in September 1882. 'Is it an error, a misdeed or a folly – or all three at once, perhaps?' The behaviour of 'that conceited scoundrel Spiridion,' his extrovert Montenegrin servant, had also stretched his patience to breaking-point, and he now replaced him with a more docile Italian called Achille Colonello, 'who looks after me much better than his predecessor'. Liszt treated his servants generously, quite apart from which his utterly unpractical nature exposed him to unrestrained abuse, and Spiridion 'saved' 4,000 thalers during his six years' service (Liszt considered that he himself needed 2,500 thalers a year at this time to meet his needs). With this and, it was alleged, with the proceeds of selling to female admirers hairs

228

combed from his master's head, Spiridion later opened a tobacconist's shop in Weimar which set him up for the rest of his life.

As to the third of his chosen commitments, his annual pilgrimage to Rome, often undertaken almost as though in a daze, he had already said the last word to Malwida von Meysenbug: 'I only come here for the sake of one person, otherwise I would not set foot in the place again.'

His eyes, too, were failing, and letter-writing became increasingly onerous – he told Ödön von Mihalovich in 1881 that in recent times he had been replying to some 2,000 letters a year. Nevertheless when he arrived for a three-week stay in Bayreuth in September of that year, Cosima found him looking better than she had expected. Wagner tried to persuade him to move to Wahnfried for good but knew that he would not – 'because you insist on your freedom'.

He had already travelled hundreds of miles that year. *Christus* had been given in Berlin and Freiburg, and the Esztergom Mass in Antwerp, with Liszt concerts in Freiburg and Baden-Baden. In the course of the winter he had played in Budapest, Sopron and Pressburg and was present at a ceremony in Raiding when a plaque, still to be seen today, was unveiled on the wall of the farmhouse in which he was born. The plaque had been paid for by the Sopron Association for Literature and Art, and Liszt's friend of long standing, Count Géza Zichy, declared his intention to acquire the house as a permanent memorial. Characteristically, however, Liszt persuaded Zichy that the money would be better used to supplement the scholarship that had been endowed in his name at the Academy of Music. The day after the unveiling, a ceremony conducted with the panoply to which he had long been accustomed, he donated a sum of 200 guilders to the school and parish of Raiding.

When he arrived in Rome in October in the company of his granddaughter Daniela von Bülow, he looked terrible. Adelheid von Schorn wrote in her memoirs:

When I first saw him I was shocked. His face was pale, his features bloated, his hands and feet were swollen and he had become quite corpulent. His mood varied with the fluctuations of his physical condition, and he was tired practically the whole time. He scarcely ever left his rooms but sat at his desk and worked, often dropping off to sleep in his chair.

As in Budapest, he played whist in the evenings with Daniela,

229

Professor Jacob Moleschott, the Dutch physiologist and philosopher, and any other friends who chanced to call on him in the Hotel d'Alibert, where he had taken rooms for himself and his granddaughter. He was especially honoured by a visit from Ernest Renan, the revolutionary Christian philosopher and historian, whose views kindled memories of his early hero Lamennais. Secular philosophy, as distinct from patterns of thought resting on independent, often pantheistic interpretations of Christianity, had no place in his reading. He and Princess Carolyne both looked into the philosophy of Schopenhauer at this time, which, with its pessimism, its cult of nirvana and its demand for self-abnegation, had claimed Wagner as one of its prominent victims. But they could make no progress against its denial of the goodness of creation and its rejection of life after death. Indeed, so narrowly and rigidly had the Princess defined the parameters of his intellectual and spiritual world that considerations of dogma, not of art, determined the permissibility or otherwise of clothing a particular subject in musical form. Thus he made no secret of the fact that he would have dearly liked to compose an oratorio on the figure of Martin Luther but that doctrinal reservations prevented him from doing so.

No such reservations, however, inhibited him in his approach to the Polish martyr St Stanislaus, whom Princess Carolyne had for years urged him to make the hero of an oratorio. A Polish libretto was prepared by Lucjan Siemienski in 1869, which the Princess translated into French; Peter Cornelius then made a German version of the French, but in so stilted a style that the mind, far from being uplifted, remains utterly earthbound. Liszt's imagination may have risen to the story of the murdered tenth-century bishop who became the patron saint of Poland, but the text given to him did not, nor, as he could not disguise, did his own musical powers. Down to within a year of his death he made desultory but fruitless efforts to complete more than the occasional fragment.

'You can try whatever you like,' sneered Wagner to the musical world in *Das Kunstwerk der Zukunft*. 'Write symphonies with chorus or without, write Masses, write oratorios – sexless operatic embryos that they are – write songs without words, write operas without libretti. Nothing you do will ever have real life in it, because you lack faith – a deep faith in the necessity of what you are doing.' In a sense Liszt had set out to demonstrate, first in his symphonic poems, then in his oratorios, that Wagner's centralization of his *Gesamtkunstwerk* on the visual impact, the dramatic spectacle enacted in the temple at Bayreuth, reflected merely his,

Wagner's, scheme of priorities. Leaving more to the creative listener's imagination, Liszt wanted to believe that a combination of words and music alone, unencumbered by an explicit visual presentation, would lead to a *Gesamtkunstwerk* experience of a higher, because freer, order. The words were to carry the intellectual message; the music was to do the rest, music as the purest and holiest of the arts, the messenger of the Almighty, the bearer of supreme spiritual experience. 'The motto of my oratorio *Stanislaus* is "Religion and Fatherland",' he proudly declared. But the 'sexless operatic embryos' remained barren, and sadly little in the output of the last twenty or more years of Liszt's life convinces us that, in the terms of his art, he had 'a deep faith in the necessity of what he was doing'.

Wagner, however, did. And Liszt shared the knowledge – gratefully, almost humbly. In July 1882, after attending the Musikverein Festival in Zurich, where *Saint Elizabeth*, the Second Piano Concerto and other pieces had been given, he went to Bayreuth for the final rehearsals and first performances of *Parsifal*. ' "Masterpiece" is an inadequate word,' he wrote to Olga von Meyendorff. 'From the opening bars to the last it rises from the sublime to the even more sublime.' To Abrányi he added: 'May the public be educated up to it.' And the day after the first performance he wrote to Hans von Wolzogen, the most zealous contemporary publicist on Wagner's behalf: 'The general feeling is that there is nothing which can be said about this miraculous work. Silence is surely the only possible response.' No gesture had given him a profounder joy than Wagner's dedication of the work to him – 'the most incredible Franz Liszt' were Wagner's words on the title-page – at the moment in 1877 when the libretto was completed.

The devotional serenity of *Parsifal*, its concepts of suffering, sacrifice and redemption, Good Friday and the Holy Grail, all absorbed into a music of pure spirituality which renders the stage action subsidiary, almost superfluous – this was for Liszt the opera to end all operas, the profoundest experience of his whole musical life, the greatest achievement of the greatest composer of the age. He was not the only one who has found himself unable to speak at the end of the performance.

Liszt moved easily and agreeably among the personalities who had come to Bayreuth for one or other of the sixteen performances of *Parsifal* which made up this, the second Bayreuth Festival. The familiar aristocratic entourage was present – save, to Wagner's chagrin, King Ludwig II of Bavaria – together with Bruckner, the young Mahler, Humperdinck, Saint-Saëns, Delibes and others from many parts of Europe. Wagner himself exhibited the tetchiness and unpredictability that accompanied his deteriorating heart condition. He had been overjoyed when Liszt arrived – 'He's our only real relative!' he cried in delight to Cosima – but when Liszt and Daniela left a subsequent performance of *Parsifal* in the middle of the third act in order to pay their respects to Count von Schleinitz and his wife, he snapped testily: 'Kow-towing to the bigwigs again! The devil take you!'

As summer moved towards autumn, Liszt's thoughts would turn, though more hesitantly as the years slipped by, to Rome. It had become his habit to celebrate his birthday there, and only the previous year the German Embassy had marked the day with a special concert. But emphases were subtly shifting. Neither this nor the following year did he go there at all. So since Princess Carolyne never set foot outside the city, and barely even outside her stuffy, smoke-filled chamber in the Via del Babuino, two years went by without their seeing each other. Instead he spent more time in Germany, while retaining his honour-bound term in Budapest at the beginning of each year. Numerous letters still passed between him and the Princess but her hold over his thoughts and actions was weakening, and after his death a huge pile of unopened letters from her was found in the Hofgärtnerei in Weimar.

The pull towards Germany inevitably had a great deal to do with Wagner, both through family ties and because of all that Bayreuth represented. Princess Carolyne's tirades had lost their power to intimidate. In the autumn of 1882, therefore, instead of going to Rome, he joined Wagner, Cosima and their children in the Palazzo Vendramin in Venice, which Wagner had rented for the winter. Here, with one of the villa's eighteen rooms at his disposal, he spent two quiet months in the family circle, attending Mass each morning at the church of San Geremia and sharing the company of the Bayreuth intimates who anxiously came to enquire after the condition of their Master – Hermann Levi, the first conductor of *Parsifal*, Paul von Joukovsky, designer of the sets, the pianist Joseph Rubinstein, the composer Engelbert Humperdinck.

'We children were all passionately devoted to our grandfather,' Siegfried Wagner recalled. 'His extraordinary kindness, and the remarkable way he concerned himself with our individual interests greatly endeared him to us.' There was also a welcome respite, said Siegfried, from Princess Carolyne's habitual attempts to control things from a distance: 'Even the Princess Wittgenstein spared my mother the admonitory letters it had become her custom to write to those with whom Liszt was staying, in which she laid down what he could eat and what not, who could be invited and who not, which subjects could be discussed and which not.'

Not that the scene between father and son-in-law was always one of unruffled geniality. 'In conversation together,' wrote Joukovsky in his memoirs, 'neither paid attention to what the other was saying. They would both speak at the same time, which often led to the most curious exchanges. Each was so accustomed to being the centre of attention that there was always a certain amount of awkwardness when they were together.'

Wagner complained that Liszt had no sense of humour – Wagner's idea of humour was not everybody's – and beneath the tension that Joukovsky observed there sometimes seemed to lie an uneasiness not without its spiky moments. Cosima told of an occasion when her father played Wagner his 'Ave Maria', with its slow crescendo rising to a climax *fortissimo*. After Liszt had finished, Wagner commented: 'I didn't know that your Virgin Mary could make such a din!' When Wagner thereupon sat down at the piano – he was no pianist – and embarked on something by Beethoven, Liszt called out to him: 'I can play it better than that!' In less competitive mood they discussed the concept of a new form of symphony in one movement – a kind of orchestral equivalent of Liszt's Piano Sonata, or a conversion into 'absolute' music of the unitary form of his symphonic poems. But the spiritual atmosphere was often overcast. 'Richard believed that he often detected in my father an air of sadness and despondency,' wrote Cosima in her diary on the dark January day that Liszt left Venice for his winter term in Budapest.

Demands on his time and his generosity continued to arrive. Hardly had he taken up his classes again at the Academy of Music than a letter from the President of the Committee of the *Presse Parisienne* asked whether he would consider playing in Paris for the victims of the recent floods in Alsace-Lorraine. 'Unfortunately,' he felt compelled to reply, 'my seventy-two years disqualify me as a pianist. My ten fingers have been out of practice for years, and I could no longer exhibit them in public without running the risk of a justifiable rebuke. I am determined to refrain from exhibiting my senility at the piano in any country.'

On 15 February, as he was sitting at his desk in his apartment in the Academy, a telegram from Venice was brought to him. Wagner had died two days earlier. At first he refused to believe it. When assured that it was true, he murmured: 'His turn today, mine tomorrow.' It was not dismissive, let alone cynical, but an obedient acceptance of the inscrutability of divine providence. 'You are aware of the melancholy view I have of life', he wrote to Princess Carolyne, telling her the news; 'it seems to me easier to die than to live. Death, even when preceded by the long, terrible agonies of "dying", as Montaigne strikingly put it, is our deliverance from a predestined yoke, the consequence of original sin.'

He offered to travel to Venice and accompany Cosima back to Bayreuth but he was secretly relieved when she declined, and he played no part in the obsequies, mourning in silence and in private.

Clustered round the name of Wagner, written from a few weeks before his death to a few weeks after, are four short works, originally for piano but later transcribed for other media, which reveal the nature of Liszt's creative musical mind in his last years. Their titles tell their own story – *La lugubre gondola* (in two widely divergent versions), *R.W. – Venezia, Am Grabe Richard Wagners* – as do those of other mournful, elegiac, sometimes almost morbid pieces from the same period – *Nuages gris, Trauervorspiel und Trauermarsch, Resignazione, Unstern*.

Much has been made of the harmonic experimentalism and originality of these last pieces, their strange sonorities and rough dissonances. A startlingly explicit title like 'Bagatelle in No Key', put to a little piece written in 1873, shows one of the directions in which Liszt's mind had been moving, and the theoretical implications of what he was doing held a nagging fascination for him to the end of his life. Arthur Friedheim relates how he called on Liszt very early one morning to find him still trying to put together a textbook on tonality which had dogged his thoughts for a number of years. But the notion of an 'experiment' in art, on the analogy of an experiment in natural science, can only mislead. An experiment in science will be performed in order to see whether something will 'work'. If it does, the result will be used to carry the developmental process to the next stage; if it does not, that particular approach will be abandoned and another tried. In either case the experiment has no autonomous value – it is a means to an end and dies the moment it has served its purpose. But in art the created work, whether 'experimental' or 'conventional', stands as a finished product and will be judged as such by the criteria proper to works of art, without consideration for what stimulative power it may possess, in its own day or in the future. Art, unlike knowledge, does not proceed by linear progression, or, like science, become 'better', more effective, more efficient. To be sure, art cannot stand still. But it develops by having new things to say, new visions to impart, each new thing and each new vision being a self-contained utterance with its own inner logic and its own inalienable qualities. It is offered to us as the work of one man's hands, for our pleasure and, perhaps, our profit.

From these late works of Liszt's it is difficult, sadly, to derive either. Their 'experimental' harmonic novelty rests almost entirely on the sequential repetition of disparate and contrasting elements, the mechanical superimposition of which is bound to lead to dissonance and incongruity. The thought-content, that is to say the thematic substance, is minimal: a short melodic pattern is repeated and repeated in sequence until stretched almost to breaking-point, and the end of the piece is reached not by the calculation of inner symmetries but through the expiration of the composer's ability to see any way forward – even, one is tempted to say, through the evaporation of his interest. Likewise only with embarrassment can we watch him helplessly trying to recapture in *Von der Wiege bis zum Grabe* the vitality and originality of his symphonic poems of the 1850s. His penetration of vision has deserted him, so too have his powers of concentration, and this last-born of his works in this genre sounds for all the world as though he had written a page or two, left it on one side, returned later to write a few bars more, gone away again, and so on until bringing the piece to a weary conclusion.

Such works point nowhere, either for Liszt or for his successors. Lugubrious, cold, almost impersonal, they stutter from the mind of a man who felt himself not so far from the eternal peace to which his hero, creator of the *Gesamtkunstwerk* on the Green Hill of Bayreuth, had already been borne in his Venetian gondola.

In Weimar the last generation of pupils was gathering round the ageing Master. His eyesight was deteriorating – the large wart above the bridge of his nose, he jocularly observed, served as a useful protuberance on which to lodge his spectacles – and parting phrases like 'Your very aged F.L.' or 'Your sorrowing old F.L.' begin to stand out in his letters. 'Writing is becoming as difficult for me physically as mentally,' he confessed to Olga von Meyendorff.

He lived to an ordered pattern. Rising at the crack of dawn, he worked at his compositions until eight, smoking incessantly as he sat; then, wearing the black cassock without which he was never seen in public, he walked to Mass in the little Catholic church down the street. After breakfast he took a nap, receiving visitors between eleven and lunch at one. In the early afternoon he returned visits or walked in the park with Gottschalg, Karl Müller-Hartung, the Weimar Kapellmeister, or another of his musical friends, then, between four and six, gave a master class in the Hofgärtnerei. A hand or two of whist, again enveloped in cigar smoke, might follow his evening meal, and he retired to bed early, usually by ten. An air of controlled refinement hung over his household, and he expected a corresponding decorum from those who shared his company, especially in the matter of table manners. His pupil August Stradal recalled in his memoirs that Bruckner particularly nauseated him by eating with his tobacco-stained fingers, picking up pieces of meat from his plate, laying them out on the tablecloth in front of him, then putting them one by one in his mouth.

Respect for the social graces had always had its place in Liszt's moral code, the product of his years in the ambience of the aristocracy and the upper classes. His youthful enthusiasm for the 1830 Revolution, for the revolt of the weavers in Lyon and similar progressive causes had long since given way to a dislike of all violence and upheaval and the cultivation of stability and spiritual repose. He had come to see in enlightened despotism, the benign rule of a single, 'given' authority, the most satisfactory form of constitutional government. 'In a republic it is always the most incompetent who are in charge,' he told Stradal. 'Only a monarchy, headed by a just and wise ruler, has real ethical significance.' Title and position had intrinsic value for him. When the Scottish composer Alexander Mackenzie, later Principal of the Royal Academy of Music in London, visited him in Rome the following winter, he noted appreciatively that Mackenzie, as a man of private means, could afford frequent such journeys to Italy and was – he underlines the word in a letter to Olga von Meyendorff – a *gentleman*.

On his strolls with Stradal through the Ilm Park in Weimar he would talk of his likes and dislikes in music and of his priorities among the composers of the past. The figure who outshone all others, the embodiment of music at its holiest, was Bach. He admired Handel but to the Frenchmen of the age of French classicism – Lully, Couperin, Rameau – he remained cold. Mozart and Haydn he loved, recalling with pleasure that his father had played as an amateur under Haydn at Eisenstadt, but Schubert he set even higher, while conceding the unevenness of his *oeuvre*. Beethoven, of course, was the Prometheus of music, the Titan who personified man at his most human, and as such a towering central experience, while to Weber, Chopin and Schumann – but not to Mendelssohn – he accorded a position of supreme importance. His early enthusiasm for Berlioz had waned, largely under the relentless dominance of Wagner, alongside whom no 'composer of the future' could be sure of survival. For Bruckner's music he had little time and his references to Brahms rarely rise above the perfunctory, whereas for the Russians – Glinka, Balakirev, Tchaikovsky, Borodin, Rimsky-Korsakov, Mussorgsky – he was full of praise.

Liszt handled his household affairs with a light hand, leaving financial affairs to his valet Achille with the sole instruction not to pester him with other than a rough account of the week's expenditure. His uncle Eduard von Liszt in Vienna had managed his investments, and the income from these continued to arrive after Eduard's death in 1879; in addition he had an income from the sale of his compositions, which in 1883 amounted to 7,300 marks. 'Particularly striking,' wrote Stradal,

> is the extreme modesty of his personal needs. He is content with everything: his various domiciles are quite unassuming, in no way luxuriously appointed, but simply with the bare essentials in each room. His diet is almost spartan . . . And if anyone presents him with a box of fine cigars, he gives them away to his guests and his pupils.

One of these guests was Grieg, who had last seen Liszt in Rome fourteen years ago and now came to Weimar at Liszt's invitation to conduct some of his own pieces. 'As well as the applause of the audience,' Grieg remembered, 'I heard Bravos from the orchestra at the best bits, and from the box on the left the grunting of Liszt – that well-known sound which you only hear when there is something he likes.'

After Wagner's death Cosima's attitude to her father, for reasons which lay deep in the past, and of which even the pages of her diary give no hint, became cool, hard, seemingly almost uncaring. It was the time of year when his thoughts would naturally turn to Bayreuth, and on 22 May, Wagner's birthday, he had conducted the Prelude and Good Friday Music from *Parsifal* at a concert in the Weimar Court Theatre. But in July Gottschalg wrote in his diary: 'Liszt is not going to Bayreuth because he felt extremely galled that Cosima would not allow her old father to stay in the Villa Wahnfried. The Master refuses to be billeted on strangers.'

So he stayed in the Hofgärtnerei for the rest of the year, leaving for Budapest in February 1884 and returning to Weimar in April. His strength was declining but he complained of nothing save his worsening eyesight. One of his last engagements before leaving Budapest for Germany took him to a concert of music by Brahms – 'that most fortunate of composers', he observed with gentle irony, 'thanks to the powerful protection of the critics'. Barely had he settled into the Hofgärtnerei again than news arrived of the death of Smetana in a mental asylum in Prague. As a boy, Smetana had written to Liszt asking for an opinion on one of his compositions, and Liszt had sent not only his encouragement but also a gift of 400 guilders towards his musical education. 'Smetana's death has deeply moved me,' he wrote in a letter of condolence to the Czech composer Karel Navratil. 'He was a genius.'

At the Musikverein Festival in May, held this year in Weimar, Liszt conducted in public for the last time – a fragment from his *Stanislaus* and Bülow's symphonic poem *Nirwana*. Then, the power of music proving stronger than his unhappiness over Cosima's behaviour, he decided to cast from his mind the indignities of recent times and go to Bayreuth for *Parsifal*, the one music-drama being performed at that year's Festival. 'The house was full and the audience enthusiastic,' he wrote, and he wove his accustomed path among the assortment of royalty, aristocracy and other dignitaries present, also attending a reception given in Wahnfried for visiting personalities.

But not only did Cosima pointedly stay away from this reception, he did not see her once during the two weeks he stayed in the town. Whether she tried to influence her family to turn their backs on him and failed, or whether she left them to strike their own attitude towards him, he gratefully took his place with them – Blandine and her husband, the nineteen-year-old Isolde and the fifteen-year-old Siegfried – in their box for *Das Rheingold* in Munich the following month.

In the bright, airy salon of the Hofgärtnerei where Liszt held his classes the atmosphere was easy and relaxed. Some twenty or twenty-five pupils would assemble in the late afternoon, six or so of whom would play in turn a piece they had practised for the occasion – a Chopin Waltz or Nocturne, a Bach Prelude and Fugue, something by Schumann, Beethoven or Brahms, a movement of a concerto, often one of Liszt's own pieces. He would listen for a few bars, then sit down at the second piano in the room and play the passage in his own way, commenting on the music at the same time, while the others sat or stood and listened, or talked quietly among themselves in groups.

When delighted with what he heard, he made no secret of his joy. A youth once played Chopin's A minor Study so beautifully that he rushed across to him and kissed him repeatedly, almost lifting him from the piano stool as he did so. His disapproval could be sometimes direct, sometimes sarcastic, sometimes even violent in tone if he found the music or the performance particularly bad. But more often it came in the form of a gentle banter with a humour in which others could good-naturedly join. 'Once,' relates the conductor Felix Weingartner, who came to the Hofgärtnerei regularly in his early twenties, 'a strikingly beautiful girl played particularly badly. When she had finished, the Master went up to her, kissed her on the forehead and said: "Go and get married, my child." Then he turned her gently round and led her towards the door.'

'I had imagined him taller,' wrote Weingartner of his first encounter with Liszt,

> though the impression he makes is largely due to his very bent shoulders and corpulent figure. The features are those one has long known from pictures, but much fatter. He riveted me with the clear, piercing gaze of his bright and shining eyes. One immediately notices his large warts, but it is too distinguished a face to be disfigured by such minor deformities. On his furrowed brow, almost in the middle, he has a wart which must be almost half a centimetre long. He uses it to rest his glasses on when he does not need them. He is long-sighted and cannot read without spectacles.

Many pupils not unnaturally thought it appropriate to offer one of the Master's own pieces as their contribution to the class. The reception he gave it, however, could be disconcerting. August Göllerich, one of an inner circle of pupils and friends, kept a diary of what went on in the classes, recording Liszt's own words. When a lady chose to play his Polonaise No. 2 in E major, he exclaimed: 'How one can choose a hackneyed piece like that is beyond me. You ought to be ashamed of yourself!' On another occasion a pupil produced two items from the *Harmonies poétiques et religieuses*: 'Pointing to the poem printed at the head of the Andante lagrimoso Liszt said: "You see, if no ideas occur to you, you just pick up a poem and everything works out. You don't need to understand anything at all about music – you just make programme music!" And he laughed heartily.'

Liszt suffered in fact considerable annoyance over the literary material that he included in his piano and orchestral pieces, for the publishers repeatedly omitted the many poems and quotations which were a vital and integral part of the musical work. 'It is only because "official" critics are against it and because "programme music" is so scorned,' he explained ironically.

He believed in sitting very upright at the piano, leaning backwards rather than forwards, in the posture depicted in paintings of him by Danhauser, Kriehuber and others. 'On one occasion,' wrote Göllerich,

> a certain young lady played Chopin's C minor Nocturne, swaying to and fro as she did so. Liszt said: 'Sit quite still, child. Don't wobble about so much!' Then he added: 'Even the estimable Clara Schumann used to sway about like this.' So saying, he sat down at the piano and gave a delightful impersonation of her.

Hand-in-hand with such frolicsome outbursts and with the dispensation of general observations on all matters musical went a serious attention to specific matters of keyboard technique – phrasing, tempo, style of execution. To make his point he would sit down at his second piano and play the phrase in question himself, adding a running commentary as he did so. His pianism had lost none of the brilliance and insight that forty years earlier had made him the most famous player in the world. The great Joachim played many wrong notes in his later years – Liszt never did. Young Frederic Lamond from Glasgow – 'the little Scotsman,' Liszt affectionately called him in his classes – could never forget the musicality of his playing. 'Let us take an example,' he wrote in his posthumously published memoirs:

> – the C sharp minor variation from Schumann's *Études symphoniques*. No other pianist – and I have heard them all – ever got that sighing, wailing, murmuring sound of the accompaniment in the left hand, and certainly no other pianist played the noble melody in the right hand with such indescribable pathos as Liszt did.

His old habit of embellishing the musical text from which he was playing had not left him. Taking Göllerich through his transcription of Schubert's 'Der Gondelfahrer', he pointed to a passage and said disarmingly: 'I took the liberty of adding this bit but I don't think Schubert would mind, if he knew.' Who could do more than smile and accept it?

Unlike Wagner, who passed over no opportunity to read or play from his works when he had a private audience at his mercy, Liszt made no effort to force his own music on to his pupils – who in many cases brought with them a fawning predisposition to drool over the Master's every note. Indeed, again unlike Wagner, he did not launch exercises in public relations on behalf of his own work, and accepted with gentle irony that the critical establishment had little sympathy for either his achievements or his aims. 'I can afford to wait,' he used to say, maybe a little ruefully but with a natural dignity.

In October he travelled to Eisenach for the unveiling of a statue to Johann Sebastian Bach in the beautiful old town of his birth, then returned to Weimar to celebrate his seventy-third birthday in the company of intimate friends. 'He is becoming perceptibly weaker,' noted Alexander Gottschalg in his diary, 'and complains for the first time about the infirmities of old age, such as the decline in his powers of sight and hearing.' He became tired in the course of the evening, and guests who called to pay their respects, including the Grand Duke's son, found him dozing in his chair. He came to depend more and more heavily on strong alcoholic stimulants to accompany his heavy smoking. 'Wine is an old man's milk – Cognac is his cream,' he quipped.

Responding to Princess Carolyne's plea, he travelled at the end of the year to Rome, taking a room in the Hotel d'Alibert close to the Via del Babuino rather than moving into the old splendours of the Villa d'Este at Tivoli. He had not seen the Holy City, or his Princess, since 1881. His letters during that time had been as frequent as ever but their tone is that of a kind of respectful matter-of-factness. He avoided subjects that he might have found it undesirable to pursue, while writing a great deal about Wagner and Bayreuth, a topic which, as he well knew, came high on her list of anathemata. The Swiss painter Arnold Boecklin, formerly a teacher at the Academy of Art in Weimar, visited him; his Rome pupils, headed by Sgambati and Nadine Helbig, animated his musical energies, while the familiar patrician company of Cardinal Hohenlohe, the German ambassadors Kurd von Schlözer and Baron Felix von Kendell, the Russian diplomat Count Anton Bobrinski and others ministered to his social needs and arranged soirées at which he played solos and duets.

But he stayed only a few weeks, and early in the New Year, 1885, he was back in Hungary, visiting with ecclesiastical dignitaries in Esztergom, Kalocsa and elsewhere but devoting most of his time to the musical life of Budapest. Of the occasional composition on which he worked – the final two Hungarian Rhapsodies, the *Historical Hungarian Portraits* – he wrote intriguingly to Saint-Saëns: 'At such and such a passage I sometimes ask myself, "Would that please Saint-Saëns?" An answer in the affirmative encourages me to continue, in spite of my fatigue and the other infirmities of old age.' But his mind remained as keen as ever. 'I sat with him one evening,' remembered Géza von Zichy, 'and he talked about art, about the misery of humankind, about politics, religion and history – indeed, about all aspects of life, and I felt as if I were standing on the summit of an immensely high mountain, with the whole earth spread out below me. Liszt is a totality, a microcosm, in the fullest sense of the word.'

The round of travels kept up its pressure. To Pressburg for a recital by Anton Rubinstein in aid of the monument to Hummel; to Vienna for a performance of Hummel's opera *Néron*; to Mannheim for *Götterdämmerung*; to Strasbourg – its home town, so to speak – to hear his *Die Glocken des Strassburger Münsters*; to Antwerp and Aachen for concerts of his music – all this in May and June alone.

Weimar itself, the person of Grand Duke Carl Alexander apart, had learned little from the presence in its midst, on and off for over forty years, of this restless genius – and the one-time Kapellmeister extraordinary knew it. He had long settled for as unobtrusive an existence as possible – a 'low profile', as the modern cant has it. When his pupil Alexander Siloti mooted the idea of a Liszt Society with its seat in Weimar, he warned him against it. 'In Weimar it is wisest to maintain a *negative* and *passive* role,' he told him. 'Therefore, my dear Siloti, do *not* try to establish a Liszt Society.' So Siloti curbed his enthusiasm, and the German Liszt Gesellschaft was founded that same year, 1885, not in Weimar but in Leipzig.

One public principle to which Liszt adhered throughout his life, from his essay 'On the Position of the Artist' of 1835 right down to the theory and practice of his last days, was that art was the concern of all, not just of a precious, privileged minority, and that the artist had both a responsibility to the whole of society and a right to the respect of the whole of society. Such was his attitude over the case of Theodor Kullak. One-time court pianist to the King of Prussia and founder of two highly successful conservatoires in Berlin, Kullak died in 1882, leaving a great deal of money, none of which, however, either he or his heirs had assigned to the promotion of music. Liszt regarded this as an abdication of artistic responsibility and was moved, despite the effort that letter-writing now cost him, to make his indignation public in a letter to Otto Lessmann, editor of the *Allgemeine Musikzeitung* in Berlin:

Dear Sir,
With regret, but with strong conviction, I again state my opinion that Theodor Kullak's negligence ought to be made good by his heirs, otherwise one will have to denounce it as a defalcation to his position as an artist. A fortune of several millions amassed from music-teaching ought not to remain buried without concern for the needs of music students. Unless his heirs choose to establish a Kullak Scholarship, I consider it their duty to add to the four existing musical scholarships at the conservatoire – those in the names of Mozart, Mendelssohn, Meyerbeer and Beethoven – an endowment of 30,000 marks each, making a total of 120,000 marks.
    Of well-known opinions, and mindful of the status of the artist, I am,
Your obedient
F. Liszt

Weimar, September 5, 1885.

In November he made his way via Munich, Innsbruck and Florence to Rome. Had he so chosen, he could have arrived in time to spend his seventy-fourth birthday with Princess Carolyne. But he did not. It was as though he were dragging his steps on a reluctant pilgrimage. Once there, he led a tired, diffident existence in familiar company; his musical imagination could rise only to *Pax vobiscum*, a short, limp piece for male voice choir, and a piano transcription of a Tarantella by César Cui. Rome, whose musical interests Liszt had at one time desperately desired to serve, had never warmed to his music, secular or religious. Comparing his fate to that of the poet Tasso, and showing Stradal the route along which Tasso's body had been borne to the Capitol in 1595, he said: 'I shall not be carried in triumph to the Capitol but the time will come when my work will be appreciated – though by then I shall no longer be among you.'
He still lived to his routine, rising at four and working desultorily at one composition or another till eight, barely able to see the paper before him in the smoke-filled atmosphere. Stradal would call to take him from his first-floor rooms in the Hotel d'Alibert, close to the Via del Babuino and the Princess, to Mass at

San Carlo al Corso or some other nearby church. San Carlo had nothing particular to offer as a building, and Stradal asked him why he chose to go there. 'Because Mass is short there,' came the curt reply.

Whatever the indifference of Rome, persistent invitations from the rest of Europe gave him no peace – from Liège, from the Philharmonic Society in London, from Paris, from St Petersburg, all clamouring for him to be present at performances of his music. And he accepted them all, committing himself to the perpetuation, half in gratitude, half in resignation, of a life lived under the aegis of transience and homelessness, a life in which his tread was becoming dull and leaden. An American agent came to Weimar and offered him two million marks to make a concert tour of the United States, playing just one piece at each concert. The idea enchanted him. 'But what can I do with two million marks at the age of seventy-four?' he complained. Mephistopheles had gone, taking his demonic power with him; the benign white-haired Abbé was left, the man, older than his years, who sighed: 'My eyesight is going from bad to worse – soon I shall no longer be able to write,' and signed the letter, 'Your not sick, but sorrowing and sad F.L.'.

At the end of January 1886, after attending a recital given in his honour by four of the faithful pupils who accompanied him throughout Europe – Bernhard Stavenhagen, August Göllerich, Lina Schmalhausen and August Stradal – he bade farewell to Rome, and to Princess Carolyne, for the last time. The train took him via Florence and Venice to Budapest, where the usual warm welcome from Ferenc Erkel and his other colleagues at the Academy awaited him. Whatever else failed to hold his attention, or had slipped beyond his powers, he still spent two or three hours a day with his students, 'several of whom', he observed with satisfaction, 'continue to display such distinction that they will soon attain the rank of first-class pianists'. At a farewell concert for him in early March, before he left for Weimar, August Stradal was to play his 'Funérailles'. Liszt walked slowly on to the platform with Stradal, stood by the piano and gazed pensively, sadly down at the applauding audience of his countrymen. Stradal wrote:

> Suddenly it flashed through my mind that Liszt felt he would soon die, and that he was bidding his last farewell to Pest. And I was supposed to play his *Funérailles*! An overwhelming sadness came over me, and I asked the Master to be allowed to help him down to his seat in the front row, for I feared he would not be

capable of remaining on his feet for long. Realizing the situation, he let me lead him back to his seat. The moment had not gone unnoticed, and many of the others present must have felt the same as I.

Two days later, accompanied by Stradal and Göllerich, Liszt took the train to Weimar. He never set foot on his native soil again.

After only a few days he left Germany again, travelling this time westwards to fulfil a group of engagements he had accepted. In Liège his Esztergom Mass was performed, together with the Second Piano Concerto and one of the Hungarian Rhapsodies. The following day he went to Paris for another performance of the Mass, at the Church of Saint-Eustache. Back in 1866, in this city of his triumphant youth, and in the very same church, the Esztergom Mass had met with surly opposition, and even those well-disposed towards him had raised a sullen wall of silence. He had no wish to relive the experience, and hesitated long before accepting the invitation to return.

He need not have done so. 'My success in Paris surpasses my wildest dreams,' he wrote jubilantly to Baroness Olga von Meyendorff. A second performance of the Mass a few days later brought thousands more to Saint-Eustache, and he happily agreed to come back to Paris the following month, after a visit to London. There was a round of social engagements with friends such as Gounod and Saint-Saëns – he was among the first to hear, at a private gathering, the complete *Carnival of Animals* – with his son-in-law Émile Ollivier, with Prince Napoleon Joseph Bonaparte (nicknamed Plon-plon) and his sister Princess Mathilde. He remembered with particular pleasure an evening spent in the company of Ferdinand de Lesseps, constructor of the Suez and Panama Canals, and his family.

Then, accompanied by Bernhard Stavenhagen, one of his most devoted pupils, he travelled from Paris to London, which he had last seen forty-five years ago. Walter Bache, a former pupil of his in Rome and the most indefatigable protagonist of his music in England, greeted him off the ferryboat in Dover; Alfred Littleton, director of Novello and Co., at whose house in Sydenham he was to stay – 'near London, where everything is so far away,' Liszt described it – even went with Alexander Mackenzie to meet him in Calais, apparently on Lord Salisbury's principle that the borders of Britain end where the coast of the continent begins. 'We were received like princes,' wrote Stavenhagen to his father.

Advising people not to be distracted by lurid reports of Liszt's personality and behaviour that may have reached their ears, George Bernard Shaw urged his readers in *The Dramatic Review* to give a wholehearted welcome to the distinguished visitor – 'of whom even hostile critics say no worse than that he has failed only by aiming too high.'

The centrepiece round which Liszt's visit had been planned was his *Saint Elizabeth*, two performances of which were given, one at St James's Hall, the other at the Crystal Palace. He had asked that Sir Arthur Sullivan conduct the work, but in the event it was put in Mackenzie's hands. At St James's Hall, wrote Bache, 'Liszt had to go into the orchestra both after the first part and at the end of the work, and the audience rose to him. Then in the middle interval the Prince of Wales went out for him and brought him to be introduced to the Princess.' The following day he went by invitation of Queen Victoria to play to her at Windsor Castle – one of his Hungarian Rhapsodies, the Miracle of the Roses from *Saint Elizabeth*, one of the free improvisations for which he had always been famed, and Chopin's Nocturne in B flat minor. There followed receptions in his honour at the recently founded Grosvenor Gallery (later the Aeolian Hall) and in the houses of the aristocracy, banquets in the company of the Prince of Wales and distinguished figures from public and cultural life, an audience of Cardinal Manning, Roman Catholic Archbishop of Westminster, a visit to the Royal Academy of Music to found a scholarship in his name, and concerts of his music at the Crystal Palace. Among those who came to be introduced to him were Sir George Grove, Sir Hubert Parry, Sir Arthur Sullivan, the poet Robert Browning, Henry Irving and Ellen Terry from the world of the theatre, and the painter Alma-Tadema. At a party in his host's villa he played one of his *Soirées de Vienne*, a Chopin Nocturne and two Studies, the Crusaders' March from *Saint Elizabeth* and – putting a probably unwise strain on the ageing fingers which he had long declined to submit to public gaze – one of his showpieces of the 1840s, the Fantasia on the Tarantella from Auber's *La Muette de Portici*. All this in the space of a little over two weeks in April.

Easter he spent with his friend Victor Lynon in Antwerp, then made his promised return to Paris, staying with the Hungarian painter Mihály von Munkácsy, who did a striking portrait of him, and attending a performance of *Saint Elizabeth* at the Trocadero. In mid-May he set out on the long train journey back to Weimar, where he was anxiously met by Göllerich, Stradal and Stavenhagen, who hardly left his side from now on.

'I could not find words to describe my feelings, so appalled was I by the Master's appearance,' wrote Stradal in his memoirs:

> we had to literally lift him out of the train and carry him to the coach, so weak had he become. But the cruellest blow of all was that he was almost completely blind. The cataract had assumed alarming proportions, and an operation offered the only hope of improvement. Dropsy had caused his feet to swell right up to his knees.

Gottschalg too found him 'greatly aged, weary and listless', and Olga von Meyendorff, who had made his well-being in Weimar her determined, sometimes arrogantly personal concern over the past fifteen years, took him to Halle, some forty miles north of Weimar, for a more authoritative opinion on his condition. The dropsy was confirmed. More alarming, however, was the state of his eyesight. 'For a month past,' he wrote to his former pupil Sophie Menter at the beginning of July, 'I have been quite unable to read and barely capable of writing, with great effort, a couple of lines. Two secretaries, Göllerich and Stradal, kindly help me by reading to me and writing letters that I dictate to them.'

The annual festival of the Allgemeiner Deutscher Musikverein took place that month at Sondershausen, thirty miles or so from Weimar, and the Grand Duke Carl Alexander put a private coach at Liszt's disposal for the occasion. *Christus* was performed in the cathedral and a number of his symphonic poems and the *Historical Hungarian Portraits* at the various concerts. Among the other composers represented was Bruckner, in whose music, however, Liszt found little interest.

He was now subdued, often uninterested, and became easily depressed. When the news reached him of the suicide of King Ludwig II of Bavaria, he was so upset that for days he tried to avoid being drawn into conversation of any kind. On the initiative of Kapellmeister Müller-Hartung a group of his pupils serenaded him with a performance of his Goethe Festival March in the garden below his window; at the end he slowly and laboriously made his way downstairs, helped at every step, to express his thanks to them. But such gestures did little to raise his spirits for more than a moment.

On 3 July Daniela von Bülow, Cosima's eldest daughter, was married in Bayreuth to Henry Thode, a young German art historian. Cosima, the mistress of Wahnfried, presided over high table; Bülow, who had remarried four years earlier and was now in charge of the court orchestra at Meiningen, did not come – sadly, but, Wahnfried being Wahnfried, to nobody's great surprise. Liszt did come. Accompanied by Stavenhagen, he left Weimar by train at six in the morning and arrived in the evening coughing violently, having caught a cold on the journey. Still being *persona non grata* to Cosima, he returned to the rooms he had occupied the previous year on the ground floor of the house of Oberforstmeister Fröhlich in what is now Wahnfriedstrasse No. 9, a stone's throw the Wagner villa. Cosima at least had the grace to invite him to the wedding ceremony and to a festive luncheon the following day in the restaurant of the Festspielhaus.

The strain, physical and emotional, of his granddaughter's wedding celebrations over, Liszt returned to the relaxing company of his friends the Munkácsys – not in Paris, where he had recently stayed with them, but in their little country château of Colpach in the Grand Duchy of Luxemburg. Here, for two serene, blissfully uneventful weeks, he quietly and peacefully vegetated. Only a visit from his old friend Cardinal Haynald, Archbishop of Kalocsa, and from the Bishop of Luxemburg, ruffled the Arcadian monotony. 'One day follows another and all resemble each other,' he wrote to Olga von Meyendorff. There would be company for dinner and in the evening he would play a few hands of whist with Madame Munkácsy and two young lady friends of hers who were also staying at the château.

'Munkácsy and I have one thing in common,' he added in the same letter, 'which is, that work makes us surly and sleepy.' But work was now virtually out of the question. If he could not see to write letters, still less could he see to write music, and since his life had always been built round a pattern of regular work, he became irritable at the enforced idleness. In some measure his incessant journeying from place to place has the character of a surrogate for the creative activity which now lay beyond him.

To close his idyll at Colpach a concert was given in his honour in Luxemburg at which he performed three short pieces. It was the last time anyone heard him play. A violent cough was now added to his complaints, plaguing him day and night. 'In order to console me,' he wrote sardonically in his last letter to Olga von Meyendorff, 'the doctor has assured me that this type of cough is very persistent. So far neither medicine, nor infusions, nor mustard plasters, nor foot baths have got rid of it.' Two days after the concert, accompanied by Stavenhagen, he left for Bayreuth with the intention of staying for all the performances of the two operas being performed at that year's Wagner Festival, namely *Parsifal* and, for the first time, *Tristan und Isolde*.

When he arrived, on 21 July, his cough was worse and he had caught a chill in the draughty compartment of the train. The Festival was due to open on the 23rd and the Wagnerians were beginning to assemble, men and women familiar to Liszt over many years. Cosima had now taken the control of the Festival into her own hands: her production of *Tristan* was to be conducted by Felix Mottl, with *Parsifal* in the traditional hands of Hermann Levi. Although, to Wagnerite chagrin, the performances turned out to be miserably attended, the sense of occasion could not be gainsaid, and the sleepy little Franconian town, boasting a mere 12,000 inhabitants, which Richard Wagner had chosen as the demonstration ground for the Work of Art of the Future, had its mind excitedly focused on one place and one man.

Feverish and weak, Liszt took refuge in his rooms, tended by a new valet, Mihal Krajner, and by Stavenhagen, Göllerich and Lina Schmalhausen, an attractive young pupil who became devoted to him during the last years of his life, and with whom, to the disdainful vexation of Cosima and her family, he probably felt more at ease than with anyone else in the sufferings of his final days. She had first become his pupil in Weimar in 1879, followed him to Rome, to Budapest, where she became what would be delicately called his housekeeper, and back to Weimar. Vienna, Antwerp, Paris, London – wherever he travelled, he sent her the most affectionate of letters, beseeching her at the last from Weimar to join him in Bayreuth, as though he knew he would need her there.

The doctor now prescribed constant and heavy doses of morphine for his cough, which left him in a permanent semi-daze; his eyes streamed and his body became more bloated than ever. 'That my eyes are failing and I shall soon be blind is probably only what I deserve,' he said ironically to Lina, 'but the dropsy is something I have not deserved.' He complained continually of thirst but could only be given frequent draughts of water, since the doctor had forbidden all alcohol.

When Cosima, told of his condition, came across from Wahnfried to decide what steps should be taken, she swept in and out of his room as though the friends at his bedside, unstinting in their love and care, did not exist. She was only one of the legion of women, and second in line only to Princess Carolyne in this, who could not bear the thought that others were performing for him the services which she herself could not, or would not, perform – and, almost worse, that he was content for it to be so.

At this moment it was the 'scheming intruder' Lina Schmal-hausen, an upstart – as his 'official' women saw her – who had somehow wheedled her way into the Master's favour, who was the particular thorn in the flesh, the last scandal in a life rich in scandal. Back in June 1885 Bülow wrote to his fellow-pupil Karl Klindworth about her: 'A charming business! Arthur Friedheim has told me the whole scandal. How sad it is for our Master's dignity!' The Master obviously saw it differently. He had never cared a fig about his 'dignity'. True affection, on the other hand, such as this young woman now gave him, was a rare possession and, especially towards the end, had a value that transcended all others.

Six months after Liszt's death Lina Schmalhausen sent his biographer Lina Ramann a sheaf of papers on which she had chronicled in close detail the events of the last ten days of his life. She stipulated that after Ramann had used this intensely personal material for her purposes, it was to be destroyed. Ramann did nothing of the kind. Not only that, but she paid not the slightest heed to Lina Schmalhausen's diary when she came to give her own account of Liszt's last days – indeed, Ramann does not even mention her. Since Princess Carolyne died over three years before the final volume of Ramann's biography appeared, and can thus hardly be implicated, we appear to be facing a conspiracy of silence between Ramann, Cosima and others to prevent Lina Schmalhausen's role in Liszt's life from becoming known for as long as possible. When Lina Ramann died in 1912, the Schmal-hausen diary was discovered among her possessions, with a provision that it should not be made public for a further fifteen years. It now lies in the Liszt Archive in Weimar – accessible but still not published, and passed over by one biographer after another. Even August Göllerich, who had known Lina Schmal-hausen from the moment she entered Liszt's life, says nothing about her in his biography, as though he too was anxious to conceal the Master's final 'indiscretion' from the world.

On 23 July Liszt dragged himself out to the first evening of *Parsifal*, and two days later, heedless of his friends' entreaties but with the doctor's assurance that there was nothing seriously wrong with him, to *Tristan und Isolde*. 'How annoying that I should have chosen Bayreuth, of all places, in which to fall ill!' he tartly observed. He watched the performances, more asleep than awake, from the Wagner family box, coughing frequently into his handkerchief. Asked his opinion of the *Tristan* production, he replied: 'It is as fine as it could possibly be.' 'After the third act,' wrote Felix Weingartner, who was sitting with him in the Wagner box, 'he did not say another word. I took him down to his coach and he was driven off into the darkness.' It was his last visit to the outside world and the last music he heard.

The following afternoon Adelheid von Schorn came with Paul Joukovsky, both of whom were Cosima's guests at Wahnfried. 'Liszt was sitting on the sofa in his living room,' she wrote,

> holding his cards in his hand and surrounded by a number of his pupils who were playing whist with him. Sitting at his side was Sophie Menter, whom I saw here for the first time. He coughed, fell asleep for a moment, then went on playing – he hardly knew who was there and could scarcely sit upright. Deeply depressed, we both left again, knowing there was nothing we could do for the Master we so loved.

Later in the day Weingartner found him lying in an armchair and clutching a thick blanket that lay draped over his legs in spite of the stifling heat.

Lina used to read to him – from French cultural and music journals, from Wagner's writings, from the Bayreuth Festival programmes – or sometimes just sit and hold his hand. '*Traurig*' ('sad') is the word she repeatedly uses to describe his state of mind. Preparing suitable food for him was difficult. On one occasion he expressed a wish for soup, and a request was made to Wahnfried that some be sent across to him. The reply came back that 'soup was only prepared twice a week', and since this was not one of the days in question, he had to go without. It is a reply that says more about the mistress of Wahnfried's attitude to her father than pages of circumstantial narrative.

By 27 July he could no longer leave his bed, and the chill he had caught on the train journey from Luxemburg had turned into pneumonia. Dr Landgraf, a local physician, could offer little help. When Cosima entered his bedroom and found Stavenhagen sitting with Lina at his side, she again ignored them and instructed his manservant Mihal that in future nobody at all was to be admitted. When she had left, Mihal laughed, called her 'a crazy witch', and said he had no intention of carrying out her orders. Indeed, when on the 29th Cosima had a bed put up in the salon and announced her intention of taking over the nursing arrangements herself, Mihal said it was mere show on her part, for since she kept the door between the salon and Liszt's bedroom shut when she was asleep, she could hardly have heard him call for help. Eva and Isolde, brought in to help their mother, seemed to Lina emotionally unconcerned and rather bored with the whole proceeding.

If Lina's account is to be believed, Liszt continued to call for her, and since Cosima spent most of the day attending to the affairs of the Festival, Lina could creep into his bedroom without hindrance and sit with him. He was now coughing up lumps of phlegm and becoming slowly weaker, but he was fully aware of the situation round him. Olga von Meyendorff, to whom Lina's name was like a red rag to a bull, had announced that she would be coming to Bayreuth on 2 August; if she were to find Lina in this position of privileged intimacy, Liszt warned, she would make a scene and join forces with Cosima to ban Lina from the house. So he and Lina agreed she would have to leave the day before the Baroness was due to arrive, and he secretly gave her the money for her fare back to Budapest. It all has the delightful flavour of a surreptitious adventure. But it was not to be played out in those terms.

When Professor Fleischer, a physician from the nearby University of Erlangen, was brought in the next morning to give a second opinion, he diagnosed pneumonia of the right lung and confirmed that there was little chance of recovery. Asked whether there was anyone he wished to see, Liszt replied, 'in a deep, almost booming voice,' according to Cosima, 'Nobody!' She did not hear him speak again. That night, around two o'clock, he somehow found the desperate strength to get out of bed. Stumbling round the bedroom, he clutched at his heart and cried 'Air! Air!' By the time Dr Landgraf arrived, he was lying across the bed as though dead, exhausted with pain and in a semi-coma.

Saturday 31 July dawned. Barely a flicker of life remained. Strong wine was poured down his throat in an attempt to revive him but to no avail. Cosima was hurriedly summoned from the Festspielhaus. The only sound that came from his lips was an occasional moan, then at half-past ten in the evening, according to some accounts – but not Cosima's – he murmured 'Tristan' and became quite still. The doctor gave him two injections in his chest; his body convulsed violently two or three times, then fell back, lifeless.

In the moonlit garden outside the house Stradal, Sophie Menter, Stavenhagen and a few others had gathered, waiting for the message they knew must come but which they were afraid to hear. Shortly after midnight Mihal came to the door and told them that the master's sufferings were over. Slowly and as though in a daze they made their way past the Villa Wahnfried and down into the town to the Hotel Angermann, to leave the news there for Richter, Mottl and Hermann Levi. Only then did they go their separate ways.

Next day the death mask was taken in the presence of Joukovsky and Mihal. A bust of Wagner stood at the head of the bed and a crucifix hung at the foot; the only decorative motif in the room was a single forget-me-not. The grandchildren watched as the body was photographed but to Lina Schmalhausen's reproachful incomprehension, they displayed little emotion. She was particularly shocked by the revelation that no one had thought to call for a priest to administer to him, an ordained Abbé, the last rites of his Church.

Arthur Friedheim, Bernhard Stavenhagen, August Stradal, Liszt's servant Mihal and others mounted a guard of honour round the body for the rest of that day and through the night. It was high summer, and the heat next day was intense. Flies settled on Liszt's face, and a piece of muslin was laid across it to protect him. But Frau Oberforstmeister Fröhlich, his landlady, was afraid that the corpse might begin to smell, and she insisted that it should be immediately put in a coffin and the coffin sealed, 'because she had other lodgers to consider'. Shocked by this insensitivity, Cosima hastily had a coffin made and carried across to Wahnfried, where it was placed on a catafalque in a side room, surrounded by flowers. Here it lay in state between ten and twelve noon that day, as a file of curious citizens made their way out from the town to look for the last time upon the legendary, larger-than-life figure who had chanced to die in their midst.

Tuesday, 3 August 1886, the day of the funeral, was overcast, humid. But it was also the day the German Crown Prince Friedrich was due to arrive for the Wagner Festival, an occasion announced and eagerly anticipated, like the Festival itself, for a long time. Bayreuth was bedecked with flags, the atmosphere festive, and the name on everyone's lips was not Liszt but Wagner. Even the news from the house of Oberforstmeister Fröhlich spread through the town as 'Wagner's father-in-law has died'.

So the demands of the Work of Art of the Future, like those made by the music of the man who created that work of art, thrust all else to one side. The Crown Prince came, the Festival took place precisely as planned, Cosima carried out her roles as administrator and producer to the letter, and the final self-congratulatory banquet was held in the Festival restaurant. No performance was cancelled. No word was spoken from the stage to the audience who may, or may not, have known what their hero

253

owed to the man who had just died a mere mile away. No attempt was made to mount an act of commemoration – a piano piece or two, a symphonic poem, a choral movement – which, given the wealth of singers and players assembled in the town at that moment, would have been a simple and natural gesture.

Felix Weingartner spoke for many:

> The Wagner family showed no outward sign of grief. The daughters dressed in black but that was all. We fully expected that at least one of the festival performances would be cancelled, but since the majority of those present came from other places, we had to admit that it would be impossible to close the opera house. Then we hoped there would be some kind of musical commemoration in the Festspielhaus, but no such announcement came. If only they had at least taken down the flag on the roof or flown it at half-mast! Yet not one of these things happened, not the slightest hint of reverence or respect. Nor did they put off the receptions at Wahnfried for a while. It seemed as though they were going out of their way to emphasize that Franz Liszt's passing was not sufficiently important for the halo that glowed over the Bayreuth Festival to be dimmed for even a moment by a veil of mourning.

At eight in the morning Stadtpfarrer Korzendorfer arrived to pronounce blessing over the body. At twelve noon the funeral carriage, drawn by four horses – Wagner's hearse three years earlier had been drawn by six, as connoisseurs of such significant symbols weightily observed – left Wahnfried and set off down the Richard-Wagner-Strasse, the Maximilianstrasse and the Erlanger Strasse to the town cemetery. Acolytes and the Catholic clergy of Bayreuth walked in front of the coffin, Siegfried Wagner, Daniela von Bülow's husband Henry Thode and two privy councillors representing the Grand Duke Carl Alexander followed it, with Cosima, Daniela, Princess Hatzfeld and Baroness Olga von Meyendorff in a closed carriage behind. Black flags hung from some of the houses along the route, the street lamps were shrouded with black cloths and the shops in the main streets were closed. At the graveside Bürgermeister Theodor Muncker and Eduard Reuss, the senior of Liszt's pupils present, each spoke a brief tribute, and, Festival or no Festival, hundreds gathered to hear the litany of 'Dust to dust, ashes to ashes . . .' Among the wreaths was one from the Crown Prince Friedrich. The next day a Requiem Mass was celebrated in the Catholic church, at which Bruckner played an organ improvisation on the opening motif from *Parsifal* – the theme that Wagner had taken from Liszt's *Die Glocken des Strassburger Münsters.*

Those musically closest to him, his last and most devoted pupils, maintained that honour and propriety required that he be buried in the garden of Wahnfried. Others, prominent among them the Grand Duke Carl Alexander and Baroness Olga von Meyendorff, called for his reinterment in Weimar, thinking to turn the Villa Altenburg into his mausoleum. Cosima, however, in whose mouth the name Altenburg left an unpleasant taste, thought in grander terms. If in Weimar, she declared, then only in the family vault of the Grand Dukes, where Goethe and Schiller also lay – anything less would be unworthy of his name. So the Weimar case fell through inner dissension. The prime honour denied it, the town committed itself, at the instance of Carl Alexander, to preserve the Hofgärtnerei as a museum containing manuscripts, books, photographs and other of his personal possessions, which it has remained ever since.

Members of the Liszt family in Vienna, a tinge of Austro-Hungarian pride in their thoughts, considered that the body should be brought there to join his Uncle Eduard, for whom he had always had a special affection, while from Budapest and Raiding came patriotic voices proclaiming that his only proper resting place lay in the soil of Hungary. 'Hungary's greatest and most illustrious artistic genius,' the *Pressburger Zeitung* called him in its obituary. Rome, it seems, made no claim for the earthly remains of its famous Abbé.

Back in 1869 Liszt had instructed Princess Carolyne that his body should not be removed from one cemetery to another: 'I desire no other spot for my body than the cemetery being used in the place where I happen to die.' Which is to say: I am everywhere and nowhere at home.

So Bayreuth kept him. Eleven years after his death a vault in the form of a miniature Romanesque chapel was erected over his grave, with the inscription, in German, 'I know that my Redeemer liveth' above the front arch and 'The upright shall dwell in Thy presence' inside. Nearby lie the graves of the novelist Jean Paul, of Siegfried, Winifred and Wieland Wagner, of Houston Stewart Chamberlain, of Hans Richter and others who made Bayreuth the centre of their lives.

In April 1945, during the fighting in the very last weeks of the Second World War, two shells landed in the Bayreuth cemetery. One struck a corner of the nearby chapel, destroying the organ; the other hit Liszt's tomb. Nothing else in the cemetery was damaged. His coffin was found to be still intact, and in 1976 the vault was rebuilt in its original form by the Hungarian Liszt Society. Even in death the serenity he craved was denied him.

Princess Carolyne von Sayn-Wittgenstein, appointed by Liszt his sole heir, received the news of his death in a letter from Adelheid von Schorn. It came as no surprise, and like the final frustration of their desire to wed, like the subsequent course of their separate lives and, indeed, like everything that happened in the world, she received it as an act of God, recalling what he had once written to her: 'One can do nothing but obey and submit in all humility. This is the prime duty of a Catholic, a duty absolute and immutable.' Seven months later, in the exaltation of having finally completed the twenty-fifth and final volume of her *Inner Causes of the External Weakness of the Church*, she joined him in death, and her body was laid to rest in the German cemetery at St Peter's in Rome – the cemetery, like Liszt's, 'that was being used in in the place where she died'.

The day after Liszt's funeral Lina Schmalhausen went back to Budapest. Six weeks later, Wagner's Festspielhaus shuttered and silent, the town back in its old meandering pattern of life, she returned quietly to Bayreuth to relive the last hours of a precious relationship. She found his apartment completely changed – new furniture stood everywhere, the floors had been freshly polished, the rooms redecorated. The Liszt era was already over. Today the house bears a simple plaque:

FRANZ LISZT

✝

31 Juli 1886

– a plain memorial to a man who once had the whole of Europe at his feet but who died without home, without worldly goods.

And also, in the deepest sense, without family. Perhaps, despite his passionate concern for his children during their formative years, and his affection for his grandchildren, he could not be a family man in the conventional sense. Cosima, at least, did not think so. In a letter to Daniela in 1885 she wrote: 'Your father and your grandfather are near-geniuses (not to be confused with semi-geniuses) and therefore have not made their final external break with nature, but they have no real sense of family.' Her persistent inability to come to terms with the course that her father's life had taken found utterance in a bitter, almost sadistic observation some years later, that 'his death was for me nothing other than the last twenty-five years of his life'.

*

'My biography is far more a matter of invention than of documentation.' Liszt knew that his life would provoke a mass of fiction masquerading as history. Or: 'Liszt's career must always give the impression of being an inspired improvisation' – the words of Liszt's grandson, Siegfried Wagner. The gypsy and the Franciscan, the virtuoso and the recluse, the hedonist and the Abbé, Art and Life and the Romantic as the Real. Maybe only through inspired improvisation could all these survive side by side in the life and mind of one man – the man Franz Liszt.

Postscript

It would have been something of a miracle if the controversy that raged round Liszt the man and Liszt the musician during his lifetime had gracefully subsided after his death. The extremes of adulation and opprobrium that greeted him wherever he went seem to have set the obligatory tone for all subsequent reception of his works, inviting us to see him either as one of the greatest musicians the world has ever known or as one of the most shameless charlatans and pernicious influences that posterity has had to endure – noble, original, magnificent to some, garish, exhibitionistic, shallow to others. Indeed, one is almost expected to declare in advance to which camp one belongs before venturing a statement on his historical position or expressing an innocent opinion on this work or that.

In broad terms the aesthetic banners behind which the rival forces have entrenched themselves bear the familiar slogans Classic and Romantic. 'The Classic is the healthy,' said Goethe, 'the Romantic is the sickly', and that is the way those of the Classic persuasion see it. Clarity, order, poise, the maintenance of the golden mean, the assertion of the calculating intelligence, a loyalty to the ethic of formal purity – such are the values on which Classicists thrive, and such were the values they found recalcitrantly absent in the music of Franz Liszt. Order and symmetry, in their view, had here given way to an arbitrary formlessness; the cool, objective joys of precept and principle were smothered in a welter of subjectivity and self-indulgence; literary and pictorial stimuli had been improperly called upon to stimulate the activity of an imagination which, expressing itself in music, should have remained faithful to music. In a word, the ideals of true art had been betrayed.

A special source of infuriation and frustration was the multiplicity of influences that fed into Liszt's music and the disturbing unevenness – equally disturbing to his admirers – of his work as a whole. Hardly had the sceptics finished sneering at his pseudo-gypsy Rhapsodies than they found themselves forced to mount an assault on the sanctimonious religiosity of his Church music, then quickly to turn and deliver a few salvos at the tinsel emptiness of his fantastically difficult pianoforte studies. The target would never keep still. And in all this there were moments recognized – to the chagrin of his detractors – to be not without a sudden beauty or effectiveness, alongside other moments – to the pained confusion of his followers – to be bafflingly banal or in distressingly vulgar taste.

The problem was then further compounded by the flamboyant zeal with which he pursued his extreme goals, both as pianist and as composer. Had he gone about his seditious purposes quietly and unobtrusively, he would have aroused less resentment and animosity; as it was, he gathered round himself a noisy retinue of acolytes and worshippers who ensured that the musical world should not be allowed to forget for one moment what he stood for. Not only the message itself but also the manner of its presentation was offensive: at its most extreme the response was outrage but even at its mildest it was embarrassment.

And so it has remained. 'I can only call his compositions terrible,' said Clara Schumann: 'a chaos of excruciating dissonances, with a perpetual rumbling in the bass and tinkling in the treble, with boring introductions and so on. I could almost detest him as a composer.' 'As an original composer he was like a child,' wrote George Bernard Shaw a few weeks after Liszt's death, 'delighting in noise, speed, and stirring modulations, and indulging in such irritating excesses and repetitions of them that decorous concert-goers find his Infernos, his battles, and his Mazeppa rides first amusing, then rather scandalous, and finally quite unbearable.' Or: 'This is false, bogus music characterized by tangible symptoms of decay, not a music that represents the glories of a superior mode of art. How many of Liszt's large-scale works can claim to fulfil even that most modest of requirements, *viz.* not to be boring?' – thus the sharp-tongued Eduard Hanslick in 1894. And because Liszt's fate, both personal and artistic, was indissolubly linked to that of Wagner, who attracted a not inconsiderable body of enemies of his own, the two could be conveniently yoked together as objects of disapproval, presenting a target correspondingly easier to hit. As early as 1856 the satirical Berlin journal *Kladderadatsch* published a cartoon showing a grim, emaciated Liszt crawling on all fours through the gateway of Wartburg Castle – a kind of Promised Land – with a smirking Wagner, dressed as the Minnesinger Tannhäuser and carrying a harp, sitting triumphantly on his back.

On a more serious note, the kind of problem with which critics found it hard to come to terms is that underlying Edward Dannreuther's description of Liszt's symphonic poems in the *Oxford History of Music* in 1905 as 'mere sketches arranged in accordance with some poetical plan, extraneous, and more or less alien, to music.' Such an attitude – it is in essence the Classicistic stance – assumes that the individual arts exist in sealed compartments, that the principles, the needs, the values of poetry have no meeting-point with those of sculpture, or the inspirations of painting with those of music. But it was precisely to the destruction of such barriers and to the establishment of a unitary principle of creation that should embrace not only all the media of art but also philosophy and religion – the ideal of the *Gesamtkunstwerk* – that the Romantics pledged themselves, and in this context Liszt, the composer of programme music, is the archetypal Romantic. 'The renewal of music through the spirit of poetry' – such was his statement of intent to accompany his symphonic poems. It is at the same time a statement of his originality and his historical importance – but also of his contentiousness.

Yet for all the wilful reluctance to understand what he was about, for all the haughty attempts to dismiss his music as that of a Flash Harry, the list of composers – starting with the greatest, Richard Wagner – who explicitly or implicitly made clear their indebtedness to him redresses the balance far more effectively than can any critical counter-argument. Setting his own symphonic poems in the tradition of Liszt's, Smetana begs him in a letter of 1880 to remain 'what you have always been to me – my teacher and master, my patron and my friend.' The generally unemotional Saint-Saëns enthusiastically recalled in his memoirs that as an eighteen-year-old he 'already regarded Liszt as a genius', while in the 1880s the young Hugo Wolf, champion of the New German School, sent one glowing article after another on Liszt to the *Wiener Salonblatt*. Forty years later Ravel, at the height of his powers, wrote of Liszt in the *Revue musicale* of the International Society of Musicians: 'Do not these composers [Richard Strauss, César Franck, the Russian school, the contemporary French school], otherwise so dissimilar, owe the best of their good qualities to the prodigious musical generosity of this great precursor?'

Liszt's 'break with the comfortable habits of traditional form', as Schönberg put it, in particular the dissolution of traditional tonality through the extension of chromaticism; his employment of chromatic intervals such as augmented second and augmented fourth, not only in melodic sequences but also as structural harmonic components, pointing his last works in the direction first of Scriabin, then, radically and programmatically, of Webern; the spiritual bond that links 'The Fountains of the Villa d'Este' to Ravel's *Jeux d'eau*, and 'St Francis of Assisi Preaching to the Birds' to Messiaen's *Catalogue d'oiseaux* and *Oiseaux exotiques* – indeed, the deep affinity between Messiaen's mystic-Catholic cosmos as such and the tendencies of Liszt's own part-pantheist, part-mystical Catholicism: – how deeply has he penetrated the world of twentieth-century music! Busoni, who himself, particularly as pianist and as transcriber for the piano, seemed like a modern reincarnation of Liszt, and who intellectualized the relationship more fully than most of his contemporaries, summed up the matter unequivocally. 'In the last analysis we are all descended from Liszt, not excluding Wagner,' he wrote in 1920, 'and we owe to him whatever inferior things we have been able to achieve. César Franck, Richard Strauss, Debussy, the recent Russian school – all are branches of his tree. And what modern composer has managed to produce a *Faust Symphony*, or a *Saint Elizabeth* or a *Christus*?'

Of all those anxious to acknowledge their affiliation to the Lisztian line of succession perhaps the proudest, for reasons equally national as musical, was Béla Bartók. While at pains not to ignore the variety and the at times apparent incompatibility of the influences that Liszt absorbed, and while far from blind to his weaknesses and imperfections, Bartók joyously allied himself both in his writings and in his music to the lineage of the greatest of all Hungarian composers. The true Magyar folk tunes that he and Zoltán Kódaly went out into the countryside to collect proved to be very different from the gypsy music which Liszt had forty years earlier put forward as the indigenous music of the Hungarian people, but Liszt's error made him no less of a patriot, and in any case the tziganes formed an integral part of Hungarian musical life, together with the music they played. When Bartók was elected a member of the Hungarian Academy of Sciences, he used his inaugural address in 1936 to make clear Liszt's position of seminal inspiration for those who came after him:

Liszt's work is more important for the development of music than Wagner's. Not that Liszt's works are more perfect than

Wagner's – the opposite is the case. But Wagner exploited and developed to the full all the possibilities arising from his own inventiveness, whereas much of Liszt's invention indicates possible developments which he himself failed to exploit and which were only fully utilised by his successors.

In other words, Liszt's music is open-ended, leaving others to carry the argument further, if they accepted the premises of that argument. It provokes, stimulates, cajoles, annoys, and has an importunate tone that cannot but bring discomfort to those resentful of being addressed in such a manner. 'People do not yet understand him,' said Princess Carolyne von Sayn-Wittgenstein, 'and to a far lesser degree than Wagner. Liszt has hurled his lance much farther into the future. A number of generations will pass before he is fully understood.' Wagner's 'work of art of the future' quickly became a 'work of art of the present' and even more quickly a 'work of art of the past': it pronounced the triumphant last word on a century of Romantic music, satiating, not stimulating, a glorious art bearing the stigmata of its own death. Liszt, by contrast, pointed now in this direction, now in that, opening doors rather than closing them, and however far he may have hurled his lance, or lances, there was always something for later generations to retrieve – though opinion has usually divided over whether the retrieval has produced a major pleasure or profit. Perhaps this disunity is as it should be. Given Liszt's multi-faceted and sometimes contradictory personality, why should we expect his bequest to the world to be one-dimensional and uncontroversial? Indeed, would he himself have wished it to be so? Yet undisputed by friend and foe alike during his lifetime, and thus a binding judgement for posterity, was his natural integrity as man and musician. This is the Liszt that George Bernard Shaw, for one, would have us remember. 'He was a man,' wrote Shaw in his obituary notice for the *Pall Mall Gazette*, 'who loved his art, despised money, attracted everybody worth knowing in the nineteenth century, lived through the worst of it, and got away from it at last with his hands unstained.'

'A man who is a musician and nothing but a musician can establish no relationship to Liszt's works. One has to bring to them a certain poetic empathy.' So Siegfried, son of Richard and Cosima Wagner, characterized his grandfather. They are wise words, bearing both an explanation and an exhortation. Most of those who cannot, or will not, come to terms with Liszt take their stand on musicians' ground and present their case as 'nothing but musicians'. Much of their evidence may rest on the truth, but it can never be the whole truth, and selective truths quickly become distortions. The context is a wider one, whether it be called poetic, with Siegfried Wagner, or philosophical, or spiritual – or Romantic. For this concept of universality, of the union of the creative and the critical, of the oneness of knowledge and experience, above all an awareness of the mystical aura that embraces the whole of existence and absorbs its conflicts – this lies at the heart of Romanticism. And it is the pulse of Romanticism that throbs through the life and work of Franz Liszt.

Bibliography

LISZT'S WORKS

Articles, Essays et sim.

Gesammelte Schriften, 6 vols, Leipzig, 1880–83. These are translations, by Ramann and others, of pieces written by Liszt in French – he wrote no essays in any other language – and although they may convey accurately enough the direction of his thought, the actual words are not his. The original French texts are available of the monograph on Chopin (1852), most of the articles of 1834-40 for the *Revue et Gazette musicale* (reproduced in Jean Chantavoine, *Franz Liszt, Pages romantiques*, Paris, 1912) and *Des Bohémiens et de leur musique en Hongrie* (1859).

A selection of his writings has been made under the title *Franz Liszt, Schriften zur Tonkunst* (Leipzig, 1981).

Music

The only completed attempt at any kind of substantial collection of Liszt's musical works is the Carl Alexander Ausgabe in thirty-three volumes (Leipzig, 1901–36), but in spite of its succession of distinguished editors, among them Busoni and Bartók, it failed to achieve the comprehensiveness one would have hoped for. A new, complete edition (ed. Zoltán Gárdonyi, Imre Suljok and István Szelenyi, Budapest), arranged under ten generic headings, has been in progress since 1970, of which seventeen volumes, all of piano music, have so far appeared.

A full inventory of Liszt's compositions – over 1,300 in all – was made by Peter Raabe, curator of the Liszt Museum in Weimar from 1910 to 1944, a year before his death, and published in the form of a numbered *catalogue raisonné* in Volume II of his *Franz Liszt: Leben und Schaffen* (Stuttgart, 1931; rev. Felix Raabe 1968). This invaluable list remains the standard source of information on the dating of Liszt's individual works, their genesis and the circumstances surrounding it, as well as on the numerous transcriptions and arrangements which he made of his own works. The catalogue by Humphrey Searle (*The Music of Liszt*, 1954; rev. 1966), updated for his article on Liszt for *The New Grove Dictionary of Music and Musicians* (1980), is based on Raabe's.

Correspondence

At the last count (Charles Suttoni, 'Franz Liszt's Published Correspondence: An Annotated Bibliography', *Fontes Artis Musicae* 26, 1979) some 6,000 letters by Liszt had been published in 300 different printed sources, but the existence of hundreds more in manuscript is known – in the Weimar Archive, for instance, in the Richard-Wagner-Archive in Bayreuth and in the Bibliothèque nationale in Paris, apart from the many still in private hands. The Weimar Archive also holds nearly 2,000 letters to Liszt from Princess Carolyne von Sayn-Wittgenstein and a large number from other correspondents.

The first, and still the most comprehensive collection, is *Franz Liszts Briefe* ed. La Mara (pseudonym of Marie Lipsius), 8 vols, Leipzig, 1893–1905. Other important collections are:

Correspondence de Liszt et de sa fille Madame Émile Ollivier 1842–1862, ed. Daniel Ollivier, Paris, 1936

Correspondence de Liszt et de la Comtesse d'Agoult, ed. Daniel Ollivier, 2 vols, Paris, 1933–4

Franz Liszts Briefe an Baron Anton Augusz, ed. Wilhelm von Csapó, Budapest, 1911

Franz Liszts Briefe an seine Mutter, trans. from the French and edited by La Mara, Leipzig, 1918

Briefwechsel zwischen Franz Liszt und Carl Alexander, Grossherzog von Sachsen, ed. La Mara, Leipzig, 1909

Franz Liszts Briefe an Carl Gille, ed. Adolf Stern, Leipzig, 1903

Franz Liszts Briefe an den Fürsten Felix Lichnovsky, ed. Hans von Wolzogen (*Bayreuther Blätter* 30, 1907)

Briefwechsel zwischen Franz Liszt und Hans von Bülow, ed. La Mara, Leipzig, 1898

Briefwechsel zwischen Wagner und Liszt, 2 vols, Leipzig, 1910

The Letters of Franz Liszt to Olga von Meyendorff 1871–1886, trans. William R. Tyler, Washington DC, 1979

Franz Liszt, Briefe aus ungarischen Sammlungen 1835–1886, ed. Margit Prahács, Budapest, 1966

Letters of Liszt and Borodin, ed. Rosa Newmarch, London, 1895

Jacques Vier, *Franz Liszt. L'artiste – Le clerc*, Paris, 1950: some fifty hitherto unpublished letters held by Blandine Ollivier.

A two-volume selection of Liszt's letters to various correspondents, sometimes inaccurately and hilariously translated into a heavily dated English, was published in 1894 by Constance Bache, who also translated the Liszt-Bülow letters (London, 1896). The Wagner-Liszt correspondence was translated by Francis Hueffer, London, 1888. Howard Hugo translated 215 letters from Liszt to Princess Carolyne von Sayn-Wittgenstein's daughter, Marie von Hohenlohe-Schillingsfürst (*Letters from Franz Liszt to Marie zu Sayn-Wittgenstein*, Cambridge, Mass., 1953).

MEMOIRS AND PERSONAL RECOLLECTIONS

d'Agoult, Marie, *Mémoires 1833–1854*, ed. Daniel Ollivier, Paris, 1927

Apponyi, Count Albert, *Memoirs*, London, 1935

Belgiojoso, Cristina, *Souvenirs dans l'exil*, Milan, 1946

Bernhardi, Theodor von, *Aus dem Leben Theodor von Bernhardis*, Leipzig, 1893–1906

Berlioz, Hector, *Mémoires*, Paris, 1870; trans. by David Cairns as *The Memoirs of Hector Berlioz*, London, 1969

Boissier, Auguste, *Liszt pédagogue: Leçons de piano données par Liszt à Mlle. Valérie Boissier en 1832*, Paris, 1927

Bülow, Hans von, *Briefe und Schriften*, 8 vols, Leipzig, 1895–1908

——*Neue Briefe*, ed. Richard Graf du Moulin-Eckart, Munich, 1927

——*Letters of Hans von Bülow*, trans. Hannah Waller, London/ New York, 1931

Chanler, Margaret, *Roman Spring*, Boston, 1934

Chorley, Henry F., *Music and Manners in France and Germany*, 3 vols, London, 1841

Cornelius, Peter, *Ausgewählte Briefe nebst Tagebuchblättern*, 2 vols, Leipzig, 1904–5

Eliot, George, *Letters*, ed. Gordon S. Haight, 12 vols, New Haven, 1954

Fay, Amy, *Music Study in Germany*, Chicago, 1881

Friedheim, Arthur, *Life and Liszt*, New York, 1961

Genast, Eduard, *Aus dem Tagebuche eines alten Schauspielers*, 4 vols, Leipzig, 1862–6

Gottschalg, Alexander Wilhelm, *Franz Liszt in Weimar*, Berlin, 1910

Gregorovius, Ferdinand, *Römische Tagebücher*, Stuttgart, 1892

Hallé, Charles, *Autobiography*, 1896; new edition by Michael Kennedy, London, 1972

Hanslick, Eduard, *Vienna's Golden Years of Music 1850–1900*, trans. Henry Pleasants III, London/New York, 1950

——*Aus dem Konzertsaal*, Vienna, 1870

Hebbel, Friedrich, *Briefe*, 8 vols, Berlin, 1904–7

Heine, Heinrich, *Musikalische Berichte aus Paris, 1844* (in *Französische Zustände* II)

——*Florentinische Nächte*, 1836

——*Über die französische Bühne*, 1837

Jerger, Wilhelm, *Franz Liszts Klavierunterricht von 1884–1886, dargestellt an den Tagebuchaufzeichnungen von August Göllerich*, Regensburg, 1975

Joachim, Joseph, *Briefe an und von Joseph Joachim*, ed. Andreas Moser, 3 vols, Berlin, 1911–13

Kellermann, Berthold, *Erinnerungen. Ein Künstlerleben*, Zurich/Leipzig, 1932

Lachmund, Carl Valentine, *Mein Leben mit Franz Liszt. Aus dem Tagebuch eines Liszt-Schülers*, Eschwege, 1970

Lamond, Frederic, *Memoirs*, London, 1949

Mackenzie, Sir Alexander, *A Musician's Narrative*, London, 1927

Madden, Richard, *The Literary Life and Correspondence of the Countess of Blessington*, London, 1855

Mason, William, *Memoirs of a Musical Life*, London, 1901

Meysenbug, Malwida von, *Memoiren einer Idealistin*, Berlin/Leipzig, 1927

Moleschott, Jacob, *Für meine Freunde*, Giessen, 1895

Moscheles, Ignaz, *Aus Moscheles Leben, nach Briefen und Tagebüchern herausgegeben von seiner Frau*, 2 vols, Leipzig, 1872–3

Neumann, Philipp, Baron von, *The Diary of Baron Philipp von Neumann*, trans. E. Beresford Chancellor, London, 1928

Ollivier, Daniel, ed., *Autour de Madame d'Agoult et de Liszt* (Alfred de Vigny, Émile Ollivier, Princesse de Belgiojoso: Lettres publiées avec introduction et notes), Paris, 1941

Pictet, Adolphe, *Une course à Chamonix*, Paris, 1838

Rubinstein, Anton, *A Conversation on Music*, trans. Mrs John P. Morgan, London/New York, 1892

Saint-Saëns, Camille, *Musical Memories*, trans. E.G. Rich, London, 1921

Salaman, Charles, 'Pianists of the Past' (*Blackwood's Magazine*, September 1901)

Sand, George, *Lettres d'un voyageur*, Paris, 1869

——*Journal intime*, ed. Aurore Sand, Paris, 1926

Scharlitt, Bernhard, 'Franz Liszt an Marie von Kalergis. Unbekannte Briefe' (*Die Musik* XI, 1912)

Schloezer, Kurd von, *Römische Briefe 1864–1869*, Stuttgart/Berlin, 1913

Schorn, Adelheid von, *Zwei Menschenalter*, Weimar, 1913

Schorn, Carl, *Lebenserinnerungen*, 2 vols, Bonn, 1898

Shelley, Lady Frances, *Diary*, London, 1912

Stanford, Charles Villiers, *Pages from an Unwritten Diary*, London, 1914

Stasov, Vladimir, *Selected Essays on Music*, trans. Florence Jonas, London, 1968

Stradal, August, *Erinnerungen an Franz Liszt*, Bern, 1929

Strelezki, Anton, *Personal Recollections of Chats with Liszt*, London, 1893

Thurn und Taxis, Marie von, *Memoirs of a Princess*, London, 1959

Wagner, Cosima, *Franz Liszt: Ein Gedenkblatt von seiner Tochter*, Munich, 1911

——*Das zweite Leben: Briefe und Aufzeichnungen 1883–1930*, Munich, 1980

——*Die Tagebücher*, 2 vols, Munich, 1976–7; trans. Geoffrey Skelton as *Cosima Wagner's Diaries*, 2 vols, London, 1979–80

Wagner, Richard, *Briefe an Hans von Bülow*, Jena, 1916

——*Mein Leben* (vollständiger Text), ed. Martin Gregor-Dellin, Munich, 1963; trans. Andrew Gray as *My Life*, Cambridge, 1983

Wagner, Siegfried, *Erinnerungen*, Stuttgart, 1923

Weingartner, Felix, *Lebenserinnerungen*, Stuttgart, 1928; trans. Marguerite Wolff as *Buffets and Rewards: A Musician's Reminiscences*, London, 1937

Weissheimer, Wendelin, *Erlebnisse mit Wagner, Liszt und vielen anderen Zeitgenossen*, Stuttgart, 1898

Wohl, Janka, *François Liszt*, Jena, 1887

Zichy, Count Géza, *Aus meinem Leben: Erinnerungen und Fragmente*, 2 vols, Stuttgart, 1911–13

BIOGRAPHIES, CRITICAL WORKS

Abrányi, Kornél, *Die ungarische Musik im 19. Jahrhundert*, Budapest, 1900

Armando, Walter G., *Franz Liszt*, Hamburg, 1961

Bory, Robert, *Une retraite romantique en Suisse. Liszt et la Comtesse d'Agoult*, Geneva, 1923
——'Diverses lettres inédites de Liszt' (*Schweizerisches Jahrbuch für Musikwissenschaft* 3, 1928)
——*Liszt et ses enfants Blandine, Cosima et Daniel*, Paris, 1936
Chantavoine, Jean, *Liszt*, Paris, 1911
——'Die Operette Don Sanche' (*Die Musik* 3, 1904)
Cornelius, Carl Maria, *Peter Cornelius*, Regensburg, 1925
Creuzberg, E., *Die Gewandhauskonzerte zu Leipzig*, Leipzig, 1981
Cronin, Vincent, *Four Women in Pursuit of an Ideal*, London, 1965
Csekey, István, 'Franz Liszts Vater, nach bisher unveröffentlichen Dokumenten dargestellt' (*Die Musik* 29, 1937)
Czeke, Alexander, 'Über ungarische Musik und Zigeuner' (*Westermanns Jahrbuch* 4, 1858)
Eckardt, Julius, *Ferdinand David und die Familie Mendelssohn-Bartholdy*, Leipzig, 1888
Federhofer, H. and Oehl, K. (eds), *Peter Cornelius als Komponist, Dichter, Kritiker und Essayist*, Regensburg, 1977
Franz, Robert (Olga Janina), *Souvenirs d'une cosaque*, Paris, 1874
——*Mémoires d'une pianiste*, Paris, 1874
Göllerich, August, *Franz Liszt*, Berlin, 1908
Gros, Johannès, *Une courtisane romantique: Marie Duplessis*, Paris, 1929
Gut, Serge, *Franz Liszt. Les éléments du langage musical*, Paris, 1975
Haldane, Charlotte, *The Galley Slaves of Love: The Story of Marie d'Agoult and Franz Liszt*, London, 1957
Hamburger, Klara, *Franz Liszt*, Budapest, 1973
Haraszti, Emile, *Franz Liszt*, Paris, 1967
——'Liszt, Author Despite Himself', (*The Musical Quarterly* 33, 1947)
Hecker, Jutta, *Die Altenburg*, Weimar, 1955
Helm, Everett, *Franz Liszt in Selbstzeugnissen und Bilddokumenten*, Reinbek, 1972
Horváth, Emmerich Karl, *Franz Liszt: Eine Studie auf der Grundlage der bekannten Quellen, Biographien und zeitgenössischen Darstellungen*, Eisenstadt, 1978
Huneker, James, *Franz Liszt*, New York, 1911
Ille-Beeg, Marie, *Lina Ramann: Lebensbild einer bedeutenden Frau auf dem Gebiete der Musik*, Nuremberg, 1914
Joubert, Solange, *Une correspondence romantique: Madame*

d'Agoult, Liszt, Henri Lehmann, Paris, 1947

Kalischer, A.C., 'Der Knabe Liszt und Beethoven' (*Neue Zeitschrift für Musik* 42-3, 1891)

Kapp, Julius, *Franz Liszt*, Berlin, 1909

——*Liszt-Brevier*, Leipzig, 1910

——*Wagner und Liszt, Eine Freundschaft*, Berlin, 1908

Koch, Ludwig, *Liszt Ferenc: Bibliográfiai kisérlet. Franz Liszt: Ein bibliographischer Versuch* (text in Hungarian and German), Budapest, 1936

Kraft, Günther, *Franz Liszt. Leben, Werk und Vermächtnis*, Weimar, 1961

La Mara (Marie Lipsius), ed., *Aus der Glanzzeit der Weimarer Altenburg*, Leipzig, 1906

——ed., *Bilder und Briefe aus dem Leben der Fürstin Carolyne von Sayn-Wittgenstein*, Leipzig, 1906

——'Aus Franz Liszts erster Jugend' (*Die Musik* 5, 1906)

——*Briefe hervorragender Zeitgenossen an Franz Liszt*, 3 vols, Leipzig, 1895–1904

——*Liszt und die Frauen*, Leipzig, 1911

——ed., *An der Schwelle des Jenseits: Letzte Erinnerungen an die Fürstin Carolyne von Sayn-Wittgenstein, die Freundin Liszts*, Leipzig, 1925

Lange, Fritz, 'Im Heimatsdorfe Franz Liszts' (*Der Merker* 2, 1911)

Legány, Dezsö, *Ferenc Liszt and His Country 1869-1873*, Budapest, 1983

Liszt, Eduard Ritter von, *Franz Liszt: Abstammung, Familie, Begebenheiten*, Vienna/Leipzig, 1937

Litzmann, Berthold, *Clara Schumann: Ein Künstlerleben*, 3 vols, Leipzig, 1902

Millenkovich-Morold, Max, *Dreigestirn: Wagner-Liszt-Bülow*, Leipzig, 1911

Moser, Andreas, ed., *Briefe an und von Joseph Joachim*, 3 vols, Berlin, 1911–13

Moulin Eckardt, Richard Graf du, *Cosima Wagner*, 2 vols, Munich, 1929–31; trans. Catherine Alison Phillips, New York, 1931

Newman, Ernest, *The Man Liszt*, London, 1934

——*The Life of Richard Wagner*, 4 vols, London, 1933–47

Noack, Friedrich, *Deutsches Leben in Rom*, Stuttgart/Berlin, 1907

Nohl, Walter, 'Der elfjährige Liszt und Beethoven' (*Neue Musikzeitung* 14, 1927)

Pourtalès, Guy de, *La vie de Franz Liszt*, Paris, 1926

Raabe, Peter, *Franz Liszt: Leben und Schaffen*, 2 vols, Stuttgart,

1931; rev. Felix Raabe, 1968

——*Grossherzog Carl Alexander und Liszt*, Leipzig, 1918

Raff, Helene, *Joachim Raff*, Regensburg, 1925

Ramann, Lina, *Franz Liszt als Künstler und Mensch*, 3 vols, Leipzig, 1880–94

Rellstab, Ludwig, *Franz Liszt*, Berlin, 1842

——*Aus meinem Leben*, Berlin, 1861

Schilling, Gustav, *Franz Liszt: Sein Leben und sein Wirken aus nächster Beschauung*, Stuttgart, 1844

Schindler, Felix Anton, *Biographie von Ludwig van Beethoven*, Münster, 1840

Schrader, Bruno, *Franz Liszt*, Berlin, 1917

Searle, Humphrey, *The Music of Liszt*, London, 1954; rev. 1966

Segnitz, Eugen, *Liszt und Rom*, Leipzig, 1901

Sitwell, Sacheverell, *Liszt*, London, 1934; rev. 1967

Szabolcsi, Bence, *The Twilight of Franz Liszt*, Budapest, 1959

Thode, Henry, *Franz Liszt*, Paris, 1911

Vier, Jacques, *La Comtesse d'Agoult et son temps*, 6 vols, Paris, 1955–63

Voelcker, Bruno, *Franz Liszt: Der grosse Mensch*, Weimar, 1955

Walker, Alan, *Franz Liszt, Vol.I: The Virtuoso Years 1811–1847*, London, 1983

——ed., *Franz Liszt: The Man and His Music*, London, 1970

Wallace, William, *Liszt, Wagner and the Princess*, London, 1927

Waters, Edward N., 'Liszt and Longfellow' (*Musical Quarterly* 41, 1955)

Weilguny, Hedwig and Handrick, Willy, *Franz Liszt*, Leipzig, 1980

Weimar: *Das Liszt-Haus in Weimar* (guidebook to the house, 1963)

Whitehouse, H. Remsen, *A Revolutionary Princess: Christina Belgiojoso-Trivulzio, Her Life and Times, 1808-1871*, New York, 1906

Winklhofer, Sharon, 'Liszt, Marie d'Agoult and the Dante Sonata' (*Nineteenth-Century Music* I, 1977)

Zorelli, Sylvia (Olga Janina), *Les amours d'une cosaque, par un ami de l'Abbé X*, Paris, 1875

——*Le roman du pianiste et de la cosaque*, Paris, 1875

Index

General Index

Abranyi, Kornél 210, 216, 231
Agoult, Countess Marie d' 19, 38, 39,
    40–5, 47, 50–1, 53–7, 59, 61–3, 65, 66,
    68, 70, 72, 74, 77, 85, 88, 91, 97, 107,
    135, 140, 144, 151, 152–3, 165, 175,
    178, 185, 199, 217–18, 227;
    background and character 39; first
    meets Liszt 40; development of
    relationship with Liszt 41; with Liszt
    in Switzerland and Italy 42–58; break
    with Liszt 59; her salon in Paris 151;
    as Daniel Stern, author of *Nélida*
    61–3, 185; sees Liszt for the last time
    185; death 217
Agoult, Count Charles 39
Albert, Eugen d' 209
Alkan 27, 33
Alma-Tadema, Sir Laurence 246
Altenburg, Villa xiv, 86, 103, 104,
    106–7, 109–11, 113–14, 121, 130,
    132–3, 134–8, 141, 159, 161–4, 166,
    168, 173, 176, 178, 179, 193, 194, 207,
    209, 255
Amadé, Count Thadé 7
Anderson, Miss (Marie von
    Sayn-Wittgenstein's governess) 103
Andrássy, Count Gyula 203
Anna Amalia, Dowager Duchess of
    Weimar 100
Apponyi, Count Albert 29, 55, 210, 214
Apponyi, Count Antal 7
Arnim, Bettina von 79, 86, 127
Auber, Daniel François Esprit 20, 246
Augusz, Baron Antal 69, 148, 212

Bach, Carl Philipp Emanuel 100
Bach, Johann Sebastian xiv, 7, 66, 74,
    79, 96, 100, 110, 141, 142, 156, 177,
    215, 236, 238, 241

Bach, Wilhelm Friedemann 100
Bache, Walter 189, 245, 246
Bakunin, Mikhail 117
Balakirev, Mily Alexeivich 82, 237
Balzac, Honoré de 33, 61, 204
Bartók, Béla 144, 156, 261
Bartolini, Lorenzo 66
Baudelaire, Charles 165, 199
Bayreuth 128, 171, 187, 192, 206–8,
    210, 215, 218–19, 225, 229, 230–1,
    234, 235, 237–8, 241, 247–8, 249, 250,
    252, 254–6
Bayreuth Festival 58, 187, 205–7, 213,
    218, 231, 248–9, 251–4
Beethoven xiv, 1, 8, 9, 10, 11, 18, 22, 48,
    50, 54–5, 65–6, 69, 74–5, 77, 79, 81–2,
    84, 89, 90, 96, 106, 121, 124, 139, 141,
    156, 177, 184, 195, 202, 207, 211,
    213–14, 219, 232, 233, 237, 238, 243
Belgiojoso, Princess Cristina 40, 45, 49,
    50, 58
Bellini, Vincenzo 3, 45, 130
Belloni, Gaëtano 64–5, 76, 91
Beresford, Lady Louise 74
Berlin 70, 78–81, 83, 86, 117, 131, 135,
    149, 151–2, 160, 177, 179, 192, 200,
    202, 208–9, 229, 242–3
Berlioz, Hector 23–5, 27, 33–4, 45, 49,
    67–8, 89, 90, 93, 103, 106, 119, 123–4,
    128, 130, 132, 138–9, 141–3, 149, 153,
    185, 237
Bernhardi, Theodor von 109
Bismarck, Otto von 200–1, 205
Bizet, Georges 214
Blessington, Countess Marguerite 75
Bobrinski, Count Anton 241
Boecklin, Arnold 241
Boissier, Auguste 30–3, 47, 209
Bonn 65, 74, 89, 90, 121, 150

Borodin, Alexander 81–2, 180, 220, 237
Brahms, Johannes xi, 52, 71, 95, 133–4, 141, 150, 157, 225, 237–8
Brassin, Louis 189
Brendel, Franz 103, 171, 176, 179, 189, 192
Bronsart, Hans von 226
Browning, Robert 246
Bruckner, Anton 218, 231, 236–7, 247, 254
Budapest 44, 54, 68–70, 79, 81, 148, 154–5, 158, 173, 185–6, 192, 197, 203–4, 206, 208, 210, 212–14, 216–17, 219, 223–4, 228–9, 232–3, 238, 242, 249, 252, 255–6
Bülow, Blandine von 186, 238
Bülow, Daniela von 186, 210, 229, 232, 247, 254, 256
Bülow, Hans von 92, 109, 114, 129, 130–1, 134, 136, 141, 149, 151–3, 157, 160–1, 163, 165, 173, 177–9, 181, 189, 202, 207, 211, 216, 219, 220, 223, 226, 238, 247, 250
Bülow, Madame von (Hans von Bülow's mother) 135–6, 151
Busoni, Ferruccio xii, xiv, 222, 261
Byron, Lord George xi, 39, 63, 75, 122, 172

Canning, Lord George 75
Carl Alexander, Grand Duke of Weimar 85–6, 98, 101–2, 105, 115, 126, 128, 153, 154, 162, 164, 177–9, 190–4, 207, 215, 218, 242, 247, 254–5
Castlereagh, Lord 75
Chamberlain, Houston Stewart 255
Chanler, Margaret 221
Charles X, King of France 18, 21
Chateaubriand, René 19, 39, 86
Cherubini, Luigi 12, 33
Chesterfield, Lord 75
Chopin, Frédéric xi, xii, xv, 1, 15, 20, 23, 28–30, 33, 45, 49, 52, 54–5, 66, 71, 79, 81, 83, 110, 116, 125, 128, 176, 207, 209, 225, 237–40, 246
Chorley, Henry F. 67, 127
Clementi, Muzio 12
Coleridge, Samuel Taylor 75
Colonello, Achille 228, 237
Conradi, August 66, 122
Constant, Benjamin 39
Cornelius, Carl Maria 114, 168

Cornelius, Peter 95, 114, 131–2, 134, 149, 153, 161, 165, 168, 182, 230
Couperin, François 236
Cramer, Johann Baptist 12
Cranach, Lucas 100
Cui, Cesar 82, 243
Czerny, Carl 8–10, 12–15, 23, 67, 68

Dannreuther, Edward 189, 260
Dante 51, 77, 82, 95, 110, 144–6
Debussy, Claude 1, 261
Delacroix, Ferdinand Victor Eugène 28, 59, 125
Delibes, Leo 224, 232
Dessauer, Joseph 93
Diabelli, Anton 9, 66
Dingelstedt, Franz 153–4
Donizetti, Gaetano 44, 74, 82
Dostoevsky, Fyodor 1
Dresden 54, 76, 117–18, 131, 145, 160
Dürer, Albrecht 100, 106
Dumas, Alexandre père 33, 89, 93
Duplessis, Marie 88, 196

Eliot, George 150
Enfantin, Barthélémy Prosper 50
Erkel, Ferenc 216, 244
Esterházy, Prince Nicholas II 5
Esterházy, Prince Nicholas Joseph 3, 4, 5, 7
Esterházy, Prince Paul Anton 5
Esterházy, Count Michael 7
Esterházy, Count Paul 55

Fauré, Gabriel 221
Faust 143, 184
Fay, Amy 200, 204, 209, 211
Fazy, James 45
Festitics, Count Leo 69, 155
Fétis, François Joseph 48–9, 127
Flaubert, Gustave 204
Flotow, Friedrich von 130
Francis II, Emperor of Austria 7
Franck, César 260–1
Franz Joseph, Emperor of Austria 148, 158, 187
Franz, Robert 96, 127, 208, 213
Freiligrath, Ferdinand 93, 95
Freytag, Gustav 86
Friedheim, Arthur 234, 250, 253
Friedrich, Crown Prince of Prussia 253, 254

Friedrich Wilhelm IV, King of Prussia 78, 79, 86, 89, 158

Gade, Niels 189
George IV, King of England 12, 14, 73
Gille, Dr Carl 145, 176–7
Glinka, Mikhail 82–3, 237
Gluck, Christoph Willibald 123, 130
Goethe, Johann Wolfgang von 9, 37, 39, 52, 75, 77, 79, 85, 86, 93, 94–5, 101–2, 104–5, 110, 122, 126, 142–3, 150, 153, 162, 194, 203, 219, 255, 258
Gogh, Vincent van xi
Göllerich, August 4, 209, 239, 240, 244–7, 249, 250
Gottschalg, Alexander Wilhelm 107, 199, 228, 236–7, 241, 247
Gounod, Charles 165, 245
Gregorovius, Ferdinand 173–4, 176, 180, 182, 184, 215, 219
Grieg, Edvard 195–6, 218, 237
Grove, Sir George 246
Gutzkow, Karl 86, 127

Hagn, Charlotte 79, 88
Hähnel, Ernst 66
Hallé, Sir Charles 33–4, 89, 218
Handel, George Frederic 1, 79, 96, 177, 236
Hanslick, Eduard xi, 134, 141, 225–6, 259
Hatzfeld, Princess 254
Haydn, Joseph 4, 5, 12, 32, 236
Haydn, Michael 12
Haynald, Cardinal 248
Healy, George 188
Hebbel, Friedrich 103, 130, 159
Hegel, Georg Friedrich Wilhelm 124
Heine, Heinrich 24, 28, 34–5, 77, 93–5, 125
Helbig, Nadine 194, 241
Herder, Johann Gottfried 85, 101, 123, 127, 194
Herwegh, Georg 77, 149, 150
Herz, Henri 59, 66
Heyse, Paul 86
Hillebrand, Karl 218
Hiller, Ferdinand 28, 33, 65, 70, 125
Hoffmann, Ernst Theodor Amadeus 37, 124, 140
Hoffmann von Fallersleben, August Heinrich 95, 109, 110, 149

Hohenlohe, Cardinal Gustav von 161, 181–2, 194, 221, 241
Hohenlohe-Schillingsfürst, Prince Konstantin von 159
Hohenzollern-Hechingen, Prince Konstantin von 181
Hölderlin, Friedrich 90
Hugo, Victor 31, 33, 51, 86, 93, 123, 204, 226
Humboldt, Alexander von 103, 125
Hummel, Johann Nepomuk 4, 8, 9, 10, 12–13, 139, 242
Humperdinck, Engelbert 232
Huneker, James 35

Ibsen, Henrik 171
Indy, Vincent d' 209
Ingres, Jean Auguste Dominique 30, 57, 59
Irving, Sir Henry 246
Ivanovsky, Peter von 97

Janin, Jules 127
Janina, Olga (Olga Zielinska) 196–200, 208
Jean Paul, see Richter, Jean Paul Friedrich
Joachim, Joseph 112, 132–4, 149, 150, 224, 240
Joukovsky, Paul von 232–3, 251, 253
Jung, Bertha 132, 182

Kalkbrenner, Friedrich 31, 79
Karl August, Grand Duke of Weimar 78, 85, 101, 143
Karl Eugen, Duke of Württemberg 78
Karl Friedrich, Grand Duke of Weimar 85, 101, 105
Karlsruhe 87, 148, 177, 178
Kaulbach, Wilhelm von 123, 178
Keller, Gottfried 149
Kierkegaard, Søren 88
Kleist, Heinrich von 90
Klindworth, Karl 139, 189, 250
Knezevics, Spiridon 214, 225, 228, 229
Kódály, Zoltán 156, 261
Königsberg 80, 158
Kossuth, Lajos 68
Krajner, Mihal 249, 251–3
Kullak, Theodor 242–3

La Mara (Marie Lipsius) x

Lamartine, Alphonse de 33, 50, 73, 123, 138
Lamennais, Félicité de 35–6, 42, 59, 77, 147, 204, 210, 230
Lamond, Frederic 209, 240
Lassen, Eduard 211
Laussot, Jessie 187, 189
Leipzig 44, 65, 70, 78, 149, 195–6, 210–11, 242
Lenau, Nikolaus 10, 93, 138, 143, 180
Lenbach, Franz von 214
Lesseps, Ferdinand de 245
Levi, Hermann 215, 232, 249, 253
Lewald, Fanny 171
Lewes, George Henry 150
Lichnovsky, Felix von 80–1, 85, 89, 91, 95, 99, 106, 116, 139
Linzen, Karl 105
Liszt, Adam (L's father) 2–4, 7–15, 17–19, 38, 181
Liszt, Anna (L's mother) 2–3, 6, 9, 13, 18–19, 21, 30, 42, 59, 62, 69, 85, 91, 97–8, 135, 153, 175, 179, 182
Liszt, Blandine (L's daughter) 47, 51, 58–9, 91, 135, 151–3, 165, 174–5, 179, 201
Liszt, Cosima (L's daughter) 23, 51, 55, 57, 59, 63, 91, 109, 110, 131, 135–6, 141, 151–2, 160, 165, 169, 174–5, 178–9, 186–7, 202, 206–8, 210, 212–13, 215, 217–20, 229, 232–4, 237–8, 247–56, 262
Liszt, Daniel (L's son) 16, 57, 59, 91–2, 114, 135, 151, 160, 175
Liszt, Eduard (L's uncle, usually addressed as 'cousin') 3, 159, 164, 169, 208, 214, 216, 219, 225, 237, 255
Liszt, George Adam (L's grandfather) 2, 4
Liszt, Franz
  birth 1–2; parents 3–4; and Hungarian language 2, 208; and the gypsies 70, 154–7; health 3, 6; first piano lessons 6–7; first concert 7; studies with Czerny 8–9; earliest compositions 9; Beethoven's kiss 10; visits to England 12, 17, 73–5, 245–6; his school education 15–16; as child prodigy 7, 8, 10–13; and Paris 15, 17, 48–50, 72, 73, 165; gives his first piano lessons 18; and politics 21–2, 115, 201; and Berlioz 23–4, 67, 89,
  90, 142, 185; and Chopin 28–30, 81, 124–5; teaching methods 20–33, 210, 239; manner of playing 32, 67, 68, 74, 211; and Lamennais 36; music and society 13, 36–8, 242; and Countess Marie d'Agoult 38–63, 165, 179, 185, 217–18; and birth of Blandine 47; rivalry with Thalberg 48–50; and birth of Cosima 51; and programme music 44, 51, 122–4; and birth of Daniel 57; his recital programmes 7, 12, 58, 66; break with Marie d'Agoult 59; European tours 65–99; and Hungary 68–70, 88, 116, 148, 155, 212, 223–4; and Mendelssohn 70–1; and Wagner 75, 86, 116–18, 127–9, 149, 178, 201–2, 205–8, 233–4; and Weimar 85, 86, 193–4, 220, 235–6; as Kapellmeister 100–164; manner of composition 88, 120; and song-writing 93–4; and Princess Carolyne von Sayn-Wittgenstein 97–8, 100–165 and passim; and religion 35, 36, 105, 137, 144–5; and orchestration 121–2; symphonic poems 122–3; and Brahms 133–4; relationship to Cosima 91, 135–6, 202, 237, 248–52; and Bülow 130–1, 151–2, 179, 186; and Schumann 71–2, 133, 150–1; and death of Daniel 160; and Allgemeiner Deutscher Musikverein 162–3, 189, 226, 231; in Rome 167–91, 212, 221, 243–4; and Church music 170, 174, 187; and death of Blandine 174–5; takes minor orders 181–2; and Bayreuth 206, 215, 218, 231; declining health 228–9, 241; death 252
Loewe, Carl 76
Logier, Bernhard 31
London xi, 12, 25, 37, 73, 79, 189, 236, 244, 245, 249
Longfellow, Henry 188, 213
Louis Philippe, King 21
Ludwig I, King of Bavaria 11, 89
Ludwig II, King of Bavaria 5, 171, 173, 178, 214, 218, 231, 247
Ludwig I, Grand Duke of Hessen 78
Lully, Jean Baptiste 236
Lytton, Lord Henry Bulwer 59, 72, 75

Macaulay, Lord 75, 86

Mackenzie, Sir Alexander 236, 245, 246
Mahler, Gustav 232
Maltitz, Baron Apolonius von 137
Manning, Cardinal John 246
Marx, Karl 205
Mason, William 133
Massard, Lambert 58
Massenet, Jules 224
Massmann, Hans Ferdinand 125
Mazzini, Giuseppe 201
Mendelssohn-Bartholdy, Felix xi, xii, 15, 21, 65–6, 70–2, 77, 103, 121, 139, 141, 156, 213, 237, 243
Mendès, Catulle 218
Menter, Sophie 217, 247, 251–2
Menzel, Adolf 218
Merimée, Prosper 204
Messiaen, Olivier 261
Metternich, Prince Klemens von 6, 12, 34
Meyendorff, Baroness Olga von 146, 203–7, 212–13, 215–16, 218, 221, 224, 231, 235–6, 245, 247–8, 252, 254–5
Meyerbeer, Giacomo 28, 33, 44–5, 77, 89, 125, 127, 130, 139, 156, 165, 187, 243
Meysenbug, Malwida von 160, 213, 218, 229
Michelangelo 1, 52, 57, 150
Mihalovich, Ödön von 154, 208, 210, 229
Milan 51, 53, 55, 58
Moleschott, Jacob 149, 230
Monteverdi, Claudio 57
Montez, Lola 88–9, 196
Moore, Thomas 39, 75
Moscheles, Ignaz 13, 17, 31, 59, 65–7, 71, 79, 89
Moscow 85, 86, 112
Mosonyi, Mihály 187
Mottl, Felix 249, 253
Mouchanov-Kalergis, Countess Marie von 92, 193, 202, 210
Mozart, Wolfgang Amadeus xiv, 4, 9, 11, 15, 17, 19, 32, 45, 67, 106, 141, 149, 214, 236, 243
Mozart, Leopold 17
Müller-Hartung, Karl 236, 247
Munich 78, 86, 114, 173, 178, 191, 194, 214, 217, 238, 243
Munkácsy, Mihály von 246, 248
Munker, Theodor 254

Musset, Alfred de 30, 33, 46
Mussorgsky, Modest 81–2, 237

Napoleon I, Bonaparte 6, 53, 66, 90, 103, 200, 201
Napoleon III, Emperor of France 152, 188, 201
Napoleon, Prince Joseph Bonaparte 245
Napoleon, Prince Louis 75
Navratil, Karel 238
Nerval, Gérard de 127
Nicholas I, Tsar of Russia 83, 99, 104, 111
Nicholson, Alfred 12
Niemcewicz, Julian 28, 125
Nietzsche, Friedrich 171, 204–5, 218
Nonnenwerth 77, 85, 91
Novalis 140

Ollivier, Daniel (L's grandson) 43, 174, 185
Ollivier, Émile (L's son-in-law) 152–3, 179, 185, 201, 245
Orsay, Count Alfred d' 75
Ortigue, Joseph d' 67, 147, 170, 185
Overbeck, Johann 215

Pacini, Giovanni 49, 55, 74
Paer, Fernando 12
Paganini, Nicolò 23, 25–7, 35, 59, 93, 103, 187
Paderewski, Ignacy 214
Palestrina, Giovanni Pierluigi da 57, 170, 183
Paris xi, 3, 11–15, 17–18, 25, 27, 28–31, 33–4, 39–40, 42, 44–50, 53, 56, 58–9, 61–2, 64, 67, 72–3, 75, 77, 79, 83, 85, 89, 91, 96, 103, 106, 115, 116–17, 125–7, 135–6, 142, 147, 151, 154–5, 160, 165, 170, 179, 182, 185, 192, 197–8, 201, 204, 214, 217, 225, 233, 244–6, 248–9
Palmerston, Lord 75
Parry, Sir Hubert 218, 246
Patersi de Fossombroni, Madame 135, 151
Pavlovna, Maria, Grand Duchess of Weimar 85, 99, 104, 111, 113, 123, 136–7, 153, 158
Petrarch 52, 57, 77, 95
Pictet, Adolphe 45, 60

Pius IX, Pope 161, 166–7, 170–1, 176–7, 181, 187, 190, 201–2
Pixis, Johann Peter 66
Plater, Countess Pauline 33
Ponsard, Francis 73
Potocka, Countess Delphine 29, 45, 88
Potocki, Count Bernard 73
Pressburg (Bratislava) 3, 7, 229, 242
programme music 23–4, 53, 110, 123–4, 142, 172, 174, 187, 222, 240, 260
Proudhon, Pierre Joseph 199, 205
Prunarède, Countess Adèle de la 33, 41
Pückler-Muskau, Prince 55
Pushkin, Alexander 82

Quinet, Edgar 33

Raabe, Peter 163
Raff, Joachim 121–2, 130–1, 133, 189, 210
Raiding (Doborján) 1, 3, 15, 47, 70, 97, 99, 208, 229, 255
Ramann, Lina xiii, 7, 11–12, 17, 35–6, 44, 46, 48, 135, 137, 196, 226, 227, 250
Ranke, Leopold 102
Raphael 52, 57
Rauch, Christian Daniel 125
Ravel, Maurice xiv, 260–1
Rellstab, Ludwig 80, 95, 125
Reni, Guido 100
Reményi, Ede 133, 149, 180, 187
Remmert, Martha 217
Renan, Ernest 230
Reuss, Eduard 254
Richter, Hans 213, 215, 253, 255
Richter, Jean Paul Friedrich (Jean Paul) 37, 255
Ries, Ferdinand 7, 12
Rilke, Rainer Maria 132, 193
Rimsky-Korsakov, Nicolai 237
Romanticism xii, 1, 124, 140, 157, 262–3
Rome 44, 52, 57–9, 160–1, 164–8, 170–1, 173–6, 179–80, 185, 187, 188–90, 192, 194–7, 202–5, 212–16, 220–1, 224, 227, 229, 232, 236–7, 241, 243–5, 249, 255–6
Ronchaud, Louis de 73, 217
Rosenthal, Moritz 209
Rossini, Gioacchino 14, 33, 44–5, 49, 53, 130, 165, 180, 185

Rousseau, Jean-Jacques 39, 228
Rubinstein, Anton xiv, 68, 130, 189, 214, 220, 232, 242
Rückert, Friedrich 95

Saint-Cricq, Caroline de 18–19, 22, 41
Sainte-Beuve, Charles Auguste 33, 39, 59, 139
Saint-Saëns, Camille 189, 214, 218, 220–1, 224, 232, 242, 245, 260
Saint-Simon, Claude Henri 22, 39, 42, 77
St Petersburg 80–3, 86, 92, 166, 244
Salaman, Charles 13, 73–4
Salieri, Antonio 9
Sand, George 18, 28, 33, 40, 42, 45–7, 50, 61, 125, 199
Sarasate, Pablo 224
Sauer, Emil 209
Sayn-Wittgenstein, Princess Carolyne von 16, 41, 43, 62, 69, 80–1, 88, 97, 99, 103–11, 113–14, 116, 118, 121, 125–6, 132, 134–9, 145–9, 151, 153, 156, 158–70, 175, 178–9, 181–3, 185, 187–8, 190, 193–4, 197, 199, 200, 202–4, 206–8, 212, 216–17, 227–8, 230, 232, 233–4, 241, 243–4, 249–50, 255–6, 262
first meets Liszt 97; leaves Russia 103; in the Villa Altenburg 103–160; and religion 107–8, 137, 146, 169; character 97, 108–10; divorce proceedings 136–7, 160–1, 163–4, 166, 169; in Rome 167–256 passim; and her Inner Causes of the External Weakness of the Church 108, 170, 190, 256; and Liszt's assumption of minor orders 183; death 256
Sayn-Wittgenstein, Marie von (Princess Carolyne's daughter) 97, 99, 103, 107, 110, 113–14, 136–7, 149, 158–9, 161, 164, 166
Sayn-Wittgenstein, Prince Nicholas von 97, 104, 111, 113, 136–7, 160, 169
Scarlatti, Domenico 54, 79
Scriabin, Alexander 261
Scheffer, Ary 31, 107, 142
Schiller, Friedrich von 75, 78, 85, 101, 104, 126, 143, 194, 255
Schindler, Anton 10
Schleinitz, Countess Marie von 210, 215
Schleinitz, Count von 232

Schlesinger, Maurice 76
Schlözer, Kurd von 179–82, 184, 241
Schmalhausen, Lina 244, 249–53, 256
Schönberg, Arnold 261
Schopenhauer, Artur 84, 124, 230
Schorn, Adelheid von 104, 108, 111,
   166, 168, 193, 199, 227, 229, 251, 256
Schorn, Henriette von 193
Schorn, Karl 86, 89
Schubert, Franz xi, 9, 32, 44, 52, 55, 66,
   68, 76–7, 79, 82, 93, 95–6, 178, 180,
   187, 237–8, 240
Schuberth, Julius 197, 199–200
Schumann, Clara 47, 54, 64, 68, 71, 79,
   83, 106, 133–4, 149, 151, 240, 259
Schumann, Robert xii, 15–16, 21, 29,
   33, 38, 44, 49, 52–4, 65–7, 70–2, 95,
   106, 124–5, 130, 133–4, 139, 150–1,
   189, 214, 225, 237, 240
Schwind, Moritz von 171, 172
Scott, Sir Walter 39
Semper, Gottfried 117, 149
Servais, Adrien François 114
Servais, Franz 114, 189
Sgambati, Giovanni 196, 241
Shakespeare 1, 39, 95, 102
Shaw, George Bernard 25, 246, 259, 262
Shelley, Lady Frances 5
Siemienski, Lucjan 230
Siloti, Alexander 209, 242
Simonfly, Kálmán 157
Sipka, Miska 207, 214
Sismondi, Sismonde de 45
Smetana, Bedrich 173, 238, 260
Smithson, Harriet 24
Sopron (Oedenburg) 1, 2, 5, 7, 70, 208,
   229
Spohr, Louis 89
Spontini, Gasparo 14
Stanford, Sir Charles Villiers 211, 218
Stasov, Vladimir Vassilevich 81, 194–5
Stavenhagen, Bernhard 244–6, 248–9,
   251–3
Stern, Daniel see Agoult, Countess
   Marie d'
Stradal, August 236–7, 243–7, 252–3
Strauss, Johann 148, 260–1
Street, Agnes 134, 142, 178, 181
Strelezki, Anton 68, 224
Sullivan, Sir Arthur 246
symphonic poem ix, 119–20, 122–4,
   130, 132, 136, 138, 140, 144, 148–9,

213, 222, 230, 233, 235, 247, 254, 260
Szapary, Count Gyula 7
Széchenyi, Count Imre 208
Szitovski, Cardinal Primate of Hungary
   148

Talleyrand, Baron 113–14
Tausig, Karl 149, 163, 168, 209
Tchaikovsky, Peter Ilyich 218, 237
Terry, Ellen 246
Thackeray, William Makepeace 86
Thalberg, Sigismund 48–50, 54, 59, 62,
   74, 79
Theiner, Father Agostino 176
Thiers, Maurice 86
Thode, Henry 247, 254
Thurn und Taxis, Princess Marie von
   188
Tichatschek, Josef 117
Tieck, Ludwig 37, 109
Trefort, Agoston 216, 225

Uhland, Ludwig 93, 95
Unger, Karoline 10, 88
Urhan, Chrétien 18

Varnhagen von Ense, K.A. 125
Varnhagen von Ense, Rahel 109
Venice 43, 54, 56–8, 232–5, 244
Verdi, Giuseppe xii, 21, 130, 187, 214
Viardot-Garcia, Pauline 83, 88
Victoria, Queen 73, 89, 246
Vienna 2, 3, 5, 6, 8, 9, 11, 15, 23, 25, 28,
   43, 54–5, 64–6, 68–9, 78–9, 81, 83, 91,
   99, 103, 118, 148, 149, 155, 159, 160,
   164, 192, 194, 200, 208, 214, 217, 219,
   225–6, 237, 242, 249, 255
Vigny, Alfred de 59
Villa d'Este 194–5, 197, 222
Virgil 144
Vischer, Friedrich Theodor 149
Vitzthum, Baron von 136
Vogt, Hortense 204
Voltaire 202

Wagner, Cosima see Liszt, Cosima
Wagner, Eva (Wagner's daughter) 186,
   215, 251
Wagner, Isolde (Wagner's daughter)
   186, 215, 238, 251
Wagner Minna (Wagner's first wife) 76
Wagner, Siegfried (Wagner's son) 215,

232, 238, 254–5, 257, 262–3
Wagner, Wieland (Wagner's grandson)
  255
Wagner, Wilhelm Richard xi, xii, 206–8,
  210–11, 213–15, 218–20, 226, 229–34,
  237, 241, 249–51, 253–6, 259–62
Wagner, Winifred (Wagner's
  granddaughter) 255
Watzdorf, Minister von 113–14, 166
Weber, Carl Maria von 9, 49, 54, 66, 74,
  93, 96, 103, 124, 130, 180, 187, 211,
  215, 237
Webern, Anton 261
Weimar xiv, 7, 8, 17, 20, 36–8, 44, 52–3,
  62, 78, 80, 85–6, 98–105, 109, 111–23,
  126–8, 130–3, 135–6, 138, 142–3,
  148–51, 153–4, 158–64, 168–73,
  177–80, 183, 187, 190–4, 197, 199,
  202–4, 206–11, 214–15, 217–21,
  224–5, 228–9, 235–8, 241–2, 244–50,
  255

Weinert, Susanne 215
Weingartner, Felix 239, 250–1, 254
Weissheimer, Wendelin 163
Wesendonk, Mathilde 152, 218
Wesendonk, Otto 218
Wieck, Clara see Schumann, Clara
Wieland, Christoph Martin 100, 143
Wieniawski, Adam 214, 224
Wilhelm I, German Emperor 79, 201,
  218
Wilhelmj, August 187, 215
Witt, Franz 216
Wohl, Janka 224
Wolf, Hugo 95, 134, 260
Wolff, Pierre 25, 27
Wolzogen, Hans von 231
Wordsworth, William 75

Zichy, Count Géza 225, 229, 242
Zola, Emile 204
Zumbusch, Kaspar von 171

Index of Liszt's Musical Works
Referred to in the Text

Album d'un voyageur 44, 116, 119
Am Grabe Richard Wagners 234
Années de pèlerinage 44, 51–2, 60, 66,
  93, 119, 128, 222
Arbre de Noël 216
'Au bord d'une source' 44, 222
'Aux cyprès de la Villa d'Este' 222
'Au lac de Wallenstedt' 44
'Ave Maria' 138

'Bagatelle in no Key' 234
Beethoven Cantata (1879–80) 202
'Bénédiction de Dieu dans la solitude'
  138
Bravura Allegro (1824–5) 14
Bravura Rondo (1824–5) 14

'Cantique d'amour' 138, 180
Ce qu'on entend sur la montagne 110,
  195, 226
Christus 111, 161, 173, 187, 208, 210,
  212, 226, 229, 247, 261
Consolations 139

Danse macabre 195
Dante Sonata 50, 51, 52, 195
Dante Symphony 40, 53, 129, 138, 142,
  144–7, 222
'De profundis' (1835) 36
Diabelli variation (1821) 9
Don Sanche ou le Château d'Amour 14,
  17, 59

Esztergom Mass (Messe de Gran) 71,
  138, 147, 148, 185, 226, 229, 245
Études d'exécution transcendante ix, 14,
  27, 119, 222
Études d'exécution transcendante
  d'après Paganini 25–7, 93

Fantasia and Fugue on 'Ad nos' for
  organ 141
Fantasia on Bellini's *I Puritani* 44, 48,
  58
Fantasia on Bellini's *Norma* 77
Fantasia on Berlioz's *Lélio* 35
Fantasia on Donizetti's *Lucia di
  Lammermoor* 44, 74, 82
Fantasia on 'God Save the Queen' 77
Fantasia on Halévy's *La Juive* 44, 48
Fantasia on Meyerbeer's *L'Africaine*
  187
Fantasia on Meyerbeer's *Les Huguenots*
  44
Fantasia on Meyerbeer's *Robert le
  Diable* 77
Fantasia on Mosonyi's *Szep Ilonka*
  187
Fantasia on Mozart's *Don Giovanni* 67,
  77, 82
Fantasia on the Cavatina from Pacini's
  Niobe 49, 55, 74
Faust Symphony 40, 53, 129, 138,
  142–4, 163, 171, 222, 226, 261
Festklänge 132, 136
'Feuille d'album' 92
'Funérailles' 139, 244

Galop chromatique 74, 82
Glocken des Strassburger Münsters, Die
  213, 226, 255
Goethe Festival March 247
Grandes Etudes (1839) 14, 27, 54
*Grande Fantaisie sur la Tyrolienne de
  'La Fiancée' d'Auber* 20
'Grosses Konzertstück' on
  Mendelssohn's *Lieder ohne Worte* 35

Hamlet 144

Harmonies poétiques et religieuses 35, 71, 138, 180, 239
Héroïde funèbre 23
Historical Hungarian Portraits 242, 247
Hungaria 148, 226
Hungarian Coronation Mass 87
Hungarian Fantasia for piano and orchestra (derived from Hungarian Rhapsody No 14) 211
Hungarian Rhapsodies ix, xii, 139, 155, 222, 242, 245
Hunnenschlacht, Die 123, 195

Ideale, Die 226
'Il Pensieroso' 60, 128
Impromptu on themes from Rossini and Spontini 14

Jeanne d'Arc au bûcher 226
'Jeux d'eau à la Villa d'Este' 222, 261

'La chapelle de Guillaume Tell' 44
'Les cloches de Genève' 44
La lugubre gondola 234
Legend of Saint Cecilia 174
Les Préludes 53, 110, 123, 148
Legend of Saint Elizabeth 111, 161, 171–3, 185, 215, 219, 231, 246, 261
Liebestraum No 3 93, 128
'Lyon' 116

Macbeth 53
Malédiction 17
Mazeppa 123, 148
Mephisto Polka 143
Mephisto Waltzes 40, 143, 180
'Miserere d'après Palestrina' 138
Missa choralis 187, 226

Nuages gris 234

Orpheus 123, 148

'Pater noster' 138
Pax vobiscum 243
'Pensée des morts' 35
Piano Concerto No 1 119, 149
Piano Concerto No 2 119, 149, 162–3, 231, 245
Piano Sonata in B minor 71, 129, 139–41

Piano Transcriptions:
Berlioz, *Symphonie fantastique* 24, 33–4
— Overture *Les francs juges* 93
Beethoven, Septet 77, 90
— Adelaïde 82
— 'An die ferne Geliebte' 139
— Symphonies 90
Cui, 'Tarantella' 243
Hummel, Septet 139
Rossini, 'La charité' 180
— *Soirées musicales* 44
— Overture *William Tell* 53, 58, 66, 82
Schubert, 'Auf dem Wasser zu singen' 96
— 'Der Atlas' 96
— 'Erlkönig' 55, 68, 82, 180
— 'Der Gondelfahrer' 240
— 'Die Rose' 44
— *Schwanengesang* 96
— 'Ständchen' 55, 82
Verdi, *Don Carlos* 187
Wagner, 'Liebestod' from *Tristan und Isolde* 187
Weber, Overture *Der Freischütz* 93
— Overture *Oberon* 93
Prayer to Saint Francis of Paola 174
Prelude and Fugue on BACH for organ 141
Prometheus 122–3, 144, 148, 162
Psalm No 13 149, 174
Psalm No 19 174
Psalm No 23 174

Rákóczy March (Hungarian Rhapsody No 15) 69
Resignazione 234
'Revolution Symphony' 22–3, 115
Rosario 222
R.W. – Venezia 234

'St Francis of Assisi Preaching to the Birds' 161, 174, 185, 261
'St Francis of Paola Walking on the Water' 161, 174, 185
Saint Stanislaus 188, 230, 238
Septem Sacramenta 222
Soirées de Vienne 246
Songs 34, 77, 93–5, 110
'Sunt lacrimae rerum' 222
'Sursum corda' 222

INDEX OF LISZT'S MUSICAL WORKS REFERRED TO IN THE TEXT

'Tantum ergo' (lost) 9

Tasso 53, 110, 122, 123, 144

Trauervorspiel und Trauermarsch 234

Twelve Studies (1826) 14, 27

Two Episodes from Lenau's *Faust* 138, 143, 180, 195

Unstern 234

'Vallée d'Obermann' 44

Variations on 'Weinen, klagen' for organ 141

Via Crucis 222

Von der Wiege bis zum Grabe 235

'Workers' Chorus' (1848) 116